Political Parties in Western Democracies

Political Parties
in
Western Democracies

LEON D. EPSTEIN

PALL MALL PRESS
London

FOR SHIRLEY

Published in Great Britain in 1967 by
The Pall Mall Press Limited
77-79 Charlotte Street, London W.1, England

© 1967 by Frederick A. Praeger, Inc.

Printed in the United States of America

Preface

My work falls short of an attempt, originally considered, to assemble a great deal of information about political parties in all Western democratic nations. I have often relied very heavily on American and British material. In the introductory chapter, I describe the difficulties of the broader task for any author and notably for me. To these difficulties I should add that I took so long to write and revise the material, which I had collected mainly in 1963 and 1964, that there is by this time new information that would have been useful for my purposes. I have tried, while writing and revising, to note events and research of the last few years, but there are certain recent works that I have not been able to use. One example is Giovanni Sartori's insightful conceptual treatise on political parties. Thanks to his generosity, I had the opportunity to read his work in a mimeographed version, but only after I had completed my manuscript.

Material that I had previously included in articles written for various academic journals is indicated in footnote references. In one instance, "British Class Consciousness and the Labour Party," published in the *Journal of British Studies,* I have used here substantial portions of my original article, and for permission to reproduce them I am grateful to the *Journal* editor, Professor Willson H. Coates. I should also note that a preliminary sketch of the ideas for this book was given in a paper presented in the fall of 1964 at Indiana University, later published in a shortened version in *Essays in Political Science,* edited by Edward H. Buehrig (Bloomington: Indiana University Press, 1966), and then republished in its original length in *Political Parties: Contemporary Trends and Ideas,* edited by Roy Macridis (New York: Harper & Row, 1967). The ideas discussed in that paper were modified considerably in the process of writing the present book, and what appears here represents a more recent and revised judgment than does the paper in either of its published versions. The later judgment owes a good deal to critical suggestions of colleagues who read the original paper.

I am indebted to many helpers during the long period that I spent preparing this work. Financially I am glad to acknowledge the support of the Rockefeller Foundation and the Social Science Research Council, which together made it possible for me to devote the entire academic year of 1963–64 to research and writing, and the support of the Graduate Research Committee of the University of Wisconsin, which provided summer salary and also funds for research assistants. These assistants, serving in turn while graduate students, were William Simpson, John Kingdon, Judith Langenfeld, and David Griffiths. I am grateful to each chiefly for bibliographical work but occasionally for tabulating data. Similarly I am grateful to Joyce Pajala, an undergraduate student who typed the first draft and checked bibliographical references, and to Geraldine Hinkel, who managed to type most of the final draft while still performing her principal task of administrative service for the College of Letters and Science at the University of Wisconsin. I have been fortunate to have such help.

I have been equally fortunate in my colleagues in political science at the University of Wisconsin. Individually and collectively they have stimulated and supported my efforts. My gratitude extends to all of them, as indeed it does also to the rest of the university of which I am a member. I must thank one colleague in particular. Professor Austin Ranney not only provided intellectual stimulation and comfort at every stage of my undertaking, but he read and commented on the first draft of the entire manuscript.

My wife has contributed so much in so many ways that I cannot even try to express my gratitude except in the largely unspoken manner of the dedicatory page.

Leon D. Epstein

Madison, Wisconsin
April, 1967

Contents

Political Parties in Western Democracies

I

Introduction

Writing about political parties in Western democracies is not a novel enterprise. It is several decades since political scientists, once preoccupied with constitutional forms, ceased to neglect parties. Much of our best scholarly talent and effort have been devoted to the study of parties in the United States and in other advanced nations. It is true that American and European experiences have seldom been brought together in roughly equal measure, as will be attempted here particularly for American and British experiences, but there have been notable comparative European texts, as well as works on parties in individual countries. Therefore, what chiefly distinguishes the subject matter of the present work is the inclusion of considerable material on American parties within the comparative frame of reference. Or, relative to American parties' texts, what is different is that certain European parties are analyzed along with the American.

The scope is potentially a little wider than the United States and Europe. I do not use the phrase "Western democratic" in a strict geographical sense. Outside of Europe, it clearly includes Australia and New Zealand as well as the United States and Canada. It seems reasonable to add Israel as an extension of Western political culture despite its newness as a nation. On the other hand, Japan, though surely advanced and currently democratic, is marginal because of its non-Western background. The Union of South Africa is more readily excluded even though both advanced and Western in background; its democratic system is tenuous and narrowly based. Putting aside all of the rest of Africa, Asia, and Latin America, despite exceptions like Uruguay and Costa Rica, this leaves fifteen European nations as clearly Western democratic: the four Scandinavian nations plus Iceland, Britain, Ireland, Switzerland, Austria, France, West Germany, Italy, Belgium, the Netherlands, and Luxembourg. It will be noted that Portugal and Spain are excluded, obviously because they are nondemocratic as well as unadvanced. Greece and Turkey are also excluded, because of their limited economic development and their unstable democratic experience. The same can be said for various other nations, especially new ex-colonial ones, which have begun democratic experiments in non-Western social and economic circumstances. Their exclusion is not on the basis of their regimes, which may closely resemble those in the West, but on the basis of their non-Western culture in other respects. The relevant nations are those which have participated actively in the special Euro-American development of the last few centuries—not the nations which have latterly been affected and now infected by that development. This definitional method seems more defensible than one based solely on the nature of regimes, which come and go even in Europe. Admittedly, however, there are some problems in applying the definition to particular nations. "Advanced," after all, is not an exact term, and to have counted Italy but not Greece is to differentiate between degrees of development. Also, a few Latin American nations, as noted, appear qualified, but they are excluded mainly because the whole of Latin America is customarily treated along with developing nations.

More difficult to justify, in certain respects, is the exclusion of Eastern Europe along with Russia. Some of this area, certainly Czechoslovakia, participated in the great Euro-American development, industrially and otherwise, and intermittently adopted Western democratic institutions. Really, therefore, it is no more than the important recent accident of Russian imposition of non-Western political regimes that causes the exclusion of all of Eastern Europe from the scope of this study. But, except for the interwar experience of the Czechs, there is little democratic experience, meaning electoral competition, in which political parties can be observed. The Communist one-party system, as will be indicated later, represents a different political phenomenon from the subject matter of our study.

Altogether, one can count, with Israel but not Japan or Latin America, twenty Western nations as now democratic in the customary sense of having electoral competition for public office. What they have in common, besides the democratic process, is the predominantly European (or Western) origins of their populations or at least, in the Israeli case, of their cultures.

Within the narrowly defined Western democratic category, a study of the various ways in which political parties function in at least several of the twenty nations should permit us to generalize with respect to differences and similarities. How relevant such generalizations can be for the non-Western world is another matter. Insofar as Western parties are responses to circumstances now developing in Asia, Africa, and Latin America, perhaps a case could be made for the universality of what we learn about parties in the West. But it is by no means clear that the new emerging nations will respond so much to Western-type circumstances where these occur, as they will to their own already existing and quite diverse conditions. This view is if anything reinforced by what will be seen to be a principal point of the present study: that even among Western nations, basically similar though they are relative to the rest of the world, there are distinctive national or regional conditions making for significantly different political parties.

In comparing parties in the Western universe, two disparities adversely affect the analysis. The first is that the units of comparison are of very different sizes—as, for example, the United States and Norway. National parties in these two nations are so different in scale that they may be hard to compare in other ways. In terms of size, the parties in American states, or in Canadian provinces or Australian states, might more readily be compared with Norwegian national parties. It is true that state or provincial parties do not deal with foreign policy, defense, and certain major domestic policies that national parties, even in a small country, have to face. But state parties, in the United States or other larger federal systems, function in environments whose social homogeneity and size more nearly resemble those of a small nation than do those of an entire continental nation. Furthermore, in federal systems where important subjects like education are left largely to the states, the parties at the state level may be dealing with many of the same issues which in smaller unitary nations are the business of national parties. For these reasons, it seems proper to discuss state parties along with national parties, even though what is being undertaken is a cross-national study.

The second disparity is more difficult to meet. It is the unevenness of information about the twenty nations. This is partly an unevenness in fact, since, no doubt, there are fewer studies of Icelandic parties, for instance, than of British parties, just as there is much less useful scholarly knowledge about some American states than others. But there is another kind of unevenness which flows from limitations on the author's time and linguistic ability. With a few exceptions (in the case of French political literature), I have relied on data and analyses written in English. This has hardly meant the elimination of non-English-speaking nations. Fortunately, both American and British political scientists have written a good deal about countries other than their own, and other political scientists, notably the Scandinavian, the Israeli, and the Dutch, often write in English. Nevertheless, my heavy reliance on the English language, plus the fact that much more is actually available on the United States and Britain than on most other nations, does mean that parties in English-speaking nations are over-represented. In behalf of such over-representation, it can be said that Great Britain and the United States are especially important as the only major powers maintaining democratic systems over a long period of time, and that Britain's highly developed party system is an especially good example of a European style juxtaposed against the American. But the comparison is not meant to be so narrowly limited. The more broadly comparative ambition will be met by illustration, if not by comprehensive accounts, from studies of certain non-English-speaking nations. No effort to be comprehensive or encyclopedic, however, is intended. That is another kind of task, better suited to a group of variously specialized scholars than to an individual. What I hope to establish is a frame of reference, or a set of hypotheses, for more comprehensive studies as well as for specific national studies.

Maurice Duverger, in the early postwar years, made a most notable attempt to provide just this kind of theoretical framework for understanding political parties.[1] While he included material on the United States, it is fair to say that he regarded the European party, especially the socialist party, as a norm for the modern world. Because this norm now seems misleading is a reason for another attempt to provide a theoretical point of departure. How mine differs from Duverger's may already be apparent from the scope of the subject matter, especially the prominence I have given to American material. The aim is to show that American parties, so often regarded as underdeveloped by European standards, are really responses to American conditions which cannot, in their entirety, be regarded as the marks of a backward nation supposed eventually to resemble Europe. Similarly, in this perspective, European parties, insofar as they differ from American ones, are seen as responses to European conditions which may, in some crucial particulars, be changing in an American direction. Admittedly, this puts the methodological purpose too starkly. The deliberate Americanist bias is for emphasis. It does not eliminate consideration of the ways in which American parties may, in certain respects, come to resemble European ones. Nor does it eliminate the genuinely supranational view that American and European parties may really be coming to resemble each other as they respond to increasingly similar circumstances: Americanization of Europe in some re-

[1] Maurice Duverger, *Political Parties*, trans. Barbara and Robert North (New York: John Wiley & Sons, 1954).

spects, and Europeanization of America in others. The West at least may yet become one world.

Still, there is a usefulness in an American emphasis. For the last generation or two, political scientists who specialize in the study of political parties, in the United States and elsewhere, have tended to regard the mass-membership, cohesive, and issue-oriented party of Western Europe and especially of Britain as a superior, because a more highly developed, form of political life. American specialists, notably of the responsible-party school, have explicitly wanted parties in the United States to develop in a similar way. They have been bolstered in their position by European political scientists who, like Duverger, found American parties backward both organizationally and ideologically.

This by now conventional attitude is linked to an exaltation of their subject matter by many students of political parties. Perhaps this began as a reaction against the old formalism and legalism of political science. If so, the reaction has substituted for the former neglect a belief in a nearly overwhelming importance of parties in the modern political process. They are seen as "the main agents of public affairs."[2] And they are said to have "created democracy," which "is unthinkable save in terms of the parties."[3] With such views, it is no wonder that scholars would idealize the stronger and apparently more highly developed parties, believing them to be the agencies most likely to serve democratic goals. Less developed parties, meaning those in the United States, must thus be reformed. Whatever might be wrong with the American political system and its policy outputs would be dealt with most effectively by building responsible parties—organized, centralized, and cohesive. Party reform, rather than constitutional reform, is the aim. Understandably, the party specialists regarded their subject or, it might be said, their clients, as the most suitable point of entry for changing the political system.

Here, then, is another departure in the present work. I do not regard parties as so obviously crucial. And I certainly do not exalt

[2] Sigmund Neumann, *Modern Political Parties* (Chicago: The University of Chicago Press, 1956), p. 4.

[3] E. E. Schattschneider, *Party Government* (New York: Rinehart, 1942), p. 1. A more modest but still large claim in behalf of parties is made by Avery Leiserson: "The political party, or party system, provides the major connective linkage between people and government, between separate, formal agencies and officials of government, and between officials and non-official (extra-governmental) holders of power." *Parties and Politics* (New York: Alfred A. Knopf, 1958), p. 35.

them. Of course, this is hardly novel among general works in political science. Many books on government have been written without stressing parties. But there is something different about a book *on parties* that does not emphasize their importance. It may even seem an inherent contradiction, since to write a book on a subject is itself to call attention to that subject. But again this is a matter of emphasis, or perhaps one should say relative de-emphasis. Obviously the subject has to be of some importance to warrant studying it at length. This would be true even if the purpose were to show that parties were evil and should be abolished. The present work is as far from that purpose, however, as it is from an exaltation of parties. What I have sought is a middle ground on which parties can be viewed as important but not overwhelmingly important political agencies. After all, they do exist in every modern democracy. But they differ considerably in organization and function from one political culture to another. For example, parties are especially impressive in Britain. They will be observed, as organized entities, actually to govern the country in a way that parties do not in the United States. But that cannot be assumed to make the American political system less effective. It is only the parties as such that may be less effective. Why should they be thought so important that their effectiveness determines the effectiveness of the system?

This more limited way of looking at political parties means that they are not regarded as primarily causal. It is plain that they do not cause democratic government to exist, since we have cases of nations ceasing to be democratic despite the existence of highly developed parties, as in Germany in 1932. In other words, parties are not a *sufficient* condition for democracy. There is more reason to believe that they are a *necessary* condition since no modern democracy exists without parties despite some attempts, notably by American municipal reformers, to do without them. But the parties that exist in modern democratic nations differ radically, as I have said, from each other. My concern is to understand the differences, as well as the similarities, among parties in different nations, and this requires an emphasis on parties as responses to their environments rather than as makers of those environments.

This sounds, in the language of recent social science, as though parties are to be treated as dependent variables. Often this will seem to be the case. But it may be acknowledged that I have really conceived parties as intervening variables—dependent in the sense of being determined in their type and form by basic national circumstances, but in turn partly independent or determining with respect both to matters like voting behavior or electoral representation and to some of the circumstances like the constitutional arrangements which themselves helped to mold the parties. These circumstances indicate a mutual interaction that is in no way denied by the thrust of the present analysis. The fact that I emphasize conditions influencing the nature of parties does not mean that I deny that parties can influence the political system and even the social system. Admittedly, however, the emphasis here, compared to that of party reformers, does reduce the relevance of parties as agencies for political change. Indeed, that is the intention. Parties do not seem as susceptible to change by intellectual formula as party reformers often believe. Not only are parties the products of their respective circumstances, but they are fairly durable products even after some of the originally determining circumstances may have changed. Like most social institutions dependent on habit and tradition, parties have lives of their own. They only seem more mutable than constitutions because their codes are less formal. Instead of being easier to change than the legal framework, for example, they may sometimes be more deeply rooted—so deeply rooted that they thrive without constitutional status. This holds for particular parties as well as for party types. They represent, at least in stable democratic societies, the accustomed and the accepted form of political behavior.

It is time to define what is meant by a political party. I have no desire to depart from common understanding. Almost everything that is called a party in any Western democratic nation can be so regarded for the present purpose. This means any group, however loosely organized, seeking to elect governmental office-holders under a given label. Having a label (which may or may not be on the ballot) rather than an organization is the crucial defining element. This allows the use of the word "party" for a group of office-holders or aspiring office-holders who have no organized followers but who merely decide to seek votes under a collective name in addition to their own personal names. Conceivably, even one man seeking office could similarly adopt a label and also qualify as a party. That may fairly be dismissed as unusual. And so, in modern times, can the idea of a group without any organized following. Some degree of organization seems characteristic of modern parties, except for sporadic manifestations here and there. In fact, the degree of organization is often taken as an important mark distinguishing a party from a faction, or a modern party from an eighteenth-century British parliamentary faction that called itself a party. But it seems better not to make so sharp a distinction. Insofar as even a very loose aggregation of politicians present themselves to an electorate under a given label, even if it covers diverse views, why not call it a party? Insistence on more than a label as the mark of a party, or of a modern party, immediately raises serious questions about the obviously loose American parties. How highly organized would *they* have to be in order to qualify? In some states or constituencies they might meet the standard, but not in others. And it would certainly defy our common understanding to question their status as parties.

Much the same trouble exists when "party" is defined, in a traditional way, "as an association organized in support of some principle or policy which by constitutional means it endeavors to make the determinant of government."[4] The "constitutional means" phrase can be accepted since it does not exclude even a Communist or fascist party in its bid for votes (as opposed to any subversive acts in addition to its electoral participation). But "support of some principle or policy" seems too limited unless it includes, as is surely not intended, the policy of winning offices for their own sake. Not all office-seekers are without principle or policy, in the usual sense of those terms, but those who are might well run under a label commonly understood as that of a party.

Although it is wrong to deny the use of the word "party" to groups of office-seekers who are either unprincipled or unorganized (or both), it can be said that the most significant entities that qualify under the broad definition are, in fact, distinguished by more than mere labels. Modern parties are characterized, as William Chambers has indicated, by a relatively durable or regularized relation between leaders and followers, by continuing procedures for performing the key functions of selecting candidates and managing public business, by the range, density, and stability of their support, and by a distinguishable set of perspectives with emotional overtones.[5] These general characteristics seem to be those of virtually all parties which we customarily consider significant in Western democracies, and elsewhere for that matter. No large modern party, even in the United States, would be excluded by a definition including these four characteristics since, as Chambers describes them, they are really very

[4] R. M. MacIver, *The Modern State* (London: Oxford University Press, 1964), p. 396.
[5] William N. Chambers, *Political Parties in a New Nation* (New York: Oxford University Press, 1963), pp. 45–49. A briefer but similar definition, noting "a stable structure," is presented by Frank J. Sorauf, *Political Parties in the American System* (Boston: Little, Brown, 1964), p. 13.

broad. The structural quality, for instance, need not involve a mass membership in order to meet the requisite durable and regular relation between leaders and followers. Chambers allows even the early American Federalists to qualify as a party according to his defined model. All he seems to mean, therefore, is that a party is more stable and identifiable than a faction in either pre-democratic or contemporary politics. This is not so different from defining parties, as I have done, to be simply those groups that bear the label of parties. This too would exclude certain pre-modern "factions" because they were not clearly labelled. And while it would *include* certain minor parties that Chambers would exclude because they were small or ephemeral, this does not make much substantive difference since they will receive little attention anyway. The only difference is a methodological one: the desire to adhere to a definition that counts as a party any group seeking votes under a recognizable label. No matter how small the vote or how special the occasion, no minor party is so minor as not generically to be a party. The single criterion is the functional one: seeking votes for a labelled candidate or candidates. Although the minor parties may still be put aside because they are unimportant, at least individually, in any modern democracy, this is because they are small and not because they are not parties. After all, if there were enough minor parties in any one nation, together they would be important.

Furthermore, if minor parties are not parties, what are they? Sometimes they are said to be interest groups because, relative to large parties, they have only the narrow, specialized appeals characteristic of most interest groups. This seems to make sense when applied to the American Prohibition party, for instance, since that party usually fields candidates not primarily to get votes and certainly not to win office, but mainly to publicize its cause through the election machinery as it also tries to do through other means. The same has been said of the American Socialist party in its later days.[6] But still, Prohibitionists and Socialists are putting up candidates for public office even if they do so as interest groups. In this respect, they are not unlike the Peasant party of Fourth Republic France. Unquestionably it was a party as well as an interest group. The fact that it represented an even more clearly defined interest than the American Socialists did not mean it was any less a party. It was a party because it functioned like one in presenting candidates under its label, just as Prohibition-

[6] David B. Truman, *The Governmental Process* (New York: Alfred A. Knopf, 1951), p. 282.

ists and Socialists presented candidates under their labels. The difference lay in the greater size of the Peasant party and in its much greater chances of electing candidates—and thus also in the greater seriousness with which it presented candidates. It was really trying to win votes in order to win offices. We are back, then, to the mere question of size and not to the difference between an interest group and a party. Thus if we exclude minor parties from the definition of parties, we must do so on the ground that they are so small as to make their pursuit of votes incidental rather than for the purpose of electing public office-holders. But this is not very firm ground, since even very small parties may be serious, though unrealistic, about future election victories in spite of present hopelessness.

Distinguishing parties from interest groups is a broader matter than deciding whether minor parties are parties. Most interest groups are plainly not parties even by our broad definition. They do not run candidates under their group label although they often support candidates, or a set of candidates, by endorsement, money, and votes. An interest group may support a party in these ways, but that does not make it a party unless it actually provides its label instead of a party label. The United Automobile Workers may endorse, finance, and campaign for Democratic party candidates in Michigan without becoming a party. It may even, through its leaders, influence or dominate the Michigan Democratic party without transforming itself into a party. To go a step farther, when the British National Union of Mineworkers, like most large British unions, actually affiliates itself organizationally to the Labour party, it becomes a section of a party in addition to retaining its identity as an interest group. The distinction here between the American and British union practices is not, for definitional purposes, so great. Both unions stop short of becoming parties on their own, even though, in their different organizational ways, they function with other groups to make and run a party.

There are many similar examples of active interest-group involvement in party politics. Different in kind, however, is the pattern exemplified by the French Peasant party in which an interest group (or a set of closely related interest groups) coincides with a party. This is much likelier on a large scale in a multi-party system than in a two-party system, as will be observed later, but wherever it happens to exist, it need not blur the analytical distinction between interest group and party. Two distinct functions remain—interest-group pressure and vote-getting—although they are performed by the same agency if an interest group is also a party. It is true that such a party cannot, within itself, be in as good a position as a more broadly based party to "aggregate" interests in order to arrive at a common policy result.[7] The aggregation must then be done among parties rather than within one. This distinction is explored in Chapter III and again in Chapter X. What is worth emphasizing here is that such interest-group parties cannot be dismissed as more primitive political agencies because their specialized bases tend to limit their size and prevent the achievement of majority status in election results. By any sensible functional definition, they are as fully parties as are the larger aggregative entities.

Another kind of group that is related to political parties is a "social movement." This is taken to be considerably more than an interest group although it may contain a well-defined interest, perhaps of an entire class. Social movements are said to be integrated by a set of constitutive ideas, or ideology, which a political party may not always have.[8] Thus, a social movement may become a party or adopt a party as its instrument, and when it does so, it marks the party with a distinctive ideology. But not every party is so marked by a social movement, and not every social movement takes the form of a party. A party is no more or less a legitimate party because it is also a social movement. It is thereby a special *kind* of party, and this will be remarked on at length subsequently in this work.

From this as from previous points, it is evident that I am deliberately avoiding a normative approach. No one type of party is assumed to be more "normal" than any other type that exists in Western democratic practice. The only thing I regard as normal is the existence of some kind of party, according to our extremely broad definition. Even here, "normal" means only that parties exist in each democratic nation, not that they must exist in every democratic system. Electoral competition and the subsequent management of government might conceivably be ordered without parties although, given Western experience, it is hard to imagine such a state of affairs.[9] There is no need to do so, although the possibility is noted in Chapter IV. Nor is there any need to answer the abstract question

[7] "The mode of performance of the aggregative function is crucial to the performance of the political system as a whole." Gabriel A. Almond and James S. Coleman, *The Politics of the Developing Areas* (Princeton: Princeton University Press, 1960), p. 44. The question of how crucial requires subsequent discussion.

[8] Rudolf Heberle, *Social Movements* (New York: Appleton-Century-Crofts, 1951), pp. 10–11.

[9] James Bryce put the point more strongly: "To begin with, parties are inevitable. No free large country has been without them. No one has shown how representative government could be worked without them." *Modern Democracies* (New York: Macmillan, 1921), I, 119.

whether a democratic nation must have political parties. At the level of empirical analysis, one can rest content with the view that, so far, parties have developed in every democratic nation. Ordinarily, they perform two functions: structuring the voting choice and conducting the government. Quite separate and different organizations may perform each function, although the same label ordinarily covers individuals both as candidates and as governing officials. The linkage between electoral and governing parties may be close or remote, and the way in which each function is performed may be of varying effectiveness or pervasiveness. Moreover, parties may perform other functions as well. It is only that parties usually seem to perform the electoral and governing functions in *some* degree. All parties, of course, do not perform both functions, since minor parties are unlikely to have a chance to manage governmental affairs.

So far, while talking about party functions, the word "functional" has not been used. Maybe it would be safer never to use the word, since it has so many more elaborate methodological meanings than any intended here. For example, it has meant starting from certain functions assumed to be common to all political systems, like political communication or rule-making, and then observing the various agencies which perform those functions in the several political systems.[10] In that approach, parties are among the agencies observed to perform the functions from which the analysis began. In the present work, however, I start from parties, study the functions they perform in certain political systems, and discuss only parenthetically how these functions may be performed by non-party agencies in other systems. In other words, the units of analysis are parties, not functions. But the parties as analytical units are defined by their functions. This is true in the literal sense that parties are defined primarily by their function of labelling candidates for public office. And it is true more broadly in that I intend to distinguish between parties in terms of their different functions in different societies at different times. Parties, as has been said, are the products of their respective societies, and so their functions are conceived as relevant to the maintenance of their respective systems.[11] What is functional in one system might be

[10] Almond and Coleman, *op. cit.*, p. 17.

[11] Ernest Nagel's especially lucid analysis of functionalism expresses considerable doubt about both its usefulness and its distinctiveness as a methodological approach in the social sciences. *The Structure of Science* (New York: Harcourt, Brace & World, 1961), pp. 525, 532, 533. See also Robert Merton, *Social Theory and Social Structure* (New York: Free Press of Glencoe, 1957), chap. 1.

dysfunctional in another. How and why this is the case is a cardinal concern of this work.

Whether or not this approach qualifies as genuinely functional, in contemporary social science, is doubtful. But the emphasis that it places on functions makes it different from Duverger's method of starting with organizational anatomy as the distinguishing characteristic of modern parties.[12] Although Duverger grants that organization is itself influenced by social factors, nevertheless he regards the degree of party organization as so important as to mark the difference between modern developed parties and old-fashioned ones. The more organizationally developed that parties are assumed to be, the more functional they are said to be in a twentieth-century nation. It is contrary to this assumption to start, as I do here, from the view that the degree of organization, like other party characteristics, is a response to the particular society and to the functions which parties are to perform in its political system.

This approach contains a naturalistic bias. Contrary to both Duverger and American party reformers, it tends to accept any existing parties in a working democratic system as suited to that system, because they do, in fact, function in that system. It is tempting to say that this approach is value-free, but it is only relatively so, since it shows a preference for a democratic system, presumably with parties of some kind.

From this position, an approach is made to three distinctive democratic theories of parties. Each of these, starting from a given value premise, leads to a party model of a particular kind. The first is the majority-rule theory. According to it, more than half of a community's electorate may be mobilized to support a policy or set of policies, and the majority thus mobilized ought to have the means to enact its policy. The means are to be provided by an organized party. "How else," asks a leading spokesman of the responsible party school, "can the majority get organized? If democracy means anything at all it means that the majority has the right to organize for the purpose of taking over the government."[13] The debatable point, however, is whether a majority in this sense can be said to exist. The fact that a majority may vote for the candidates of a given party does not mean that this same majority, or any majority, supports a given policy even if all of the party's candidates champion it.[14] Of course, it is possible

[12] Duverger, *op. cit.*, p. xv. See Aaron Wildavsky, "A Methodological Critique of Duverger's *Political Parties*," Journal of Politics, XXI (May, 1959), 303–18.

[13] Schattschneider, *op. cit.*, p. 208.

[14] The difficulty is not entirely avoided by shifting from a belief in a ma-

that the majority of voters supports the policy as well as the candidates of the victorious party. This is more likely in some societies, perhaps relatively homogeneous ones, than in others. But it is hard to accept as a general principle unless one also accepts the idea of a well-defined majority class within a community. Thus, the majority-rule position is especially compatible with the Marxist view of an industrial working-class, constituting a majority with distinctively socialist policies, juxtaposed against the minority interests of a minority capitalist class. The socialist working-class party, as will be shown, is the ideal model for the responsible-party school. But the members of this American school are not Marxists. The nearest they come to Marxist policy positions is in their advocacy of moderate measures of social amelioration, presumably to be supported primarily by the industrial working class they are designed to benefit. This resemblance is less important, for analytical purposes, than the purely theoretical one of accepting the validity of majority rule. It is this which leads the responsible-party advocate, like the Marxist, to believe that a party can and should represent clear-cut majority views and that it can and should be highly organized in order to translate these views into law.[15]

The second democratic theory relevant to a party model is one that can be labelled pluralist rather than majoritarian. The basic idea is that, rather than majority and minority in a democracy, there are groups of various types and sizes seeking to advance their views.[16] The crucial point is the denial of the existence of a well-defined majority view. This makes it unnecessary to question the claim of any such majority, if it did exist, to rule in its own behalf and against the desires of a minority, or of minorities. The fact is, however, that pluralists do tend to champion the legitimacy of minority interests

jority to a belief in majorities—that is, by substituting for the idea of a durable majority supporting a settled policy the idea of different majorities on different issues. It may be just as hard to know whether even a temporary majority supports a given policy when it votes for party candidates. Carried far enough, however, the majority-rule position would not clearly support a preference for a cohesive and responsible party model, since the majorities in support of a party would presumably shift so much from time to time that the party would have to be very loose in order to accommodate its majorities. See Austin Ranney and Willmoore Kendall, *Democracy and the American Party System* (New York: Harcourt, Brace, 1956), p. 28.

[15] A popular statement of the majoritarianism underlying the responsible-party advocacy is made by James MacGregor Burns, *The Deadlock of Democracy* (Englewood Cliffs, N. J.: Prentice-Hall, 1963), p. 335.

[16] Robert A. Dahl, *A Preface to Democratic Theory* (Chicago: The University of Chicago Press, 1956), p. 131.

(sometimes by talking about minority rights) against the claims of majority rule. What is significant is that in one way or another pluralist democrats can and do accept a much looser party model than the majoritarians. The pluralists do not need a party to stand for any settled majority, but only for one or more of the minorities which they see as constituting the body politic. A multi-party system would be compatible with the pluralist position, but so is a two-party system in which each of the two parties represents an aggregate of certain minorities. At most, each aggregation would represent policy tendencies more or less shared by several minorities. Plainly, this model is represented by present American national parties, and this is not surprising since pluralism is adopted by defenders of the American system.

The third theory is individualist, as opposed to both the majoritarians and pluralists. It is really so extreme that the party model to which it leads must be presented in the abstract rather than by reference to any existing organization. Individualism at the very end of the spectrum is what we are talking about. It assumes that the individual himself is the only valid unit to be represented in a democratic order and that any organization between voter and public officeholder is obtrusive and wrong. Roots of this approach may be found in Rousseau, or at least in some of Rousseau's ideas understood in certain ways, but the approach itself was actually brought to bear on modern parties by one of the first students of the subject, Ostrogorski.[17] Opposed to all of the organizational developments in the American and British parties that he studied, Ostrogorski suggested a model more suited to his assumption of atomistic individuals: a league of voters created from time to time for particular elections but without any institutional structure.

Connected though each of these models may be to certain value premises, they nonetheless serve our analytical purposes. Even the individualist one, not found in practice at the national level in any Western democracy, represents a useful polar point of comparison. And municipal nonpartisanship in the United States is an attempt to work with the individualist model in a limited way. The majoritarian and the pluralist models are of greater usefulness in analysis, since most of the parties we shall examine can be seen as approximations of one or the other. This is not to suggest that a nation whose parties conform to one of the two models has deliberately adopted the given model because of a theoretical preference for majoritarianism or plu-

[17] M. Y. Ostrogorski, *Democracy and the Organization of Political Parties* (London: Macmillan, 1902).

ralism. No such primacy for ideas or ideals seems reasonable. Rather, it is likely that a nation's parties come to resemble one model or the other as a result of many circumstances, and that a particular democratic theory develops at the same time partly to justify the model. The developmental circumstances must therefore be discussed, as they are in Chapter II, before describing the parties themselves.

This is not meant to downgrade the importance of ideas. On the contrary, it will be plain in much of this book that the pluralist conception of democracy is essential if there is to be a happy acceptance of my main interpretations of party development. What I contend is that there is no trend toward the kind of party favored by majoritarians, particularly not toward the mass-membership party, and that there are good reasons to welcome apparent tendencies in the other direction.

II

Developmental Circumstances

By speaking of developmental rather than determining circumstances, I do not deny the basic idea that parties should be considered more as responses to than causes of their environments. But I shall soften the implied determinism by indicating that parties develop along with their circumstances in such a way as subsequently to affect in turn at least some of those circumstances. Especially is this true for the relation of parties to certain matters like election arrangements.

The circumstances relevant to the development of political parties are broad and various. Topics they include are the enlargement of the suffrage, the social structure, the constitutionally provided executive-legislative relationship, the degree of federalism, and the election arrangements. Each affects the development of parties but, because of differences in timing as well as in substance, not in the same way in each national community. My discussion of each circumstance will be brief, the object to sketch in their nature and relevance rather than to describe in detail their effect on particular parties. The latter is the subject of most of the rest of the book.

1. *Enlargement of the Suffrage*

There is every reason to believe that modern political parties emerged with the extension of the vote to a fairly large proportion of the populace. Theoretically, parties might have functioned even when the suffrage was restricted to a small hereditary class or to large property-owners; and in some sense parties did then exist. In any representative assembly, however limited the franchise on which its members were elected, groups were formed. And it was not unusual, for example, in ancient Rome[1] or eighteenth-century Britain, for rep-

[1] Lily Ross Taylor, *Party Politics in the Age of Caesar* (Berkeley and Los Angeles: University of California Press, 1961), pp. 6–23, gives an illuminating comparison between Roman political groups and modern European and American parties.

19

resentatives to seek their own re-election and the election of their friends by indicating a group identity. Labelling, however, tended to be sporadic and unclear. Even according to the broadest definition, such groups are not clearly parties.[2] As long as voters were few, there was less need for the definite labelling we associate with modern parties. Nor was there the same need for extra-parliamentary organization. Without mass voting, there must have been more economical means for individuals to seek election than by organizing a political party. Just how many voters there had to be in order to justify a party in anything like the modern sense is uncertain. We do know that there were organizational responses before the establishment of universal manhood suffrage. Even when sizable groups were still excluded for racial or economic reasons, the franchise was sometimes wide enough for parties to function.

The leading case is found in early American society. Late eighteenth-century and early nineteenth-century United States fell short of full manhood suffrage, but the existing property qualifications for voting were loose and varied enough so that in a community consisting of many farm-owners, there were numerous eligible voters even before 1800. Furthermore, they lived in a revolutionary society which had just declared itself for republican principles compatible with popular participation. It is hardly an accident that this new nation, the first to enfranchise fairly large numbers, had the first modern parties, or the first parties of any kind if we adhere to the strict definition. They had functions to perform in the United States that did not exist elsewhere. That modern democratic parties originated in the United States is thus obvious. But it needs to be stressed anyway since this simple fact alone should cast doubt on the notion that American parties are retarded. Certainly they have had the most time to develop. They started first.

There is nothing brash about this assertion. It has been amply demonstrated by American political historians, most recently and most pointedly by William Chambers. Accepting the Federalists as well as the Jeffersonian Republicans as modern parties, Chambers regards their development, in the new, fairly democratic conditions, as an attempt to order politics in a way that personal factions could not do (but as they could and did in a predemocratic society).[3] Par-

[2] The institutional development of parties can be traced to intragovernmental organizations. Austin Ranney and Willmoore Kendall, *Democracy and the American Party System* (New York: Harcourt, Brace, 1956), pp. 111–15.

[3] William N. Chambers, *Political Parties in a New Nation* (New York: Oxford University Press, 1963), p. 147.

ties were needed to provide clarity and continuity for an enlarged electorate. The Jeffersonians were an especially new political phenomenon because they started as an opposition seeking (successfully) the peaceful transfer of power, and so performed a characteristic function of a democratic party.[4] More clearly than the Federalists, then, the Jeffersonians, before they too disintegrated, provided the prototype for the more highly developed parties of the Jacksonian and post-Jacksonian periods. Notable in Chamber's lucid analysis is that party development was most advanced in the most nearly modern American states; for example, Pennsylvania, with a large electorate and an absence of dominance by a traditional elite, was most congenial to the earliest parties.[5]

It is true that Chambers, by counting the Federalists along with the Jeffersonian Republicans, interprets American party development a little differently from other historians. It is more usual to regard the Federalists as pre-modern, like eighteenth-century English parties, and as merely presenting their actions to the country for approval or disapproval. This is Edgar E. Robinson's view. It is also Wilfred E. Binkley's; in his case, the reason for rejecting the Federalists is that they themselves denied the legitimacy of party organization.[6] Both Robinson and Binkley, however, have no doubt about the modern democratic character of the Jeffersonians. Indeed, they deliberately contrast the Jeffersonians, "the product of conditions peculiar to America,"[7] to the Federalists. They do not place the emergence of modern parties at a much different time from that used by Chambers. From either viewpoint, the United States in 1800 had at least one party developed as was none other in the world.

If that one were to be dismissed, as seems unreasonable, because it disintegrated after routing the Federalists and establishing a virtual monopoly, there would still be the Jacksonian parties to be counted well ahead of any European development of the same period. By the second quarter of the nineteenth century, there can be no doubt that distinctively modern American parties existed in response to the nearly universal white manhood suffrage. One of these parties, as we know, turned out to be most durable. Granted, the development was uneven. In certain respects, parties were more highly developed in

[4] V. O. Key, Jr., *Politics, Parties, and Pressure Groups* (5th ed.; New York: Crowell-Collier, 1964), p. 203.

[5] Chambers, *op. cit.*, p. 81.

[6] Wilfred E. Binkley, *American Political Parties* (New York: Alfred A. Knopf, 1943), pp. 50–51.

[7] Edgar E. Robinson, *The Evolution of American Political Parties* (New York: Harcourt, Brace, 1924), p. 75.

the northern states where popular participation was on a larger scale.[8] Northern cities, in particular, became the strongholds of organized parties. Not only did this begin early, but it continued throughout the nineteenth century, especially in response to the continued enfranchisement of new immigrants.

No nineteenth-century observer was likely to regard American parties as underdeveloped. Instead, they seemed the most highly organized political agencies in the world—the very expression of the mass democracy which the United States then represented almost alone. Henry Jones Ford, an American writing in the 1890's, spoke of the elaboration of American party structure, giving to party organization a massiveness and complexity unknown in governments like Great Britain's. An American party was able to govern and to secure votes in a way that Ford thought that British parties did not then do. In the 1890's, James Bryce, the most famous of British students of American politics, described "the tremendous power" of American party organization in even stronger, though less favorable, terms: "It enslaves local officials, it increases the tendency to regard members of Congress as mere delegates, it keeps men of independent character out of local and national politics, it puts bad men into place, it perverts the wishes of the people, it has in some places set up a tyranny under the forms of democracy."[9] He spoke of "the remarkable cohesion of parties in America."[10] Victories at the American ballot box had to be won by "the cohesion and docility of the troops."[11] No American, he said, would dream of offering himself for a post unless chosen by his party. Candidacies were controlled by parties through their representative bodies.[12]

The total picture is of American parties performing more functions more fully in the nineteenth century than either their defenders or their critics would credit them with in the middle of the twentieth century. And Bryce was by no means alone in his view of the relative importance of parties in the United States. Instead, in this respect, his impressions were typical. Bryce in particular is cited here both because of the special weight of his authority and because he does link the early growth of American parties to the early advance of popular suffrage in the United States.

[8] Henry Jones Ford, *The Rise and Growth of American Parties* (New York: Macmillan, 1898), p. 142.

[9] James Bryce, *The American Commonwealth* (Chicago: Charles Sergel, 1891), II, 491–92.

[10] *Ibid.*, p. 48.

[11] *Ibid.*, p. 72.

[12] *Ibid.*, pp. 74, 77.

In expecting European parties to become increasingly important as the suffrage was extended, neither Bryce nor anyone else had to assume that their organizational form would be identical with that pioneered in the United States. Bryce wanted Europe to avoid what he regarded as many evil American results. In at least one respect, he had reason to think that European parties would be different. They were developing mainly after administrative reforms had established the principle of employing civil servants on the basis of merit or, at any rate, some kind of career consideration. American parties, on the other hand, had developed before civil-service reforms and so had come to depend on the spoils system as a significant organizational ingredient. It is uncertain whether nineteenth-century American parties could have substantially developed without this ingredient. But European parties, starting only near the end of the nineteenth century, found a different organizational base.

What this suggests is that while the enlargement of the suffrage accounts for the development of modern parties, the timing of this enlargement in relation to other factors helps to account for the particular nature of parties in particular environments. The parties' relation to civil-service reform is only one of many possible consequences of the time at which the suffrage is extended on a large scale. Much more significant may be the temporal relation of suffrage extension to the economic stage reached by a given national community. The parties that respond to nearly universal white manhood suffrage when introduced in a still largely agrarian society, like the United States in the early nineteenth century, may be very different from the parties that respond to a similar suffrage extension in an already industrialized nation, like Britain of the late nineteenth century. In the latter case (to be analyzed at length in a subsequent chapter), there existed a large urban proletariat potentially organizable by a party and perhaps already organized in trade unions or even in social movements before most members of this proletariat had the right to vote. British political parties were faced with a large and well-defined class that had not existed in anything like the same degree when American parties first developed.

No such difference would exist if the mass extension of the suffrage came automatically at the same stage of economic development in each nation. But plainly the relationship is not automatic if by economic development we mean industrialization and urbanization. By that criterion, Great Britain should have been ahead not only of the United States but also of the rest of the world in its introduction of the universal franchise. On the other hand, if economic development

means relatively high per-capita wealth and income, the early introduction of the mass franchise in the United States, compared to
Britain and other nations, would be explicable without introducing
non-economic factors. Still, it is doubtful whether any purely economic explanation of suffrage extension is entirely satisfactory. The
much less tangible factor of a community's values, derived from a
multitude of sources, plays some part.[13] It helps to explain why all
European nations, whose values included a recognized class structure
and a respect for traditional authority, were slower to extend the
franchise than was the new American community—itself often rebelling against European culture.

In discussing Europe in this connection, it is worth noting that
extension of the franchise was not the only democratic practice that
many nations adopted at a later date than the United States. Political
power was often not effectively transferred from hereditary rulers to
representative assemblies, no matter how narrow their electorates,
until late in the nineteenth century. In Germany at least, there is
doubt whether that power was ever effectively transferred until after
World War I; therefore, the existence of manhood suffrage in the
Reich from 1867 may not have the same significance it would have
had in a polity with a more powerful parliamentary authority.[14] This
observation only strengthens the case for the comparative slowness of
Europe to adopt democratic practices.

British experience here is especially convincing, even though Parliament effectively exercised authority throughout the nineteenth
century and perhaps earlier. The point is that members of the House
of Commons were elected by a very small portion of the population
until 1867, when the ballot was first extended to most urban males. It
is impossible to give mass democracy an earlier date in British history.
The Reform Act of 1832, while eliminating the worst maldistribution
of seats, enfranchised relatively few new voters. Property qualifications remained major barriers for most Englishmen so that as late as
1866 only about one adult male in eight had the vote.[15] Even the
enfranchisement of 1867—the famous "leap in the dark"—did not
extend the vote either to all urban males or to most of the rural popu-

[13] That national values play a very large part is argued by Seymour Martin
Lipset, The First New Nation (New York: Basic Books, 1963), chap. 7.

[14] The constitutional exclusion of the Reichstag from responsibility for gov-
ernmental policies made political parties into pressure groups of a special sort.
Guenther Roth, The Social Democrats in Imperial Germany (Totowa, N.J.:
Bedminster Press, 1963).

[15] Sir Ivor Jennings, Party Politics (Cambridge: Cambridge University Press,
1961), II, 116.

lation. Not until 1885 were rural and urban males treated pretty much alike, and not until 1919 was the principle of universality clearly enacted. Still, 1867 is the most appropriate date since the Reform Act of that year created sufficient voters for parties to develop organizationally and for the British themselves, often with misgivings, to believe that they were now adopting democracy. Mark well that this was fifty to seventy-five years after roughly the same circumstance existed in the United States.

The significance can be grasped by appreciating the nature of British politics before 1867. Party competition, in the sense long established for the American electorate, remained largely unknown in Britain. In fact, competition for parliamentary seats was not general; many candidates for the House of Commons were elected unopposed.[16] They did tend to subscribe to a parliamentary faction and a leader, which together had some of the characteristics of a party. But personal loyalty was the vital element. However much the parliamentary factions came to resemble modern parliamentary parties (and the resemblance was close despite less cohesion and discipline), they did not yet maintain the electoral ties of modern parties. Looser and more personal methods suited the nondemocratic franchise.

Most other European nations also lacked the crucial basis for modern parties until at least fairly late in the nineteenth century. Many were even later than Britain. Belgium did not significantly extend its franchise until 1893, when manhood suffrage was granted. The Scandinavian nations, now apparently models of stable democracy, were all slow to establish democratic electorates. Denmark's manhood suffrage dates from 1901, Norway's from 1898, and Sweden's from 1909. Perhaps France is the nearest to a major exception. It introduced manhood suffrage in 1848, but, save briefly, voting did not take place in a nonauthoritarian environment until 1875. Elsewhere there is nothing approximating universal manhood suffrage before 1867. Canada, Australia, and New Zealand were not yet nations before that date.

Even many nations that broadly extended the franchise late in the nineteenth century tended to limit its democratic impact by various provisions. The German Reich, as already indicated, is a well-known case. But elsewhere also, on occasion, the franchise was extended only for the election of a parliamentary body with limited authority. In addition, votes could be unequally weighted by classes (as in Prussia until 1919), plural voting allowed for privileged groups, or balloting

16 *Ibid.*, p. 5.

made public rather than secret. The last of these provisions is treated as especially important in Stein Rokkan's most useful comparative survey of political participation.[17] Rokkan shows that only very late in the nineteenth century or very early in the twentieth did many European nations adopt effectively secret voting along with manhood suffrage. And it was only late in the nineteenth century that the United States instituted the same practice. But the absence of secret voting, as Rokkan indicates, may have been more likely to intimidate poorer citizens in Europe, because older class relations persisted, than in the United States, where bribery seems to have been the chief disadvantage of public voting. The point is arguable, however, and since the secret ballot is only indirectly related to the development of conditions for modern parties, it is expedient here again to concentrate on the suffrage itself. Its relative lateness of arrival on a mass basis in Europe is entirely plain, and so is the relative lateness of modern parties.

The significance of this difference in timing is indicated in two ways. First, if large-scale party organization is understood as a strong *early* response to mass enfranchisement, it is possible to account for the fact that American parties reached their organizational peaks in the nineteenth century. Second, it is also possible to account for the different and, in some respects, greater party organization subsequently developed in Europe, because it took place in nations different from the United States by virtue of both their general background and their considerable urban industrialization prior to mass democracy. The setting for the first modern parties was sharply different in Europe than it had been in the United States. And this matter of timing is even more significant since a nation's first modern parties may establish durable patterns of behavior. The first parties themselves often remained for many decades or as long as a century under their original labels, and even when succeeded by others the original organizational forms ordinarily remained. As S. M. Lipset has observed in a roughly similar context, institutionalized behavior, once established, fosters ideologies helping to sustain the behavior.[18] Parties affect their political environments if only by maintaining themselves once they have been brought into existence.

---

[17] It is from this survey that the dates for suffrage extension are taken. Stein Rokkan, "Political Participation" (Paper presented to International Political Science Association, Paris, 1961). Additional information may be found in Douglas V. Verney, *Parliamentary Reform in Sweden 1886–1921* (London: Oxford University Press, 1957), pp. 91, 110–11, 212–13.

[18] Lipset, *op. cit.*, p. 196.

2. Social Structure

I have suggested that the social structure of a nation helps to mold the character of political parties at crucial developmental stages. And it is ordinarily taken for granted that the social structure continues to exert influence. This is especially so when the term is understood, as it is here, to include, along with economically based classes, the ways a nation is divided (or united) by religion, race, ethnic background, language, educational levels, and manners or styles of life. All Western nations are divided in some or all of these ways, but the degrees of particular divisions and their combinations differ significantly. They also differ when division by geographic sections is taken into account. That kind of division, obviously important both on its own and because of its interaction with other aspects of social structure, is excluded only for the time being; it can usefully be discussed later as part of the impact of federalism on political parties.

There is a tendency to analyze this complex matter of social structure with socio-economic class as the base point, on the assumption that the fundamental division in a modern Western nation is between the industrial working class and the bulk of the remaining, heavily middle-class, population. Then each nation is analyzed to learn the extent to which it conforms to this pattern or to which other identifiable social factors produce deviations. Parties in or out of the parliamentary arena, as well as voting behavior, can also be analyzed from this point of view, and I have generally adopted this approach here. There is nothing wrong with the procedure, provided that the class division is not treated as a norm to which all nations, after but transient deviations, are expected eventually to conform.

In this perspective, however cautiously understood, class appears to have been more important in European than American politics. That is, the European working class, more sharply set apart from the middle class than was the American working class, fashioned more nearly its own agencies and so gave a more distinctively class character to European politics. The presence in the twentieth century of large socialist or communist working-class parties in all West European nations is the evident result. The greater class-consciousness producing this European result is attributable to several factors. Europe, unlike the United States, entered the industrial age with a pre-existing class structure, in fact and in principle, which segregated the mass of the population from its social betters. Before the rise of industrial capitalism, it was customary in both groups to think in terms of upper and lower classes, and continuation of this established custom, especially in the early stages of the new industrial order, was natural. These class orientations were accentuated by (although they also had much to do with causing) the exclusion of most of the European population from the franchise. So while the industrial working class may have been new, conditioned by the new industrial society, not all of its characteristics were purely the consequences of that new society. Its very existence as so distinctive a group owed much to earlier history. Classes, as Schumpeter has sagely remarked, "bear the marks of different centuries on their brow."[19]

. They were also, it must be stressed on the other side, the product of their own times. Here too the European working class differed from the American because it was considerably less prosperous. European nations, as they industrialized, were simply not as rich as the United States. At least partly because the total wealth and income were smaller, there was less for the workers. They were not only less well off than American workers; they also seemed poorer relative to their richer fellow-countrymen than American workers seemed relative to their capitalist employers. These economic reasons for greater class consciousness in Europe persisted well beyond the early capitalist days. Into our own time (though perhaps not beyond the 1960's) the European worker's standard of living remained sufficiently below the American so as alone to account for a different kind of working-class politics. The lower standard, derived from a lower starting point, rose less continuously than it might have otherwise because of the shattering effect of the two world wars on the European economy. The class pattern, associated with an originally abysmal poverty, existed for a long time, until the rapidly increasing prosperity of the 1950's began to affect it. "Classes," again to quote Schumpeter, "once they have come into being, harden in their mold and perpetuate themselves."[20]

But this simplified European-American comparison of class, while it has validity and usefulness, should be qualified in two ways. First, there are similarities as well as differences between European and American classes. After all, some class consciousness does exist in the United States, where the working class is fairly well organized for economic, and to an extent also for political, purposes. And, on the other side, European workers have not been so conscious of their separate class identity as to be organized only on class lines. A classless United States cannot be juxtaposed with a class-conscious Europe.

[19] Joseph Schumpeter, *Imperialism and Social Classes,* trans. Heinz Norden (Oxford: Basil Blackwell, 1951), p. 145.
[20] *Ibid.*

This would imply that social mobility existed in the United States in an altogether different way than in Europe, but that has been shown not to be the case. Considerable intergenerational social mobility appears in every Western industrial society. The rise in status of talented and ambitious children of the working class is not peculiar to the United States.[21] It may be more frequent and easier in the United States—which is significant enough to help explain some of the political phenomena with which we are concerned—but this kind of difference ought not to be exaggerated into a total difference in kind.

Secondly, neither Europe nor the United States, with respect to the working class, should be treated monolithically. Only in the broadest sense can one speak of Europe in contrast to the United States. For some purposes, there is a spectrum in which all Western nations can be located at various points in relation to each other. In the matter of class consciousness and party politics, the United States is far enough away from all the European nations on such a spectrum so as to be considered a case apart. Yet in this as in other respects, there are also great differences among individual European nations.[22] British working-class politics during the first half of the twentieth century, for example, were milder than those of Germany and France; Italy's, befitting the least prosperous of Western democratic nations, remained the sharpest into the 1960's. And it is also important to appreciate differences within each nation. This is best exemplified by the United States because it is so large and diverse. Working-class consciousness has been present in large northern cities as it has not been in the south or in the midwestern prairies, and the consequent political organization varies from region to region. In some places more than others, the class division resembles that of Western Europe.

In making this qualification, non-class factors come into play. The degree to which a society is rural or urban is obviously one such factor: class consciousness in rural areas differs from that which I have just discussed. Not only would rural society not produce in its own area an industrial working-class base for a political party, but insofar as that rural society was important in the national community, it would limit the pervasiveness of working-class politics in the nation as a whole. Furthermore, rural society might exert this kind of influence not only by its present importance but by having been important

[21] David V. Glass (ed.), *Social Mobility in Britain* (London: Routledge and Kegan Paul, 1954), pp. 260–65, 344–46.
[22] The point is made convincingly in another connection by Leonard Krieger, "A View from the Farther Shore," *Comparative Studies in Society and History*, V (April, 1963), 269–73.

in an earlier period when political parties first developed. American national parties were originally shaped by the then prevailing rural character of the United States, and perhaps they still bear some of the marks of that environment, even though organizationally there were always urban influences.

It is equally evident that racial, ethnic, religious, and linguistic differences serve to complicate class politics in one way or another. Most frequently, such differences cut across class lines. Not only does religion, for example, often help to account for voting behavior, but it may also account for a political party specifically designed (like the Catholic-inspired Christian Democrats of continental Europe) to compete for working-class loyalties on a confessional basis. Politics derived in one way or another from such a non-class factor is not readily washed away. A party based on defending a religion may out-live the day when the religion was threatened. Similarly, ethnic blocs outlive the discrimination that made for ethnic consciousness. Such politics persist when several factors coincide, as do ethnic, religious, and linguistic differences in Canada.

Education and style of life stand somewhat differently in their relation to class because they are so much the product or accompaniment of class. But they are not entirely so. Although the amount of formal education an individual receives is linked to his class status (for example, working-class children usually have fewer years of formal education than middle-class children), a nation's public policy may provide a great deal of education for everyone and so diminish the difference between classes. As early as 1870 the United States had 57 per cent of its five- to seventeen-year-olds enrolled in public schools, and this was at a time when almost everywhere else any widespread education beyond the most elementary years was virtually unknown. The contrast remained sharp at the secondary-school level even in 1950, when the American percentage of fifteen-year-olds attending school was between two and three times as high as the English or French percentage, and still higher for sixteen- and seventeen-year-olds.[23] Or, looked at from another angle, when in 1949 only

[23] Seymour Martin Lipset and Reinhard Bendix, *Social Mobility in Industrial Society* (Berkeley and Los Angeles: University of California Press, 1959), pp. 93–94. Complementing these figures is another study showing that in the mid-1950's, the ratio in the United States of those over age fifteen enrolled in secondary schools to the total age group was above 60 per cent, contrasted to European ratios of 17–18 per cent for Germany and Britain, 25–28 per cent for Belgium, France, and Switzerland, and 30–35 per cent for the Scandinavian nations. J. Frederick Dewhurst *et al.*, *Europe's Needs and Resources* (New York: The Twentieth Century Fund, 1961), pp. 315–16.

about 12 per cent of the English adult population had been through any kind of secondary school,[24] American high schools had been attended by larger numbers for almost a half-century. The result, in the United States, has been the facilitation of a certain kind of upward mobility and a reduction in one vital way of the social distance between classes.

The American style of life may also be said to reduce class differences. Despite evident extremes of wealth and poverty, where stark differences surely exist in substance as in style, there has been a pervasiveness, even uniformity, of consumption patterns that Europeans always notice in contrast to their own societies.[25] Mass production of quality items, along with mass advertising media, was a striking feature of American society before taking hold on the same scale elsewhere. The early wealth and prosperity of the United States was essential to this development, but it owed something also to the levelling tendencies of American culture, including the commitment to equal educational opportunities for everyone. Therefore, it is not certain that European mass production of quality items will have the same effects.

Although education and style of life, when relatively uniform from class to class, serve to reduce class differences, they can reinforce class differences when they markedly differ. British education is a case in point. Its limited scope and internal demarcations between fee-paying and government-supported schools and (among the latter) between academic and nonacademic secondary training, tend to maintain the separation of the working and middle classes. So does the maintenance of different cultural values associated with earlier class traditions.

3. *Federalism*

Federalism is both a social and a structural phenomenon. A nation's governmental structure is likely to be significantly federal only if its society is sectionally diverse, or was at the start. For, to have a continued vitality in opposition to the centralizing pressures of recent times, structural federalism must have had a social basis strong enough to have left major residues. From the other side, structural federalism, once it exists, helps to sustain some degree of social federalism by providing an organized political outlet for the original regional diversity. The two are intimately related and only separable

[24] Glass, *op. cit.*, p. 105.
[25] Morris Rosenberg, "Perpetual Obstacles to Class Consciousness," *Social Forces*, XXXII (October, 1953), 22–27.

for certain analytical purposes. Together they furnish an importantly different environment for political parties than does a unitary nation, particularly when the parties have emerged in a period before much centralization. Then, instead of being formed nationally, with local branches, they are formed primarily to contest regional elections. They may long remain so oriented and only federated for national elections. In other words, party organization tends to parallel governmental organization, particularly the governmental organization prevailing when parties originally developed.

This is generally borne out by the histories of Canada, Australia, Switzerland, and the United States, whose parties started to function in federal circumstances. In each, the major national parties are federations of regional parties, be they at the state, province, or canton level. A somewhat different case is presented by the present West German republic. Admittedly it is federal, if less clearly so than the others, but this federalism is a postwar creation while German *parties* have an earlier history of democratic experience in less federal circumstances, which gives them a more national character than parties of the older, more continuous federal systems. Yet even the German parties now have federal aspects that parties in persistently unitary nations do not have.

Switzerland is in some ways more federal than the larger nations. Socially, its regions contain distinct ethnic and linguistic groups. And structurally, the authority of its regional units, the cantons, is strongly preserved vis-à-vis the national government. It is appropriate, therefore, that Swiss parties should be especially strong at the cantonal level and that their national organizations should be truly confederational.[26] Like the Swiss system generally, they have been exposed to less centralizing or nationalizing pressure than parties in the United States or Australia. It is possible that Canada, where federalism is sustained by the coinciding religious, ethnic, and linguistic distinctiveness of Quebec, is closer to the Swiss pattern. And Canadian parties remain strongly provincial in their organization. However, even Australian federalism, based though it is on a less diverse society, has state parties that count for more than national ones.[27] Structural federalism in Australia seems strong enough to sustain these state parties as basic units perhaps because they existed, in the states, before the Australian Commonwealth was established. Thus, as in the United

[26] George A. Codding, *The Federal Government of Switzerland* (Boston: Houghton Mifflin, 1961), pp. 124–30.

[27] J. D. B. Miller, *Australian Government and Politics* (London: Gerald Duckworth, 1964), p. 64.

States and Canada, national parties are "loosely-knit federations of state organizations."[28]

Australia is not the only nation to provide evidence for the persistence of federalism, as an influence on parties, long after originally determining circumstances have changed. The United States is also a case in point. American parties did not antedate the federal union, but they developed in an earlier, much less centralized society. In the nineteenth century, national and state political stakes were more nearly equal than they are now. Although from the beginning American parties competed for national as well as state offices, their organizations were built primarily at the state level. Perhaps they would be so built even now, for the states would still seem important units for the accumulation of power, despite the centripetal forces of American economic and social life. Significantly, however, state governments have become less powerful relative to the national government than state parties have relative to their respective national parties. These shifts cannot be readily measured, but it has not been observed that party power has moved to Washington as much as governmental power, although the one accompanies the other to some extent. American parties have even brought divisive state and local influences to bear on national policy-making.[29] The United States does not yet, at any rate, have basically national parties, despite the development of increasingly national policies, as in the labor and welfare fields, ever since constitutional interpretations yielded to the pressures of the American economy.[30] In this respect, the Constitution changed before political parties.

We can see the enduring effect of federal forms even more clearly if we examine the sharp contrast of American and British experiences. By the time modern parties were created, Britain was not only constitutionally unitary, as it had long been, but to a great extent geographically unitary. There were the Celtic fringes of Ireland, Scotland, and Wales, but the most unassimilated of these, Ireland, was soon to become independent. Most of Britain was simply English, and it had neither the large area nor the diverse and geographically segregated

<hr />

[28] L. C. Webb, "The Australian Party System," *The Australian Political Party System*, ed. Australian Institute of Political Science (Sydney: Angus and Robertson, 1954), p. 115.

[29] Morton Grodzins, "American Political Parties and the American System," *Western Political Quarterly*, XIII (December, 1960), pp. 974–98.

[30] Before the 1930's it could be argued that the American Constitution was interpreted so as to limit national powers to the extent of making broad social and economic policies inappropriate for national parties. Arthur N. Holcombe, *The Political Parties of Today* (New York: Harper, 1924), chap. 2.

population to make for social federalism. By the mid-nineteenth century, the nation was already united by railroads—sufficient, in so small a country, to bring almost everyone within a day's journey of everyone else. Social, economic, and governmental power were all primarily in London. The bases for political parties then were overwhelmingly national, and it is no wonder that they organized nationally from the start. There could hardly have been a less federal environment, and there could hardly be less federal parties than those of Britain. Local party units and regional groupings exist for little more than administrative convenience. Local elections are contested as well as national ones, but the parties are not organized around local government so as to provide power bases for regional factions. In this regard, it is true, Britain is extreme even among unitary nations. France's parties, for instance, are not always so completely national, although they are more so than those of federal nations.

4. *Executive and Legislative Authority*

A more purely constitutional circumstance for the development of political parties is found in the provisions for the relations of executive and legislative authority. By describing these matters as "constitutional," I mean not only those spelled out in a written document, although they may be of considerable importance, but also the customary and legal bases for the structure of government.

Broadly speaking, the structure is either that of a parliamentary system, in which the executive authority rests on majority support in the legislative body, or that of the American presidential-congressional system, in which each authority is directly and separately elected. Variations of each type exist, but almost every democratic government is of one type or the other. Fifth Republic France is a hybrid, and Switzerland is a special case. Otherwise, all of our Western democracies have the parliamentary system except for the United States.

At the outset, I must insist that the structure of executive-legislative authority, like the degree of federalism, may be taken as "given" in relation to the development of political parties, even though we know that constitutions are often changed and that parties help to build new executive and legislative structures. Existing or reincarnated parties did so in making the postwar constitutions in France, West Germany, and Italy. In each of these cases, however, the basic parliamentary mold was not changed, and the parties helped to perpetuate the general constitutional structure to which they were accustomed. Only in 1958, with the beginning of the Fifth Republic, was an effort made to establish a genuinely different structure in which the old parties would have to fit as best they could, and this was by the will of one man and not that of the parties. Putting aside this one case, whose lasting effect is not yet established, it is safe to argue that Western democracies have maintained the general constitutional types with which they began. And, in each nation, the constitutional type existed in some form from before the parties. The parties, in other words, grew in the conditioning environment of a given governmental structure. They had to adapt organizationally and electorally to it. What they could become was fixed, within certain limits, by the constitution as well as by the social conditions of the nation.[31]

This is another way of saying that especially in this respect there were different possibilities for parties in the United States than elsewhere.[32] The American separation of executive and legislative powers gives parties two electoral targets in the national arena: the presidency and the congress. And because control of the executive branch flows exclusively from presidential election, it is possible for a party to be victoriously united, with majority support, only in that election and still gain an obviously important goal. Moreover, the executive power can be retained without continuous majority support in the legislative branch. Consequently, there is absent in the American system the strongly compelling force for legislative party unity that exists in a parliamentary system. I will stress the significance of this difference in a later explanation of the limited governing function of American parties. Here it is enough to note the durability of the constitutional structure and so of its impact on parties.

The practical political difficulty, perhaps the near impossibility, of substituting a parliamentary system for that of the separation of powers has led many Americans who want more united national parties to start their reform with the parties themselves. This involves trying to achieve congressional party unity, especially by a majority of the president's own party, without the parliamentary system's incentives for unity. What the parliamentary system so neatly provides elsewhere would, in the United States, have to be imposed by a party

[31] A cogent argument for the influence of constitutional structure has been made by Samuel H. Beer in a critical review of Maurice Duverger's work. "Les Partis Politiques," *Western Political Quarterly*, VI (September, 1953), 516–17.

[32] Denis W. Brogan makes the point that American parties have functioned to maintain an awkward constitutional system but that by so doing they have sacrificed other possible party functions. *Politics in America* (New York: Harper, 1954), pp. 91–92.

organization for programmatic purposes. It cannot be said that more united American parties would be impossible to produce. The separation of powers allows for the possibility of relatively united parties, and, after all, American legislative parties are united to some degree and for some purposes already. The one major qualification is that it would be difficult for the American system to work with very strongly united parties if a different party from the president's happens to control the houses of congress. Party reformers assume that this difficulty could be avoided if parties were so united that voters would elect presidential and congressional candidates of the same party, but something would have to be done about off-year congressional elections and about holdover U.S. senators.

The fact is that the shrewdest advocates of party reform have been well aware of the deterrents imposed by the American constitutional system. Certainly this was true of Woodrow Wilson, who did not turn to party reform, under presidential leadership, until after he had argued for the adoption of the parliamentary system.[33] And it is true of E. E. Schattschneider, a recent and eloquent advocate, who has plainly said that in Britain it is cabinet government that has given that nation the foremost example of the kind of party government he admires. On the other hand, provisions of the United States Constitution "have made impossible the rise of responsible cabinet government and all that a responsible cabinet system might mean in terms of party government."[34]

In the contrasting West European situation, parliaments, though originally sharing power with monarchs, gradually made executive government (the ministries) responsible to elected representatives. By reducing the monarchs to figureheads or by substituting weak presidents, there was a drift away from the separation of powers or an avoidance of it through "government by assembly" in the French republican tradition. In either case, power was to be monopolized by the elected representative body. This often occurred, as it did in Britain, before the democratic age of modern parties. When parties did develop—indeed, as they developed—they could foresee full executive and legislative control by obtaining a parliamentary majority. This was as true in Canada, Australia, and New Zealand, where the British parliamentary system was transplanted, as in Western Europe.

[33] Wilson's interesting shift from constitutional to party reform is analyzed by Austin Ranney, *The Doctrine of Responsible Party Government* (Urbana: University of Illinois Press, 1962), pp. 39–42.

[34] E. E. Schattschneider, *Party Government* (New York: Rinehart, 1942), p. 126.

5. Election Arrangements

Grouped under the heading of election arrangements are various governmental rules, distinguishable from constitutional structure by their readier alterability. In fact, many election arrangements are so readily altered that their inclusion here among developmental circumstances might well be questioned. It is best at the outset to grant their marginal status in this respect, since I shall discuss some of the ways of conducting elections (for example, by proportional representation or by single-member, simple plurality) as more the results than the causes of party systems. Yet, election arrangements also have a causal relationship to parties.[35]

The most conspicuous and the most discussed differences in elections are found in the ways of choosing members of legislatures. Even if we ignore deliberate rigging to give preponderance to a group or section of voters, and limit our attention to acceptable democratic practices, a great variety is still possible. The simplest, it is true, is to carve the geographical area being represented into roughly equal constituencies, each electing as its member the candidate with more votes than anyone else. Only one ballot is required. This single-member, simple-plurality arrangement has been widely used, and it appears to suit situations in which there are no more than two strong candidates. When there are more than two, the simple-plurality feature can be qualified by use of a preferential ballot on which the voter ranks each of several candidates; his second choice is then counted if there is no first-choice majority. Another way to elect by majority, when there are more than two strong candidates in a single-member district, is to have a run-off election when no candidate obtains a clear majority on the original ballot. It is common in the United States to allow only the two leading candidates on the second ballot, so ensuring a majority for one of the candidates. But France has not so restricted candidates when using this second-ballot procedure (although they tend to restrict themselves), and consequently a member may be elected without a clear majority of votes even in the run-off.

Opening the way for greater variation is the multi-member district. When legislative elections are held on this basis, voters are usually asked to vote for as many members as are to be elected from a given district. Voters may also be asked to number their choices or to vote for a particular bloc of party candidates. The latter system—party-list proportional representation—is the usual form for elections in multi-

---

[35] Interestingly, election arrangements have been treated as even more emphatically influential by a sociologist. Lipset, *op. cit.*, chap. 9.

member districts in Europe. The number of members elected from each district varies greatly from country to country and even from district to district. The more members from each district, the greater the possibility of mathematical equality in representation for each party presenting lists of candidates.

So brief a summary barely touches the intricacies of methods of legislative election. There are many ways in which the methods may be modified and combined. Some of these will subsequently have to be taken into account, but for the time being it is enough to note the basic difference between single-member, simple-plurality election and multi-member, proportional representation. In national elections at least, the first of these methods is used in the United States, Canada, New Zealand, Great Britain, and, with an important modification, Australia. But almost all of continental Western Europe plus Eire uses or has recently used some form of proportional representation. West Germany elects half of its national legislature by proportional representation and the rest in single-member districts. France, having employed proportional representation in the Fourth Republic, in the Fifth Republic returned to the Third Republic's customary single-member district with second-ballot run-offs. But the French change their electoral system so frequently that this particular shift cannot be regarded as the start of any trend.

How did legislative elections come to be so differently arranged? Historical antecedents do not help here, since all the nations we are discussing entered the democratic age with a variant of the single-member system. The simplicity of this system would originally have been responsible for its use. Proportional representation was not even invented until the middle of the nineteenth century, and it was not adopted, in its now familiar party-list form, by any continental nation until after some experience with democratic parliamentary elections in single-member districts. When that experience coincided with the emergence of more than two strong parties, as it did in continental Europe during the late nineteenth and early twentieth centuries, proportional representation was adopted in order more equitably to represent the several parties. Undoubtedly party-list proportional representation better serves this purpose since it enables a party that would get a minority of, say, 20 per cent of the vote in every one of five small single-member districts to obtain one of five seats when these districts were combined in one large district electing five members according to party proportions. If the same vote distribution held nationally, the party with 20 per cent of the vote would, with proportional representation, receive 20 per cent of the parliamentary seats.

With the single-member system, there could be no such result unless the party's 20 per cent was so highly concentrated in certain districts (as is unlikely) that its candidates could win pluralities in those districts. A minority party with evenly distributed votes might win no seats. Moreover, supporters of a minority party could be discouraged from voting for their party because its chances of winning seats were so slight. It is no wonder, then, that minority parties, or parties with votes distributed nationally and not just sectionally, have urged that proportional representation be established. It is also no wonder that these parties succeeded in getting the election system changed when they were, in the aggregate, numerous enough to be a majority.[36] Self-interest here bolstered the appeal of mathematical equity that proportional representation undoubtedly had for egalitarian socialists and liberal intellectuals.

Regarding it as historically demonstrated that proportional representation owes its establishment largely to the prior existence of parties and specifically of several parties, it is nevertheless also possible to regard proportional representation, like any other election system, as subsequently an important circumstance for political parties. Once proportional representation is established, it helps not only to perpetuate the parties that established it, but also to facilitate the emergence and continuance of other nonsectional minority parties. At least, proportional representation makes it easier for such parties to exist and to be politically influential. This much can safely be said without falling into exaggerations about the influence of an election method. It is not necessary to believe that in the absence of a social basis for multi-party politics, proportional representation could create them. Nor is it necessary to believe that single-member, simple-plurality election could create pure two-party politics without other factors being present. Even in Britain the rigor of single-member, simple-plurality election has not liquidated the Liberal party, although it has decisively restricted its parliamentary influence. In other words, election methods exert their influence within the limits of other more basic circumstances. Thus, despite the admitted aid that proportional representation gives to the perpetuation of more than two parties, it is conceivable that a multi-party system could be transformed into a virtual two-party system without first abolishing proportional representation. This may have been happening in West Germany during the last decade. But one can still make the modest claim that the

[36] How this came about is convincingly presented by John G. Grumm, "Theories of Electoral Systems," *Midwest Journal of Political Science*, II (November, 1958), pp. 357-76.

change to a two-party system would have been facilitated if complete single-district, simple-plurality election had first been adopted.

What has to be faced is that proportional representation is the method of legislative election in most Western democratic countries. Besides West Germany (where it may not be the settled one) and Italy, there are, among others, such stable democracies as those of Scandinavia, Belgium, Switzerland, and the Netherlands, all of which have used proportional representation during most of the twentieth century.[37] The fact that all of these nations, except possibly Switzerland, have parliamentary systems does not mean that there is any inherent relation between such systems and proportional representation. At least there is not the same kind of obvious relation as there is between the system of the separation of powers and the popular election of the chief executive—by far the single most important officer in the American system (and even more so in de Gaulle's French system, where the president's power is much greater than parliament's). A collegial executive, such as Uruguay has had, is possible even with the separation of powers, but it is not a Western democratic practice. Switzerland has a collegial executive, but it resembles a parliamentary system's cabinet in its method of election and, to some extent, in its lines of responsibility. The single popularly elected chief executive is the established form. Since there is no way for one man to be elected by proportional representation, he must be chosen by plurality or majority election. Popular votes may be totalled nationally, as they are in France, or by electoral units like the American states. In one way or another, voters must choose a single candidate for the office. They may do so on more than one ballot, as is required in France if no presidential candidate receives a popular majority on the first ballot. The United States also requires a majority election (in this case of electoral votes); the House of Representatives, not the electorate, does the second balloting if there has been no electoral majority. These provisions for election only by majority cannot be regarded as absolutely inevitable concomitants of a strong independently elected chief executive, but they do seem appropriate. It is unlikely that the framers of any democratic system would want to have so powerful an officer as the American president elected without a kind of majority support. That his support can be in an electoral college and not always in the popular vote is now regarded as a defect, although a minor one, of the American system.

[37] Data on nations using proportional representation before World War II are presented by James Hogan, *Election and Representation* (Oxford: Basil Blackwell, 1945), pp. 3–4.

The required majority election of the president in the United States has long been observed to influence the American party system. We noted earlier that presidential election itself allows national parties to be but loosely united. The majority feature, however, militates in favor of there being no more than two such entities seriously engaged in presenting candidates for the presidency. To obtain a majority requires that a vast diversity of interests and groups unite, at least for this purpose, in order to have any chance to win. Third parties have not been absent from presidential contention, but they are usually unsuccessful and short-lived. The incentives are overwhelmingly in favor of very different kinds of politicians joining under one of two banners in order to secure the fruits of executive office. It is doubtful that without the presidency and its method of election there would have been sufficient other incentives in the American system to have produced, especially in the past century, as regular a two-party alignment in a nation so large and so diverse.

There is another American election arrangement that is sharply distinguishable from arrangements elsewhere. It is the presence of a very large number of elective offices. Even at the national level, where the phenomenon is least striking, American voters make three choices: representative, senator, and president plus vice president. This contrasts with the parliamentary system, in which voters ordinarily elect members of but one legislative chamber or, less often, of two. And at the state and local levels, where other nations adhere to their national pattern of electing only their legislators or councillors, the United States has its voters choose several state executive officers, numerous county and municipal administrators, many state and local judges, and school board members, in addition to legislators and councillors of the state, county, and city units. American ballots, at general elections (not yet to discuss primaries), are staggeringly long, especially when, as is usual, the national, state, and county offices are being filled at the same time. No other country, it must be emphasized, places such demands on its citizens. There is no way to explain the American pattern except to say that it resulted from an excess of democratic spirit. Direct popular election of numerous office-holders was an article of faith among the Americans who established the new or reconstituted state and local governments of the early nineteenth century. And the populist and progressive forces of the late nineteenth and early twentieth centuries extended the established Jacksonian principle of popular election.

Although the growth of modern American parties coincides with direct popular election of a host of officers, the parties do not appear to have been responsible for the widespread extension of the principle. Rather, they seem to have adapted to it. Their relatively early growth may even have been influenced by the long ballot. American voters clearly needed help in making their many ballot choices, especially in cities where even the local governmental candidates could not be known personally to the electorate. Parties furnished this help in the form of slates of candidates on ballot papers originally prepared and distributed, it should be noted, by the parties themselves. The fact that preparation and distribution of ballots was in party hands increased the power of parties, as Bryce observed,[38] but even after governmental authorities took over the task in the late nineteenth century, the power to influence voter choice was left to the parties, since their labels continued to be printed on the ballot to identify candidates. Identification of this kind has not been usual in Britain or in the English-speaking Commonwealth, where, with only one legislative representative to be chosen, there is less need for it. Labels would still be useful, however, and in continental European nations they have been printed on the ballots, whether prepared by government or parties, even for legislative elections in single-member districts. With party-list proportional representation, the party label is necessarily the crucial item on the ballot.

It can be observed from the comparison of the American, British, and continental European experiences that the presence of the party label on the ballot is not positively related to the present-day strength of the political parties. Everyone would acknowledge that British parties are now stronger than American, in almost every respect, and at least as strong as those in Europe. This is not to say that the ballot form never contributes to the strength of parties. It is not certain, for example, that American parties, contending against various hostile elements in the environment, would be even as strong as they are without their labels appearing on the ballot to structure voting decisions. And in the nineteenth century, American parties may have developed as fully as they did because of the labelling need imposed by the multitude of elective offices. It is true that after governmental authorities took over ballot-preparation some of the bases for party organization, namely financing and distributing ballots, did disappear. But no one is likely to claim that this alone led to a subsequent weakening of party organization.

Yet there is something about the long American ballot that may now weaken party organization, even though it helped to produce it

[38] Bryce, *op. cit.*, p. 138.

in the first place. The very fact that the label is on the ballot, through no organizational effort, means that a party does not have to expend resources in order to inform voters ahead of time as to who the party candidates are. By performing this service for the parties, the government adds to the value of the label. Any candidate securing a place on a party ticket will derive benefit from the label even without his active participation in any collective party enterprise. He may, therefore, find it expedient to concentrate his efforts and those of his friends on an individual, non-party campaign seeking votes beyond those to be received on a straight party basis. He does not have to tell voters about his party identification in order to receive the electoral benefits of that identification. In other words, the very existence of the party label on the ballot, while it certainly facilitates straight-ticket voting, is compatible with the fragmentation of campaign organization so readily observed in committees for individual candidates. Still, this fragmentation is not the simple result of the labelling. Having a party-list, proportional-representation ballot has no such effect. On the contrary, collective party effort is maximized by the party-list system since it is the party and not individual candidates that the voter is choosing. It is really the multiplicity of elective offices (including so many executive ones) that, even with the party label, encourages individual campaign organization. Without the label on the ballot, there might be even more fragmentation.

This does seem to be true in cases where American cities and states have taken the labels off the ballot, establishing what are known in the United States as nonpartisan elections (but which I will call nonpartisan *ballots*). Observing their effect is complicated, as will be noted in a later chapter, by the fact that they coexist with partisan-ballot elections for some state and national offices. Thus, the parties, functioning anyway for these latter purposes, may have more significance in the nonpartisan ballots than would be the case if there were no party balloting at all. At least, however, it is plain that nonpartisan ballots in the United States do not cause parties to become stronger than they are or were with partisan ballots. American parties do not thereby come to resemble British parties which, without the labels, acquaint the voters so thoroughly with the names of their candidates. But this should not be surprising. Compared to the simplicity of letting voters in each British constituency know the name of their party's candidate for a single legislative office, the task for an American party would be staggering, although admittedly not impossible. Generally, the idea of challenging American parties with universally nonpartisan ballots, like Britain's, is intriguing. They might collapse entirely, abdicating the field to individuals and ad hoc organizations, or they might become much stronger, given the need to do much more in order to survive at all. Curiously, this is one possible reform available from the arsenal of British practice that no advocate of stronger American parties has proposed. Perhaps it seems like a shock treatment from which the patient would never recover.

Americans are now so accustomed to legal control of party candidate selection, along with a host of other governmental controls over parties, that it is hard to appreciate how unusual it is among Western democratic nations. What has been done in the United States is to convert what were originally private associations into quasi-official entities whose "members," especially for candidate-selection purposes, are legally stated to be some portion of the electorate instead of merely those who happen to belong to associations (as one might belong to any club). Other nations, even the European ones that place party labels on their ballots, do not seek to determine party membership by law. They leave party members, in the usual associational sense of the term, to select candidates although there may be some legal regulation of parties in other respects. In the United States, in contrast, the portion of the electorate legally entitled to participate in selecting a party's candidates may be as broad as all voters who want to participate on the given day of the "primary election"—the name given to the governmentally-provided balloting to decide which candidates shall have the various party labels in the subsequent general election. Less broad than this open primary, but still much different in kind from strictly associational control, is the primary closed to all except those numerous citizens who have previously registered, with the government's election agency, as voters for the party in whose primary they now want to vote. It is true that the primary, open or closed, does not prevail for all American offices. Presidential candidacies most notably are only indirectly affected by primaries, and some states retain the older party conventions for choosing candidates for certain offices. Even then, convention delegates themselves are chosen by a legally controlled process that gives at least nominal power to voters who are not associational members. Generally, however, primaries are the characteristic American method for choosing party candidates in the twentieth century.

The consequences of this conspicuous American divergence from other Western nations needs to be explored at various later points in this book. Here it is enough to note that primaries make the organizational task more complicated but not impossible. Other legal regulations of parties have similar effects, but this cannot be said of all of the American election arrangements.

In summary, constitutional and social circumstances have by no means been entirely unfavorable to the development of American parties. The early extension of the suffrage produced modern parties in the United States before they emerged elsewhere. Linked to this historical disparity, the significant difference between American and European class structures made for different, but neither better nor worse, kinds of parties. Likewise, the parliamentary system and the separation of powers, or federal and unitary systems, are distinguishing circumstances in the limited non-normative sense. Having identified these circumstances and having indicated the nature of their force, most of the remainder of this work can be concentrated on the political parties that developed under them. Instead of starting from the predicated independent variables, the presentation from now on is organized around the dependent or intervening variables—that is, the parties—in order to understand how they have been shaped by what has already been discussed.

III

The Nature of Competition

The number of competing parties is a first concern. Some writers, discussing this subject, say they are discussing the "party system," but that term has broader connotations which make it inappropriate to use simply for the number of parties existing in a given place. Although the number of parties is related to the *kind* of parties, the relation is reciprocal rather than unidirectional. Both the number and the kind of parties are viewed as responses to broader circumstances. The number of parties is worth separate analysis here in order to emphasize how, in fact, it is a response of this nature. Displaying the variety among Western democratic nations, in numbers of parties, should help to illustrate this point and at the same time raise questions about the view that there is any right number for democratic societies generally.

1. *The One-Party Possibility*

To have more than one party seems a democratic norm. This follows from the assumption that political democracy requires competition to give the voters a choice. It is hard to take serious exception to this reasoning unless one argues that there need be no parties at all but only competition purely between individual candidates, as some American states and localities have attempted (as will be discussed in the next chapter). But the universality of party development accompanying the mass franchise argues against the feasibility of individual competition at the national level. Given one party, the competitive desideratum calls for at least one other party. It is conceivable, however, that there could be competition between a single party and individual candidates of no party.[1] And it is by no means inconceivable

[1] In one careful and highly sophisticated effort to construct an index of political development for all countries, based heavily on the role of parties, having even one party is rated as in some degree advanced. Phillips Cutright, "National Political Development," in Nelson W. Polsby, Robert A. Dentler, and Paul A. Smith (eds.), *Politics and Social Life* (Boston: Houghton Mifflin, 1963), pp. 569–82. Cutright does award more development points to a nation

that competition among candidates within a single party, as in American primaries, could provide voters with meaningful choices.

It is not this American kind of one-party arrangement that adherents of party competition are usually trying to define as violations of the democratic norm. Rather, it is the totalitarian party in a totalitarian nation. Certainly the Communist party of the Soviet Union, for example, is different in kind from a competitive party (even a Communist party as long as it is out of power) in a Western democratic society.[2] But the Communist party of the Soviet Union is different, or nondemocratic, not primarily because it is the only party in the country. Being the only party is not what keeps it from having internal competition open to the electorate or from otherwise operating as a democratic party. It has functions to perform for the Soviet state that are incompatible with electoral competition. Because of these functions, it is the only party, and it monopolizes political power in a well-defined undemocratic way. Therefore, there is no need to place all one-party arrangements beyond the democratic pale in order to dispose of the Soviet case.

Whether the one-party arrangements now frequent among the new nations should be classified with the arrangement in the Soviet Union is open to question. It seems reasonable to do so, as for the fascist regimes in Europe between the wars, whenever a single party monopolizes political power and allows for no competitive electoral process to affect its holders of power. This has happened especially in Africa. A new nation makes a single party the instrument for achieving national solidarity, otherwise absent, in much the same way that the Soviet Union has used the Communist Party as the instrument for class unity.[3] Only one legitimate interest is recognized in either case, and it is appropriate that there should be but one chosen instrument for that interest.

By definition, however, Western democratic nations do not elimi-

---

with at least two parties represented in parliament than to a nation with only one.

[2] C. W. Cassinelli, "The Totalitarian Party," *Journal of Politics,* XXIV (February, 1962), 11–41. For an account influenced by recent East European experience, see Jerzy J. Wiatr, " 'One-party' Systems—The Concept and Issue for Comparative Studies," in Erik Allardt and Yrjo Littunen (eds.), *Cleavages, Ideologies and Party Systems* (Helsinki: Academic Bookstore, 1964), pp. 281–90.

[3] Rupert Emerson, *Political Modernization: The Single-Party System* (Denver: University of Denver Social Science Foundation, 1963), pp. 24–25. The Mexican case is illustrative, as in Robert E. Scott, *Mexican Government in Transition* (Urbana: University of Illinois Press, 1964), pp. 106–9.

nate competition for any such reason (except, interestingly, in emergency periods). Therefore, where there is a one-party arrangement, its basis must be different. However poorly it may function, in terms of providing meaningful electoral competition, it cannot be dismissed as undemocratic. In one sense, there is a great deal of one-partyism in democratic countries. National party competition conceals many one-party constituencies. Certain localities, even large states or regions, are often almost entirely dominated by a single party. This is more obvious in countries with national two-party systems than it is in multi-party countries which, with proportional representation, enlarge the opportunities for minority parties to elect a few candidates in a constituency where there is only one large party. No such opportunities exist for a minority party in a two-party nation with single-member, simple-plurality elections. For example, as many as two-thirds of British parliamentary constituencies and of American congressional constituencies are "safe," from one election to the next, for periods of several decades, for the candidates of one party or the other. Only certain secular trends are likely to upset one-party area domination in nations, like the United States and Britain, whose politics are otherwise stable. This domination is often stronger for local elections than for national ones held in the same area. One-party politics characterizes local government for long periods in most large British and American cities, with the minority party's role confined to permanent opposition. All that saves this opposition from utter futility is the chance to win minority legislative or council representation, or the chance to contribute as many votes as possible to a potential majority in a large constituency of which the locality is a part (for example, for a gubernatorial candidate). Whether these chances mean that there is really two-partyism depends on the point of view. Strictly in terms of local government, there is still no significant inter-party competition for power. But even a locally permanent minority belongs to a genuinely competitive party in the larger arena.

The same question arises in a federal system where state or regional units dominated by a single party coexist with national party competition. The single party in such cases may be affiliated, in varying degree, with one of the two major national parties, as is ordinarily true in the United States,[4] or it may be primarily regional, as has been true in some Canadian provinces. Either way, however, two-party

---

[4] Whether states have one-party patterns, or something in between, is of considerable concern to American political scientists. Austin Ranney and Willmoore Kendall, *Democracy and the American Party System* (New York: Harcourt, Brace, 1956).

politics is not effectively institutionalized below the national level. And sometimes, as for a long period in the American south, one party may be so dominant as to preclude even nationally competitive politics within the region. From this and other American experiences, a good deal is known about the possibilities of one-party politics. The outstanding point is that they can be electorally competitive. The basis for competition is intra-party, and its form is the party primary officially conducted by the state in the manner of a general election. Indeed, the American primary (to be discussed at greater length in a subsequent chapter) may have been adopted for the very purpose of giving voters a choice of candidates in areas committed to one-party politics for sectional reasons growing out of the Civil War. Whether that purpose has been fulfilled is debatable.

One-party Democratic politics in the American south provides the best-known experience with this purpose of the primary election. The experience has been most fully described by V. O. Key in one of the great landmark studies of American political science. Southern one-party politics, he said, tends to consist of fluid factions that cannot be counted on to present voters with a clear-cut choice between the ins and the outs in the manner of two-party competition. Often, factions are so chaotic that electoral followings become little more than personal ones based on a friends-and-neighbors approach. Other times, especially in certain states, a clear enough bifactionalism grows around the dominating personality of a given politician and his heirs so as to allow voters to choose much as they might if there were two competing parties.[5] Still, there remains the institutional difference that internal one-party competition takes place without benefit of ballot-labelling in the style of American general elections. No matter how sharp the bifactional alignment, or how much each faction might itself use a label, candidates of both factions are all Democrats on the ballot. Thus southern factions of the Democratic party, to identify their candidates to their followers, would have to carry the message as effectively as do British parties in the absence of ballot labels. That would be most arduous for the whole of a long ballot, but conceivable with respect to a few leading offices. It is doubtful, therefore, that the absence of factional labels on the ballot is fundamentally what prevents southern primaries from being more consistently contested by recognizable factions.

[5] V. O. Key, Jr., *Southern Politics in State and Nation* (New York: Alfred A. Knopf, 1950). pp. 11–12, 128. A close look at bifactionalism in a single southern state is given by Allan P. Sindler, *Huey Long's Louisiana* (Baltimore: Johns Hopkins Press, 1956), pp. 282–86.

A more lasting and coherent bifactionalism developed in the favorable environment of at least one northern state. Wisconsin, during most of the first half of the twentieth century, was sufficiently Republican to make Republican nomination to state-wide office tantamount to election, and Wisconsin did have sharp enough issue conflicts to produce two identifiable factions, progressives and stalwarts, contesting the primary elections established principally to settle Republican nominations. Each faction had slates for state-wide offices, the legislature, and county offices. Each faction also had an organization that was no less highly developed than most American party organizations. In fact, they both were parties in virtually all of their state functions. They were not so nationally, except insofar as one or the other could control Wisconsin's formal Republican organization and so be part of the national Republican party. For this and other reasons, the state's Republican bifactionalism was uneasily related to national politics. Wisconsin voters came to prefer Democratic presidential candidates on occasion, and eventually often. The state was not insulated from national two-party competition either as long, or to the same degree, as southern states. Consequently, one-party Republican politics, after first giving way temporarily to three-party competition (during a decade when the progressive Republicans were formally a party instead of a faction), finally disappeared in favor of inter-party competition with the Democrats.[6]

It should also be noted that the open form of primary is most like a general election and so most nearly satisfies the democratic norm of electoral competition when there is only one party likely to win (but where a substantial minority belongs to another party). There can be no doubt that this norm was often fulfilled in Wisconsin, when primary turnouts were about as large as general election turnouts and when the primary election presented a choice between coherent factions. There also can be no doubt that on these occasions what existed was really two-party competition in all but name. Such competition, we know from British experience, can exist without ballot labels. All, therefore, that distinguishes the Wisconsin experience from that customarily regarded as two-party competition in the United States is that the names and organizations of the state's competing groups were different from those of the two national parties.

More significantly distinguishable from two-party competition is the absence of coherent factions within a single-party framework. This was true even in Wisconsin some of the time and in south-

[6] Leon D. Epstein, *Politics in Wisconsin* (Madison: University of Wisconsin Press, 1958), chap. 3.

ern states much of the time. Then, electoral competition is more purely individualistic than in any two-party or multi-party situation. It is bound to appear old-fashioned or underdeveloped if the structuring of politics by parties is viewed as the modern accompaniment of the mass franchise. Observing the American southern states as relatively backward in various ways is compatible with this perspective. But it is not absolutely certain that party competition is always more advanced than competition among individuals. Experiences with nonpartisan elections in American cities, including some new suburbs, should give pause before generalizing with finality.

Besides considering whether inter-party competition is more advanced and more nearly meets the democratic norm, we can also make a comparison with internal one-party competition in terms of policy results. Again, the American states are the laboratory, but this time for more exacting analyses. Let us begin with the hypothesis that two-party politics leads to greater governmental responsiveness to public demands for certain policies, especially ones concerning welfare services, to be carried out if the candidate wins office. The problem is to learn to what extent favorable policy outputs are correlated with two-party competition (as opposed to one-party politics). One study, confined to the six New England states, makes a case for positive correlation. On tax load and apportionment issues, along with state services, chiefly welfare, this study found more favorable legislative results in the three states (Massachusetts, Connecticut, and Rhode Island) with two-party competition than in the three states (Maine, Vermont, and New Hampshire) with largely one-party politics.[7] Because these two sets of states differ from each other in various aspects of social and economic life—like degree of wealth and urbanization— which may affect policy outputs as much as party competition does, it is hard to be convinced that the hypothesis has been established, despite the author's effort to allow for socio-economic differences in his analysis. It is even harder to be convinced after a subsequent study, by other authors, of all the American states. Here, while the same kind of favorable results in terms of welfare policies were found to be positively related to party competition, they were also found to be positively related to socio-economic factors, especially per-capita income. And, most telling, the rank-order correlation between per-capita income and welfare policy is much higher with party competition held constant (by grouping competitive states and noncompetitive states) than is the rank-order correlation between party competition

[7] Duane Lockard, *New England State Politics* (Princeton: Princeton University Press, 1959), chap. 12.

and welfare policy with per-capita income held constant.[8] As the authors rightly observe, party competition does not seem important even as an intervening variable in determining policy results.

What also emerges from this kind of analysis is that party competition itself is more likely to develop under certain socio-economic conditions than under others. The factor most often associated with party competition is urbanization, but this of course is understood to be accompanied by high per-capita incomes, manufacturing, etc. Since in Britain, Germany, and some other European countries, political parties did not develop until industrialization was well established, the generalization that party competition is an urban phenomenon is bound to hold in these nations unless the rural districts could be shown to have more party competition than the cities. And there is no such evidence. On the other hand, competitive parties did develop in the United States, Canada, Australia, and New Zealand before pervasive urbanization, and this may also be argued for France, Norway, Denmark, and Italy. Evidently, then, party competition can exist in non-urban environments. A good twentieth-century example is the persistence of active two-party competition in the Rocky Mountain states.[9]

The question remains whether party competition in less urban areas differs significantly in degree or kind from that in more urban areas. Party competition, although not entirely absent either in nations or in states that remain predominantly rural, might still be less pervasive and especially weak in the rural communities within the larger unit. A finding in support of this view emerges from a study of the mixed urban and rural state of Ohio. Ohio generally has two-party competition, but this competition is more highly associated with urban than rural counties, evidently because of the cities' more widely divergent groups, more complicated class structure, greater division of labor, greater economic rivalry, and wider range of ideas.[10] Undoubtedly these factors distinguishing an urban county, especially a metropolitan one, from a rural county, provide a socio-economic basis

[8] Richard E. Dawson and James A. Robinson, "Inter-Party Competition, Economic Variables, and Welfare Policies in American States," *Journal of Politics*, XXV (May, 1963), 265–89. See also the authors' "The Politics of Welfare," in Herbert Jacob and Kenneth Vines (eds.), *Politics in the American States* (Boston: Little, Brown, 1965), chap. 10.

[9] Thomas W. Casstevens and Charles Press, "The Context of Democratic Competition in American State Politics," *American Journal of Sociology*, LXVIII (March, 1963), 536–43.

[10] Heinz Eulau, "The Ecological Basis of Party Systems: The Case of Ohio," *Midwest Journal of Political Science*, I (August, 1957), 125–35.

for two-party division that is absent in a more homogeneous community. Thus, at the urban county level, we would expect more organized party competition. But there is no reason to expect a greater degree of competition within each of the smaller units (districts, wards, or suburbs) composing that county. These units may be just as homogeneous as small rural towns and offer equally limited bases for party competition. An industrial working-class ward may be as overwhelmingly Democratic in its voting behavior and in its potential leadership, or a middle-class suburb as overwhelmingly Republican, as a rural town is overwhelmingly committed to one party or the other. But because the smaller urban units are combined with others within a county they become part of a heterogeneous community that provides a basis for two-party competition in a way unlikely for a rural county. Looking at the matter in this perspective lessens the significance of any showing, like that in Ohio, of the association of urbanism with party competition. In any event, the universality of the Ohio finding has been questioned in a study of another state.[11]

Whether there is a basis for party competition within a given unit of government, then, depends on more than simply the degree of urbanism. Apart from the many factors more or less associated with urbanism, we must consider the relation of the given unit to the politics of the larger community of which it is part. Generally, party attachments are made at levels beyond the local unit—the national level in a unitary nation and both state and national levels in a federal one. Then, in some degree, these attachments are reflected at local levels, in organization as in voting behavior. This happens even in the United States, where locally organized parties are contained within state parties, although occasionally a large-city party organization may dominate the state party organization. Thus, while parties at the higher levels are divided primarily, let us say, between working-class support of and middle-class opposition to social-welfare policies, there may be little support and overwhelming opposition in rural communities, so that the two-party competition of urban communities is simply inapplicable. On the other hand, if national or state parties are divided primarily on some less exclusively urban issue, then the rural communities might have an equal basis for two-party competition.

Federal systems display the operation of this principle in the relation of state or provincial parties to national parties. Entire American

[11] David Gold and John Schmidhauser, "Urbanization and Party Competition: The Case of Iowa," *Midwest Journal of Political Science*, IV (February, 1960), 62–75.

states, as we know, have often been so overwhelmingly committed to the stand of a particular national party that the other party can secure almost no following. Canada provides roughly parallel instances. The long Liberal party dominance in Quebec is the best known, but there is another kind of example, both in Quebec and in the prairie provinces, showing the domination of provincial politics by a single party other than the two major national ones. The long hegemony of the Social Credit party in Alberta is the leading case. It depended on the preponderance in Alberta of small-propertied independent commodity producers who thought neither of the two eastern-based national parties adequately represented their interest. (In this respect, Social Credit, gaining power in 1935, had succeeded another exclusively prairie party, the United Farmers, which had ruled since 1921.) Maintaining provincial control with overwhelming majorities continuously from 1935 into the 1960's, Social Credit virtually eliminated party competition except in national elections. However, because open party opposition, although ineffective, has persisted, one-partyism may not be the correct label. Preferable, perhaps, is "quasi-party" competition, to borrow a term applied in the major work on politics in Alberta.[12] Assuredly there is nothing like two-party or multi-party competition in the usual sense.

Nor can it be said that two-party or multi-party competition exists in Northern Ireland. Here, where both structural and social federalism exist as a unique instance within the United Kingdom, the Ulster Unionists dominate politics in much the same way as Democrats have done in Alabama. This holds for elections to what might be called the state parliament, sitting in Belfast, and to the national parliament in London (where Ulster Unionists function with British Conservatives). In Northern Ireland no less than in the American south or in Alberta, the dominant party serves a sectional interest transcending the two-party alignment of the rest of the nation. The Ulster Unionists are the clearest case of all, since they unite Protestants, including many industrial workers who might otherwise be drawn to the Labour party, in opposition to the minority of Catholics favoring ties to Eire rather than Britain.

Altogether, there are so many similar examples of the absence of party competition at one or another level that it is necessary to qualify any generalization about party competition being a norm in Western democratic nations. It is not certain that one-partyism is only a transient characteristic of backward areas. Perhaps one is encouraged to

---

[12] C. B. Macpherson, *Democracy in Alberta* (Toronto: University of Toronto Press, 1953), p. 246.

think so by the recent development of two-party competition in an increasing number of American states, including even southern states to some degree, as more states are urbanized and industrialized and fit the party pattern set by an urban and industrial nation. But there may be counter-trends within each state as, in urban and especially metropolitan communities, there is an increase in de facto segregation in separate governmental units of various blocs of voters. Congressional districts, as well as other sub-state constituencies, may thus become more one-party rather than less. This process would be expedited by a continued nationalization of politics, since making each national party stand everywhere for the same policies would intensify its appeals to some groups and curtail its breadth of appeal.[13]

There is no reason to think that this is a peculiarly American phenomenon. And, of course, it is not peculiar to federal systems since it does not rest on units like states or provinces. For that reason, local one-partyism may not be quite so significant a phenomenon as state one-partyism even though it is more nearly universal. City wards and districts, or suburbs, do not provide the same loci for political power that states or provinces do. They are not so likely, therefore, to serve a sectional interest, as it was possible for the southern Democratic party in the United States, Social Credit in Alberta, and the Ulster Unionists in Northern Ireland. Nevertheless, the absence of party competition at local levels forces us to appreciate that the two-party competition we take for granted in national or state politics is often based on aggregations of different one-party constituencies. Only a minority of the local constituencies in a nation or state may be genuinely competitive, and perhaps only temporarily, while they move from being safe for one party to being safe for the other. This kind of competition is more important in a parliamentary system with no nation-wide or state-wide constituencies to elect presidents or governors. But some parliamentary systems create inter-party competition by having large multi-member constituencies that offer more fertile ground for competing groups than the smaller single-member constituencies could. This is one result of proportional representation.

2. The Two-Party Pattern

So far, I have discussed two-party competition only in the limited context of a comparison to one-party politics. That is indeed a narrow American perspective. Among Western democratic nations, two-party

[13] The point was cogently made in reply to a manifesto from the responsible-party school. Julius Turner, "Responsible Parties: A Dissent from the Floor," *American Political Science Review*, XLV (March, 1951), 143–52.

competition is regularly viewed as the alternative to single-party dominance only in the United States (and occasionally in other federal systems). Much more often it is juxtaposed to multi-party competition.
This significantly changes the terms of discussion. Inter-party competition of some kind is assumed to be not only desirable but also usual.
The question remains whether two-party competition is better suited
to democratic purposes. Another way of putting the question is to ask
whether two-party competition does not represent a norm for democratic societies.

There are two related reasons for considering two-party competition as a norm. One stems from the belief that there is a natural
dualism about public responses to political issues—that voters and
politicians are either for or against a given policy.[14] So it seems natural to choose between only two sets of candidates presumably pledged
to two opposing issue-positions. The trouble with this is that even
with clear pro and con positions on any one issue, there are likely to
be several issues or sets of issues at any one time, and there is then
the basis for more than one dualism of opinion. It cannot be assumed
that the several dualisms will always coincide so that the same voters
and politicians opposing each other on one issue will do so on the
others. The degree of coincidence depends on the nature of the issues
and of the society where they emerge. Thus contemporary Britain,
without major ethnic, religious, or other noneconomic divisions cutting across an overwhelmingly urban industrial society, seems more
hospitable than Canada or France, for example, to a dualism at least
with respect to domestic issues. France of the Third and Fourth Republics is really a leading case of the noncoincidence of opinion
cleavages. French divisions on social-welfare legislation, religious
education, and constitutional structure overlapped but were far from
being identical. They hardly provided the basis for two-party competition, as even a believer in natural dualism like Maurice Duverger
has admitted. He found similar noncoinciding cleavages in most of
continental Europe (as of 1951), and he recognized that, as in
France, these cleavages made for a multi-party pattern.[15] Still, Duverger thought that there was a natural movement of societies toward
two-party competition, although it was countered in many places by
opposite tendencies.

The second reason for regarding two-party competition as a norm
lies in the belief that it is the simplest and likeliest way to have effec-

[14] Maurice Duverger, *Political Parties*, trans. Barbara and Robert North
(New York: John Wiley & Sons, 1954), p. 216.
[15] *Ibid.*, pp. 229, 232.

tive democratic government. Partly this is a matter of thinking that voters should have a clear-cut choice between prospective governing groups and that this is possible only when there are but two parties, one or the other of which regularly emerges as a majority to be held accountable for managing the government. There is also the point that the government itself might be more stable when majority party support is almost automatically provided by two-party competition— particularly in a parliamentary system requiring continuous majority support in the legislature to sustain the executive in office. So strong is the belief in the usefulness of two-party competition in this situation that changes in parliamentary election systems, usually from proportional representation to single-member districts, have been advocated in order to try to substitute two parties for several existing ones. Whether such an engineered change is practical or even desirable without other more fundamental socio-political changes is open to doubt. In a way, it has been tried in Fifth Republic France, where single-member districts with second-ballot runoffs were reinstated after the Fouth Republic's proportional representation. The result, in 1962, it is sometimes said, was the first parliamentary majority for a single party in the history of republican France. It is true that this new majority (for Charles de Gaulle's favored Union for the New Republic [UNR]) could not have been achieved under proportional representation, since the UNR lacked a majority of popular votes.[16] But neither could it have been achieved without de Gaulle. And being for or against de Gaulle is an impermanent dualism. Moreover, without him or anyone like him under the Third Republic, the same single-member, double-ballot system failed to produce a majority party, not to mention two-party competition, which even the Gaullist republic has not so far created. Popular presidential election in France may be more consequential in this respect, but, again, other circumstances are also essential.

These two arguments for two-party competition involve different conceptions of the competitive norm. With the first, the norm, assumed to be desirable, is seen to be a natural one toward which societies tend to develop. But with the second, the norm is simply very desirable. Whether or not two-party competition is natural, or more natural than multi-party competition, the believers in its desirability want to engineer its establishment. The existence of issue-dualism is not necessary as a foundation for their position. Instead, they may

[16] Seymour Martin Lipset, *The First New Nation* (New York: Basic Books, 1963), pp. 298–99, attributes this new majority in France to the change in election methods.

seek to manufacture this dualism by creating two-party competition. Within limits, this is perhaps possible, as may be seen in the way that the two American national parties manage to channel the opinions of a large and diverse nation. The limits are that the two parties must be loose and accommodating rather than strictly doctrinal on every issue. Thus, with each party containing many adherents who on certain issues agree with the other party, the parties are unlikely to present clear-cut policy alternatives. But this is not at all what advocates of two-party competition want. Part of their argument for two-party competition as a desirable norm is that it provides a clear-cut choice between groups standing for opposing policies. Certainly, this is what the responsible party school is talking about. And it makes a good deal of sense. Without each of two parties representing definite policies, much of the presumed advantage of two-party competition is lost. Two-party competition might still be more desirable than the multi-party variety, simply by providing a choice between two potentially governing parties rather than between several parties none of which could secure a majority to govern alone. This advantage is sufficient for those, like the author, who believe that elections are democratically meaningful even if simply between competing candidates, or groups of candidates, but it is not enough for those who insist that each group of candidates, as the representatives of a party, must stand for clearly distinguishable policies. It might be impossible in a diverse nation like the United States to secure this result and still have only two parties.

One other aspect of the two-party model must be noted. It is the approximation to it that comes when there is a majority or near-majority party facing two or more minority parties. The French UNR has been in this situation since 1962, and Scandinavian Social Democrats, notably those in Norway and Sweden, have enjoyed a similar status for even longer.[17] Technically, only half of the model is present under these conditions. There is *a* majority or potential majority party capable of governing, but there is no alternative of the same nature. Instead, there is at most a coalition. How near the coalition is to being a recognizable alternative depends on how united the parties composing it are in presenting themselves as a governing combination and on how united they turn out to be as a government. In Scandinavia, the coalition is identifiable as a non-socialist or anti-socialist alternative, but still it is not so united a force as the Social Democratic parties.

[17] Henry Valen and Daniel Katz, "The Norwegian Party System: Decision-Making, Oligarchic Tendencies, and Democratic Functioning" (Paper delivered at the American Political Science Association, Washington, 1962).

Unity is difficult since there are several minority parties. It is easier in Australia where, facing the larger Labor party, there has been a combination of two other parties, the large Liberal party plus the smaller Country party. The Australian situation differs from the Scandinavian in another way. Australia began with something more like two-party competition and subsequently developed minor parties, but Scandinavian nations have a history of multi-party competition that, with the growth of the Social Democrats, came in one respect to resemble two-party competition. It is reasonable still to regard Scandinavian politics as less two-party than multi-party.

The fact is that there are not many Western nations with two-party competition. If it is the democratic norm, it is a norm that is not usually met. This is entirely apart from local one-partyism concealed beneath national two-partyism. Even at national levels, two-party competition is less frequent than multi-party competition, despite a definition of two-partyism broad enough to include nations with substantial third or fourth parties, like Britain, Australia, Canada, and Austria, along with the United States and New Zealand. In each of these nations, it is at least customary and reasonable to expect either of two parties to secure a majority or a near-majority so as to be able to govern with, at most, the help of a small minority party. Including Canada is surely generous, since there for a long period only one party seemed able to obtain a majority, and at times recently neither has been able to do so. Austria, for other reasons to be discussed, is also marginal. Nor is there anything ungenerous about the exclusions. West Germany is the closest to eligibility of those excluded, but it cannot be said to have two-party competition so long as only one of its parties, the Christian Democratic Union, can achieve majority status (and then only once) and the next largest party, the Social Democrats, receives less than 40 per cent of the vote. Thus, figuring West Germany as no more than on the verge of changing from a multi-party pattern, we have only six cases of two-party competition among twenty Western democratic nations. Admittedly, the balance would be more even if populations and not individual nations were counted. The United States, over three times as large as any other Western democracy, tips the balance. Even by that unlikely method of counting, however, two-party competition can hardly be said to be pervasive.

This is confirmed when we realize that the minority of nations with two-party competition are all English-speaking, except the most marginal, and heavily influenced by British institutions. Austria can temporarily be put aside because of its brief experience and the unusual way in which competition has taken place. Rather special circumstances, then, may be required for two-party competition. What these five nations have in common, besides their language and British background, is not national homogeneity. In fact, the United States and Canada are not all that homogeneous. But, except for the United States, all five managed to move into modern democratic times without the internal revolutions that mark the history of the continental democracies, and with less bitter class politics than was usual on the continent. Even Britain, Australia, and New Zealand, while having labor parties in many ways comparable to European social democratic parties, had more moderate movements than the Marxist ones characteristic of continental nations in the late nineteenth and early twentieth centuries. Thus it is sometimes said that the five Anglo-American nations could afford two-party politics because feelings would not run so high as to make it impossible for one party to tolerate governmental control by the other party. Arthur Holcombe put the point this way: "The double party system is doubtless a convenient system for contented peoples, but it is not an efficient system for the expression of public opinion when the variety of opinion and intensity of conviction are great."[18]

Both variety and intensity, then, must be taken into account. Variety of opinion alone would not seem to be decisive since the American two-party pattern has accommodated considerable variety. As suggested earlier, this accommodation is easier in a presidential-congressional system than in a parliamentary system. Yet even American two-partyism ceased to work, in 1860, when the intensity of conviction was too great for a large share of those in one party to accept government by the other party. Intensity is surely a relative term, changing over time. Accordingly, if the greater intensity of conviction has so far prevented continental nations from developing two-party competition and if that greater intensity derives from earlier historical experience, it is possible for the intensity to decline as the historical experience recedes farther into the background, and for conditions for two-partyism to become more propitious. But multi-party patterns, once started, tend to perpetuate themselves. In any event, there is no assurance that two-party competition will suit a nation just because intensity of conviction has diminished. All that can even be claimed is that only in nations where convictions have not been intense does two-party competition flourish.

[18] Arthur N. Holcombe, "Parties, Political," *Encyclopedia of the Social Sciences* (New York: Macmillan, 1933), XI, 592.

It seems more sensible to put the point this way than to emphasize the role of two-partyism in muting intense convictions. Admittedly, some such muting does take place when various groups have to compromise in order to remain under a single banner and attract the crucial marginal voters needed for a majority victory. And multipartyism does not impose this kind of internal compromise at the electoral stage. But for two-partyism to work successfully in this way or to exist at all requires the absence of intense convictions which are uncompromisable. America's pre-Civil War two-party pattern could not survive the strains of the slavery controversy in 1860. Two-partyism ought, then, to be considered not so much a means making compromise possible as a means to facilitate compromise made possible by other circumstances.

The five English-speaking nations, where two-partyism has been the apparently durable pattern, do not seem to have further common factors, vis-à-vis the continental European nations, beyond those derived from their British background and their less intense class consciousness. The four Commonwealth nations are parliamentary, while the United States is not. Britain and New Zealand are unitary; Canada, Australia, and the United States are federal. With reference to this latter distinction it is true that among the Commonwealth nations the two with unitary systems, Britain and New Zealand, have more firmly established two-party patterns than Australia and especially Canada, the most decentralized of the four. So there is a case for arguing that in nations having the forms of British parliamentary government, two-partyism is more strongly associated with unitary than federal systems. The argument has been made by Leslie Lipson, with reference to South Africa as well, but he did not insist that the degree of federalism was itself causal.[19] Both federalism and the number of parties, he wisely allowed, were based on common social factors. There is, however, good reason to question the association between federalism and the number of parties when analysis is extended beyond the Commonwealth nations. The unitary system in continental Europe has not coincided with two-partyism, and, on the other side, the United States, surely more federal than any of the others except Canada, has the most firmly established national two-party pattern. True, American parties are weakly organized by comparison with those in the other nations, but that only suggests that a certain kind of two-partyism suits a nation that is both nonparliamen-

[19] Leslie Lipson, "Party Systems in the United Kingdom and the Older Commonwealth: Causes, Resemblances, and Variations," *Political Studies*, VII (February, 1959), 12–31.

tary and federal. Or, to be precise, two loosely structured parties are possible in a nation that is also nonparliamentary.

This precision derives from a comparison of Canada with the United States. Canada's parties cannot be as weakly organized as the American because both the Liberals and Conservatives must be cohesive enough to support a parliamentary government. Yet, looser parties might better suit the nation's federal circumstances. As things now stand, Canadian two-partyism is almost continuously threatened by third parties representing forces that neither of the major parties seems able to absorb. S. M. Lipset has forcefully put the point:

> Canada's political party problem is a result of the fact that its social structure and bases for political division are essentially comparable to the American and French pattern, but it retains a form of government which requires disciplined parliamentary parties, and which does not permit cross-party alignments in the House of Commons, sharp divergences among the federal programs of the parties from province to province, or democratic methods of solving internal party cleavages.[20]

The "party problem" of which he writes is the appearance of third and fourth parties formed by groups in disagreement with the dominant groups in each of the major parties. Since these third and fourth parties are regionally based but contest national elections, it is reasonable to infer that the major national parties are prevented by their tight parliamentary discipline from giving effective representation to certain regional or provincial interests in the Canadian federal society.[21]

Indeed, Canada's two-party pattern has been extensively qualified in the last forty years. Although the old competition between Liberals and Conservatives, well established before World War I, has remained dominant, at least nationally, it has not even monopolized national attention. In the thirteen elections to the Canadian House of Commons between 1921 and 1963, third parties secured more than 10 per cent of the popular vote eleven times, and more than 25 per cent five times. The low point was 6 per cent in 1930, and the high point 32 per cent in 1945. The two third parties of the early 1960's, Social Credit and the New Democrats (formerly the Cooperative

---

[20] Seymour Martin Lipset, "Democracy in Alberta," Canadian Forum, XXXIV (November and December, 1954), 175–77, 196–98, at p. 197. A contrary view is put by Dennis Wrong, "Parties and Voting in Canada," Political Science Quarterly, LXXIII (September, 1958), 397–412.

[21] C. B. Macpherson agrees with Lipset on this point in his otherwise critical response to Lipset's review of his book, "Democracy in Alberta: A Reply," Canadian Forum, XXXIV (January, 1955), 223–25.

Commonwealth Federation), polled a total of 26 per cent in both 1962 and 1963. Although third parties have not been represented in the Commons in the same high proportion as they have in total votes, they have had enough M.P.s to keep either of the major parties from a legislative majority in six of the first thirteen parliaments elected since 1921. These six parliaments, however, sat for only twelve of the forty-three years from 1921 to 1964, and during several of these twelve years, the Liberals, as after the 1963 election, were only just short of majority status. Until 1962, when Social Credit won localized support in Quebec, third-party M.P.s were mainly from the western provinces. The New Democratic party, like the old CCF, has sought to become national on a basis of trade-union support, and it has begun to show strength outside of western Canada, especially in Ontario. But it remains to be seen whether this is the beginning of a large-scale change, which would probably mean the displacement of the Liberals or Conservatives as a major party, or whether it is only a temporary advance, as by the CCF in 1945. At any rate, the CCF-NDP has so far been only somewhat less sectional than Social Credit or the old prairie Progressives of the early 1920's.[22]

It is this sectional characteristic that makes Canadian third parties relevant in considering the view that two major national parties cannot, in a parliamentary system, contain the diverse interest of a federal society. Plainly, in Canada, they have not done so. Not only have both the CCF-NDP and Social Credit elected M.P.s from the prairies, but one or the other has controlled the governments of the three westernmost provinces over long periods—thirty years for Social Credit in Alberta and twenty years for the CCF in Saskatchewan. Add to these prairie cases the long and fairly recent tenure for the National Union party in Quebec, and it is even plainer that third-party strength has persisted in Canada as it has not done in the United States. The Canadian combination of federal and parliamentary systems may not be the only likely explanation for the difference,[23] but

[22] Origins of prairie third parties are analyzed by W. L. Morton, *The Progressive Party in Canada* (Toronto: University of Toronto Press, 1950). In explaining the discontent with the two major Canadian parties before World War I, Morton writes (p. 9): "The western member, in short, was a party man and subject to caucus, and therefore easily aroused the suspicion of having sacrificed the interests of his section to national policies. By the end of the period under review, the belief was growing in the West that the 'national' parties were controlled in caucus by majorities drawn from central Canada, to the advantage of the East."

[23] Other reasons are given by J. R. Mallory, "The Structure of Canadian Politics," *Canadian Politics* (Sackville, N.B.: Mt. Allison Publications, 1959).

it is a persuasive one. (Quebec's third party could otherwise be explained, since the province is distinctive from the rest of Canada in a way that no American state or even group of states is from the rest of the United States.) The prairie provinces pretty much resemble American prairie states in their relation to the east. Some of these states, like the Canadian provinces, also had third parties—Populist, Non-Partisan League, and Farmer-Labor—but they did not persist, being fairly rapidly absorbed both at the national and state levels by one or the other of the major parties even though this often meant changes within the latter.

It is even safe to generalize that third parties are characteristic of what we call two-party competition and that their fairly ready disappearance in the United States is the unusual case. The term "third party" here is artful. It does not mean minor parties that poll no more than a few percentage points of the total vote nationally or in any large constituency and that almost never elect anyone. Nor does it mean the fairly large minority parties operating in a multi-party pattern. Rather, a third party is any party that regularly breaks the two-party competitive pattern in a nation or region by winning or threatening to win enough offices to influence control of the government. (As in Canada, there may be more than one such party at a time. It is convenient to speak of these as third parties even though technically some are fourth or fifth.)

The familiar effects of single-member, simple-plurality election might seem likely to discourage third parties in Canada as in the United States or Britain. But, in a federal system, while this may hold nationally, it is not true regionally for a third party based on sectional interests. Indeed, the Canadian prairie protest parties were encouraged by their ability to win in almost all of the single-member districts in certain provincial legislative elections. Contrast this to the problems of a third party like the British Liberals whose strength, even insofar as it has been regional, cannot be converted into the kind of governmental control possible in a Canadian province.

Among the persistent third parties in the English-speaking parliamentary nations, the British Liberal party is exceptional not so much because it has lacked power but because the interest it represents is so ill defined. Standing between the parties of business and of labor, and against big political and economic organization, the Liberals do not have a strong class base any more than a sectional one. The more typical third party in the Commonwealth nations is both class-oriented and section-oriented. Its base, like that of the Canadian prairie parties, is agricultural. But, in twentieth-century Britain, this seems unlikely. There are not enough British farmers for a national party, and there is no sizable section of the country whose government they could dominate even if there were such a regional government. Canada, Australia, and New Zealand, however, have large and important agricultural minorities, in some instances only recently become a minority, and their existence as such is apparently essential for third-party movements. In the past, as long as farmers constituted a majority or even a near majority of the populace, they were obviously represented by at least one major party, which continued until the farming community diminished, as is the tendency in Western societies, to a minority position. Only then are farmers likely to feel left out, the political struggle now occurring between major parties appealing mainly for urban votes. They still may not form their own party, except sporadically, if the major ones are accommodating, as they seem to be in the United States, although American farmers now display their politics of protest by large-scale switches from one major party to the other[24]—an apparent present-day substitute for the earlier involvement with Populism and the Non-Partisan League. The latter was especially strong in the North Dakota wheat area during and just after World War I, and its experience contrasts significantly with the nearly simultaneous development of a protest movement by Canadian wheat farmers just across the border. Instead of becoming a fairly durable third party, as did the movement in Saskatchewan (first as Progressives and then as the CCF), the North Dakota Non-Partisan League captured the Republican party by winning its primary election as early as 1916–18.[25]

Third parties have institutionalized the special interest of farmers and allied small-townsmen in Australia as in Canada since the 1920's, and to a lesser extent in New Zealand since the 1950's. The Australian Country party differs from the Canadian CCF and the original Social Credit party in that its ideology is not socialist or otherwise economically radical, but its conservatism does not mean that it is any less clearly tied to the special agrarian interest. In some ways, it represents an especially explicit defense of rural interests against the urbanization of the nation. Farmers have felt most acutely the danger of being overwhelmed by urban Australia. Lacking majority status within a single Australian state, the Country party has been unable to secure the governmental control possible for the CCF and Social Credit in the Canadian prairie provinces. Understandably, it has ad-

[24] Epstein, *op. cit.*, pp. 70–72.
[25] Seymour Martin Lipset, *Agrarian Socialism* (Berkeley and Los Angeles: University of California Press, 1950), pp. 13–14, 124–25.

vocated the establishment of one or more new states to be carved out of the present ones so as to produce a rural majority in an important governmental unit.[26] Not achieving this unlikely goal, the Country party has nevertheless managed to share power in certain states and in the national government (for the first time in 1923) by electing parliamentary representatives in sufficient numbers for them to be needed, on occasion, in the formation of a government by the major-party Liberals. Nationally, while contesting elections on its own, the Country party seems to have become a permanently necessary governing partner for the Liberals. Its continued national parliamentary representation is facilitated, but not necessarily caused, by the use of preferential voting. This method, whereby voters number their preferences for candidates in single-member districts, requires that for election a candidate receive either a majority of first preferences or, failing that, a majority composed of these same first preferences plus the second preferences they receive on ballots where the first preferences were for the lowest-ranking candidate or candidates. The method favors the Country party in that it gives it slightly more representatives in the lower house of parliament than its percentage of the popular vote would indicate.[27]

Yet the Country party is by no means an artifact of the election method. It is strong enough regionally to prosper, it is believed, as it does in several states, without preferential voting. The Country party wins non-Labor votes, and therefore parliamentary seats, which the main non-Labor party, the Liberals, would ineffectively mobilize.[28] Although in this light the Country party seems less like a completely separate party and more like a regional extension of the Liberals, nevertheless it maintains an autonomous organization devoted to interests of its own besides the maintenance of Liberal-Country coalition governments. As Miller observes, the Country party is "a compact, efficient, determined political institution which is a response to specifically Australian conditions."[29] How significant it is that there is this third political entity depends on how much emphasis is placed on organizational form. Having their own party does not mean that Australian farmers have representation that American farmers cannot

[26] Ulrich Ellis, *The Country Party* (Melbourne: F. W. Cheshire, 1958).

[27] J. D. B. Miller, *Australian Government and Politics* (London: Gerald Duckworth, 1964), p. 101.

[28] L. C. Webb, "The Australian Party System," in *The Australian Political Party System* (Sydney: Angus & Robertson, 1954), pp. 103–4.

[29] Miller, *op. cit.*, p. 79.

secure through control of state organizations of the national Republican party, for example, in the Dakotas, Kansas, or Iowa. In either the Australian or the American way, agrarian interests are politically represented.

New Zealand's more recent party of rural protest, under the Social Credit banner, has not converted its votes into national representation. And there are no regional units like states. After receiving 11 per cent of the popular national vote in its election debut in 1954, the Social Credit party evidently stabilized its strength at the level of 7–9 per cent of the electorate. As such, the party was an alternative conservative party, much like the Australian Country party, mainly for farmers and small-townsmen. Its appeal also extended, as is typical of Social Credit parties, to minor urban capitalists—small shopkeepers and self-employed skilled tradesmen.[30] That is to say, it is a characteristic twentieth-century development when other groups likely to feel overwhelmed by the forces of bigness in modern society join the farmers in a minority protest movement. Poujadism in the Fourth French Republic displayed the same phenomenon more dramatically if briefly.

The point here is not primarily that these similar phenomena suggest the usefulness of a comparative study of rural protest movements. What is of relevant concern is that these movements have so frequently modified the pattern of two-party competition. They seem to characterize most of the third parties rupturing the two-party pattern in those few nations where the pattern has existed at all. Yet, as is known from the persistence of the minority electoral strength of British Liberals, primarily rural protest is not necessary for a third party to survive. The British example enables one to say that two-party patterns in parliamentary systems are marked by viable third parties even in national politics. Only in the United States, with its separation of powers, is there no persistent third party at the national level. But there have been sporadic third parties contesting the presidency in the twentieth century: Theodore Roosevelt's Progressives of 1912, LaFollette's Progressives of 1924, Wallace's Progressives of 1948, and various right-wing and southern parties from 1948 into the 1960's. In American state politics, third parties controlled the governments of Wisconsin and Minnesota as recently as the 1930's, before they lost their separate identities, and in New York the third-party Liberals

[30] R. M. Chapman, W. K. Jackson, and A. V. Mitchell, *New Zealand Politics in Action: the 1960 Election* (London: Oxford University Press, 1962), pp. 272–75.

survived in a special way into the 1960's, when third-party Conservatives also appeared.[31]

These transient American examples support the paradoxical conclusion that a third party is a functioning element in two-party competition. In a sense, a third party represents dysfunction. If two-party competition functioned perfectly, the two major parties would contain all important political forces (really *all* political forces, so that there would not be any minor parties). But two-party competition is never perfect. It comes closest to being so in the United States, where the parties can be loosely organized and hospitable to divergent views. And it comes fairly close in Britain and New Zealand, where they function in especially homogeneous circumstances.

This leaves one other nominally two-party competitive nation to discuss. Postwar Austria's party contests were, until 1965, really unlike any others in the democratic world. Between them, the Catholic People's party and the Socialists polled enough of the votes and secured enough of the representation to give the appearance of two-partyism, but they competed against each other in only a limited way. They did not, through election of a parliamentary majority, obtain separate control of the government. There was no contest between the ins and the outs, no opposition party facing a governing party so that the electorate chose one group or the other to govern the nation. Instead, the People's party and the Socialists were in continuous coalition, governing the country together, for the twenty years after World War II. What opposition there was came from the lesser, minor parties. Elections were not meaningless, however, since their outcome determined the distribution of offices and power between the two parties when they formed or re-formed the coalition government. When, for example, the Socialists gained votes in a general election, they were in a favorable position to bargain for more ministerial positions.[32] With these positions went patronage and influence so that each party had a well-defined organizational stake in perpetuating the coalition as well as in improving its position within it.

[31] New York state law, permitting an individual to be nominated by more than one party, gives the Liberal party a role, but a peculiarly auxiliary one, even with a decided minority of the total vote. Its nomination of an individual who is also a candidate of a major party may provide him with the crucial votes he needs for victory. The Liberal party can use its nomination as a bargaining weapon in influencing a major party's nomination. V. O. Key, Jr., *Politics, Parties, and Pressure Groups* (New York: Crowell-Collier, 1964), pp. 274–75.

[32] F. C. Engelmann, "Haggling for the Equilibrium: The Renegotiation of the Austrian Coalition, 1959," *American Political Science Review*, LVI (September, 1962), 651–62.

In the language of economic organization used by a close observer of Austria, the coalition was "a cartel formed to mitigate party competition."[33] Originally an apparently temporary postwar affair that then included the Communist party, the Austrian coalition became a long-term means of mitigating the competition between the two major parties whose intense rivalry in the 1930's had produced civil war. Coalition was a way to avoid the orthodox consequence of two-party competition whereby one party or the other controlled the government. Austrians decided, in effect, that they were not to be among those nations tolerating this all-or-nothing consequence of two-party-ism. After all, altogether there were not many such nations since two-party competition itself was so unusual. The continental nations generally had coalition government imposed by the necessities of multi-partyism. Austria's coalition differed because it was based on two-partyism, which in turn, made for greater stability from one election to the next. But it did not eliminate electoral competition either between the two parties or with the lesser parties.[34] What it did was to change the nature of two-party competition from the pattern cherished by advocates who believe in the virtue of electoral choice between two alternate policies represented by two possible governing parties. (Whether the West German grand coalition of 1966 will have this effect is open to doubt.) Insofar as the Austrian practice fell short of the democratic norm, so does American two-party competition as long as the two major parties do not represent contrasting policies to be carried out subsequent to election. The trouble is that the norm is really too narrowly conceived. The kind of two-party competition that meets it is rare.

3. *The Multi-Party Pattern*

Enough has been said to indicate that if, on the shaky ground of frequency of occurrence, any number of competing parties could be said to be the norm, it would be more parties than two. At least twelve of the twenty Western democratic nations are multi-party ones—fourteen if France and West Germany, on the basis of recent experi-

[33] Herbert P. Secher, "Coalition Government: The Case of the Second Austrian Republic," *American Political Science Review*, LII (September, 1958), 791. The Austrian coalition may have a counterpart of even longer and more durable standing in Switzerland, where all four major parties hold positions on the Federal Council (the executive authority). Roger Girod, "Geography of the Swiss Party System," in Allardt and Littunen, *op. cit.*, pp. 132–61.

[34] Otto Kirchheimer, "The Waning of Opposition in Parliamentary Regimes," *Social Research*, XXIV (Summer, 1957), 127–56.

ence, are added to Switzerland, Sweden, Norway, Denmark, Finland, Iceland, Belgium, the Netherlands, Luxembourg, Eire, Italy, and Israel. The classification is a usual one and would not often be questioned even currently, except for West Germany.

It can also be argued that multi-partyism is a norm in another more substantial sense. In a modern society, it may be more natural. If one starts not with the "naturalness" of two sides confronting each other but rather with the existence of a variety of interests and opinions, then one would expect multi-partyism unless there were unusual circumstances that channeled the variety into only two parties. Why should all the inevitable cleavages coincide with respect to such diverse issues as welfare, civil rights, foreign policy, religious education, and the nature of governmental authority? Failing that unlikely coincidence, why should citizens necessarily submerge or compromise some of their positions on these issues in order to fit a two-party pattern? The alternative of allowing for cross-cleavages by having several parties surely seems natural. It is true that there is difficulty in finding a reasonable limit to combinations of opinions justifying separate parties. Seventy parties might be even more "natural" than seven.

Perhaps, however, for each society there is some modest number that seems natural. A Dutch defender of multi-partyism, thinking of other systems in addition to his own nation's, has said that there are about five natural trains of thought that ought to be separately represented.[35] Since this is near the number of sizable parties actually existing in most multi-party nations, it is tempting to accept it. But than we must first accept that parties are supposed to stand for principles or underlying trains of thought. Here the multi-party advocate, while consistently insisting on party-list proportional representation, is curiously in agreement with a belief of the responsible two-party school: that parties should clearly stand for programs and policies. The difference is that the multi-party advocate is on stronger ground since clear-cut programs and policies are easier for a party when it is one among several minority parties than when it is one of two striving to obtain a majority.

Competition among five or more political parties has earned a bad name because of the instability of governments and of the democratic order itself in the major European nations with a multi-party system —the Third and especially the Fourth Republic of France, Weimar Germany, and Italy before and after Mussolini. Whether or not

[35] George van den Bergh, *Unity in Diversity* (London: B. T. Batsford, 1955), p. 45.

multi-partyism can be blamed as a causal factor of instability, the association with failure is clear. Only in the smaller nations has multi-party competition coincided with the maintenance of democratic government over a long period. The Dutch experience is noteworthy because multi-partyism in the Netherlands is such a pure type. No single party has more than about one-third of the total vote, and at least five consequential parties have existed for many years. These represent sharply different positions within the community. Besides two secular parties, Labour and Liberal, there are two Calvinist parties (one aristocratic and the other plebeian), and a Catholic party.[36] The absence of a majority or potential majority party has not prevented stable government. Long bargaining sessions precede cabinet formations, but once formed the governments are durable. From 1880 to 1958, omitting the years of World War II, there were only eighteen Dutch cabinets. Of these, thirteen remained in office until subsequent elections.[37] Only three persons were premiers between 1918 and 1940.[38] Coalitions since World War II have included a cabinet formed by the two largest parties, Catholic and Labor, and another formed by Catholics, Liberals, and Calvinists.[39]

Dutch political stability therefore cannot be dismissed as due simply to the preponderance of a single large party, like the Social Democrats in Sweden[40] or Labor in Norway.[41] There are other similar examples. Israel is only a slightly less pure case of working multi-partyism. Although one party (Mapai) is the largest and is always at the center of coalition governments, it polls only about one-third of the total vote, and the coalition's composition changes at the margins from time to time in order to reflect election results.[42] But there is no alternation, actual or potential, between one party and another in the Israeli or Dutch case. Obviously there could be none in a genuine multi-party pattern, and it is improbable even between

[36] Hans Daalder, "Parties and Politics in the Netherlands," *Political Studies*, III (February, 1955), 1–16.

[37] Ernest Van Raalte, *The Parliament of the Kingdom of the Netherlands* (London: Hansard Society, 1959), p. 50.

[38] Daalder, *op. cit.*, p. 8.

[39] Robert C. Bone, "The Dynamics of Dutch Politics," *Journal of Politics*, XXIV (February, 1962), 23–49.

[40] Dankwart A. Rustow, *The Politics of Compromise* (Princeton: Princeton University Press, 1955), pp. 209, 216–17.

[41] Henry Valen and Daniel Katz, *Political Parties in Norway* (Oslo: Universitetforlaget, 1964), pp. 40–41.

[42] Amitai Etzioni, "Alternative Ways to Democracy," *Political Science Quarterly*, LXXIV (June, 1959), 196–214.

groups of parties.[43] When electoral competition is structured so that generally left-wing parties face generally right-wing parties, as sometimes occurs in France, the effect of gains made by one group at the expense of the other tends to be only a shift of the coalition to represent more heavily the winning group or, at most, the displacement of one party by another. Most of the parties composing the old coalition are likely to continue in the new one. In this way, multi-partyism readily avoids alternation in office by opposing parties or groups.

The absence of alternation may be claimed as a distinguishing feature of multi-partyism. And it may also be claimed as an advantageous feature either because nations value continuity or because they find it hard to tolerate exclusive governmental control by one party or group. Compromise government of the center is the characteristic result of multi-partyism. Curiously, however, the same result was achieved by the Austrian two-party coalition. Thus, if the presence or absence of party alternation is the definitive element in discussing competitive patterns, postwar Austria must be classed with the multi-party nations. Much can be said for this classification. Austrian voters, like those in multi-party nations, were asked to determine how large a share in the government a given party should have, not whether it should have full control. Moreover, they made this determination in an election conducted by party-list proportional representation—the very method suited to show degrees of strength rather than to produce a government majority. True, even with this method Austrian voters could give one of the two parties so much strength that it would be emboldened to break the coalition and govern alone. And indeed, this finally happened in 1965, while with genuine multi-partyism it is not even possible since no party is anywhere near a majority position. But it is surely reasonable to say that as long as it was only a possibility in Austria and the coalition remained intact,

---

[43] Descriptions of multi-party situations in various Western nations in addition to those already noted may be found in Basil Chubb, "Ireland 1957," in David E. Butler (ed.), *Elections Abroad* (London: Macmillan, 1959), chap. 3; Roger Girod, "Geography of the Swiss Party System," in Allardt and Littunen, *op. cit.*, pp. 132–61; Morris Davis, *Iceland Extends Its Fisheries' Limits* (London: Allen & Unwin, 1963), pp. 53–56, 99; Val R. Lorwin, "Conflict and Compromise in Belgian Politics" (Paper delivered at American Political Science Association, Washington, 1965). Interwar Czechoslovakia is another example of a working multi-party pattern as described by Malbone Graham, "Parties and Politics," in R. J. Kerner (ed.), *Czechoslovakia* (Berkeley and Los Angeles: University of California Press, 1940), pp. 137–70, and by Edward Taborsky, *Czechoslovak Democracy at Work* (London: Allen & Unwin, 1945), pp. 37–40, 85–86, 94–98, 107–11.

Austrian party competition for twenty years more closely resembled the multi-party than the two-party pattern. Naturally, this casts doubt on the significance of a simple classification according to the number of competing parties, although admittedly Austria is so small a country and its democratic experience so brief that the functional resemblance of its two-party pattern to the multi-party pattern is not enough to destroy the distinction based on numbers. Austria might be only the exceptional case. Not enough is yet known about the somewhat similar German attempt, begun in 1966, to maintain a grand coalition of the two leading parties.

There is another reason for arguing that multi-party competition is substantively different from two-party competition. Each of the parties in a multi-party pattern is said to articulate interests but not to aggregate them, as do the parties in a two-party system. With multi-partyism, each party is more like a large interest group; it performs the functions of a party but it also performs functions that, in the two-party pattern, only an interest group performs. This distinction is the familiar one drawn from Gabriel Almond's well-known introductory chapter in *The Politics of the Developing Areas* and particularly from his contrast between Britain and France. British parties, he says, are aggregative in the sense of seeking "to form the largest possible interest group coalitions by offering acceptable choices of political personnel and public policy."[44] Interest groups and parties are differentiated in Britain but not in France (of the Third and Fourth Republics), where parties and interest groups interpenetrate one another. Some parties control interest groups, and some interest groups control parties. Thus, French parties have not aggregated interests to the same degree as British parties. Almond grants that an interest-group party aggregates to some extent, and that even an interest group that is not a party at all may be aggregative from certain standpoints. But an interest group or a party based on a particular interest cannot be *distinctively* aggregative. It must also articulate its interest. So when political competition is between several parties each based mainly on an interest, the agencies performing the aggregative functions are not differentiated from the interest-articulating agencies. They tend to be the same. Almond, incidentally, regards this undifferentiated quality as a sign of a less modern, less developed political system.

It is not necessary to hold a normative view when emphasizing the relatively nonaggregative characteristic of parties as an index for dis-

[44] Gabriel A. Almond and James S. Coleman, *The Politics of the Developing Areas* (Princeton: Princeton University Press, 1960), p. 37.

tinguishing multi-partyism from two-partyism. Nor is it necessary to believe that multi-partyism causes parties to be nonaggregative. It is at least as likely that interests in the society in question cannot be readily aggregated. Perhaps the interests are too sharply conflicting for compromises to be possible under only two party labels. In other words, broad interest aggregation may be difficult for the same reasons that two-party competition is difficult. There is really the same phenomenon, virtually by definition, in discussing the nonaggregation of interests and multi-partyism. And, in fact, those advanced democratic nations whose parties do not aggregate interests often have more than two parties.[45] It does not, therefore, make any more sense to say that nonaggregation causes multi-partyism than to put it the other way around.

The question remains whether relative nonaggregation of interests is significantly descriptive of multi-partyism. Granting that parties in this pattern are less aggregative than parties in the two-party pattern, is this difference meaningful? This is another way of asking how much less aggregating is done in the one case than the other. The point is relevant because it is essential to speak of relative aggregation or nonaggregation rather than of two absolutely different methods of representing interests. In this perspective, there is an overlapping of the two patterns just as there is between two-partyism and multi-partyism. For example, the Swedish Social Democrats, although opposing more than one important rival party, strive for a majority just as clearly as the British Labour party does against only one main rival. These Social Democrats, no more than the British Labour party, can afford to represent the interests of only the organized industrial working class. The similarity, with the Swedish Social Democrats an aggregating party, is clearly related to the similarity of Swedish multi-party competition to the two-party pattern. On the other side, in an apparent two-party pattern, the Austrian People's party and the Austrian Socialist party are each closely linked to rather imperfectly aggregated interest groups. Furthermore, any labor or socialist working-class party is usually based heavily on one interest group even if engaged in two-party competition. This is true of British Labour, much as it tries to escape the public reputation for being a trade-union party. It is more sharply the case in Australia, where the Labour party, like its competitors, has a strongly syndical charac-

---

[45] This is reflected in the systematic classification by Arthur S. Banks and Robert B. Textor, *A Cross-Polity Survey* (Cambridge: M.I.T. Press, 1963), par. 130, where among Western democracies only the six two-party nations are listed as having significant interest aggregation by parties.

ter.[46] Also in the United States a party may be closely tied to a single interest group at least at the state level, in the manner of the Democrats and the United Automobile Workers in Michigan.[47] It might be added that third parties, notably the prevalent agrarian type, are almost always non-aggregative within the national two-party pattern.

What can still be said is that nonaggregation of interests is more characteristic—perhaps considerably more so—of multi-partyism. Unquestionably this is a meaningful distinction at a certain level of analysis. Parties that aggregate are different from parties that do not. But the political systems to which the parties belong may not be so different as a result. Aggregation will be performed in the system—if not by the parties, presumably by a coalition government. The parties, representing interests, then bargain with each other instead of having interest groups bargain with each other within a party. The difference is important procedurally, and since procedure is the business of political scientists, the difference should certainly be discussed (as it is at later points), but it is not overwhelming.

The last statement is meant as a warning against those who assume that multi-partyism is inferior because its parties do not sufficiently aggregate interests. Their assumption is that interest groups should be submerged at the earliest possible stage of the political process. Significantly, however, not all two-party patterns are sufficient for this purpose. The parties in them must be strong enough to *"shut out the pressure groups."*[48] Thus British parties are preferred to the looser American ones, which aggregate interests before the electorate but not so successfully in the legislatures. Still, the two-party pattern as such makes possible a submergence of interests that multi-partyism allows and encourages. But all this rests on a pejorative view of interest groups. If, on the other hand, one considers them legitimate and useful (as I do for other purposes in Chapter X), one cannot make this case against multi-party competition. Having each party clearly associated with an important interest group then becomes just another way of providing representation. It might even seem a better way, since interest groups and therefore interest-group parties are likely to be closer to the citizens' most immediate concerns. Against this must be set the argument that parties have a different function to perform from that of interest groups and that merging these func-

---

[46] Miller, *op. cit.,* p. 65.

[47] Stephen B. and Vera H. Sarasohn, *Political Party Patterns in Michigan* (Detroit: Wayne State University Press, 1957), pp. 68–69.

[48] E. E. Schattschneider, *Party Government* (New York: Rinehart, 1942), p. 192.

tions might make either or both less effective.[49] Neither argument is entirely persuasive. It seems safest to regard multi-party competition, like two-party competition, as a workable democratic method. This is another way of saying that the difference between the two forms of competition does not appear so fundamental as do the circumstances making for one form or the other.[50]

Western democratic government surely functions when competition is between several parties instead of between two.[51] It even functions, within limits, when competition is primarily within one party (fortunately, since this state of affairs often holds in large areas of formally two-party nations). In fact, two-party competition actually providing two clear-cut alternatives is rather exceptional. It is marred not only by sizable one-party monopolies, but also by the prevalence of third parties. And the likeliest way to preclude third parties is to have the two major parties as weakly organized as they are in the United States, and so fail to meet the true standard of providing two clear-cut policy alternatives.

[49] Harry Eckstein offers discerning discussion of the separate uses of interest groups and parties. The former can relate special opinions to special policies while parties, aggregating in the British manner, relate only broad ranges of opinion to general policies. *Pressure Group Politics* (London: Allen & Unwin, 1960), pp. 162–63.

[50] This puts the author in agreement with G. E. Lavau's criticism of Duverger for emphasizing electoral systems and the number of parties. *Partis Politiques et Realités Sociales* (Paris: Armand Colin, 1953), pp. 164–65.

[51] Enough has been said earlier to indicate that there is not always a sharp distinction between two-party and multi-party competition. The conception of a continuum with respect to the number of parties is fully explored by Douglas Rae, *The Politics of Electoral Law* (Ph.D. dissertation, University of Wisconsin, 1966), chap. 2.

IV

Structuring the Vote

Structuring the vote is the minimum function of a political party in a modern democracy. Even by the broad definition of a political party as a group seeking to elect government officeholders under a given label, it is not possible for a group to qualify as a party unless it does structure the vote. All that is meant by the awkward word "structuring" is the imposition of an order or pattern enabling voters to choose candidates according to their labels (whether or not the labels appear on the ballot). The structure may be little more than that provided by the label itself and the voters' acquaintance with it, or it may involve a vast educational and campaigning apparatus mobilizing voters for a party cause. In one way or another, parties provide a basis—although not the only one—for electoral choice. Voters may still make their choice on some other basis, like individual candidate appeal, but party labels, persisting over many elections and many candidates, simplify the voter's decision. Indeed, they become most relevant for new mass electorates. Structuring the vote, regularly and systematically, was not a characteristic of what were called parties in pre-democratic times.

Like those pre-democratic parties or factions, modern parties may also perform governing functions. Vote-structuring, however, is their essential minimum modern function. A party can be said to exist as long as it structures the vote even though it does nothing else. Of course, modern parties do other things as well. But while they vary greatly in which of these other things they do, Western democratic parties are substantially similar in their structuring of the vote. Universality in this respect suggests that parties are a democratic necessity. No other means to structure the vote seems likely. Insofar as groups not calling themselves parties were regularly to propose slates of candidates, they would be parties for functional purposes. In other words, if there is any organized structuring of the vote, parties exist by definition. But the question of whether it is necessary to have structuring of any regular kind cannot be entirely foreclosed. It is worth examining the efforts to do without it at local levels of American politics, and the attempt of a single important individual to stand apart from political parties in seeking executive office.

Here, I should like to focus attention on the structuring that generally does exist. One more preliminary point is in order. Vote-structuring occurs whether parties are thought to stand for principles or merely for the election of candidates carrying the party label. It is not even certain that the structuring is any firmer in the former instance, or that it is any firmer when parties are highly organized. The label may stand for a sufficient traditional or habitual pattern so as to make for stability in voting behavior without program or machine.

1. National Patterns

The best way to appreciate how vote-structuring is inherently a function of political parties is to start with American parties. It is generally agreed that their labels represent less by way of both programmatic principle and organized membership than the labels of most Western democratic parties. Moreover, American parties, in any organized sense, often cannot even control the bestowal of their own labels. The result of direct primaries may be to label candidates unwanted by party leaders and by whatever there is of an organized membership. Yet American voters, as will be observed, are heavily influenced by party labels. Perhaps they are not so thoroughly influenced as British voters, who are faced with a sharp choice between sets of candidates each committed to a united policy-making party, but party remains the single most important determinant for American voters, although by no means the only one.

The attachment of Americans to political parties has been called a "psychological identification." It is very often handed on from one generation to the next. It is persistent for individuals in that a large majority continue to identify with the party for which they first voted. And a smaller majority but still a majority never cross party lines despite the manifold opportunities and temptations on the American ballot. It is fair to conclude with the authors of the leading study of voting behavior that American party identification, once established, is an attachment not easily changed.[1] Certainly it accounts for most of the votes in national elections, notably in those not involving the personal popularity of a presidential candidate. For example, in the 1958 congressional election, only one vote in twenty was cast by

[1] Angus Campbell et al., The American Voter (New York: John Wiley & Sons, 1960), pp. 121, 147–49.

those without any sort of party loyalty; and of the great majority with party identification, only one in ten voted against his usual party. Consequently, about 84 per cent of the vote was cast by people following their usual parties.[2] The percentage is not quite so high in the enlarged electorate of a heated presidential contest, when there are more new voters and more infrequent voters. These groups have been found to have less firm party attachments than the regular voters.[3] They constitute important exceptions to the stability with which parties structure voting behavior, and their marginal character may decisively influence election results. But they are exceptions to the general pattern.

These party attachments determine voting behavior even though they do not seem as important as certain non-party attachments. American voters rate party below their other group loyalties.[4] In one study in a particular state, they even declared that they were more likely to take political advice on candidates and issues from non-party associations like farm or business organizations.[5] Parties ranked low on the influence scale. Whether or not this would be true elsewhere, the finding is really not incompatible with the general influence of parties on voting behavior, for the influence seems to be habitual rather than direct. It is the party label, not the party association and its leaders, which provides the guide. In this respect, it is a different kind of influence operating in a different way and at a different level from other associations. In fact, an American party does not seem to be an association in the same sense as business or farm groups. Or if it is, its influence *as an association* is limited while its influence *as a psychological identification* for voters is great. The party does not have to tell voters what to do in order to influence them. It may try to tell them in order to be organizationally still more effective. But the party's continued existence is itself an influence. It might be thought that an influence so dependent on the mere habit of label-identification would wear away with time, especially if the habit was originally formed when party principles were clearer and organizations stronger, as might be the case in the United States. But there is

[2] Warren E. Miller and Donald E. Stokes, "Constituency Influence in Congress," *American Political Science Review*, LVII (March, 1963), 54.

[3] William N. McPhee and Jack Ferguson, "Political Immunization," in William N. McPhee and William A. Glaser (eds.), *Public Opinion and Congressional Elections* (New York: Free Press of Glencoe, 1962), chap. 6.

[4] Robert E. Lane, *Political Life* (Glencoe, Ill.: Free Press, 1959), p. 300.

[5] Howard E. Freeman and Morris Showel, "Differential Political Influence of Voluntary Associations," *Public Opinion Quarterly*, XV (Winter, 1951–52), 703–14.

no evidence of any decline in party preferences over the last few decades.[6]

American parties thus structure the vote to a considerable extent, but it may still be true that they do so less than parties in other nations. Our evidence on this point is slight because there have been few systematic crossnational comparisons. Such comparisons are difficult in any case. Unlike things are being compared when Europeans are asked, as were Americans in the studies noted, for their usual party identification and for their votes in a particular election. In Europe these two questions seem to be about the same thing, since elections are ordinarily assumed to be between parties, especially with party-list proportional representation and in the absence of popular election of executive offices, rather than between individual candidates bearing party labels. But this is another way of saying that European voting is probably more highly structured by parties than American, and that remains to be seen.

The most impressive comparative study is of French and American voters. By concentrating on party identification alone, this study avoided the problem of relating party identification to voting behavior. The comparison is simply between the respective percentages of American and French respondents who classified themselves as of a particular party. The results are surprising, even if it is borne in mind that the French figures date from the fall of 1958, when party lines were more fluid than usual because of the development of a new Gaullist party along with the Fifth Republic. While 75 per cent of the Americans regularly counted themselves as Republicans or Democrats, fewer than 45 per cent of the Frenchmen answering the question classified themselves in one of their country's many parties or splinter groups. Another 10–15 per cent, who associated themselves with a fairly recognizable broad tendency (say, of the left or the right), could be added to the 45 per cent to secure a liberally comparable figure. On the other hand, the 10 per cent of the French sample (in contrast to a tiny fraction of an American sample) who refused to answer the question about party identification cannot be assumed to be identifiers.[7] Even without counting them one way or the other, however, it is plain that significantly fewer Frenchmen than Americans identified with parties.

The finding cannot be explained away as a difference peculiar to

[6] Lane, *op. cit.*, p. 301.

[7] Philip E. Converse and Georges Dupeux, "Politicization of the Electorate in France and the United States," *Public Opinion Quarterly*, XXVI (Spring, 1962), 1–23.

1958 as far as France is concerned. True enough, interviews were conducted during the campaigns for the new Fifth Republic constitution and for the subsequent parliamentary elections, and this was a time when an important new party was being formed and some of the old ones were declining at least temporarily. But 1958 was not an entirely unusual year. Parties, especially on the right, have often come and gone in recent French politics. The UNR was a reincarnation of a party that had existed in the late 1940's and early 1950's. Its existence or re-existence might be thought to make available a party identification desired by many voters who would otherwise lack any attachment. But the presence of the UNR along with so many others, some long established, simply did not produce a high percentage of party identifiers. At the minimum, what this means is that many parties, each representing a distinctive position, do not guarantee greater party identification than that prevalent in the United States with its two not sharply distinctive parties. That much can be said, although the large number of parties in France may not alone or primarily account for the low percentage of identifiers. The percentage may be low *despite* the many parties. What the authors of this comparative study believe is that the French parties, while offering clearer policy positions for the more involved voters than American parties do, are too varied, changing, and complex for many ordinary French citizens to follow sufficiently to establish identification with them.[8] The proliferation of French parties may be useful to the politically interested, but it is meaningless to many others. Whether this is equally true for other multi-party patterns, particularly more stable ones, is an open question.[9]

A comparative Norwegian-American study is related to this question since the Norwegian multi-party pattern is more stable than the French. In this study, also using survey data, percentages of identifiers are not compared. Instead, the analytical question is whether the identifiers in one nation are more likely than those in the other to vote in accord with their identification. The answer, as might have been expected, was a higher percentage for the Norwegians; that is, they less frequently switched than American party identifiers. This

[8] *Ibid.*, p. 22.

[9] A fairly low degree of party identification in Belgium's multi-party competition is revealed in a 1962 survey by the Centre de Recherche et d'Information Socio-Politique, *Une Etude D'Opinion en Belgique* (Brussels, February 22, 1963), p. 6, but this is partly accounted for by an especially low number of socialist party identifiers (that is, especially low in relation to the number of socialist votes in an election). Perhaps, as we know from surveys in other nations, left-wing voters may be reluctant to reveal their party identification.

finding accompanies others showing that Norwegian identifiers see greater policy differences among their parties than Americans do between theirs, and that they have more distinctive issue-positions than do Americans.[10] It is possible, therefore, that the Norwegian parties not only structure the vote more thoroughly but do so because of their policy positions. In turn, it could be argued that these positions are distinctive partly because the multi-party pattern encourages them to be so. In light of the French case, however, it cannot be argued that multi-partyism alone made for the greater party identification.

The French-American and the Norwegian-American comparisons might be interpreted as placing American parties in between the French and the Norwegian with respect to their degree of vote-structuring. But the two studies are not alike enough to permit this ordering to be made with any assurance. Two different though related phenomena have been compared: simple party identification in the first instance, and the relation of party identification to party voting in the second. Possibly American parties would rank high on the first in comparison to any other nation's parties[11] but generally low on the second. Relative to other nations, the United States may have a high percentage of party identifiers, but a less high percentage of these identifiers may regularly vote for their party's candidates. The second seems more properly to measure vote-structuring, but it may be of limited importance to know that parties consistently structure the vote of their identified followers if the latter are only a small portion of the total electorate. In other words, American parties may structure the vote for a relatively large share of the total electorate because they start with so many identifiers in the first place that they compensate for the many voters whose loyalty is not sustained from election to election.

This suggests that party identification has a different meaning in the United States than in Europe. Apparently an American is less likely than a European to vote regularly for the candidates of the party with which he identifies. He is a partisan, but not an intense

[10] Angus Campbell and Henry Valen, "Party Identification in Norway and the United States," *Public Opinion Quarterly*, XXV (Winter, 1961), 505–25. See also the survey data on party identification in Stavanger, Norway, shown by Henry Valen and Daniel Katz, *Political Parties in Norway* (Oslo: Universitetsforlaget, 1964), p. 217.

[11] There is an implicit comparison to what is called the relatively weak party identification of the recent Canadian electorate. Howard A. Scarrow, "Distinguishing Between Political Parties—The Case of Canada," *Midwest Journal of Political Science*, IX (February, 1965), 61–76.

one. This is indirectly supported by data on types of partisanship contained in a major cross-national survey of high civic attitudes. The American percentage of what are called "open partisans," as opposed to apathetic, intense, or parochial partisans, is notably higher than the percentage for any of the other three sets of Western nationals (British, German, and Italian). The American figure is also higher if open and apathetic partisans are lumped together (although the American percentage of apathetic partisans is the lowest).[12]

Despite this partisanship, or perhaps because of the kind of partisanship, it is thought that American elections are seldom as dominated by party considerations as European ones. No observer of the United States would be able to dismiss the appeal of individual congressional candidates in the way that Sir Ivor Jennings could when he wrote that his reason for having said nothing about British parliamentary candidates was that "they do not matter much."[13] This can be demonstrated in various ways. Jennings himself did so by citing the inter-war experience of two-member constituencies which showed no great difference between the votes cast for the two Labour candidates, or between the two Conservative candidates. More recent experience with nearly uniform national swings, regardless of constituencies or candidates, confirms the observation. Less than 1 per cent of a district's vote is about all that is ever attributed to the appeal of the personality or campaign of a candidate. Similarly, party voting tends to dominate Australian parliamentary elections.[14] In those countries with party-list proportional representation, the question of individual candidate appeal is not even likely to arise except when, as in Italy, individual preferences are indicated on the ballot. On the other hand, it is known simply from American election returns that there must be a great deal of candidate-voting in congressional and other races. There are usually large differences between the total votes polled by candidates of the same party, and survey work on the voting behavior producing these differences reveals even more split-ticket voting than appears from the election results.[15]

[12] Gabriel A. Almond and Sidney Verba, *The Civic Culture* (Princeton: Princeton University Press, 1963), p. 155.

[13] W. Ivor Jennings, *The Queen's Government* (London: Penguin, 1954), p. 60.

[14] J. D. B. Miller, *Australian Government and Politics* (London: Gerald Duckworth, 1964), p. 105, and D. W. Rawson, *Australia Votes* (Melbourne: Melbourne University Press, 1961), p. 167.

[15] Leon D. Epstein, *Votes and Taxes* (Madison: University of Wisconsin Institute of Governmental Affairs, 1964), pp. 26–30. This is a study of an off-year election in which more than half the voters reported that they had split

Some party-identifiers vote for only some of their party's candidates.

How much of this American phenomenon can be explained simply by the opportunity to elect candidates to so many different offices? Might not voters in other nations, no matter how strong their parties, be tempted to deviate in favor of individual candidates if they had the same opportunity? It is likely, but there is no way to test it directly. The old two-member British parliamentary constituencies, noted earlier, do not offer quite the right test since election only to a single parliamentary body was involved. The same holds for present-day local British council elections. Only slightly nearer the point is any difference in voting behavior between a national and a regional or local election held within a year or so (but not at the same time, as in the United States). It would not indicate the kind of difference displayed in American split-ticket voting, since a shift from one to another set of candidates might indicate a shift from one party to another, rather than a shift determined by the qualities of the individual candidates.

There is also another reason why it is hard to analyze the difference between American and European parties with respect to party and candidate preference. The United States, by directly electing its executive officers, tends to separate personal appeals from those of party. Americans who liked Eisenhower could vote for him for president and still vote for Democrats for other offices. But those who live under a parliamentary government and who like a party leader for his personal qualities must vote for his party's parliamentary candidate (or candidates) in order to make him prime minister. Thus his appeal must become an element in his party's appeal if it is to do him any good at the polls. On the other hand, an American party leader, as candidate for president or governor, can get himself elected without a legislative victory for his party. His personal appeal may help to elect other candidates in his party (the coattail effect) but not as clearly as it helps his own election.[16]

This leads to the observation that in structuring the vote, as in other matters, national party patterns are greatly influenced by the constitutional circumstances. Everywhere, including the United States, parties structure the vote on a large scale. But different incentives in the different systems importantly affect the way the structuring oc-

their state and/or county tickets, and in which nearly one-quarter of the voters reported that they had split their gubernatorial and U. S. senatorial ballots.

[16] Philip E. Converse and Georges Dupeux, "De Gaulle and Eisenhower: The Public Image of the Victorious General" (Mimeographed paper delivered at the Paris Congress of the International Political Science Association, 1961).

curs. Thus, although American parties like parties elsewhere have incentives to structure the vote, these incentives are not so pervasive as those in a parliamentary system whose only election is for legislative members who are potentially part of a majority maintaining an executive in office. In such an election, the party's interest in each parliamentary seat is much greater than an American party's interest in obtaining a legislative majority. Not only parties but voters function differently under the two systems. Voting for a party is more compelling when party is so clearly the basis for government. Choosing a legislative candidate for his own virtues makes little sense when his chief political importance is to form part of the support for, or opposition to, a government.

2. The Class Basis

So far, parties as objects of voter identification have been treated as though their attraction were independent of other social forces. Especially may this have seemed to be the case in describing the traditional or habitual pattern for structuring the vote, but such a pattern is likely to be derived from an explicable source. The division of votes between parties may reflect another, perhaps more basic division in the community—by socio-economic class, ethnic group, religion, language, region, or even temperament. Of all these possibilities, class regularly receives and probably deserves the most attention because it seems to divide twentieth-century parties, in substantial though varying degrees, in every Western democracy. To the extent that class does underlie party divisions, it can tell us a good deal about the difference between parties. In particular, it may tell whether the parties that structure the vote most rigorously do so in nations where class lines are fairly rigorous. Party identification may, in other words, be an artifact of class identification, even in a nation, like the United States, whose parties are not class-conscious in the European sense. The political saliency of class seems lower in the absence of an openly socialist working-class party, but it may be sufficient for a substantial association with party voting.

What is now chiefly meant by the class division in advanced Western nations is that between the industrial working class, consisting mainly of blue-collar manual workers, and the middle class, consisting mainly of white-collar employees and businessmen. Any upper class, too small to count much in terms of votes, is lumped with the middle class. The line between working and middle class is not easily drawn since occupational basis does not always coincide with income; many manual workers earn more than many white-collar clerks.

There is an understandable tendency to classify the latter, especially when they work at routine manipulative tasks, with the working class. Manualists, regardless of how skilled they are or how high their income, always remain in the working class. Farmers constitute a special problem unless they are dropped from analysis, as is possible in studies of purely urban communities, or unless they are classified separately. They may, however, be divided between working and middle classes according to their status as farm employees or owners and managers.

Despite the difficulties of classification, complicated greatly in cross-national work, one substantial comparative study of class voting has been made, in addition to numerous national or local ones. It consists of secondary analysis of survey data from the four major English-speaking democracies: Great Britain, Australia, the United States, and Canada. The rank of class voting was found to be in the order named. That is, class status was most closely associated with party preference in Britain and least closely in Canada. The association, however, was substantial except in Canada, and it did not disappear within age groups, religious groups, regions, or large cities. The "index of class voting" persisted when each of these factors was controlled. (This index was defined simply by subtracting the percentage of non-manual workers voting for "left" parties from the percentage of manual workers voting for "left" parties.[17])

Interesting attempts are made to explain the differences in degree of class voting among the four nations. Britain and Australia are poorer countries, in per-capita income, than the United States and Canada, and it is possible that the lower income levels of the working classes there have been conducive to greater class consciousness. Or perhaps the degree of class voting has to do with the nation's degree of urbanization, low proportion of middle class in the labor force, limited educational opportunities, limited mobility, and relatively little income stratification among industrial workers.[18] What is striking about these correlates with class voting, including per-capita income, is that all except degree of urbanization seem everywhere to be changing in a direction associated with less rather than more class voting. Each of the four nations, along with others in the Western world, is increasing its per-capita income, middle-class proportion of the labor

[17] Robert R. Alford, *Party and Society* (Chicago: Rand McNally, 1963), pp. 101–2. "Left" parties were the Labour parties in Britain and Australia, the Democratic party in the United States, and the Liberal party plus the CCF (or NDP) in Canada.

[18] *Ibid.*, pp. 121–22.

force, educational opportunities, social mobility, and (less definitely) income stratification *among* workers. These tendencies, now more characteristic of the United States and Canada than of Britain and Australia, are becoming more general with further economic development. Urbanization too is becoming more general, but in this case it is already even more characteristic of Britain and Australia than of the United States and Canada. It would have to be assumed that urbanization is the dominant factor, among the several noted, in order to believe that socio-economic change was likely to cause American and Canadian voting to become more class-based, as in British and Australian voting. It seems more reasonable to believe that socio-economic change is working in the other direction, so that with increasing per-capita income, larger middle-class proportion of the labor force, greater educational opportunities, increasing mobility, and greater income stratification among workers, Britain and Australia would come more nearly to resemble the less class-based voting patterns of the United States and Canada.

Reasonable though this appears, other possibly countervailing forces may be at work. The lower frequency of class voting in the United States and Canada can be explained at least in part by factors other than the socio-economic ones already mentioned. Both nations have marked sectional, religious, and ethnic cleavages which cut across class so as to reduce its importance as a voting determinant. Their importance is underlined not just in comparison with Britain and Australia, but also by the comparison of the United States with Canada. It is appropriate to associate the fact that there is less class voting in Canada, economically so much like the United States, with the existence of the combined linguistic, ethnic, religious, and sectional cleavage between French and English Canada. The United States, despite its sectional, ethnic, and even racial differences, has no present-day non-class cleavage to rival the dominating Canadian one. If, then, non-class cleavages help to account for lower levels of class voting (only more so in Canada than the United States), one might infer that class voting would increase as sectional, ethnic, religious, and language differences were worn away by national assimilation processes.[19] Of course, this assumes that assimilation processes *do* wear away non-class differences, and, especially for Canada, one cannot be sure of this. Even insofar as it does hold, however, it perhaps cannot be associated with an increase in class voting. While a decrease in non-class differences would make class factors become more influential determinants of voting, the class factors may themselves

[19] *Ibid.,* pp. 331–32.

recede so sharply with socio-economic changes that they would be no more influential than they were in the face of strong non-class determinants.

What is being questioned is the belief that there is an irreversible trend in modern political societies toward class-based voting and therefore toward an increasingly well-defined economic division between parties. This question is raised despite the admission that class is the most pervasive factor accounting for party-identification in Western democracies, the United States included. Obviously, class does not account for all of the party division, for if it did, a working-class party would win all of its elections in an industrial nation. But it accounts for a great deal—more, it is usually thought, in certain continental democracies than in the English-speaking ones for which we have so far cited comparative data.[20] To have voters divided largely by class is even regarded as a distinctively modern element in what seems a democratized version of Marxism. Class consciousness, in this perspective, gradually supersedes such "pre-modern" groupings as those of section or religion. Evidence to support this doctrine seemed to be provided by the history of the first half of the twentieth century. Working-class parties and basically middle-class parties grew almost everywhere. Even in the United States, the Democratic party, without a working-class party label, began in the 1930's to assume a strongly class character in its voting appeal, especially in the northern cities. Apparently all that prevented class from becoming even more influential (and so, incidentally, giving the working-class party a permanent majority) were various residual (often non-class) factors, among which nationalism should be counted. Specifically Christian parties in continental Europe thus viewed religion as a means of cutting across the growing class consciousness of industrial workers. Like the other non-class appeals, it was believed, by many socialists, to be effective only temporarily.

Granting that the first fifty years of this century show considerable evidence that class voting is increasing, it is still doubtful that this is an irreversible trend into our own time or into the proximate future. Predominant or at least heavy class voting may be declining or about to decline. Unfortunately, no available data bear directly on this possibility. Inferences are possible although uncertain. Studies of Britain give reason to suspect a decline in such voting. The most likely piece of evidence shows that the average level of class voting is lowest in London and the southern region, which are the most metropolitan, the most urban, and the most economically advanced areas of Brit-

[20] Campbell and Valen, *op. cit.*

ain.[21] The social and political character of these areas may well be what a modernizing Britain will increasingly be like in the next few decades. This would be true with respect to a smaller percentage of manual workers voting Labour, as happened in London and the southern region, and to a smaller percentage of manualists in the total population, as is unquestionably a general trend in Britain as in all advanced societies. The latter seems especially significant since the previously observed high degree of British class voting may be associated with the fact that Britain has had a higher proportion of manual wage-earners than other Western nations[22] over a considerable period of time, which helps to account for the successful growth of a working-class party. This is not to neglect the negative influence of Britain's homogeneity in respects other than class. Class tended to be an important division not only because it was so intrinsically but also because there was little else to divide the nation.[23] Therefore, there is no assurance that a decline in working-class numbers or consciousness will make for less class voting. On what other bases the vote will be divided is not clear. British Conservatives may receive more working-class support than the approximately one-third of recent years, but how could Labour receive more middle-class votes unless it greatly changed its working-class character?[24]

A similar observation can be made for Australia. Here too, in a nation with generally high class voting, the most populous and advanced regions show class voting below the national average. Moreover, the working-class deviants from Labour voting are found, in one significant category, to be upwardly mobile members of their class.[25]

American class voting, a good deal lower generally than the British

[21] Alford, *op. cit.*, p. 150. After Alford's study, there is a report of a slight increase in Labour's percentage of the middle-class vote and a slight decline in Labour's percentage of the working-class vote between the 1959 and 1964 general elections. David E. Butler and Anthony King, *The British General Election of 1964* (London: Macmillan, 1965), pp. 296–97.

[22] John Bonham, *The Middle Class Vote* (London: Faber, 1954), p. 195.

[23] Jean Blondel, *Voters, Parties, and Leaders* (Baltimore: Penguin, 1963), p. 26.

[24] The working-class support received by the British Conservative party has been divided into deferential and secular voters. The former are older, with lower incomes and less concern for social mobility. They are probably declining in number. But the secular working-class Conservative voters are likely to be young, prosperous, and upwardly mobile. Moreover, they belong to an expanding class. Robert T. McKenzie and Allan Silver, "Conservatism, Industrialism, and the Working Class Tory in England" (Mimeographed paper delivered at the Washington Congress of the International Sociological Association, 1962).

[25] Alford, *op. cit.*, pp. 201–2.

or Australian, has shown no substantial shift since the 1930's. It declined in the presidential elections of 1952 and 1956, but it was at a high point in 1948.[26] Increasing urbanization would seem to be conducive to increased class voting, since rural and small-town America have offered only a narrow base for a predominantly working-class party.[27] Therefore, unless class voting was increasing, for which there is no evidence, it is probable that other economic factors associated with low class voting effectively countered urbanization.

Canada has so little class voting that no downward trend is likely. Even if a downward trend is predictable for truly advanced societies, Canadian class voting may well rise before it begins to fall. There is every reason to believe that the non-class cleavages are so strong in Canada that class voting there is below what might be expected for an urban, industrialized nation.[28] For example, in Quebec, the Liberal party received considerable support from relatively high socioeconomic levels although generally, in the Canadian data, the Liberal party is counted as a "left" party for purposes of measuring working-class support.[29]

On the basis of the data from these four English-speaking democracies, but with little evidence from the United States and virtually none from Canada, there is at most an argument that a decline in class voting is possible. A few additional studies indirectly support this argument by indicating that working-class voting is especially intense in transitory stages of industrialization and urbanization. For example, the shock of rapid industrialization in a previously agrarian society has been associated, in northern Europe, with extremist working-class movements.[30] Working-class consciousness has been shown, in one impressive American study of Detroit in 1960, to be at a higher level among the recently uprooted than among blue-collar workers who had long lived in an urban industrial setting. Among workers of Polish and Ukrainian descent, those coming to Detroit directly from non-industrial European backgrounds were more class-conscious than those born in the northern United States, and among Negroes, the southern-born were more class conscious than the northern-born.

[26] *Ibid.*, p. 226.

[27] Leon D. Epstein, *Politics in Wisconsin* (Madison: University of Wisconsin Press, 1958), pp. 68–69.

[28] Alford, *op. cit.*, p. 284. See also Paul R. Opferkuch, "Southern Ontario Voting Patterns 1945–1959" (M.S. thesis, University of Wisconsin, 1963).

[29] Groupe de Recherches Sociales, *Les Electeurs Quebecois* (Montreal, 1960), p. 11.

[30] Seymour Martin Lipset, *Political Man* (Garden City, N.Y.: Doubleday, 1960), pp. 68–72.

The author attributes these differences partly to the fewer skills and experiences enabling the uprooted to adjust to industrial society and partly to the tenacious class lines of their pre-industrial societies.[31] What this points toward is a flat contradiction of the Marxist view that class consciousness will grow with "preparation" in industrial situations. If class consciousness means extremism or militancy, this view is surely contradicted by the whole history of advanced nations as well as by the particular study. But this is not the same thing as establishing a diminution in class voting generally. Working-class status may be associated, just as much as ever, with voting for a particular party even though it and its voters are moderate.[32] One cannot be sure that less intense class consciousness also means less class voting.

Another approach is suggested by data on the differences in voting behavior between workers who classify themselves as working-class and workers who classify themselves as middle-class. In several countries, the former were consistently found to vote more frequently for the party of the left than did the latter. British studies are especially convincing on this point. The difference in the percentages voting Labour is substantial.[33] Similarly, in the United States there is evidence that, within identical objective categories of occupation, income, and education, those who perceive themselves as working-class tend to be Democrats more frequently than those who think of themselves as middle-class.[34] A study of Swedish workers shows the

[31] John C. Leggett, "Uprootedness and Working-Class Consciousness," *American Journal of Sociology*, LXVIII (May, 1963), 682–91.

[32] This appears to be the explanation offered by Seymour Martin Lipset for his finding that parties of the left have maintained their percentages of the total vote during a period of decline in ideological distinctiveness. "The Changing Class Structure and Contemporary European Politics," *Daedalus* (Winter, 1964), pp. 271–303.

[33] Mark Benney, A. P. Gray, and R. H. Pear, *How People Vote* (London: Routledge & Kegan Paul, 1956), pp. 115–20; Mark Abrams and Richard Rose, *Must Labour Lose?* (Harmondsworth: Penguin, 1960), pp. 15, 18; A. H. Birch, *Small-Town Politics* (London: Oxford University Press, 1959), p. 109. An especially interesting division between the voting behavior of grammar-school educated voters of working-class background and the voting behavior of nongrammar-school educated voters of the same background is presented by Glen H. Elder, Jr., "Life Opportunity and Personality: Consequences of Stratified Secondary Education in Great Britain," *Sociology of Education*, XXXVIII (Spring, 1965), 196–97.

[34] Homer C. Cooper, "Social Class Identification and Political Party Affiliation," *Psychological Reports*, V (1959), 337–40; Oscar Glantz, "Class Consciousness and Political Solidarity," *American Sociological Review*, XXIII (August, 1958), 375–83.

same result with respect to support for the Social Democrats, who receive 72 per cent of the votes of workers classifying themselves as working-class but only 55 per cent of those classifying themselves as middle-class.[35]

No matter how well established these findings, they would indicate a diminution in class voting only if the numbers of workers subjectively identifying with the middle class were increasing. On this, the evidence is not so clear, although at least one of the studies mentioned above implies such an increase.[36] And it is widely believed that the most advanced industrial societies facilitate middle-class identification for urban workers through fairly high earnings, mass distribution of durable consumer goods, more years of formal education, and pervasive communication media. While an impoverished 10–20 per cent may remain, including the unemployed and many of the aged, the industrial working class itself, especially at its upper levels, can move toward the middle-class standard, if not style, of life. Any such trend would more likely contribute to the destruction of the class basis of party strength than would the increase in the middle classes, which, while it does diminish the size of the working-class vote, does not necessarily decrease voting by class. It might even increase it if the middle class became large enough to support the party of the right so handsomely that the working class was abandoned to the party of the left. It is safe to say that enough of a working class will always remain in an industrial society, however advanced, to maintain one large party able to attract the bulk of that class's votes. But if the subjective identification of workers with middle-class status grows, the class reason for voting for the party of the left would be seriously threatened since we know that identification with the middle class is associated with middle-class voting patterns.

All of this is meant to suggest—but no more than suggest—that the class basis for party voting, so usual in Western nations, may be eroded by social and economic forces now at work.[37] Perhaps this seems less consequential for Canada, where non-class factors are apparently more important, and for the United States, where non-class

[35] Bo Sarlvick, "The Role of Party Identification in Voters' Perceptions of Political Issues: A Study of Opinion Formation in Swedish Politics 1956–1960" (Mimeographed paper delivered at the Paris Congress of the International Political Science Association, 1961).

[36] Abrams and Rose, *op. cit.*, pp. 23, 53.

[37] The possibility of voting behavior being strongly influenced by policy preferences more complex than class voting is explored by V. O. Key, Jr., *The Responsible Electorate* (Cambridge: Harvard University Press, 1966), pp. 58–59.

factors have always been considerable.[38] But in Europe, where so much of modern politics has been based on class divisions, any erosion of those divisions will substantially change many parties. They may have to find new ways to structure the vote if the significance of the difference between working class and middle class diminishes in large degree. Or, as seems likely (in ways to be described in subsequent chapters), European parties may modify their organization and appeal so as to be less exclusively class-conscious, although still representing class interests clearly enough to encourage strong class voting. This would resemble the American pattern of the last few decades.

3. The Nonpartisan Alternative

There may be no reason to believe that modern parties, in the absence of the class consciousness characterizing early twentieth-century Western society, could not have responded to other bases for structuring the vote. And there may, therefore, be no reason to think that parties will not survive in a less class-conscious society. They might even prosper on an entirely different basis. Surely their function of structuring the vote is as relevant in one kind of society as in another, so long as there is a mass electorate. Nevertheless, it is true that most important modern party competition has rested on the division between classes and that where that division did not exist, because of the nature of the economy, there was often no competition. Moreover, when existing class divisions seemed inappropriate to the political issues at hand, attempts were made to manage politics without parties. The leading examples come from American nonpartisan experience, mainly in cities but also in some states. The crucial question is whether mass voting can be structured without parties or whether in attempting to do so parties are not re-created under a different name. Unfortunately, as will be seen, there can as yet be no firm answers.

The essence of an American nonpartisan election is simply that no party labels appear on the ballot. No legal restrictions prevent party organizations from endorsing and working for candidates. Technically, the situation resembles that in Britain and other Commonwealth nations where party labels are regularly omitted from the ballot. Practically, there may also be a resemblance since, in some nonpartisan American cities, parties structure the vote in one way or

[38] For the early importance of ethnic and religious differences in party voting, see Lee Benson, *The Concept of Jacksonian Democracy* (Princeton: Princeton University Press, 1961), p. 165. The persistence of these differences is clearly portrayed by Nathan Glazer and Daniel P. Moynihan, *Beyond the Melting Pot* (Cambridge: M.I.T. Press, 1963).

another. This might well be expected in an environment where partisan elections are characteristic of state and national politics. It is really surprising that American parties are hampered at all by the nonpartisan ballot. Yet they do seem less effective in a way that the absence of the ballot label in other countries would not lead us to predict. Of course, the nonpartisan ballot is designed in the United States to make them less effective. Municipal government, it has been thought, would be improved by curbing parties. Dropping their labels from the ballot was the simplest of several reforms undertaken to purify city politics early in the twentieth century. The meaning of the omission of party labels was thus different in the United States. This is because Americans had been accustomed to the labels, both before and after ballots became governmental rather than party documents,[39] and because American parties found it harder than parties elsewhere to structure the vote without the help of the ballot label—given the large number of American offices to be filled at every election. Accordingly, there is more than legal significance involved in the nonpartisan ballot's reduction of the American political party to the same status as that of all other groups in a local community.[40] Parties must compete on nearly equal terms with non-party groups endorsing candidates. For really strong parties, this should not have been serious, despite the long ballot, but for American parties the effect has been described as "debilitating" by a leading student of the subject.[41]

American parties, where thus weakened, must have been relatively weak to begin with. Indirect support for such a view comes from studies of nonpartisan municipal politics which show that where national and state party loyalties are strong they carry over into municipal politics.[42] Chicago is perhaps the leading example. Much seems to depend on the kind of city and on the kind of party the city would support, with or without the nonpartisan ballot.[43] A systematic

[39] Eldon Cobb Evans, *A History of the Australian Ballot System in the United States* (Chicago: The University of Chicago Press, 1917), p. 6.

[40] Eugene C. Lee, *The Politics of Nonpartisanship* (Berkeley and Los Angeles: University of California Press, 1960), p. 97.

[41] Charles R. Adrian, "Some General Characteristics of Nonpartisan Elections," *American Political Science Review*, XLVI (September, 1952), 768.

[42] Phillips Cutright, "Nonpartisan Electoral Systems in American Cities," *Comparative Studies in Society and History*, V (January, 1963), 225; J. Lieper Freeman, "Local Party Systems: Theoretical Considerations and a Case Analysis," *American Journal of Sociology*, LXIV (November, 1958), 282–89.

[43] Edward C. Banfield and James Q. Wilson, *City Politics* (Cambridge: Harvard University Press and M.I.T. Press, 1963), pp. 151–52. For the continued partisan influence in a nominally nonpartisan situation, see Harold F. Gosnell, *Machine Politics: Chicago Model* (Chicago: The University of Chicago Press, 1937), p. 30.

analysis of six California cities, all with a nonpartisan government, shows a considerable variation in party influence.[44]

The extent of the nonpartisan ballot in American politics should be emphasized. More than 60 per cent of American cities of more than 5,000 population use ballots that do not identify parties, and the number increased between 1940 and 1959.[45] Minnesota and Nebraska elect their state legislatures on nonpartisan ballots. Local school boards, when subject to popular election, are usually chosen on nonpartisan ballots. (I single this out for mention since education is typical of the subjects Americans have tried to insulate from party politics. Rather than not being important enough, it has been considered too important for parties to manage. It is not from lack of policy implications that local education matters are protected from party competition.)

How well nonpartisanship works when it works—that is, when parties are unable to influence voting—is as hard to estimate as the relative effects of one-party politics and two-party competition.[46] Policy outputs, which ought to provide the criteria, are hard to measure and compare. Nonpartisan American municipal governments appear less corrupt than partisan ones, but their lack of corruption may well be inherent to the city. A corrupt city, managed by a really strong party organization, can prevent the adoption of a nonpartisan ballot, along with other reforms. On the other side, the nearly complete ascendancy of the nonpartisan form in middle-class suburbs does not *cause* the high level of educational and other public services ordinarily provided by these communities.[47] Their wealth and social status would make such services likely whatever the ballot form and probably help to account for the form itself.

In the American environment, it is generally middle-class culture which is associated with the nonpartisan ballot and with the whole effort to take politics away from parties. This is true of the earlier municipal reforms and of the contemporary suburban patterns. It is in the absence of middle-class strength, as in large cities abandoned to the working class by the middle-class flight to the suburbs, that organized parties retain municipal strength. A fair question is whether the general growth of the middle class will also mean the growth of

[44] Lee, *op. cit.*, p. 98.

[45] *Ibid.*, pp. 3, 24.

[46] An interesting early effort to measure the effect of nonpartisan elections was made by Robert E. Cushman, "Non-partisan Nominations and Elections," *Annals of the American Academy of Political and Social Science*, CVI (March, 1923), 83–96.

[47] Data on the nature of suburban populations are reported by Robert C. Wood, *Suburbia* (Boston: Houghton Mifflin, 1958), p. 111.

nonpartisanship. If so, however, there is still no sign of any substantial extension of nonpartisanship beyond the local level. National politics and ordinarily state politics seem even in the United States to retain parties to structure the vote. All that can be said to qualify this is that local nonpartisanship can spill over to influence voter attitudes toward even national politics, and that it can do so without producing any movement for a nonpartisan national ballot. The number of unattached voters in national elections may simply be increased by the habits of independent voting for individual candidates for local offices.[48] Thus nonpartisan local elections can affect partisan national elections just as the national partisan patterns are usually said to affect nonpartisan local contests.

Some of the effects of nonpartisan balloting have been carefully studied in an unusual small-scale research project. In his work on Oberlin, Ohio, Aaron Wildavsky took the opportunity to test several familiar propositions on the basis of this small town's voting experience before and after the adoption of the nonpartisan ballot for city council elections.[49] Among other findings, he disproved the proposition that misunderstanding and apathy would develop and reduce electoral participation (Oberlin's increased after adoption of the nonpartisan ballot), and his evidence also disproved the proposition that campaigns would increase the emphasis on personalities at the expense of issues. Wildavsky quite reasonably grants that his findings may not apply everywhere, particularly to large cities that have had genuine party competition, but he strongly suggests that the Oberlin experience might be duplicated in the many similar situations where there had been no effective party competition.

It may seem odd to end a chapter on how parties structure the vote by stressing the possible importance of an exception to this party function. Yet the emphasis is deserved, even though the exception is limited, apparently, to only a segment of American politics. Nonpartisanship in the United States is not an individualistic anachronism. It is a twentieth-century reaction to previously established parties, and it tends to be strongest in communities which, in social type, are becoming more rather than less common. Why, therefore, should it be dismissed as an attempt to preserve pre-modern rural or small-town values? Instead, nonpartisanship may be an attempt to take a political step beyond parties, to ask voters even in a mass elec-

---

[48] *Ibid.*, pp. 152–56. Nonpartisan views of local citizenship spill over to national and state campaigns.

[49] *Leadership in a Small Town* (Totawa, N.J.: Bedminster Press, 1964), pp. 47–51.

torate to choose candidates as individuals or as members of groups more narrowly defined than parties, and to break what are seen as artificial cleavages imposed by parties. However, many things stand in the way of the argument—besides the main thrust of Western democratic experience. One is the clearly useful tendency of elected office-holders to form governing groups. Another is simply the difficulty of making a voting decision unstructured by parties. Curiously, however, it is in the United States, where the long ballot imposes the greatest difficulty, that the nonpartisan effort has been made. Its success and its future are still doubtful enough so that structuring the vote without parties is no more than a possibility, but it is a possibility that cannot be disregarded completely.

V

Organization

1. Bases

Just as political parties have been functional responses to voting by a mass electorate, so their nongovernmental or extra-parliamentary organizations have been means created by party leaders, including candidates, to help win votes and secure office. Organization in one degree or another always exists for this electoral purpose. It may have other purposes as well and still be regarded as that of a party, provided the electoral purpose is prominent, if not dominant.

This straightforward functionalism omits important cases. The most obvious are Communist and fascist parties. Their members are recruited for more demanding purposes than vote-seeking, and these other purposes—quasi-military, revolutionary, or subversive—may dominate most of the time even in democratic nations. Where this is so and where electoral activity is minor, as it is for Communists in Britain, their organizations can be dismissed, as unlike those of political parties in any usual sense. But where, as in France or Italy, Communists receive about one-quarter of the total vote, their organizations plainly function as important vote-getting agencies among other things. Their vote-getting may even be a dominant function. In any event, they are too important electorally to be excluded from consideration. What can be said, though, is that much of the Communist organizational apparatus, like the fascist, has been created and maintained for nonelectoral purposes. Membership selection, training, and discipline are more developed than would be justified by pure vote-getting considerations. The nonelectoral purposes of the Communist cell are made clear not only by what its members do, but also by the simple fact that ordinarily the cell does not coincide with a geographic constituency.[1] Thus, while neither Communists nor fascists can be excluded from a typology of party organizations, they ought to be recognized as exceptional. Because many of their functions are aber-

[1] Maurice Duverger, *Political Parties*, trans. Barbara and Robert North (New York: John Wiley & Sons, 1954), pp. 27–36.

rant in relation to the usual objectives of parties in competitive democracies, their organizations are also aberrant. They may be highly effective as vote-getting agencies, but they are developed in ways that vote-getting itself does not require.

The same holds for the historical development of certain present-day democratic party organizations. Those which began as working-class "movements" in nineteenth-century Europe did not at first seek votes so much as advocate a cause by propaganda or economic pressure, simultaneously organizing trade unionists and socialists. They were electoral machines only secondarily, or they subsequently became electoral in response to a delayed popular franchise. Then socialists sought votes as well as members. It is hard to say, in the instances of prospering socialist organizations, just when gaining members became secondary or ancillary to gaining votes. Some organizations never made the transition. Mostly these appear as minor parties, except of course for certain Communist parties. For present purposes, more significant among parties that grew from the earlier "movements" are the large socialist, labor, or social democratic parties throughout Western Europe. We can expect them to bear the marks of their origin and early history, even though now their electoral function dominates. Organizationally they will differ from parties that were originally electoral, even though they no longer differ functionally. The different historical origin of parties helps to explain the differences in their organizational types.

In particular, it may help to explain the differences between the loose cadre organization, typical of parties in the United States and also typical of traditional conservative and liberal parties in Europe, and the more highly structured, mass-membership organization, typical of working-class parties, whether labelled socialist or not and perhaps also typical of other more recent European parties.[2] The cadre type characterized, from the start, parties with primarily and almost entirely electoral functions. The mass-membership party of the socialists—using the term loosely for any democratic party based primarily on the class consciousness of industrial workers—began as movements concerned with other functions, but, organized in branches, they seemed to be so efficacious in vote-getting that non-socialist parties, it is argued, tended to adopt the same pattern in order to compete. This is Duverger's familiar argument, expressed by the term "contagion from the left."[3] But whether it does account for the organizational

[2] Frank J. Sorauf, *Political Parties in the American System* (Boston: Little, Brown, 1964), chap. 1.

[3] Duverger, *op. cit.*, p. xxvii.

form of non-socialist European parties may be doubted, since it is not clear that they adopted the socialist pattern in a permanent or full-fledged way, or that, when non-socialist mass-membership does exist (as for British Conservatives), it came as a response to socialist developments. The question is of considerable import since, if cadre organization is typical only of pre-socialist and not generally of non-socialist parties, there is ground for accepting Duverger's view that cadre organization is old-fashioned and mass membership is the modern form. But if non-socialist parties have successfully competed without adopting the socialist pattern of mass membership, then it would be difficult to accept the modernity of that pattern. Of course, American non-socialist parties have successfully competed, but not against strong socialist opposition. Opportunity for contagion from a socialist left has not arisen in the United States. It is in Europe plus Australia and New Zealand where the influence of socialist or labor party organization on other parties can be assessed.

Instead of starting from Duverger's hypothesis that the typically socialist mass-membership organization is the modern party form, I look at this organization (separately in the next chapter) as the response of a movement originally concerned with more than elections and thus likely to be different from parties committed almost solely to electoral functions. This basic presumption causes us to look skeptically not just at organizational imitation by non-socialist parties but also at the idea that mass membership remains consequential in socialist or labor parties. Any decline in membership, and evidence of only limited imitations by non-socialist parties, would justify the belief that the socialist organizational type is a special feature of a time and place rather than a form typical of advanced democratic nations. American organizational experience is also relevant since the absence of mass membership in the United States tends to strengthen the argument that socialist parties are special phenomena. On the other hand, substantial growth in mass-membership party organization in the United States, even if entirely non-socialist, would raise doubts about this hypothesis.

The distinction between socialist working-class and non-socialist parties, as organizational types, is a principal theme of this inquiry, but it is not the only one. There is also a rural-urban distinction. Party organization, with or without mass membership, tends to be more highly developed in cities than in small towns or farm areas. For example, American patronage machines, while important in some rural areas, are characteristic of cities, especially large cities. And party clubs with dues-paying members are distinctively urban, notably among middle-class activists. But middle-class activists obviously provide a different organizational base than an equally urban working class. The consequent pattern, especially in predominantly middle-class suburbs, will differ from both city patronage machines and socialist organizations. And if there is an urban and suburban middle-class organizational pattern, it may be found in other Western nations besides the United States. Therefore, the tentative typology is slightly more complicated than the distinction solely between cadre and mass organizations. Besides the barest skeletal party, often characteristic of rural communities, there may be three distinct, mainly urban types: patronage, middle-class, and socialist working-class. The last two are similarly mass-membership parties in their European manifestations, and will be discussed together, although the socialist working-class party is also treated separately in the next chapter.

Another preliminary observation must be made: while certain social and economic circumstances seem to be prerequisite for certain party organizations, they do not automatically cause these organizations to develop. There must be other incentives. In other words, the organization must be considered useful for party purposes if it is going to be created and maintained. Here the incentives to organize on the part of leaders and candidates are plain: they will probably want an organization to help win votes and elections of which they are the potential beneficiaries. But what of the ordinary party workers and rank-and-file members? For them, the incentives are plainly material or utilitarian only if patronage is available to be dispensed to the more active among them. Or sometimes, necessarily less often, today's party worker will look forward to the material reward of a subsequent candidacy leading to elected government office. Or he may hope to have his activity rewarded by access, for private material purposes, to elected officials of his party, although a financial contribution to the party, without active membership, ordinarily suffices to gain this advantage. The fact is that only the old large-scale, American-style distribution of the spoils of office provides the *material* incentive for any large amount of rank-and-file party work.

Consequently, other kinds of incentives have to be considered. Two have been identified and applied to parties,[4] the solidary and the purposive; along with material incentives, they very well may exhaust the kinds of incentives that will encourage organizational work. The solidary kind includes the intangible values of socializing, congenial-

---

[4] Peter B. Clark and James Q. Wilson, "Incentive Systems: A Theory of Organizations," *Administrative Science Quarterly*, VI (September, 1961), 129–66.

ity, sense of group membership, conviviality, and general enjoyment. Purposive incentives, while also intangible, derive from the stated goals of an association, such as enactment of reform legislation, rather than from the simple act of association itself. Both kinds are considered less useful for maintaining continuity than material incentives, now greatly decreasing in the United States. Indeed, it is doubtful that party organizations can be maintained only by solidary and purposive incentives.[5] Pessimism may well be justified. With respect to solidary incentives, it is hard to see how parties can compete very well against *non*political associations organized primarily for social congeniality. Certainly political parties will be unlikely to attract members on this basis in the first place; at most, solidary incentives would retain members who enjoyed their party associations after joining for other reasons—reasons perhaps related to purposive incentives, often the foremost ones in the early stages not only of an individual's membership but also of a party itself (especially a reform party). A party's purposive incentives tend to recede, or to become less pure and attractive, as electoral functions impose the need for policy compromises. Adherence to policies may not always be compatible with electing candidates. Still, policy compromises may not lose all of a purposively motivated membership. Many members may regard candidate-election as a means to an eventual policy goal, however compromised that goal is in the short run. Or the election of candidates may itself become a satisfying purposive goal even if it was not so initially. Perhaps this is to suggest a fourth kind of incentive that is not exactly like any of the others but combines certain purposive and solidary qualities. The incentive is simply to win as for one's team in a game. In this light, a party member is less than a full-fledged team member but more than a spectator. He can work for his side as well as cheer for it.

It is plain that neither this fourth organizational incentive, if it exists, nor the solidary and purposive incentives are reasons as clear and strong for joining and working for an organization as are material incentives. Unfortunately for parties, their most meaningful material incentives—patronage jobs—have been disappearing even in the United States. Other material incentives adequate for many members are hard to come by. Parties really cannot rival unions, trade associations, or other specialized groups in representing economic interests. The electoral need for parties to make broad appeals usually prevents

[5] *Ibid.*, p. 165.

consistent interest-group representation. Analogously, parties also suffer by comparison with other organizations in respect to solidary and purposive incentives. Just as the necessity for broad appeals makes it difficult for a party to compete materially for members against economic interest groups, so breadth gives a party less solidary or purposive attraction in competition with groups whose sociality or normative goals can be more narrowly defined.

Organizationally, then, one should expect parties to be small, weak, and intermittent in comparison with many other associations, including some that participate in politics. Where this is not the case and parties are organizationally strong, despite the absence of patronage, it is reasonable to seek the explanation in unusual circumstances —such as the class consciousness of a large social sector supporting a socialist party. Purposive and material incentives may there be linked and made virtually identical in a most efficacious organizational manner.

Generally there seems in political parties to be an unusually large gap between the organizational incentives of the leaders and of other members. For it is plain that the leaders, here including candidates, prospective candidates, and a few of their peers in the hierarchy, have strong incentives—that is, to gain office—which, in the nature of things, most members cannot share in the absence of large-scale patronage. This is true whether the attractiveness of government office is viewed as strictly material or in less tangible terms of power.[6] Rank-and-file members must be recruited on the basis of entirely different incentives. This is by no means so apparent in the early stages of a new party, especially one that originated as a movement, for then the leaders seem to share the purposes of their followers. It is when a party approaches electoral victories, especially in two-party competition, that the leaders' incentives can be demonstrably different from those of organizational members.

[6] Amitai Etzioni, *Complex Organizations* (New York: Free Press of Glencoe, 1961), pp. 42, 75–76. Administrative or other leadership positions within the party organization ought to be added to the governmental offices providing material incentives (or power-oriented incentives) for a fairly small number of potential party members. In this respect, party organizations resemble other voluntary associations whose core members necessarily differ from a mass membership. This characteristic of voluntary associations is well stated by Theodore Caplow: "A major problem of voluntary associations is 'apathy.' Successful voluntary associations often escape from this threat by enlisting a cadre of militants or bureaucrats, for whom participation is a career." *Principles of Organization* (New York: Harcourt, Brace & World, 1964), p. 130.

2. Patronage

No such difference in aspirations appears within a party organization built on patronage. Everyone, whether candidate or precinct worker, has the same incentive: to get a job in the government through winning the election. Ideology, principle, program, and policy, if they exist at all, are equally instrumental at every organizational level. There is a strictly business arrangement, rational and efficient for the narrow purpose at hand. Organizational membership in any formal sense can be kept fairly small. What is needed is one "member," or precinct captain, for each set of several hundred voters. Additionally, some of these voters can be organized informally to encourage their electoral loyalty. But they remain a source of votes, not of dues or policies. For example, the political clubs often organized by American big-city machines seem more like auxiliaries than like mass-membership parties.[7]

There is a degree of oversimplification in describing patronage politics solely in terms of government jobs. Other favors are also available to the winners—contracts for private businesses and preferential treatment for licensed occupations. Many of these opportunities are open primarily to financial contributors rather than to campaign workers, however, and they may continue and even increase in importance after job patronage substantially declines. They may help any kind of party organization, including one based heavily on patronage, but they do not appear to be essential. Government jobs alone could sustain an organization dedicated to vote-getting. Even if such jobs have not in practice been the only possible rewards, they have characterized the organization of patronage machines.

Size, it must be emphasized, is not an object of an organization of this type. Only enough "members" are needed for efficient vote-getting. Mass followers are not organized as members. Party work is done by the leaders—little bosses at the neighborhood level and big bosses higher up. This kind of organization can thrive, as it obviously has, within the party framework created by American state laws. The legally prescribed party committeeman, from ward or precinct through the county and state level, may simply coincide with the machine organization. The committeemen are the vote-getters. Thus the patronage machine is compatible with the cadre or skeletal form of organization that is often said to characterize American parties, in contrast to European ones. But the patronage organization should really

[7] Roy V. Peel, *The Political Clubs of New York City* (New York: Putnam's, 1935).

be distinguished from the purely cadre organization for the latter may exist without patronage. Then, to be sure, it is not much of an organization. Committeemen at the precinct level may be entirely inactive if present at all, with little remaining but a handful of top party leaders plus candidates and aspiring candidates. Their communication with the voters tends to be confined to the mass media and to ad hoc election campaigns. Without patronage or European-style mass membership, this strictly cadre organization characterizes parties in many areas of the United States. It may always have characterized parties in many rural areas.

The patronage machine, however, is a more highly developed form, even though it seems to have reached its maturity at an earlier stage of American democracy. Indeed it seems to have originated with democracy itself. This is the view of the leading historian of American patronage. "The true cause for the introduction of the spoils system," Carl Russell Fish wrote, "was the triumph of democracy." Once large numbers of Americans had the vote, as happened by the 1820's and 1830's, there had to be an organization to bring the eligible voters to the polls. "This work requires the labor of many men; there must be captains of hundreds and the captains of tens, district chiefs and ward heelers." For the lesser agents, in particular, politics "must be made to pay" if time is to be devoted to the task at hand.[8] Fish's view of patronage as at least an accompaniment of the early triumph of American democracy is accepted by V. O. Key, who argues further that the United States has so far "contrived no system for the support of party that does not place considerable reliance on patronage."[9] There remains the question why other nations, especially in Europe, did not have parties similarly relying on patronage. Even when there was a pre-democratic background of patronage appointments—in a lush though narrow upper-class way, as in England—no large-scale spoils system accompanied the extension of the mass suffrage. Most of the social conditions ordinarily said to explain American patronage (notably the rapid growth of large cities[10]) were present in Western Europe when the suffrage was extended in the late nineteenth century. The explanation probably is to be found in other historical circumstances that distinguished early nineteenth-century

[8] *The Civil Service and the Patronage* (Cambridge: Harvard University Press, 1904), p. 156.

[9] V. O. Key, Jr., *Politics, Parties, and Pressure Groups* (New York: Crowell-Collier, 1964), p. 369.

[10] Fred I. Greenstein, "The Changing Pattern of Urban Party Politics," *Annals of the American Academy of Political and Social Science*, CCCLIII (May, 1964), 1–13.

America from late nineteenth-century Europe. In the latter, as suggested in Chapter II, there was already an established career civil service to fulfill the requirements of modern government and also (as I will stress later) an organized or organizable working class capable of sustaining a party on a non-patronage basis.

In certain structural respects, the American patronage machine may have been more highly developed than the larger mass-membership parties. Certainly, the patronage organization at its peak had a large enough cadre of more or less full-time politicians for effective vote-getting. Chicago provides one of the best examples because its political machine has enjoyed an unusually long success. Harold Gosnell closely studied it in its heyday,[11] and his study contains data for 1928 and 1936, when, despite a change from Republican ascendancy to Democratic near monopoly, the organizational system continued to be based on jobs and spoils. Probably it still does. Major figures, below the top city boss, were the ward committeemen and the precinct committeemen (or precinct captains). Although the ward committeemen (fifty for each party) were chosen in primary elections, the organization's ability to control the primary ensured their continuance, indeed near-permanence, in office. The more numerous precinct captains were appointed by the ward committeemen; here the turnover was high partly because of failure to meet the vote-getting standards set by the latter. There is no doubt about the strictly hierarchical nature of the arrangement. The precinct captain worked for his ward committeeman not only as a vote-getter but often also as a government employee in the sense that a salaried patronage job, obtained through the ward committeeman, depended on his performance as precinct captain. The number of precinct captains who held government jobs was striking. Gosnell reports that 60 per cent were government employees in 1928, and almost 50 per cent in 1936 (including three-quarters of the Democratic precinct captains, as a result of their party's greatly increased control at most governmental levels).[12] These figures were not at the time peculiar to Chicago; Gosnell cites comparable data from Philadelphia and in a group of cities in New York state.[13] Although in Chicago as elsewhere, one party at any given time would have more of its precinct captains in government jobs, there were almost always some jobs for the second party, since it might

[11] Harold F. Gosnell, *Machine Politics: Chicago Model* (Chicago: The University of Chicago Press, 1937).
[12] *Ibid.*, pp. 54–56.
[13] *Ibid.*

well be the majority party at the county, state, or national level, although a minority in the city itself.

In the Chicago model, precinct captains tended to be of relatively low socio-economic status. Their usual government jobs were not at professional or managerial levels, and those without such jobs were more often clerks, salesmen, or laborers than lawyers or executives. Furthermore, over half of the 1928 precinct committeemen and 40 per cent of the 1936 committeemen had been formally educated only through grammar (elementary) school.[14] Their status in these respects is understandable since precinct captains were rank-and-file leaders, in and of their own neighborhoods, resembling their neighborhood constituents. Naturally, precinct captains and even ward committeemen tended to belong to their area's predominant ethnic group.[15]

The manner in which precinct captains secured votes is well established. House-to-house canvassing was basic. This was essential both to make sure that one's constituents were registered and to see that they subsequently voted. It is well known that votes were occasionally bought for cash, but most of the time the precinct captain had other resources to make his canvass effective. He was the neighborhood's political go-between for a great variety of favors. And he functioned as a nonprofessional social worker, dispensing both governmental services (or access to these services) and material goods (like the famous Christmas turkey). When the precinct captain had a political club, it too was part of the social-service activity. The strictly material side of the committeeman's relation to voters should not be exaggerated. It has been pointed out that turkeys, for instance, might have been more important as tokens of friendship than as material rewards.[16] In any case, they established a debt on which the captain could draw at election time when he needed votes.

Other American city machines resembled Chicago's in most important respects except that they were not successful for so long. New York City's organization seems to have differed mainly in form. The assembly district leader, chosen either by a primary or by a committee whose members are elected in a primary, is comparable to Chicago's ward committeeman, and the election district captains, appointed by the district leader, are comparable to Chicago's precinct captains. Po-

[14] *Ibid.*, pp. 54, 57.

[15] *Ibid.*, pp. 44–45.

[16] Edward C. Banfield and James Q. Wilson, *City Politics* (Cambridge: Harvard University Press and M.I.T. Press, 1963), p. 117.

litical clubs have been more prominent, however, in New York than in Chicago. While voluntary and largely outside the formal party structure created by state law, the New York political clubs are sources of strength for district leaders.[17] Rival clubs may challenge the regular ones by trying to defeat leaders in primary elections to party posts. In their great days and in fact until recently, the established leaders had clubs strong enough to defeat such rivals and to maintain control of the formal organization. This was certainly true as long as patronage was bountiful and as long as established immigrant groups stayed in their old districts.[18]

The old-style machines have declined in American cities in the last few decades. Loss of patronage and diminishing immigrant bases are only two of several probable causes of the decline. The growth of the government's professional social services has made the boss less relevant as a humanizing intermediary between citizens, especially new citizens, and the legal enforcement machinery. Increasing education has placed more and more voters above the level of influence by precinct captains. And the new mass media have given candidates more direct access to voters. Yet it is true that where patronage remains bountiful, as in Chicago, the machine is still a vital political force. As late as the 1960's, Chicago's politicians had 15,000 city and county jobs at their disposal and another 13,000 to 14,000 state jobs.[19] Even without much of the older federal patronage, there were enough jobs to maintain at least one major party organization in the old style. Nor was Chicago unique. Pennsylvania still had 50,000 patronage positions as late as 1962. Jobs in this quantity seem more than enough to take care of precinct captains, with some left over for their friends and helpers. Altogether patronage on this scale could maintain a fairly large and effective vote-getting organization.

There are probably other ways to have larger organizations, but it is doubtful whether there is any more effective means of getting votes than to have these material rewards available for those who rounded up the votes needed to win elections. Perhaps the rewards were not always distributed so as most effectively to maximize vote-getting efforts. It has been pointed out that patronage was often divided equally by wards rather than distributed more heavily to marginal

[17] Wallace S. Sayre and Herbert Kaufman, *Governing New York City* (New York: Russell Sage Foundation, 1960), chap. v.
[18] Peter Kobrak, *The New Urban Reformer* (M.S. thesis, University of Wisconsin, 1962), pp. 14, 29, 79.
[19] James Q. Wilson, *The Amateur Democrat* (Chicago: The University of Chicago Press, 1962), p. 69.

wards where it might have enhanced the party's electoral prospects.[20] Also, it is possible that ward or precinct leaders would become more interested in controlling the organization than in broadening its electoral base. But most of the time, obtaining votes for one's party improved one's status and so maintained or increased patronage opportunities. Really the arrangement was quite rational from the standpoint of the party and its workers. Jobs were simply exchanged for party votes. What was rational and apparently effective for the party, however, was hardly so from a broader public standpoint. After all, the jobs were government jobs. Patronage was not always the best way to fill them. Nor did the men who were elected to office on the basis of jobs-for-votes always set the most desirable examples of public responsibility. Civil-service reform was aimed at the heart of the patronage system, and it now seems in the process of destroying it. Perhaps the old-style machines would die of other causes anyway, but they surely die wherever large-scale patronage is removed. The scale, it must be stressed, is all-important: only a few policy-level positions may encourage large campaign contributions, but they cannot provide the wherewithal for precinct captains.

Students of political parties now appear curiously uncertain about whether the death of bossism is a good thing—in contrast with the steady stream of intellectual, reform-minded criticism directed at the machines in their heyday. Then, even believers in strong parties had yearned for the passing of bosses in order to clear the way for the new party model. There had been complaints that the "unofficial professional politician," the local boss, had victimized both local and national government since he had to be dealt with on patronage terms by a national political leader.[21] What was wanted was a national party of amateurs directly loyal to national leadership, and this is still the view of party reformers among political scientists.[22] But there also are some recent professorial mourners for the old machines. For example, Banfield and Wilson have said, a propos of Franklin Roosevelt's dependence on big-city bosses to deliver the vote: "No President will ever again find such support in city politicians. Now that a national leader cannot expect to have large blocs of votes 'delivered' by city bosses, he must get them for himself; to do this he

[20] James Q. Wilson, "The Economy of Patronage," *Journal of Political Economy*, LXIX (August 1961), 373.

[21] E. E. Schattschneider, *Party Government* (New York: Rinehart, 1942), pp. 110, 183. See also Austin Ranney, *The Doctrine of Responsible Party Government* (Urbana: University of Illinois Press, 1962), p. 61.

[22] James MacGregor Burns, *The Deadlock of Democracy* (Englewood Cliffs, N. J.: Prentice-Hall, 1963), pp. 236–37.

may have to pay a higher price than was paid before, and a higher one, perhaps, than the nation can afford."[23] The higher price they mention would be in terms of catering to public opinion through charm, salesmanship, rhetoric, and ideology. Just why and how the price here would be higher than the local boss's price is not clear. Nor is it really so clear that city bosses were important in delivering votes to Roosevelt. He often seemed to deliver votes to them by creating Democratic majorities where there had been none before.

Still, there is something to be said for patronage organizations. Especially in the late nineteenth century, their real heyday, the machines did, as one sympathetic political scientist has said, reduce "the cost in human suffering from industrialization and urban growth."[24] It seems too much to go beyond this comment to give the machines credit for obviating the development of class-conscious parties in the United States. The most that can be said is that the ethnic groups' consciousness of their special identity, the groups on which the patronage organizations built their followings,[25] fragmented any class consciousness that might have provided the basis for a workers' party. And it is by no means clear, in any event, that American class consciousness would have been sufficient. At least the party machine was not causal. It too was partly a product of ethnic differentiation, and in this sense, it was the American counterpart to a working-class party. As a mid-nineteenth century creation, the American machine antedated class parties. It was a means, without class-conscious ideological goals, to mobilize masses of voters. But, more relevant, there were thousands of government jobs to be filled by patronage appointment. That this condition for the existence of the machine was fulfilled in the United States, and almost nowhere else to the same degree, accounts for the large-scale patronage machine's almost unique omnipresence on the American political scene. In most other Western nations, civil-service reform superseded patronage either before or simultaneously with the growth of the mass suffrage. It is a peculiarity of historical timing that in the United States a large and growing electorate existed at a time when a vast number of government positions could provide the patronage base for organized party work. And

[23] Banfield and Wilson, op. cit., p. 345.

[24] Fred I. Greenstein, *The American Party System and the American People* (Englewood Cliffs, N.J.: Prentice-Hall, 1963), p. 53.

[25] The ethnic basis provided by European immigrants and more recently by Negroes and Puerto Ricans is discussed by Elmer E. Cornwell, Jr., "Bosses, Machines, and Ethnic Groups," *Annals of the American Academy of Political and Social Science*, CCCLIII (May, 1964), 27–39, and by Nathan Glazer and Daniel P. Moynihan, *Beyond the Melting Pot* (Cambridge: M.I.T. Press, 1963), pp. 220–25.

once party organization came to be so based, a vested interest was created in maintaining government patronage. Civil-service reform had to overcome this vested interest, and victory was by no means immediate.

The party organizations based on patronage were strong enough to fight a long delaying action. This testifies to the inherently useful nature of the arrangement.[26] Material rewards, as long as they existed, made for a durable party organization. In the United States at least, it is not clear that an equally useful substitute has been found. The alternative to a patronage organization may be almost no American organizational membership at all. But this too might be workable in contemporary circumstances. At any rate, there is no point in idealizing the patronage machine. Its basis was an arrangement no longer tolerable in a modern society demanding efficient governmental services. The narrower efficiency criterion of a political party organization no longer prevails.

3. *European-Style Mass Membership*

In the absence of large-scale patronage, but not necessarily because of only that absence, many European parties developed membership organizations based largely on nonmaterial incentives. These organizations of zealous faithful party adherents had other purposes too, but they have regularly been used to perform the same vote-getting task as the patronage machine. Thus they represent a similar type of organizational response to the need to reach large numbers of voters. They vary from country to country, but their development suggests that organization of one kind or another has been a characteristic party response to a large electorate—at least in the early stage of that electorate's enfranchisement. It may still be true, however, that parties are meaningful to voters without such organizations. The party labels alone, even if representing no more than skeletal organizations, may suffice to structure the vote along party lines. The frequent occurrence of mass-membership party organizations is prima facie evidence only that they are or were originally useful, and not that they are necessary as vote-getting agencies.

British parties usually are cited as the prototype of mass-membership organizations. But they are not in all respects typical of European organizations since British party membership preceded the creation

---

[26] Recent relative advantages of patronage in local politics are supported by Phillips Cutright, "Activities of Precinct Committeemen in Partisan and Nonpartisan Communities," *Western Political Quarterly*, XVII (March, 1964), 93–108, and by James Reichley, *The Art of Government* (New York: Fund for the Republic, 1959), pp. 97–102.

of a socialist, working-class party. Unlike continental Europe, it cannot even be claimed for Britain, that right-wing parties built their extra-parliamentary organizations in response to earlier left-wing ones. Conservative and Liberal voters had been organized before the Labour party became a major force. The most that can be claimed in behalf of Labour party influence is that the mid-twentieth-century Conservative party expanded its organization in order to compete against Labour's. But precisely because British party organization cannot thus be viewed as entirely a reaction to the influence of a socialist working-class party, it is an especially good example of the relevance of membership to vote-getting. That is, nonelectoral purposes are not needed to explain the origin of Britain's mass-membership organizations.

Volunteer activists, grouped by parliamentary constituencies, created the organizational bases for British parties when they began to seek more members after the extension of the suffrage. (Patronage was already removed as a possible organizational base by the civil-service establishment.) The Liberals pioneered in the development of membership organizations, the best examples being those in Birmingham, but the Conservatives soon followed. For both, the associations were fostered by national leaders, and, while national unions were formed, the chief concern was to have effective groups of campaign workers in each constituency.[27] This remained true for the Conservative party as for the new Labour party; the Liberals, with the same type of organizational effort, declined in ways that are well known.

Today, the Conservative and Labour organizations are large and complex. In 1953, there were as many as 2,805,032 individual members (the only possible kind) in the Conservative party, but the number declined by an estimated half-million before 1961.[28] The

[27] The late nineteenth-century, or pre-Labour, organizational response of Conservatives and Liberals at the local level is well described by Frank Bealey, Jean Blondel, and W. P. McCann, *Constituency Politics* (London: Faber & Faber, 1965), pp. 62, 404–5, and more broadly for one of the two parties by James Cornford, "The Adoption of Mass Organization by the British Conservative Party," in Erik Allardt and Yrjo Littunen (eds.), *Cleavages, Ideologies and Party Systems* (Helsinki: Academic Bookstore, 1964), pp. 400–424. The classical description is by M. Y. Ostrogorski, *Democracy and the Organization of Political Parties* (London: Macmillan, 1902).

[28] Robert T. McKenzie, *British Political Parties* (London: William Heinemann, 1964), p. 187. The Conservative high point was a product of a massive postwar recruitment, apparently for the first time, in order to broaden the Party's financial support. J. D. Hoffman, *The Conservative Party in Opposition 1945–51* (London: MacGibbon & Kee, 1964), pp. 84–85.

Labour party had no more than a million members at its peak in the 1950's. Well over 5 million trade unionists, however, are indirectly members of the Labour party by virtue of paying union dues which include the party's political levy.[29] Even if we put aside these indirect memberships, Labour's total remains impressive. And the Conservative figure of more than 2 million dues-payers is even more so. No one contends that all or most of these members are active, even to the extent of attending meetings.[30] But merely to have so many enrolled members is no slight accomplishment. The more than 3 million Englishmen who pay dues directly to the two major parties constitute a substantial portion of Britain's adult population. (The nation's total population is not much over 50 million.)

Variation in the size of local party branches is great, and it appears to bear no close relation to party voting strength in the constituency (at least when studied with respect to the Labour party in Lancashire and Cheshire).[31] Marginal constituencies do not regularly have large party memberships, and neither do all "safe" seats. Rather, the pattern is that the parties recruit large numbers of members in places where middle-class voters are numerous.[32] Thus, the organizations may be biggest where they are least needed for electoral purposes. Safe Conservative constituencies, overwhelmingly middle-class, may have large Conservative and Labour organizations neither of which affect the election result. Marginal constituencies will have enough party members for campaign purposes, and, if not, outside help will often come from national and regional headquarters. Again, therefore, there is a question about the electoral usefulness of a large membership. Clearly it cannot be very useful in noncompetitive constituencies.

This assumes that the principal electoral relevance of a party membership is to provide campaign workers. It leaves aside membership as a source of dues on the ground that there are easier ways of collecting campaign funds (except perhaps for a new working-class party without trade-union support). It also leaves aside membership as a means for providing programmatic communication between leaders and followers on the ground that this is not a strictly electoral function. The basic assumption is that the effort to sustain a mass membership is justified primarily by vote-getting considerations. If

[29] McKenzie, op. cit., p. 484. The figure is now nearer 6 million.
[30] A. H. Birch, Small-Town Politics (London: Oxford University Press, 1959), pp. 50, 82.
[31] McKenzie, op. cit., p. 544.
[32] Jean Blondel, Voters, Parties, and Leaders (Baltimore: Penguin, 1963).

other purposes are also served, as is likely, they are bound to be of secondary interest to party leaders and candidates who want to win elections.

Party members, notably in Britain, do the kind of door-to-door campaigning that American precinct captains used to. This is what the British call canvassing—going through an electoral register marked, from an earlier canvass of voters, as to party preference of each voter, and seeing to it that all or nearly all of one's own party voters get to the polls. Door-to-door solicitation is the rule, and so is the provision of transportation for voters who need it. Helping to make arrangements for postal votes (absentee ballots) is another important aspect. These activities are by no means unknown in the United States, but they are pursued more fully and intensively in Britain, mainly by nonprofessional party activists. The fact that they are *directed* by a professional party agent does not detract from the amateur status of most of the campaign effort. Even with the now widespread use of paid agents at the local level and with the growth of professional staffs at national and regional party headquarters, Britain does not have very many full-time political personnel.[33] Only an enormous increase in paid help, at great expense, would displace the members' efforts in canvassing. But the real question is whether intensive canvassing is to be maintained at all. Ad hoc campaign organizations are an alternative.

There are many reasons why canvassing in Britain so developed as to require this effort by volunteer activists. Some of these reasons may be related to time and place. British election law imposes a modest limit on campaign expenditure in behalf of a parliamentary candidate, so the local party cannot spend much money even if it wanted to. But there is no limit on unpaid voluntary campaigning. And this campaigning at the local level accomplishes one task not undertaken by the vast and expensive national party efforts: acquainting local voters with the name of the candidate. The absence of party labels from the ballot makes this a necessary campaign function,[34] whose importance does not diminish with the nationalization of politics. (On the contrary, the more that voters make their electoral decision on the basis of national party preferences, the more essential it is for them to be told which parliamentary candidate represents which party.) The only way to eliminate or lessen this campaign function would be to

[33] W. L. Guttsman, *The British Political Elite* (London: MacGibbon & Kee, 1963), p. 196.

[34] Mark Benney, A. P. Gray, and R. H. Pear, *How People Vote* (London: Routledge & Kegan Paul, 1956), p. 76.

put the party label on the ballot. Similarly, new legislation could reduce the importance of party organization with respect to postal voting. (British law now not only imposes strict terms for postal-voting eligibility, but requires that application forms be submitted two weeks before polling day.)

General canvassing does not, however, seem entirely dependent on features of British electoral law. There is a point to trying to get all of a party's adherents to vote no matter what the legal circumstances (except when voting is legally compulsory, as in Australia and Belgium). That British party activists do canvass on a large scale can be assumed, although it is by no means universal to have a marked register. Some idea of the extent is given in a Gallup report that about half of British voters had been approached by a party representative during the 1959 campaign.[35] This contrasts with the figure of 15 per cent reported for the United States in 1956.[36]

Whether canvassing is effective is another question. No one can confidently ascribe any part of the large British turnout to more thorough canvassing since there are many other factors that could account for it. And from internal British evidence there is reason to doubt whether the turnout is appreciably greater in thoroughly canvassed constituencies than in more unorganized ones.[37] We do not know how many of those who are canvassed would have voted anyway. But we do know that party leaders and candidates retain their faith in the efficacy of canvassing. Especially in marginal constituencies, a party does not want to risk doing without a marked register if the competing party is working with one. If the most assiduous canvassing increases a party's vote by only two or three percentage points, still these may constitute the crucial margin for victory. And perhaps there is no other way than door-to-door solicitation to obtain the extra two or three per cent. There may be some such irreducible number that cannot be brought to the polls by the most intensive use of the mass media.

What systematic studies there have been of the efficacy of door-to-door work in the United States tend to support this view. Organizational activity was found to have a small but discernible relation to

---

[35] David E. Butler and Richard Rose, *The British General Election of 1959* (London: Macmillan, 1960), p. 140.

[36] V. O. Key, Jr., *Politics, Parties, and Pressure Groups* (New York: Crowell-Collier, 1964), p. 461.

[37] Butler and Rose, *op. cit.*, p. 163, and David E. Butler and Anthony King, *The British General Election of 1964* (London: Macmillan, 1965), p. 295.

the size of a party's vote in Detroit.[38] And, in a comparative study of eleven large eastern and middle-western cities, organizations were found to influence turnouts of partisan voters while not having much to do with the determination of partisan dispositions in the first place.[39] Door-to-door work has been shown to be especially influential in primary elections.[40] We know too that American candidates appreciate voluntary canvassing when they can obtain it. On the other hand, there are nations in which canvassing is not widely used even when there are large membership organizations. In Norway, for example, systematic canvassing is not an accepted practice partly on the ground that it is an invasion of privacy. It is not surprising therefore to have a report that local organizational activity (membership and so forth) has made no appreciable difference in votes cast in Norway. There is little variance between wards to be accounted for by differences in degree of party activity.[41] Yet Norway has, especially in the Labor party, a large membership organization. It is plain that this bears little relation to the campaign function of canvassing.

Where members *are* used for personal solicitations, it ought to be granted that there is some political benefit. This does not settle the question about the net value of mass-membership organizations. There is still the unresolved question of whether the numbers of votes the workers obtain are sufficient to justify the considerable professional efforts to organize the workers—which might better be spent on reaching voters directly through the mass media. More particularly, there is the question whether it would not be more efficient to recruit voluntary workers for each campaign, without the trouble of maintaining membership organizations between campaigns. And certainly most of a party's membership is not concerned with the function of canvassing. At most, only a few hundred in a British local party of several thousand members are potential canvassers. The others do little more than pay their dues. Most of the members, then, are not functional in an electoral sense. They may even be dysfunctional, since the time spent by local activists in recruiting them might be better used soliciting votes (or preparing to solicit votes by marking

[38] Daniel Katz and Samuel J. Eldersveld, "The Impact of Local Party Activity Upon the Electorate," *Public Opinion Quarterly*, XXV (Spring, 1961), 1–24.

[39] Charles E. Gilbert, "National Political Alignments and the Politics of Large Cities," *Political Science Quarterly*, LXXIX (March, 1964), 25–51.

[40] Phillips Cutright and Peter H. Rossi, "Party Organization in Primary Elections," *American Journal of Sociology*, LXIV (November, 1958), 262–69.

[41] Henry Valen and Daniel Katz, *Political Parties in Norway* (Oslo: Universitetsforlaget, 1964), pp. 116, 126, 145.

electoral registers). The most efficient arrangement for a British constituency, for example, might be to have only fifty or a hundred
activists enrolled as party members[42]—a cadre party, in other words,
not a mass party.

This harsh efficiency-minded analysis neglects the possibility that
a few local activists might want lots of members for their own nonelectoral purposes. Relatively little is known about the motivations of
activists who are not themselves potential candidates for public office.
Why do they volunteer for the drudgery of door-to-door solicitation,
for example, when there is no material benefit? One possible reason
is to be in a position to influence party candidate-selection and party
policy. The chances of doing so might well be increased when the
fifty to a hundred activists claim to represent a few thousand dues-
paying members and not just themselves. Their influence still could
be ineffective, but it would be harder to brush aside claims resting on
an apparently broad popular base. Of course, no problem would exist
for party leaders and candidates if their activists (plus their followers) tended to have the same policy preferences as they, but there
is evidence enough to suspect that there is a difference. In an American and in a British study, activists were found to be more partisan,
even if not more extreme ideologically, than the higher echelon of
politician.[43] Both groups, as might have been expected, are likely to
be less moderate ideologically than ordinary party voters, and the
lower level of activists pronouncedly so. Not only do they have less
incentive to modify their views than do office-seeking politicians, but
they also tend to have rather more rigid personalities and find fixed,
unaccommodating partisanship congenial.[44]

Admittedly the information about the nature of activists is so in-
complete as to support no more than a suspicion of an inherent incompatibility between electoral and membership-recruitment functions of political parties. The suspicion is slightly reinforced by the
indirect evidence of the frequent disparity between successes in

[42] Larger constituencies than those of Britain would obviously require more
member-canvassers. It would not be unusual, however, for candidates themselves to be regarded as the most effective canvassers, as has been noted for an
Irish election. Basil Chubb, "Ireland 1957," in David E. Butler (ed.), *Elections Abroad* (London: Macmillan, 1959), p. 207.
[43] Richard Rose, "The Policy Role of English Party Militants" (UNESCO
Seminar Paper, Bergen, Norway, 1961), and Edmond Costantini, "Intraparty
Attitude Conflict: Democratic Party Leadership in California," *Western Political Quarterly*, XVI (December, 1963), 956–72.
[44] Louise Harned, "Authoritarian Attitudes and Party Activity," *Public
Opinion Quarterly*, XXV (Fall, 1961), 393–99.

obtaining members and in obtaining votes, to which Duverger first called attention.[45] And there is the subsequent case of the Italian Communist party, which continued to gain votes in the 1950's and early 1960's while losing members on a large scale.[46] Altogether, there seems to be less truth to the idea of a positive relation between party membership and voting turnout than one would expect. We once liked to believe that a large mass membership was useful in getting out the vote, and the high percentage of voters in Europe, together with the presence of mass-membership parties, encouraged this view. But recently it has been observed in West Germany that turnout percentages remained high and even increased during a period of party membership decline.[47] (The decline itself is a subject for discussion in Chapter IX.)

Enough has been said to suggest that having a mass membership may complicate the task of seeking votes. This is not to say that leaders are or should be unready to welcome volunteer campaign workers, especially in the absence of a patronage-based organization. But it is to argue that it might be more efficient to recruit them in small cadre organizations or simply ad hoc at campaign time. Arguing against these suggestions is the fact that since mass-membership organizations exist in so many Western nations it is hard to believe that political leaders do not find them useful. Some might be dismissed as residual socialist organizations, begun for nonelectoral or out-of-date electoral reasons. Still others, often existing alongside socialist working-class organizations, also seem less purely electoral than, say, American parties. Indeed, the point is made in a Norwegian-American comparison that Norwegian membership parties reflect a much closer relation between interest groups and parties. Farmers' associations are linked to the Agrarian party and trade unions to the Norwegian Labor party.[48] Similar instances elsewhere can be cited to support the argument that mass membership can be associated with interest-group parties, which would help to account for the existence

[45] Duverger, op. cit., pp. 96, 101.

[46] Norman Kogan, The Government of Italy (New York: Crowell-Collier, 1962), p. 45.

[47] Samuel H. Barnes et al., "The German Party System and the 1961 Federal Election," American Political Science Review, LVI (December, 1962), 905.

[48] Stein Rokkan and Angus Campbell, "Factors in the Recruitment of Active Participants in Politics: A Comparative Analysis of Survey Data for Norway and the United States," International Social Science Bulletin, XII (1960), 69–99. Membership figures for 1957 are given in Valen and Katz, op. cit., p. 70. The Labor party then had 90,000 collectively affiliated members and 64,000 individual members.

of mass memberships despite the possibility that they are not essential for the fulfillment of strictly electoral functions. In other words, parties combining some of the functions of interest groups and of electoral parties would have large organizations capable of supplying campaign workers even though workers could, if the mass organizations did not exist for other reasons, be recruited more efficiently in other ways.

Although the British Conservatives are an exception in this respect, since they maintain a large membership organization without any interest-group base, elsewhere the really large party memberships seem to have other purposes besides electoral ones. Israel is an impressive case in point. Its parties have organized an exceptionally large portion—between one-fourth and one-third—of the electorate.[49] Most of these parties, especially the larger ones, perform many non-electoral functions—conducting businesses, distributing health and welfare benefits, providing housing, and publishing newspapers. Some are linked to trade unions, others to religious groups, and others to particular immigration movements. Most of them antedate the creation of Israel in 1948, having been formed to perform mainly non-electoral functions under the British mandate as social movements, often as colonization or pioneering associations, and so assuming economic functions before electoral ones.[50]

Different but still nonelectoral reasons account for the similarly large membership in Austrian parties. Here too, the percentage of dues-paying members is exceptionally high—one-third of the Socialists' many voters are party members.[51] For this party in particular, membership was originally like that of an order, or of a state within a state, rather than that of an electoral organization simply competing for votes. An economic link to trade unions further reinforced the Socialist strength. And in the case of Austria's other party, the People's party, membership was based on a complex business and agrarian interest-group structure as well as on Catholic affiliations.[52] (It should be added that the postwar coalition provided a consider-

[49] Benjamin Akzin, "The Role of Parties in Israeli Democracy," *Journal of Politics*, XVII (November, 1955), 523.

[50] Marver H. Bernstein, *The Politics of Israel* (Princeton: Princeton University Press, 1957), p. 55.

[51] Kurt L. Shell, *The Transformation of Austrian Socialism* (New York: University Publishers, 1962), p. 4, and Uwe Kitzinger, "The Austrian Electoral System," *Parliamentary Affairs*, XII (May, 1959), 392–404.

[52] Herbert P. Secher, "Coalition Government: The Case of the Second Austrian Republic," *American Political Science Review*, LII (September, 1958), 798.

able amount of patronage for both parties and so may have helped to sustain the membership originally recruited on other bases.)

Israel and Austria offer extreme examples both of membership size and nonelectoral bases of party organizations. But the same coincidence of large membership and nonelectoral bases can be discerned in other nations. It is generally true that a socialist working-class party with trade-union affiliations will have more members than a nonaffiliated socialist party. In fact, it is hard to find a democratic party except the British Conservatives with a large membership and without an interest-group structure.[53] This means that in many nations the only mass-membership party is the one based on trade unions. Norway is a case in point,[54] while West Germany is not, since the Social Democrats are not structurally tied to the unions but derive their large membership from the party's origin as a social movement. And the diminution of the characteristics of a social movement, as the party became more exclusively electoral, accounts for a recent decrease in membership.[55]

Sweden is a clear case of party membership on the Austrian and Israeli scale and on a similar interest-group basis. In 1948, about one-third of the voting population held membership of one kind or another (in women's or youth auxiliaries as well as in the regular organizations) in Sweden's five national parties. Even allowing for some exaggeration by counting one individual with overlapping membership more than once, there can be no doubt about the high degree of organization. At the time these figures were gathered, they were thought to represent the most inclusive party organization in the world. All the parties had local branches throughout the country, but the Social Democrats were by far the largest and most fully organized. The Agrarian party, similarly linked to an interest group, was becoming so. The conservative or business-oriented parties had fewer members, but these too were recruited on the basis of occupational distinctions. Swedish political organization has been rightly said to approximate a corporativist ideal—not just in the membership

---

[53] The New Zealand National Party, despite its large membership, does not seem a genuine exception for reasons explained by Robert N. Kelson, "The New Zealand National Party," *Political Science*, VI (September, 1954), 3–32.

[54] Stein Rokkan and Henry Valen, "The Mobilization of the Periphery," in Stein Rokkan (ed.), *Approaches to the Study of Political Participation* (Bergen, Norway: Chr. Michelsens Institutt, 1962).

[55] Uwe Kitzinger, *German Electoral Politics* (London: Oxford University Press, 1960), p. 204. Recent Social Democratic experience is in sharp contrast to the pre-1914 organization. Guenther Roth, *The Social Democrats in Imperial Germany* (Totawa, N.J.: Bedminster Press, 1963), p. 160.

base but also in the nature of party activity. Swedish political parties operated as civic clubs, pressure groups, publication media, and purveyors of leisure-time pursuits. As elsewhere, the Social Democrats took the lead in these respects, but the other parties, notably the Agrarians, followed with intensive organizations of their own.[56]

Why this should have happened in Sweden more than in most other European nations is not clear. Because Sweden is by European standards so advanced in respect of its economic organization, it is tempting to attribute its highly developed party organization to this general advancement. But the temptation ought to be resisted, and for several reasons. First, this explanation would not hold for Austria, whose party organization is most like Sweden's in scale and intensity. Second, the United States, similarly advanced economically, has parties at the opposite developmental pole. And third, Sweden's democratic political development was late, even by European standards, since the suffrage was not widely extended until 1907–9.[57] Its party organizations cannot be viewed as the culmination of a long process of democratic experience, although they might be understood as a typical twentieth-century organizational response to mass political participation of that time. Even this interpretation leaves unanswered the question whether mass party membership was, in Sweden and elsewhere, a response unique to the early twentieth century or whether it indicated a more universal pattern to which nations whose parties began earlier would eventually conform.

France provides the most useful organizational contrast to Sweden. Except for Communists and Socialists, and perhaps the postwar Movement Républicaine Populaire (MRP), French parties have never been mass-membership organizations. Nor have they been highly developed in other organizational respects. Yet the mass franchise in France is of long standing, and there has been plenty of time to develop membership organizations. Right-wing parties stay close to the cadre model, and this includes even a new party like the UNR that has been successful in polling a very large vote. And they seem never to have used large numbers of volunteer activists in campaigning. As late as 1958, election observers found door-to-door canvassing to be rare. Except in some communist areas, it was said to be regarded as an intrusion.[58] In other ways also, French parties are

---

[56] Dankwart A. Rustow, *The Politics of Compromise* (Princeton: Princeton University Press, 1955), pp. 144–52.

[57] *Ibid.*, p. 72.

[58] Philip Williams and Martin Harrison, "France 1958," in David E. Butler (ed.), *Elections Abroad* (London: Macmillan, 1959), p. 58.

less organized about campaigning, less so than British parties, for example, and organization in terms of members has also sharply declined.[59] Moreover, the French case is not the only exception to the usual frequency of European-style mass-membership organizations. Right-wing, conservative, and moderate liberal parties in several countries occasionally are not membership organizations, even though they are competing against left-wing parties of considerable size. The most notable exception, although not in every respect, is the Italian Christian Democratic party, which has many members.[60]

Australia's party experience, however, is in line with that of most European nations. The party of the right, the business-oriented Liberals, emphasizes membership and membership activity less than the Labor party. At least in one large electoral district, Liberal party branch members have been found to do little more than make an annual contribution even where they are formally organized. Often the branches come into existence only during campaigns.[61] These observations made in the single district are supported by a national report, although the latter also suggests considerable inactivity in Labor party branches.[62]

4. *The Middle-Class American Style*

There are good reasons for considering American nonpatronage membership parties separately from those of Europe. It is uncertain that they are the same phenomenon. Not only are most of them new in the United States, but they are neither widespread nor clearly permanent. Furthermore, their members come mainly from the middle class. (Of course, this is true of some right-wing European parties, but they, as we have seen, are atypical.) What one meets in the United States are efforts, both Republican and Democratic, to organize party members as alternatives to patronage machines or, in a few instances, as their rivals. Sometimes the new membership organizations are built within the legally established party apparatus (as in Michigan), simply converting it from a cadre to a membership party.

[59] Membership figures for French parties are given by François Goguel and Alfred Grosser, *La Politique en France* (Paris: Librairie Armand Colin, 1964), p. 106.

[60] Raphael Zariski, "Intra-Party Conflict in a Dominant Party: The Experience of Italian Christian Democracy," *Journal of Politics*, XXVII (February, 1965), 4–5, 21.

[61] D. W. Rawson and Susan M. Holtzinger, *Politics in Eden-Monaro* (London: William Heinemann, 1958), pp. 48–53, 148–49.

[62] D. W. Rawson, *Australia Votes* (Melbourne: Melbourne University Press, 1961), pp. 13, 23, 34.

Other times (as in Wisconsin and California) the new organizations find the statutory party too constricting and so develop "extra-legally." They then perform most political functions under a new label, but also secure control of the legally established apparatus for certain formal purposes. Either way, the point is to have an organized membership as the "party." And, it may be granted, the membership, as often in Europe, is recruited on a nonpatronage basis and on a large enough scale so as to go well beyond the limited ranks of potential candidates for elective office. Loosely speaking, the basis is ideological or policy-oriented. And, significantly, the members are called "amateurs," distinguishing them from the professional politicians who for so long dominated American party organizations.

The mark of the new amateur parties is their regularized dues-paying membership, which sets them apart from the numerous committees created mainly for particular campaigns or candidates. Dues-paying is still unusual in major American political parties—so much so that a recent text was not far wrong in asserting that "there are no card-carrying Republicans or Democrats."[63] For the national parties, as such, the statement is entirely correct. And in state parties, little is known of regular dues-paying by many members outside of California and Wisconsin. Locally, however, there are dues-paying clubs—like those in New York and Chicago. Knowledge of others is limited, except in Detroit, about whose organization of nonpatronage workers within the regular Democratic apparatus there is a notable study.[64] It is useful, however, to concentrate on the studies of the clearly distinguishable amateur organizations of California, Wisconsin, Chicago, and New York City. In each of these cases, the dues-paying membership is in a club or other agency outside of the legally established party although the agency may use the party name. (The distinction is nevertheless important because within the extra-legal party only the card-carrying dues-payers are members, while within the statutory party the membership includes all those eligible to vote in the party primary.) The dues-paying party is the only real party organization

[63] Greenstein, *The American Party System* . . . , p. 31.
[64] Samuel J. Eldersveld, *Political Parties: A Behavioral Analysis* (Chicago: Rand McNally, 1964). This Detroit area study of both Republican and Democratic organizations found, among other things, that the top party leadership believed that more party workers could be attracted if there were patronage, or some form of payment, instead of the purely altruistic incentives, that few precinct leaders were ideological in their motivation, and that there was great doubt at the top of the hierarchy about the efficacy of the organizations. See also Eldersveld's earlier *Political Affiliation in Metropolitan Detroit* (Ann Arbor: University of Michigan Bureau of Government, 1957).

in the usual sense of the term. It can, however, be built within the statutory party, so that the latter contains a dues-paying organization plus a larger "membership" of primary election voters.[65]

One accepted generalization about the new amateur organizations is that almost all of them are urban or suburban.[66] This is not novel, since all American party organizations tend to be urban. More striking is that both the new Democratic and the new Republican clubs are predominantly middle-class. The Democratic ones have links to the unions, it is true, but the unions are more likely to furnish funds and votes than working-class dues-payers. Union leaders themselves often become party members, but they do not usually bring many union members with them. The urban, middle-class nature of these new clubs is clear in Wisconsin, despite an admittedly larger working-class minority on the Democratic side.[67] Elsewhere, without any exactly comparable study, much the same pattern emerges. Especially is this so for the Democratic clubs studied by James Wilson in New York, Chicago, and Los Angeles. He finds that the "amateur club movement is, with few exceptions, a middle-class phenomenon."[68] As in Wisconsin, Democratic club strength tends to be concentrated in areas that regularly vote Republican. Wilson observed few Negroes or industrial workers in any of the clubs. Even the middle-class members were a rather select, intellectual portion of their class.

For New York City, Wilson's findings are confirmed by other studies—one on Manhattan activists generally[69] and another on one of the largest reform clubs in the Manhattan Democratic party. Here, almost the entire membership was middle class—whether measured by income, education, or occupation—and this was reflected even in the social style of club events. The fact that these events were often coffee or cocktail parties in members' apartments emphasized how alien the club was to working-class recruits, whose apartments simply would not have been large enough for the meetings.[70]

Less is known about the Republican amateurs in California than

[65] Robert Lee Sawyer, Jr., *The Democratic State Central Committee in Michigan, 1949–1959* (Ann Arbor: University of Michigan Institute of Public Administration, 1960).

[66] Frank J. Sorauf, *Party and Representation* (New York: Atherton Press, 1963), pp. 47–49.

[67] Leon D. Epstein, *Politics in Wisconsin* (Madison: University of Wisconsin Press, 1958), chap. 5.

[68] Wilson, *The Amateur Democrat*, p. 258.

[69] R. S. Hirschfield, B. E. Swanson, and B. D. Blank, "A Profile of Political Activists in Manhattan," *Western Political Quarterly*, XV (September, 1962), 489–506.

[70] Kobrak, *op. cit.*, p. 88.

the Democratic ones, but what is known suggests their overwhelmingly urban-suburban character. And the Republican Assembly of California, the extra-legal organization, has been at least as highly organized as its counterpart, the California Democratic Council. Like the Democratic Council, the Republican Assembly adopts policy positions and endorses candidates whom it hopes to nominate in primary elections.[71] The latter purpose ranks high for Californian as it does for Wisconsin Republicans, and for much the same reason: previous difficulties for "regulars" in winning primary nominations over "independents." Indeed, this is a main reason why the membership organizations were formed in the first place. Helping to *elect* candidates naturally followed.

As campaign organizations, in primary and in general elections, the amateur clubs seem clearly more advantageous for Republicans than for Democrats. Middle-class members are going to be effective in bringing out middle-class voters, and these voters are likely to be Republican. Middle-class Democratic members are simply not as well situated to maximize the Democratic vote in their party's strongest voting areas (where, incidentally, more effort may be needed to bring out the vote). This assumes that effective campaigning means door-to-door canvassing. In this respect, middle-class Democrats, like middle-class Republicans, are poor substitutes for the old patronage-fed precinct captains in working-class neighborhoods. On the other hand, these new amateur clubs may well typify the political pattern of an increasingly middle-class nation. If there is going to be party organization of the middle class, it is surely not going to be based on patronage. As has been shrewdly said of the middle class, "People who have, or pretend to have, opinions on political questions, will not give away their votes or exchange them for petty favors."[72] The question remains whether middle-class voters will give their votes to anything offered by an organized membership even of their fellow middle-class citizens. Would canvassing bring out a larger vote for a given party than would occur anyway as a result of campaigning through the mass media and a host of other pressures? If not, there is serious doubt that the amateur clubs have any usefulness in fulfilling strictly electoral aims desired by party leaders and candidates. The clubs might even

---

[71] Hugh Bone, "New Party Associations in the West," *American Political Science Review*, XLV (December, 1951), 1115–25; Currin Shields, "A Note on Party Organization: The Democrats in California," *Western Political Quarterly*, VII (December, 1954), 673–84; Winston Crouch *et al.*, *California Government and Politics* (Englewood Cliffs, N.J.: Prentice-Hall, 1964), 79–82.

[72] Banfield and Wilson, *op. cit.*, p. 122–23.

get in the way, as suggested earlier, by seeking less "marketable" policies and candidates.[73]

A special feature of these clubs is the prominence of women in their activities. Again, the contrast to the patronage machines is sharp —and so is the similarity to the British Conservative organization. Women in the American clubs do much of the canvassing (especially by telephone) and most of the office work of addressing and mailing —not to mention the home-based coffee hours. All this is a long way from the male political world of a party's saloon headquarters. The middle-class club epitomizes the change in the United States, but it has taken place elsewhere. In Britain, while the Conservatives provide the leading example, the Labour party too has many women activists, especially in its local parties in middle-class areas.

If the new American clubs resemble British organizations in this respect (as in a few others), it is still wiser to treat the American phenomenon separately. The resemblances are superficial by comparison with the differences. These American clubs are not typical of American party activity or inactivity. Their continued existence is uncertain. They have no working-class base. Even their appeal to really large numbers of middle-class citizens on a regular basis is decidedly limited compared to the appeal of service clubs and other non-political activities.[74]

5. Contagion from the Left?

This is the place to examine again Duverger's hypothesis that mass-membership political organization originates on the left, notably in socialist working-class parties, and is then imitated by parties of the right out of political necessity. Explaining the development of party organization according to this hypothesis is most successful if attention is focused on France and a few other continental European nations, and if the time period of analysis ends, as did Duverger's, in the late 1940's or early 1950's. For at that time, the working-class parties, certainly the largest and most fully structured political membership organizations in those nations, did seem to be models that were being followed by newer or recently reorganized parties of the moderate or conservative right. The pervasiveness of the mass-membership form could already be noted in Sweden and Austria, for example, and there was some reason to expect the same imitative pattern in France, West Germany, and Italy.

Even at the time, however, this pattern might be observed to have

[73] Wilson, *The Amateur Democrat*, p. 160.
[74] Reichley, *op. cit.*, p. 125.

varied outside of continental Europe. Britain's Conservative party had a mass organization that in many respects antedated any response to the Labour party. Still, the Conservatives had responded to left-wing methods to some extent, and in any event British party organizations were generally supposed to typify those of a modern democracy. The United States and Canada were more clearly exceptions, for which it was possible to account by explaining that neither had a large socialist working-class party and therefore no model to imitate.

Now, fifteen years after Duverger expounded his theory of party development, there is more reason to question the hypothesis, and especially his handling of the exceptions. Mass-membership parties have not appeared in nations where they were previously unestablished. In France, notably, mass membership is less prominent than fifteen years ago; the left-wing parties have declined, and the right-wing parties have not adopted the membership form. Elsewhere, membership has declined even where, as in Britain, the form had long been well established. And the United States and Canada have shown but few signs of developing mass memberships, despite occasional efforts. Where American membership parties have developed, they have by and large been middle-class, and as much of the right as of the left. Even if they should spread, which is doubtful, it would be hard to read into their development any confirmation of the theory of an organizational contagion from the left.

The Canadian picture is similar, except that a new and sizable socialist party provides a model for the major parties to imitate if they want to. The Cooperative Commonwealth Federation (CCF), transformed in the 1960's into the New Democratic Party (NDP), has a substantial dues-paying membership. In Saskatchewan, where the CCF was the majority party from 1944 until 1964, 8 per cent of the electorate were CCF members at the time power was secured.[75] Participation in CCF affairs was also observed to be at a high level, in the best tradition of democratic socialist movements, although this one was largely agrarian rather than industrial. The dues-paying membership formula was used in the CCF's periodic efforts to extend its power into other provinces.[76] Yet there is virtually no evidence that the Liberal and Conservative parties felt compelled to respond with

[75] Seymour Martin Lipset, *Agrarian Socialism* (Berkeley and Los Angeles: University of California Press, 1950), p. 199. See also Dean E. McHenry, *The Third Force in Canada* (Berkeley and Los Angeles: University of California Press, 1950), pp. 46–48.

[76] Leo Zakuta, "The C.C.F.-N.D.P.: Membership in a Becalmed Protest Movement," *Canadian Journal of Economics and Political Science*, XXIV (May, 1958), 190–202.

parallel membership organizations of their own.[77] Perhaps a more successful national effort by the CCF, or later by the NDP, would have forced such consideration. But evidently, in the circumstances, the typical North American cadre organization, bolstered by residues of patronage, was thought to be a sufficient match.[78] The socialist left was not organizationally contagious. Indeed, its own decline is likelier than is its influence on party patterns.

It must be granted that the American and Canadian experiences do not refute the view that large-scale membership organizations follow from successful socialist efforts. Rather, they simply show the absence of the latter. But if a successful socialist party is a prerequisite, not much remains of the view that mass membership is the distinctively modern party form unless socialist success is fairly pervasive. That surely does not presently seem to be the case, although it might have appeared so in the late 1940's. Not only are the United States and Canada still without large socialist movements, but throughout much of Western Europe such movements appear to be declining in size or in their working-class socialist character. If, then, a strong socialist working-class political movement is essential for the development of mass-membership party organization, by contagion or otherwise, the future of the latter is indeed in doubt.

Then there is the fact that, in a broader social perspective, the middle class and the middle-class style appear to be growing at the expense of working-class preponderance. This is important, for it has been argued that mass membership in political groups is more congenial to the working class, with its acceptance of the need for collective action, than to the more individualist middle class.[79] If this is so, the possibilities for highly developed membership organization would recede with the spread of the middle-class way of life. That such American mass-membership parties as exist are predominantly middle class does not refute this likelihood, since they are by no means so well established as to indicate anything like the organizational success achieved earlier by European working-class parties. The

[77] Peter Regenstrief, "Some Aspects of National Party Support in Canada," *Canadian Journal of Economics and Political Science*, XXIX (February, 1963), 59–74; and John Meisel, *The Canadian General Election of 1957* (Toronto: University of Toronto Press, 1962), chap. 4.

[78] John R. Williams, *The Conservative Party of Canada* (Durham, N.C.: Duke University Press, 1956), p. 144; and Robert Macgregor Dawson, *The Government of Canada* (Toronto: University of Toronto Press, 1957), pp. 562–63.

[79] Duverger, *op. cit.*, p. 26.

usual absence of membership organizations is the striking feature of American political life.

What I have meant to suggest is that the socialist working-class party must itself be understood as part of the explanation of political membership organization. A theory that adequately explains the rise of socialist parties is likely to account also for the presence or absence of mass membership parties. By no means is this to follow Duverger's argument. He assumed that having a large socialist party, and so large membership organizations, was the mark of a modern political society and generally the direction of future party development. Instead the view here is that socialist movements, and therefore mass-membership parties, may belong to particular places and periods that are not the most "modern."[80]

[80] Mass-membership parties appear to be significant recent phenomena in developing nations. See the description by Robert E. Scott, *Mexican Government in Transition* (Urbana: University of Illinois Press, 1964), pp. 147, 174. The Japanese experience is less clear. Robert A. Scalapino and Junnosuke Masumi, *Parties and Politics in Contemporary Japan* (Berkeley and Los Angeles: University of California Press, 1962), pp. 83, 85, 149.

VI

The Socialist Working-Class Party

1. *Organizational Necessity*

The socialist working-class party is not the only kind of party to have mass membership, but it has been the most frequent, and all socialist parties that have become major political forces have mass memberships. There is a good and clear reason for this organizational character. How could a movement that challenged the existing economic order seriously compete politically unless it organized many of the class in whose name and interests the challenge was being advanced? Patronage, even if customarily available, would be too inaccessible to provide an organizational basis for a movement originating outside the orthodox political system, and capitalists would be unlikely sources of funds. Of necessity, a working-class party has had to have a collective organization of working-class members to support its leadership, whether that leadership was middle class or working class. The organizational problem is entirely analogous to that of trade unions. Only in large numbers can there be strength. Dues cannot be high and so must come from many rather than few. And numerous members are also necessary to reach the still more numerous workers whose votes are needed.

On the other hand, it is more than just hypothetically possible for middle-class parties to function without mass memberships—both in Europe and in America. (Even though the Democrats have often had a heavy working-class vote, they have been a middle-class party in leadership and organization.) In the absence of patronage, many European middle-class parties have enjoyed long periods of electoral success. Like the American parties, they could raise sufficient funds from relatively few contributors that enabled them to mount campaigns reaching large numbers of voters. Or they have been able to achieve their purposes through individual campaigns, often supported by friendly general-circulation newspapers. This individualist style is simply unsuitable for a working-class party. The proletariat, as Michels observed in his early study of socialist parties, needs to organize in order to exert strength. Individually, workers are weak.[1] Their strength is in numbers. Although Michels was more concerned with his thesis that the workers did not and could not control their parties, he emphasized the very large working-class membership that had been organized, especially by the German Social Democrats.[2] His belief that when workers chose their leaders they were really choosing their new masters did not mean that he regarded working-class membership as an unimportant feature. On the contrary, he assumed that the membership was essential to the political purposes of the party and especially of its leaders.

Duverger's assumption was similar. He regarded the party branch as a socialist invention, along with the very concept of a regularized party membership.[3] This, it seemed to Duverger, was the way to reach a democratic electorate, typified by the industrial working class. And along with it went opportunities for articulation of party policy which looser and smaller organizations of the pre-socialist type often could not or did not have. Besides, there was something more democratic about an organization that made possible an articulation of policy through branches. Intra-party discussion has remained a value in socialist parties.[4] But no one denies that membership would be an organizational necessity for a successful working-class party even if there were little or no articulation of policy by membership branches. So the question whether there is more democratic policy-making in a mass party than in a smaller one can be left to one side. Many members systematically organized in branches were, in any event, essential for a socialist working-class party seeking power. No other way existed to accumulate the resources for the struggle.

A more complicated problem is presented by the apparent improvements introduced through Communist party organization of the working class—using the cell instead of the branch as the basic unit, often orienting membership around the work-place rather than a geographically defined electoral district, and also involving a tighter and more disciplined organization, though not always a larger one. The admirer of socialist organization, on grounds of its efficiency, almost has to admire the Communist even more. As Duverger writes of the machinery of the Communist party: "One may deplore the use made of

[1] Robert Michels, *Political Parties,* trans. Eden and Cedar Paul (Glencoe, Ill.: Free Press, 1949), p. 22.

[2] *Ibid.,* p. 270.

[3] Maurice Duverger, *Political Parties,* trans. Barbara and Robert North (New York: John Wiley & Sons, 1954).

[4] Mark Benney, A. P. Gray, and R. H. Pear, *How People Vote* (London: Routledge & Kegan Paul, 1956), p. 42.

the instrument; one cannot refuse admiration for its technical perfection."[5] Although the cellular structure and the close discipline of the Communist party were inspired by clandestinely subversive purposes, it remains true that they are also efficacious for electoral purposes in a democratic society. Communists have often been notoriously successful in competing with socialists for working-class members and votes. This cannot be attributed to organizational superiority alone, but no one would suggest that Communists have been handicapped by their structure. It is at least as effective as that of the socialists in organizing the working class on a large scale. And, if anything, there is a case to be made for its greater effectiveness. Therefore, if we consider this kind of organizational effectiveness "modern," we must surely include the Communist form as a leading illustration. And if we see a trend toward more thorough-going party organization, we may have to view the Communist party as the latest developmental stage.

Assuredly this is a real problem if one retains Duverger's argument that a large and highly organized working-class party is *the* modern political form and yet prefers, as Duverger does, a democratic society with which Communist organization is in many respects incompatible. But one does not have to accept that there is any such organizational trend if, to start with, one believes that large-membership working-class parties are a product of circumstances occurring only at certain stages of social development in certain nations, that these circumstances may be receding, and that therefore a socialist (or Communist) working-class party is not the inevitable wave of the future in every advanced nation. Where such a party has successfully developed, it is true, it has had a mass membership, because of a demonstrated organizational necessity. But it has developed only in circumstances (numerous to be sure) that prevailed in some Western nations and that may have become less prevalent even where originally they were crucial.

2. Origins

Two obvious prerequisites for a socialist working-class party are a sizable industrial working class and the felt need of that class to organize politically, as well as industrially, in its own interests. The first has sometimes existed without the second; the United States is the leading case in point. This does not mean that industrial workers are left outside the political process. Their votes, even some of their activity, may be attracted by various parties and candidates. As has been

[5] Duverger, *op. cit.*, p. 58.

stressed in Chapter IV, class is an important basis for voting in the United States as elsewhere. A party may appeal to industrial workers without its being their own class or socialist party. The difference is significant, certainly in organizational terms, but why does it exist? It is really more of a description than an explanation to say that the difference is in degree of class consciousness. Why this difference?

The formerly popular Marxist view was that the requisite class consciousness would come with time. Nations late to industrialize would be late to develop class-conscious workers' parties. It was also granted that special conditions even in some highly industrialized nations could delay the process, but only delay it. Now, however, after over a century of industrial development in the Western world, the Marxist view is untenable since it fails to account for the absence of a socialist party in the largest industrial nation, the United States, and for the apparently arrested growth of socialist parties in the most fully industrialized European nations. It is now possible to argue that the socialist working-class party is a product of a fairly early stage of industrialization, and of industrialization in specifically European socio-historical circumstances.

It was easy at the time of World War I, when European socialist parties were already highly organized and still growing, to think of these parties as the products of an advanced industrial order. They seemed a political response to already mature capitalist societies. But with continued economic change, accelerated especially after World War II, the industrial order of 1914 seems old-fashioned. And so do the political responses to that order even though they still persist. The fifty years or so from 1860–70 to 1910–20 must now be regarded as nearer the beginning than the maturity of industrialization. For almost all of Europe (except Britain), those years constituted the first half-century of wide-spread industrialization.

Certain general characteristics of early industrialization, given otherwise favorable national circumstances, help to explain the earlier rather than later rise of working-class parties. The first industrial growth has often been especially rapid and bewildering in its dislocations.[6] The sudden creation of a new urban proletariat, even when still decidedly in the minority, tended to produce at least incipient revolt.[7] Class-conscious radicalism was associated with "explosive in-

[6] Val R. Lorwin, "Working-Class Politics and Economic Development in Western Europe," *American Historical Review*, LXIII (January, 1958), 350.

[7] This is an important part of the well-known interpretation of the basis for the Russian Revolution by Leon Trotsky, *The History of the Russian Revolution*, trans. Max Eastman (New York: Simon and Schuster, 1932), I, 33, 38.

dustrialization."[8] In its early stages, the new economic order meant hardships rather than the higher standards of living that later came to be associated with it. It is understandable not only that working-class parties arose at an early stage of industrialization, but that they were more radical in their demands and methods during their first years.

Yet early industrialization alone is not sufficient explanation for the rise of socialist working-class parties.[9] Again, it must be stressed that industrialization did not everywhere lead to the rise of these parties. In the United States, even the early stages of industrialization were insufficient stimuli for a class-conscious movement of any large size. What circumstances in Western Europe provoked the rise of large socialist parties during early industrialization? Here it is worth while also to try to account for certain intra-European differences. In particular, why did Great Britain have a less radical working-class party than had most of the continental nations in the first half of the twentieth century? The British Labour party was not Marxist-revolutionary before 1914 or Leninist-revolutionary (Communist) in subsequent decades.

Generally, what can be said of Europe is that its pre-modern, feudal past made for a pervasive consciousness of class before the development of industrial society. While this was almost equally true for Britain as for the rest of Europe, it is possible to believe that its effects were softened by other aspects of British life.[10] At any rate, Europe's industrial working class was created in a political culture long based on class distinctions. Industrial workers were a new class in an old class society. They were socially and politically unequal to begin with. In fact, most of them had first been unequal as peasants. Being underprivileged economically had always meant being underprivileged socially and politically, and it still did. Only now, because of the nature of the new employment and the new urban life, organization became a real possibility, and it was fostered by the alienated

[8] Walter Galenson, "Scandinavia," in Walter Galenson (ed.), *Comparative Labor Movements* (New York: Prentice-Hall, 1952), pp. 149–50.

[9] This judgment is partly in accord with the view of Herbert Blumer that social discontent cannot be attributed to early industrialization although they sometimes coincide. He believes that the industrialization often begins to take place in situations of intense social change when strong disruptive forces are thrown into play. "Early Industrialization and the Laboring Class," *Sociological Quarterly*, I (January, 1960), 5–14.

[10] Reinhard Bendix has distinguished continental European from British experience by suggesting that the continental working class had no sense of "recognized position in the civic community in which to participate." "The Lower Classes and the Democratic Revolution," *Industrial Relations*, I (October, 1961), 115.

subculture of the urban proletariat. It was natural for workers to think of themselves as a class, virtually a nation, apart from the rest of the nation. They were outside. It was no wonder that their organization aimed, as has been aptly said of Austrian socialists, to build "a proletarian state within a state."[11] Middle-class leaders there might be, alongside those recruited from the working class itself, but the movement was always of the working class. Middle-class leaders joined it and helped to form it, but to do so they abandoned their own class and its parties. This is what having a working-class party meant.

A particular residue of pre-modern Europe was the persistence of political inequality in the restricted franchise. Almost everywhere in Europe, considerable industrialization came before the franchise was extended to the mass of the population. The working classes existed before they had the right to vote. Sweden provides a striking example. Its Social Democrats were active for twenty years before the suffrage was won just after the turn of the century. Indeed, universal suffrage had been one of their principal demands from the time of their official organization in 1889, and their mass membership was partly recruited in order to win it.[12] Finland's experience is similar. There too the Social Democratic organization antedated the constitutional right of workers to vote. By the time this right was won, in 1906, the Social Democrats were strong enough to win 40 per cent of the seats in the country's first democratically elected parliament.[13]

None of the other large socialist parties with substantial beginnings before universal suffrage seems to have been so successful as the Scandinavian, but the German Social Democrats had in other respects a more notable history. They began in the Bismarckian era as a movement recruiting supporters among the still largely unfranchised workers, and for a few decades after the franchise they were cut off from gaining power despite the workers' votes. Lassalle's original socialist party, founded in 1863, had as its only stated purpose "the peaceful and legal struggle for equal, universal and direct suffrage."[14] The programs of the unified party founded at Gotha in 1875 were in its early years also dominated by demands for extension

[11] Kurt L. Shell, *The Transformation of Austrian Socialism* (New York: University Publishers, 1962), p. 10.

[12] Dankwart A. Rustow, *The Politics of Compromise* (Princeton: Princeton University Press, 1955), pp. 43, 76.

[13] Carl Erik Knoellinger, *Labor in Finland* (Cambridge: Harvard University Press, 1960), pp. 48–49.

[14] A. Joseph Berlau, *The German Social Democratic Party 1914–1921* (New York: Columbia University Press, 1949), p. 22.

of the suffrage.[15] In other words, the party of the workers had to fight for the political freedom of the workers it was seeking to represent. The fight is significant in itself, but for the present thesis it is even more significant to note the condition that made it necessary— the political alienation of the working class, as a lower order, in imperial Germany. This alienation had pre-industrial roots, as is often pointed out,[16] and yet it persisted to give a distinctive character to German Social Democracy. It was reinforced by Bismarck's efforts to destroy and then to isolate the party. The Social Democratic organization of the working class came to be a subculture within the German community. This did not have to mean a revolutionary attitude, and for most German Social Democrats it did not. But party membership was a way of life. Or, to quote a recent authoritative work, "The fact that the labor movement became 'home, fatherland and religion' to hundreds of thousands points up their great alienation from the dominant system."[17]

Any party formed and developed before it could have an electoral impact would have special characteristics, even if not all of those associated with the broadly alienated German movement.[18] But even when socialist political organization began among an already enfranchised working class, as in France after 1870, it was still a beginning different from other parties'. A socialist working-class party was everywhere a movement outside of parliament before it was a party competing for power. Its leaders were themselves outsiders (even if of middle-class origin), and they did not hold public office first and organize their followers afterward. Organization was intended to be achieved before major electoral competition, given the assumed need to mobilize a class previously without a role in the political system. That such a class did in fact exist in Europe seems to have been established by socialist success in the late nineteenth and early twentieth centuries.

[15] Douglas A. Chalmers, *The Social Democratic Party of Germany* (New Haven and London: Yale University Press, 1964), pp. 5–6.

[16] Guenther Roth, *The Social Democrats in Imperial Germany* (Totowa, N.J.: Bedminster Press, 1963), p. 11.

[17] *Ibid.*, p. 211.

[18] Socialist parties in Belgium and the Netherlands are illustrative. The Belgian party committed itself to the struggle for the suffrage at an early mass meeting in 1890, but the goal was not achieved until the World War I period. Val R. Lorwin, "Belgium: Religion, Class, and Language in National Politics," in Robert A. Dahl (ed.), *Political Oppositions in Western Democracies* (New Haven and London: Yale University Press, 1966), p. 157. See also Hans Daalder, "The Netherlands: Opposition in a Segmented Society," in *ibid.*, pp. 205, 207.

It is too much to expect a perfectly positive relation between socialist success and the degree of alienation of each nation's working class. For one thing, the alienation can hardly be measured with any exactness, and there are always the other factors—rapidity of industrialization, general level of prosperity, or disastrous wars—which affected socialist success. But in Europe the working-class parties grew in what was already a class-conscious environment, and this was underlined when the parties began before their members were voters. Not only was this a symptom of the alienation with which socialism began, but it also left important marks on the party.

It is difficult to use the same approach to understand the development of a working-class party in Australia and New Zealand. Here are two instances of flourishing labor political movements in non-European circumstances. No local pre-modern class consciousness can account for the successful creation of workers' parties in these two new countries. In both Australia and New Zealand, they were well started early in the twentieth century and strong enough by the 1930's to dominate national politics for long periods.[19] Their growth was roughly parallel, in time and size, to that of the British Labour party, except that they secured effective governmental power earlier (if British Labour's success is put at 1945). It is true that they were moderate in their aims, certainly more so than most early European socialist parties and probably more so even than British Labour, and they tended to be more purely worker-oriented than socialist. Often they represented little more than the aims of the trade unions with whom they had close connections. Nevertheless the Australian and New Zealand parties were, in their way, class-oriented. Especially in the Australian case, the contrast to the American experience is sharp and must be explained before we can fully accept the view that working-class parties reflect only class-conscious European conditions.

Can one fall back on the idea that Australia and New Zealand, unlike the United States or Canada, were transplanted European societies in which the old class consciousness remained in the new physical environment? There is something to this, especially in Australia, and perhaps enough to account for what happened.[20]

[19] L. C. Webb, "The Australian Party System," *The Australian Political Party System* (Sydney: Angus and Robertson for the Australian Institute of Political Science, 1954), p. 91.

[20] Australia is special in that the working class, of European origin, predominated when the nation began. In this light, Richard Rosecrance has said: "In political terms Australia was the 'radical' fragment of British society." "The Radical Culture of Australia," in Louis M. Hartz (ed.), *The Founding of New Societies* (New York: Harcourt, Brace & World, 1964), p. 284. In still

There was direct British influence, more than in Canada and certainly more than in the United States, but no simple imitation, since the Australasian labor parties grew not later but in some respects earlier than the British Labour party. This was less true in New Zealand[21] than in Australia whose working-class party emerged before New Zealand's and was more largely an urban phenomenon. In fact, the Australian party presents the important special case. Unless it is to stand as a plain exception, challenging the major thesis of this chapter, it must be explained in large part as the exported product of European class consciousness.

3. *The American Contrast*

Why the United States has not had a large socialist working-class party is an important question that has long been put by European socialists. How, it has been asked, did the United States become the apparent developmental exception? When Australia and New Zealand are regarded as having working-class parties resembling those of Europe, the United States does indeed appear to be a striking exception among Western nations. Only Canada, whose socialist party, despite its persistence, does not have a large national industrial working-class base, can be added to the United States. Thus there is at most the North American exceptions, plus Ireland, to the prevalence of major socialist parties in Western nations. And an explanation of how the United States was different would likely explain the Canadian situation as well. Ireland can be disregarded because of its size and small industrial base or treated as a special case for historical reasons. It is primarily the United States that a socialist has to account for if he believes that his kind of class party comes with the development of industrial society. In this perspective, the tendency has been to believe that American circumstances were such as only to delay class consciousness and socialist party growth.[22] Many kinds of delaying factors are named: ethnic differentiation within the working class, the influence of the frontier, the country's

---

more particular terms, Israel's leftist parties could be viewed as transplanted European movements. Lester G. Seligman, *Leadership in a New Nation* (New York: Atherton Press, 1964), pp. 29–32.

[21] Leslie Lipson, *The Politics of Equality* (Chicago: The University of Chicago Press, 1948), pp. 213–28.

[22] As G. D. H. Cole wrote, ". . . when one looks beneath the surface it seems not unreasonable to conjecture that Labour in America is, on the whole, moving on a road which Labour in Western Europe has trodden already." *A Short History of the British Working-Class Movement 1789–1947* (London: Allen & Unwin, 1948), p. 8.

unusual wealth, and a large rural population even after considerable early industrialization. All of these factors except the unusual wealth were viewed as likely to diminish with continued industrial development, so that the United States would come to resemble Western Europe in providing a hospitable environment for a working-class movement. American wealth alone, in the socialist view, was not sufficient to prevent workers from eventually appreciating their unequal class status in a capitalist society.

The trouble with this explanation is not only that American socialism appears to have weakened to the point of its virtual extinction instead of merely suffering from a late start. Also, the explanation follows from the way the question is put: it was presumed that a socialist working-class party is a normal political response to Western industrialization and that, therefore, there is something abnormal or at least unusual about a nation with no such response. A major intellectual wrench is required not to look at the United States in that perspective and yet not from the narrow parochial viewpoint in which the United States itself provides the norm. The starting point has to be that neither the presence nor the absence of a large socialist party should be regarded as normal—and, concomitantly, neither the presence nor the absence of the requisite class consciousness. The United States and Western Europe then are simply different. Or, more exactly, they have differed during the decades of socialist development.

They were not so different, however, that socialist working-class movements did not spring up in the United States at almost the same time as they did in Europe. If one counts the Working Men's party of the Jacksonian era, the American movement may even be said to have antedated many European counterparts.[23] But it is not necessary to resurrect this early and largely forgotten group in order to make the point that class-conscious political organization was attempted fairly early in the United States. During the last quarter of the nineteenth century, the efforts of American socialist leaders, many of them intellectuals, were of roughly the same scale as those in many European nations, including Britain. (Germany's Social Democratic party was a rather special case whose size was envied by

[23] Edward Pessen, "The Working Men's Party Revisited," *Labor History,* IV (Fall, 1963), 203–26. This early effort to mobilize the working class was not directly frustrated by a Jacksonian Democratic party mobilization. The class character of that party's appeal has been exaggerated. Lee Benson, *The Concept of Jacksonian Democracy* (Princeton: Princeton University Press, 1961), pp. 331–32.

other socialists besides those in the United States.) Soon, in the first decade or so of the twentieth century, American socialists built a party that was not far behind the growing strength of the new British Labour party. Moreover, the Socialist Party of America was avowedly socialist in a way that British Labour was not until 1918. What the American socialists did not have, however, was the trade-union base the new British party secured in 1900. This made the American movement more purely socialist but also, in the long run, much smaller.

Significantly, the American Socialist party recruited a dues-paying membership designed to be enormous. By 1912, there were 117,984 members, and the Socialist candidate for president received 897,000 votes (6 per cent of the total popular vote).[24] Both in members and votes, the party had more than doubled its numbers since 1908, and it seemed on its way as a growing American political force. Yet by 1916, even before American entry in World War I, decline had set in; its membership was down by about one-third and its presidential vote by even more. Membership decline continued, with a temporary increase during the depression. The presidential vote rose, notably in 1920 and 1932; still, in neither year was the socialist percentage of the total popular vote as high as it had been in 1912. In other respects as well, 1912 was a socialist high point in the United States. There were then fifty-six socialist mayors of American cities, more than 300 aldermen, and one member of the House of Representatives.[25]

Special features of this socialist strength are worth noting. It was not limited to any one region. Instead, as a careful historian of the party has said, American socialists in 1912 were a coalition of regional groups and so, in this respect, resembled the major American parties. New York City was an important center, with heavy support from recent immigrants in the needle trades, but the Milwaukee party, owing much to German immigrants, was more dominant in its community. Then there was socialist strength in a new agrarian settlement like Oklahoma, in three of whose poor sharecropping counties Socialist candidates polled over one-third of the congressional vote in 1914.[26] While these examples of socialist support are representative of the strongest showing the party made at the peak of its growth,

[24] David A. Shannon, *The Socialist Party of America* (New York: Macmillan, 1955), p. 5.

[25] D. D. Egbert and Stow Persons (eds.), *Socialism and American Life* (Princeton: Princeton University Press, 1952), II, 146.

[26] Shannon, *op. cit.*, p. 106.

each, it should be stressed, represented a phenomenon that, while not untypical in America, was destined to be temporary. Both the East European Jews of New York and the Germans of Milwaukee were bound to become less heavily influenced politically by their backgrounds. And the poor sharecroppers of newly settled Oklahoma were either to become more prosperous farmers, in a few instances, or to cease being farmers altogether. Much the same can be said of the revolutionary socialists in western mining and lumber camps. The desperation of their situation was transient.

Some native American industrial workers were attracted by the socialism of 1912. The party was not a wholly foreign importation either in its program or in its following. Many of its intellectual leaders, not to mention its working-class leader, Eugene Debs, were native Americans. But most of the American working class, immigrant and native-born, remained outside the socialist fold. It was exceptional for the socialists to establish ties with what trade unions there were. The still struggling American Federation of Labor, after an initial flirtation with socialist leaders, became hostile to them, not just indifferent. This relationship, or lack of it, is usually thought to have been crucial to the socialist failure, since socialists were ordinarily as unable to establish their own rival unions as they were to secure A.F. of L. support. But the absence of a widespread socialist-unionist nexus is more a symptom of failure than its cause. In those few localities where the nexus was established, as in Milwaukee and in Reading, Pennsylvania, the socialists enjoyed political success, especially at the municipal level.[27]

Why this symptom of socialist failure almost everywhere in the United States? Part of the answer is that the already organized American Federation of Labor was itself small and heavily concentrated among craft rather than industrial workers. Craft workers, given the nature of their employment and their relatively high pay and status, were unlikely to become class-conscious socialists in a rich country. The industrial workers were not to be fully organized until the middle and late 1930's. But why weren't they? Or, more particularly, why didn't the American socialists organize industrial workers when European socialists did so, with some success, at about the same time? No doubt they wanted and even tried to, and it cannot be argued that American industrial workers were so well off that they did not want to be organized. They were willing enough to be

[27] *Ibid.*, pp. 21 and 188; and Henry Pelling, "The Rise and Decline of Socialism in Milwaukee," *Bulletin of the International Institute of Social History of Amsterdam*, No. 2 (1955), 91–103.

organized in the 1930's, when they were often better off than they had been in 1912. But their organization was not, ultimately, a socialist class-conscious movement. It was an American-style job-conscious unionism whose politics was New Deal reformist. There was enough "class consciousness," although it was seldom called that, for trade unionism and support for Roosevelt, but not for a European-style movement.

Perhaps it was only a crucial difference in timing. Restrained for several decades by special American circumstances, American industrial workers, when they were numerous enough and otherwise ready for collective organization, found that socialism had spent its force in the United States and perhaps elsewhere in the Western world. What might, then, have been socialist-oriented trade unions became instead a less distinctive political force. So largely fortuitous an explanation, however, is unconvincing. There seems to be something more basic. It is hard to disagree with Shannon in his summary estimate: "The primary reason that American Socialists never developed the strength of their comrades in other countries was that in America there is considerably less class consciousness than there is in other Western nations."[28]

There is still the question why, in the 1930's as in 1912, there was less class consciousness in the United States than in Europe. (There was more in 1912 than in the 1930's, it seems, judging by the substantial though not overwhelming socialist success in the earlier year.) Perhaps the factors formerly employed to explain the "delay" in the development of American class consciousness could explain its continued absence. But one of those factors—that the United States remained heavily rural even while building a large industrial establishment—does not seem relevant, since even a rural majority, while capable of limiting the popular impact of an urban socialist party, could not have kept it or affiliated unions from organizing. The more rural European nations, like Norway, did not lack strong socialist movements. Certain kinds of rural communities even proved good recruiting ground. Or, to seize another kind of example, the pre-1917 industrial working class in Russia was a most decided minority in a largely peasant nation but it was nevertheless organized in definitely class-conscious unions and parties. And, more directly to the point, the diminution of rural influence in the United States has not been accompanied by an increase in class consciousness among industrial workers. The same can be said for that hardy perennial, the influence

[28] Shannon, *op. cit.*, p. 263.

of the frontier: surely it declined some time ago without any marked change in worker outlooks. But exactly this cannot be said for ethnic differentiation since, despite the decline occurring after immigration was checked following World War I, important residues from the old immigration patterns remain, along with racial differentiations. Yet it is hard to believe that ethnic differentiations ever impeded the organization of American workers—some of the most class-conscious organization, as of American socialists, could be found among immigrant groups. And, as their ethnic differentiation diminished, union organization, while becoming more widespread, tended to be less and not more clearly tied to a class-conscious political movement.

This leaves America's unusual wealth as the most probable factor accounting for the continued absence of class consciousness. It will be recalled that socialists could not easily use this factor to explain what they regarded as a "delay" in American development. And the trouble is that if American wealth precluded the emergence of class consciousness it presumably would continue so to preclude. After all, the wealth itself has not diminished. If the United States was so rich that its workers had been "bribed" with large material rewards, why shouldn't they continue to be bribed? Of course, rigid Marxists among the socialists had their doctrinal economic reasons for believing that capitalists could not manage this over the long run, but these reasons were unconvincing to almost everyone else, except perhaps in depressions. Now they appear more unconvincing than ever. In short, American industrial workers, as an entire class, have not been so poor or so depressed as to believe that an improved future required a drastic change in the economic system. Instead, wealth, especially as expressed in houses and later in cars, was sufficient to be widespread.[29] American capitalists too may have been richer than capitalists elsewhere and even many times better off than their workers, but still what counted in this respect was the workers' absolute condition and, particularly, their rate of improvement within the existing system.

Here American workers had good reason to think themselves better off than workers in European nations. The American standard of living was almost continuously higher. This does not mean that the American standard in 1900 was higher than the West European standard in 1960. But 1960, by which time the European standard had risen appreciably, was not when European class-conscious poli-

---

[29] Charles A. Gulick and Melvin K. Bers, "Insight and Illusion in Perlman's Theory of the Labor Movement," *Industrial and Labor Relations Review*, VI (July, 1953), 510–31.

tics developed. Politics of this type became habitual years earlier, when the economic status of European workers was much lower than in 1960—and much lower than the status of most American workers had ever been under large-scale industrialization. The latter is the significant point in using relative wealth to explain the different American experience. Being substantially above the poverty line, even during early stages of industrial development, distinguished most American workers from the Europeans.

It is unnecessary and unreasonable, however, to attribute the different American history in regard to working-class parties exclusively to the unusual wealth of the United States. After all, it is simply not known whether the higher standard of working-class living alone can account for the differences. And the truth is that other differences also existed. One is that the right to vote was available to most American industrial workers before there were even very many of them. Just as one can argue that the rise of European class-conscious socialism was due partly to the long delay in universal suffrage, so one can try to explain that American workers were less class-conscious because they did not find themselves outside the circle of political participation. The point has never been made more clearly than by Selig Perlman:

> Another cause of the lack of "class-consciousness" in American labor was the free gift of the ballot which came to labor at an early date as a by-product of the Jeffersonian democratic movement. In other countries, where the labor movement started while the workingmen were still denied the franchise, there was in the last analysis no need of a theory of "surplus value" to convince them that they were a class apart and should therefore be "class conscious." There ran a line like a red thread between the laboring class and the other classes. Not so, where that line is only an economic one.[30]

The "free gift of the ballot" was also important as a symptom of the kind of social environment enjoyed by the working class in the United States. In order for there to be manhood suffrage awaiting the new industrial class, there had to be a more egalitarian society to begin with. The American value system was decidedly different from Europe's, even from Britain's. No socialist movement was needed, during the late nineteenth and early twentieth centuries, in order to establish the political equality of American workers. They *were* born equal.

This theme is basic to Louis Hartz's broad interpretation of Ameri-

[30] Selig Perlman, *A Theory of the Labor Movement* (New York: Augustus M. Kelley, 1949), pp. 167–68.

can political experience in comparison with Europe's. He uses the phrase "born equal" to describe not just American industrial workers but Americans generally. And he notes the absence of a feudal past to account for the pervasiveness of American liberalism, which, unlike European liberalism, was able to assimilate workers and other sectors of the populace in its scheme of values. Its success is related to the same cause as the failure of socialism. "It is not accidental," Hartz argues, "that America which has uniquely lacked a feudal tradition has uniquely lacked also a socialist tradition."[31]

Insofar as this explanation is accepted, there can be no more hope for an American socialist party in the future than in the past. There is no way to secure a feudal background if it was missing in the first place. In this respect, the explanation is as discouraging to socialists as the one which rested on America's unusual wealth. The United States is not moving nearer to feudalism any more than it is becoming poorer. Of course, the United States Government may well adopt, as it has in the past, many programs and policies that can fairly be *called* socialist not only because socialist parties have favored them but also because they involve collective and public action for the benefit of the mass of the population, particularly industrial workers. Probably the United States has been later than certain European nations to adopt some of these programs (apart from public education), but this is a far different thing from being later in having socialist parties. More if not different class consciousness is required for workers to support their own socialist party, dedicated originally at least to basic change in the economic system, than for them simply to support social legislation proposed by a liberal or reform party. American workers are now, as they have been in the recent past, class conscious enough for the latter, but not enough for the former.

From one viewpoint, this matters little if the socialist-type governmental programs are adopted anyway, with or without a socialist party. But from the viewpoint of party organization, where this analysis started, there is a considerable difference as long as mass membership seems basically a socialist form. It means not only that the United States has not had this kind of party organization because of the absence of a large socialist party, but that it *will* not have one because it is not going to have a large socialist party. In this perspective, existing American party organization cannot be regarded as archaic, as Duverger regarded it,[32] unless one believes that it will remain archaic—that is, non-socialist—forever.

---

[31] Louis M. Hartz, *The Liberal Tradition in America* (New York: Harcourt, Brace, 1955), p. 6.
[32] Duverger, *op. cit.*, p. 23.

4. The Trade Unions

American socialists failed because they were unable to recruit large-scale support in the working class. This was not because of the absence of trade unions, but because of the absence of enough socialist-organized or socialist-oriented ones. The significance of this point may be understood by observing the union connections established by the successful socialist parties in other nations. Sometimes there was formal affiliation of unions to the socialist party. Sometimes the unions were mainly organized by socialists in the first place. Whether either or both of these conditions are met, the connections are in any event substantial. The typical European "labor movement" has had two expressions, one industrial and the other political, but both based on the assumption that the working class had interests that only its own organizations could really serve. The difference from American labor was especially apparent at a time when American unions had no regular political commitment, but it is just as real now that the latter regularly support the Democratic party. This is not the workers' own party and assuredly it is not a socialist party. Rather it is a basically middle-class liberal party to which unions lend their considerable strength.[33] No European socialist party resembles the American Democratic party in being first a large middle-class party subsequently attracting organized labor.

There is no reason why a European labor movement has to be different from the American in pursuit of industrial objectives just because political objectives are pursued by its party organization. Examples exist of European unions, like those in Britain, being at least as concerned as American ones to secure non-socialist, job-conscious goals in respect of wages, hours, and working conditions. Where European unions have been less effective in these respects, like those in France, it is not clear that this is a consequence of class identification with a political party. It seems more likely to be caused by particulars of the French situation, including how the unions are politicized. The fact that British unions (and Swedish ones, for that matter) are successful makes it impossible to argue that socialist political connections are related to minimal industrial accomplishments.

[33] The prevalence of this American characteristic is convincingly illustrated by continued Democratic party discouragement of working-class participation in organizational activity even in metropolitan Detroit, where trade unions are more closely related to the party than is usual in the United States. Samuel J. Eldersveld, *Political Parties: A Behavioral Analysis* (Chicago: Rand McNally, 1964), pp. 446–47.

What marks off the labor movement's experience in Great Britain from that of many continental nations (most clearly of France and Italy) is that British unions were not organized as socialist political agencies. British unions existed prior to the formation of the Labour party, which they helped to bring into being almost twenty years before it became officially socialist in 1918. French and Italian workers, on the other hand, were often organized in unions by socialists and then by Communists and by Catholic agencies. Although individual British socialists provided leadership for unions in both their formation and their later development, the unions themselves always had a status of their own. And in this British unions significantly differ from the American even though their original industrial organization no more depended on socialists than did the American unions. The British unions turned out to be willing to join with socialists in establishing a political wing of the labor movement. Both before and after the Labour party officially adopted a socialist program in 1918, the unions provided the bulk of the support.

It is hard to see how there could have been an important British Labour party without massive trade-union support. There could perhaps have been a middle-class party, like the Liberals (or the American Democrats) receiving union money and votes. And this may still occur in the future. But if there was to be a sizable socialist working-class party, as has in fact been the British case, then the unions were clearly necessary. No socialist party anywhere else has ever been as successful as the British without union support.

On the other hand, it does not seem necessary for unions to lend support by the British method in order for a socialist party to be successful. With neither the German Social Democrats nor the Scandinavian socialist parties are unions related in the same ways. The British method is for national trade-union federations (but not the Trades Union Congress as such) to affiliate their memberships, or substantial portions of them, directly to the national Labour party. A really large union might pay party dues for a million of its own members and so have a commensurately large share of power in the party. Under twentieth-century British law, except between 1927 and 1945, unions could affiliate any desired number of their members (provided that union members did not "contract out" by specifying that their union dues not include a portion for the Labour party). But even when the unions functioned under the more restrictive legislation that permitted affiliation only of members who "contracted in" (specifying that they wanted a portion of their union dues paid to the Labour party), the unions were in a position to supply handsome, if reduced, support for the party and to dominate its counsels if union leaders collectively wanted to do so.[34] It has been usual, as in the early 1960's, for the unions, through their "indirect" members, to provide five-sixths of the total party membership. Their financial importance is especially great—not only in the matter of dues to support party headquarters, but also because they contribute additional sums for particular campaigns. Since World War II, it has been estimated, 70 per cent of Labour's central organization receipts came from unions; taking local organization receipts into account as well, the unions contributed 50–55 per cent of the party's total income. Unions do contribute to local parties, but the percentage here is not so high, despite very large contributions in some constituencies. The 50–55 per-cent figure does not include money that unions spent directly on their own political activities in behalf of the Labour party. That too is a large amount—union officials are often switched from their industrial duties to party political work during campaigns—and if counted in, the estimated total union contribution to Labour's political expenses would rise to 70 per cent.[35] There can be no doubt that the most notable feature of the dependence of the Labour party on trade unions is that it is not just for election campaigns, but also for regular operations of the national headquarters and organization. This is facilitated by the formal affiliation of trade unions to the party, so that it is literally their own party. But it is not inconceivable that similar regular support might be forthcoming without it.

The British affiliation method is unusual. The closest parallel to it is found in the Australian and particularly New Zealand labor parties. An earlier and similar Belgian arrangement of collective union membership in the socialist party was changed in 1945 to a straight individual direct membership.[36] Much the same shift occurred, also in 1945, in the Netherlands.[37] In both instances, the old affiliated union federations had been socialist in contrast to rival unions organized by other ideological movements, notably Catholic ones. It is striking that these socialist-labelled unions broke their formal affiliation with socialist parties while the British unions, never bearing a socialist tag, not only maintained their institutional links after World

[34] Martin Harrison, *Trade Unions and the Labour Party* (London: Allen & Unwin, 1960), p. 36.

[35] *Ibid.*, pp. 99–100.

[36] Val R. Lorwin, "Labor Organizations and Politics in Belgium and France," in Everett M. Kassalow (ed.), *National Labor Movements in the Postwar World* (Evanston, Ill.: Northwestern University Press, 1963), p. 146.

[37] Walter Galenson, *Trade Union Democracy in Western Europe* (Berkeley and Los Angeles: University of California Press, 1961), p. 40.

War II but actually strengthened them, partly as a result of the legal re-establishment of the "contracting-out" provision. In this respect, the British pattern differs from that in other nations besides Belgium and the Netherlands. The Austrian socialist unions, which before 1934 had been an industrial extension of the Social Democratic party, officially at least accepted a less political status, when in 1945 they joined with unions organized by Catholics and by Communists to form a non-party Trade Union Federation. Direct union financial support for the Social Democrats could then no longer be given.[38] In postwar West Germany too, where unions had never formally been part of the socialist party structure in the British manner, organizational neutrality in politics was adopted by the old socialist-inspired unions, along with the Catholic unions, as part of the arrangement for a unified trade-union movement.

Swedish and Norwegian union-party connections may also be technically distinguished from the British in this respect, even though the Scandinavian unions resemble the British in being entirely secular. They represent a unified trade-union movement to begin with and thus are affected by none of the pressure for political neutrality that socialist unions receive when they cooperate industrially with Catholic unions. The fact is that the Scandinavian unions are not organizationally neutral in politics. Yet the Swedish and Norwegian unions do not affiliate nationally to their labor parties in the manner of British unions. The formal affiliation is at the local level—local unions affiliate to local parties[39]—and at this level their weight, both financial and in terms of membership, approximates that of British unions in the Labour party. This follows from the fact that in Norway and Sweden as in Britain all trade-union members also become members of the party unless they specify to the contrary. The effect of this locally in Sweden and Norway is much as it is nationally (as well as locally) in Britain. Large portions of the party membership are indirect.

No major substantive difference, then, flows from the distinction between British and Scandinavian unions in the manner of their affiliation. Norwegian unions, for example, do almost everything for the party that British unions do. National union federations in Norway, even though not themselves directly affiliated to the national party, make large grants to the national party in addition to giving financial support through local membership affiliation. And the Norwegian unions, like the British, furnish much of the campaign

[38] Shell, *op. cit.*, p. 59.
[39] Galenson, *Comparative Labor Movements*, pp. 155–56.

apparatus at election time. As one student of Norwegian labor has said, "The trade-unions become a gigantic political machine dedicated to victory at the polls."[40] Given this much involvement, it is hard to say that the absence of national affiliation is of more than symbolic importance. Even its symbolic importance may be questioned, although a case has been made that Norway's Labor party finds it useful to avoid institutionalizing a major interest group in its national party structure because to do so would blur the image of a party of all the people. Interestingly, in its earliest days, before 1899, it functioned both as a political agency and as a trade-unions federation.[41]

Whatever the reasons for differences in manner of affiliation, or between formal and informal affiliation, there can be no doubt that close and large-scale union connections of one kind or another are associated with socialist party success—at least in the sense of there being no substantial socialist success without major union identification with the party. Therefore, it is safe to say that large, socialist-oriented unions are a necessary condition. It is not so certain whether we can say that this condition is sufficient for success. Not everywhere have socialist parties, even with strong union support, been successful to the extent that British and Scandinavian parties have, with their majorities or near majorities in national elections. The labor parties of Austria, Australia, and New Zealand rank with the British and Scandinavian, but most others fall well short of achieving majorities. Of course, this is a high standard for success. It would rule out the German Social Democrats, who have not won much more than a third of the national vote, despite close union connections; the principal Israeli socialist party, the Mapai, whose union ties are most intimate; and also the socialists (and Communists) of France, Belgium, the Netherlands, and Italy. In the latter four nations, while the parties have close union connections dating from the inception of the party organization, their unions include only a limited portion of the working class. This is so not just because of an absence of widespread unionism, although this was true for long periods, especially in France, but partly because non-socialist union organization, chiefly under the auspices of the Catholic Church, divided the working class. Thus even before the ascendancy of Communist unions in France and Italy following World War II, socialist unions could support socialist parties only on behalf of their

---

[40] Bruce Millen, "The Relationship of the Norwegian Labor Party to the Trade-Unions," in Kassalow, *op. cit.*, p. 127.

[41] Henry Valen and Daniel Katz, *Political Parties in Norway* (Oslo: Universitetsforlaget, 1964), pp. 312–13.

partial (although substantial) organization of the working class. In other words, socialist class consciousness was limited by the counter-attraction of a Christian ideology responding to Marxist and so atheist challenge. Naturally this limitation remained in force when, in France and Italy, the Communists succeeded the socialists as the militant party of the left. In Belgium and the Netherlands, where socialists remained the major party of the left, the limitation also remained.

Germany can really be included among those nations where a chiefly Catholic response to Marxism succeeded in keeping socialists from organizing industrially and politically in sufficient strength to achieve an electoral majority. Yet in Germany and in other countries socialists were strong enough to be represented by electoral shares of 30–40 per cent (for socialists alone or for Communists plus social-ists). The scale is much closer to the British or Scandinavian suc-cesses than to the American socialist failure. And, like the British and Scandinavian parties but unlike the American, all the continen-tal socialists securing one-third or more of the national vote were closely connected to large, if not dominant, trade unions.[42] All this suggests not only that closely connected unions are crucial to any substantial political success by socialist parties, but that the larger these unions are the more substantial the success. Sweden, whose Social Democrats are the most successful of all, has an extremely high percentage of its workers organized in unions supporting the party.[43]

It requires little reflection to see that the differences among Euro-pean parties in the degree of their trade-union support cannot be explained by differences in the degree of non-egalitarianism making for class consciousness. Britain and Scandinavia do not have less egalitarian cultures than continental Europe. Nor do they have more militant or bitter unions or parties—in fact, the opposite, especially in recent decades when size and representativeness, besides electoral success, exerted moderating influences. The very fact that the British and Scandinavian unions and their associated parties were able to organize most of the working class may have made for less doctrinal intransigence, but it is also likely that smaller movements always had the seeds of intransigence within them because of their position as

[42] Although German trade unions have not in recent times been formally integrated in the SPD as have British trade unions in the Labour party, they were fairly described for many years before Hitler as adjuncts of the SPD's attempt to gain power. Douglas A. Chalmers, *op. cit.*, pp. 6, 97.
[43] Galenson, *Comparative Labor Movements*, pp. 155–56.

a rival to the Catholic Church. For a socialist working-class organization simply to exist in a Catholic nation was to have a formidable enemy, both to oppose and to be opposed by. Workers organized by socialists were then doubly set apart from the rest of the community: by religion and by class.

In summary, there have been three patterns relating unions to parties. First is the American, in which there is no connection to a socialist working-class party and only nonstructural connections to middle-class parties—usually the Democratic party. Second is the British, found generally in non-Catholic areas of Europe, where most union organization is closely linked to a socialist party functioning as the political wing of the labor movement. To fit under this heading, however, it is not necessary for unions to affiliate their members in the particular manner of British unions. Third is that of continental Catholic nations in which socialist unions, representing only part of the working class, are linked to socialist parties similarly limited. Usually these unions were organized by socialists, just as Catholic unions were organized by Catholic political leaders, but it is not the fact that political organization preceded industrial organization which distinguishes this pattern from the second. Many Scandinavian unions were often organized after the socialist parties, but the resulting unified labor movement is like the British and not like the Catholic continental nations.

5. Survival

Given the association of successful socialist parties with large-scale class-conscious unionism, it should follow that diminution of this working-class base—whether in the size of the industrial working class or in the intensity of its sense of alienation—would reduce socialist party success. The full effect would not be felt immediately, since socialist parties, like other well-established social and political institutions, have a momentum of their own. Still, some adverse effect should be observed if the class base for socialism has been seriously eroded.

It is well to recall that the base is that of a large working class alienated from the prevailing system of private ownership of property and from its related social and political order. This alienation, sufficient for a separate political movement and not just for class-interest voting, is associated with the relative poverty of industrial workers, proletarian in the genuine propertyless sense, and from residual social and political distinctions like those expressed in the denial of the right to vote. These distinctions, while continuing to be felt to some degree long after the grant of an egalitarian suffrage, really must have withered with time, but this might well have happened without reducing the base for a socialist working-class party since the old distinctions were chiefly important in accounting for the *origin* of such a party. Once the separate working-class party was well established and especially after it achieved success, the social and political distinctions originally encouraging its growth would no longer be necessary to sustain it.[44] What would still be necessary, however, is a large working class with at the very least a continued sense of economic alienation.

Here we encounter two material changes in advanced economic orders that operate against the maintenance of the old working-class base. First, there is the relative decline in industrial employment in a highly developed economy, of which the American is the leading example. Manual workers in factories and mines, instead of continuously increasing as a proportion of the gainfully employed, as happened in earlier stages of industrialization, come to decline in comparison to rapidly increasing numbers of service employees, technicians, and white-collar workers.[45] While even in the United States industrial workers are still the largest single group, their dominance has decreased to a degree that virtually destroys any hope of building a political movement on a majoritarian industrial working class.[46] And in Western Europe, rapid economic development paralleling the earlier American pattern threatens to reduce the class on which traditional socialist hopes rested. Therefore, the political impact of mid-twentieth century economic trends is likely to be more notable in Europe than in the United States, since the American industrial working class, even at its peak strength, never supported a party of its own.

The consequences of economic change may already be observed in

[44] All that this suggests is that the working-class party might well remain after some of the necessary conditions for its original large-scale establishment have disappeared or greatly diminished in intensity. But the party, while remaining, would probably change its character in significant ways. It is this which Reinhard Bendix refers to when he finds "a clue to the decline of socialism" in Western Europe after "the equality of citizenship has been institutionalized successfully." *Nation-Building and Citizenship* (New York: John Wiley & Sons, 1964), p. 74.

[45] Specifically, for example, there is a decline of the proportion of factory workers in the rapidly changing French economy. Stanley Hoffmann, *In Search of France* (Cambridge: Harvard University Press, 1963), pp. 64–65.

[46] George H. Hildebrand, "The New Economic Environment of the United States and Its Meaning," *Industrial and Labor Relations Review*, XVI (July, 1963), 536.

European trade unions. In Great Britain, for example, the percentage of all wage- and salary-earners enrolled in unions declined from 45.8 per cent in 1952 to 43.7 per cent in 1960.[47] The most heavily unionized industries had themselves declined and so generally had the relative importance of manual workers. West Germany showed the same pattern. Union membership in absolute numbers was at a peak in 1951 and then remained static despite a tremendous increase in the total work force.[48] While these relative declines may not continue, it should be noted that in the 1950's and early 1960's short-run factors could not readily have accounted for loss in trade-union strength. These were prosperous years, unemployment was low, and the legal and political environment was entirely benign for union organization. In similarly favorable short-run circumstances and even before large-scale automation, unions elsewhere in Europe suffered similar declines. Finland is a good case in point.[49] Declines in French and Italian unions should be considered too, but sharply divided political control of worker organizations played a part here. On the other side, Sweden may seem like an exception, and if so a significant one, since its economy is in some respects the most advanced in Europe. Swedish unionism, already in 1950 virtually complete among manufacturing workers, did not noticeably decline as a percentage of the total labor force even though manufacturing itself suffered the relative decline characteristic of advanced economies. What happened was that the unions, more successfully than elsewhere, were extended to white-collar workers and government employees—indeed to 80 per cent of these categories[50]—but this was done mainly by unions outside the trade union federation and social democratic orbit. Even though unionism thrived, it was not the kind of unionism associated with a socialist working-class party.

There was also a decline, within the industrial category, of traditional heavy-industry employment versus employment in light manufacturing. Miners, steelworkers, and longshoremen are characteristic not so much of the newest economic order as of that of the late nineteenth and early twentieth centuries. And this older, heavy-industry employment had provided the core of class-conscious unionism and its

[47] Arthur M. Ross, "Prosperity and British Industrial Relations," *Industrial Relations*, II (February, 1963), 83.
[48] Arnold J. Heidenheimer, *The Governments of Germany* (New York: Crowell-Collier, 1961), p. 82.
[49] Knoellinger, *op. cit.*, p. 139.
[50] Galenson, *Comparative Labor Movements*, pp. 119–20.

related politics. This held particularly for those whose work put them in isolated or segregated communities.

Another point worth noting is that this declining though still considerable category of heavy industrial workers is no longer impoverished.[51] Wages, hours, and working conditions have most dramatically improved. The betterment of British miners is the best known example, but the transformation is striking almost everywhere that the older heavy industries persist. It is a different matter, of course, when employment in these industries actually ceases and the unemployed often become impoverished. This class of unemployed poor, especially in the United States, turns out to be larger than expected of a boom economy in boom times, and, also contrary to expectations, it has interested politicians.[52] But neither in the United States nor elsewhere are the very poor going to be more than a minority, however permanent. They provide no political substitute for the declining class of workers in heavy industry who once loomed so large.

Along with the changes in types of organizable labor, there are signs that unionism, in adjusting to these changes, tends to change its character. Just as the white-collar worker or the new industrial worker is less likely, if he joins a union, to do so as an expression of class identification than the mineworker of 1900, so the unions themselves are likely to be less class-conscious in the old sense. The old contrast between the ideological unionism of Europe and the business unionism of the United States may become dulled as European conditions change.[53] Strictly trade-union objectives would then take precedence over political objectives, except as the latter are related to specific union interests. This may be discerned even in Britain where, although the unions are still formally affiliated to the Labour party, they have become less willing to make sacrifices for political action.[54] This is not a matter of the Labour party being or becoming too ideologically socialist or class-conscious for the unions. The oppo-

[51] Lessened economic impoverishment does not stand alone. Carl Landauer rightly stresses the recently greater opportunities for working-class access to intellectual training and cultural advantages. *European Socialism* (Berkeley and Los Angeles: University of California Press, 1959), II, 1666–67. These changes are not entirely separable from the impact of mass suffrage on older class societies. The point is made for Sweden by Nils Stjernquist, "Sweden: Stability or Deadlock," in Robert A. Dahl, *op. cit.*, p. 129.

[52] John Kenneth Galbraith, *The Affluent Society* (Boston: Houghton Mifflin, 1958), p. 328.

[53] Ross, *op. cit.*, p. 64.

[54] Harrison, *op. cit.*, p. 347.

site, as will be observed, seems to be happening as the Labour party appeals to a broader portion of the electorate. In different ways, both the unions and the party are becoming less class-conscious. The unions do so because the workers' demands, as for material possessions, can plainly be met by unions within the economic system. And the party becomes less class-conscious in order to be effective in a society with fewer workers of the old type, since otherwise, as one Labour leader remarked after the 1959 general election, the party is in danger of fighting under the label of a class that no longer exists. Or, to be more precise but less dramatic, the class that still exists is less conscious of its own separate political cause but perhaps more conscious than ever of its specific and pragmatic economic cause.

Much of the shift in party posture in Britain and in other nations has been in the form of a continued dilution, now almost liquidation, of traditional socialist doctrine. This is most plain in Britain, West Germany, and other nations where there is a large unified socialist working-class movement. Where the movement has been divided between Communists and social democrats, as in France and Italy, the effect is hard to discern at all. While the social democrats in these nations have become decidedly non-revolutionary in program as in tactics, they do not command the largest share of working-class support. The French and Italian Communist parties, which have commanded this support to the extent of 20–25 per cent of the total national vote since World War II, can hardly be said to have become moderate reform parties even though they are no longer openly revolutionary. Their appeal is to an aggrieved and alienated working class in much the same spirit as that of early twentieth-century revolutionary socialists, whose position and support the Communists inherited. The tradition that thus persists in France and Italy has no counterpart elsewhere in Western Europe. The only other Communist party to play any important electoral role is Finland's, and it functions in special circumstances and at a lower level of support.[55] Probably, then, it is fair to count these two cases as no more than important exceptions to the view that large socialist working-class parties have become ideologically moderate. Treating France this way is readily

---

[55] The level of support is not much lower for Finnish Communists than for French Communists under the Fifth Republic. The Finnish Communist party has received 20–24 per cent of the vote since World War II. Most striking has been the heavily rural character of much of this support, reflecting a traditional backwoods radicalism. Erik Allardt, "Patterns of Class Conflict and Working Class Consciousness in Finnish Politics," in Erik Allardt and Yrjo Littunen (eds.), *Cleavages, Ideologies, and Party Systems* (Helsinki: Academic Bookstore, 1964), pp. 97–131.

understood since its Communist party, while immoderately class-conscious almost by definition, has declined, as is predictable for a working-class party unchanging in its basic appeal in a modernizing economic order. In recent years, French Communists have lost votes after losing members in the postwar years.[56] The Italian case differs since Italian Communists actually increased their vote as late as 1963, and this in a political environment where the larger of the two socialist parties also maintained much of the old militancy.[57] But with Italy as the one true exception it is easy to explain that the older doctrinal socialism still thrives there because Italy is the least developed economically, as measured both by industrialization and by wealth, of any Western democratic nation. The fact that class-conscious socialism should be increasing there even in the 1960's is consonant with the theory that European conditions are especially propitious for such political development when a given country is going through the relatively early and rapid stages of industrial development.[58] In addition, Italy's working class, like that of most other European nations a half-century ago, is fairly new to political life. Not only did universal suffrage arrive late, but its meaningful use had been suspended during more than two decades of fascism.

After detouring to account for French and Italian Communists, I can return to the democratic socialist parties that have modified their traditional doctrines. Here I shall leave the French and Italian socialist parties to one side. There is no doubt that they, especially the French, have shifted to reform programs, but these shifts are not of great significance as long as the competing Communists are the major working-class parties. Much more telling is the leading example of

[56] Jean Ranger, "L'évolution du Parti Communiste Français," Revue Français de Science Politique, XIII (December, 1963), 951–65. An important development, affecting the base of French Communist support, is the process of integration of trade unionism in French society so that unions no longer regard themselves as systematic opponents of the state. Alfred Grosser, "France: Nothing but Opposition," in Dahl, op. cit., p. 295.

[57] Raphael Zariski, "The Italian Socialist Party: A Case Study in Factional Conflict," American Political Science Review, LVI (June, 1962), 372–90.

[58] Perhaps there are better ways to make this point. Joseph La Palombara writes of the "lingering rigid social stratification and inequality of opportunity" in Italian society. Interest Groups in Italian Politics (Princeton: Princeton University Press, 1964), p. 51. Samuel H. Barnes calls attention to the recent peasant background, with all of the pre-modern characteristics of southern Italy, that marks the urban proletariat of postwar Italy. "Italy: Oppositions on Left, Right, and Center," in Dahl, op. cit., pp. 318, 320. For a recent study of the Italian Communist party, see Norman Kogan, "Italian Communism, the Working Class, and Organized Catholicism," Journal of Politics, XXVIII (August, 1966), 531–55.

the German Social Democrats. Their retreat from orthodox Marxism is long and famous. Well before World War I, the main body of Social Democrats had ceased to be a revolutionary party.[59] Yet they were still a class-conscious party dedicated to replacing the capitalist economy with a socialist order, albeit by peaceful means. Furthermore, there was a revolutionary socialist wing before World War I and a large Communist party between 1919 and 1933. Only after 1945 or perhaps 1949 were the Social Democrats again *the* working-class party for almost all practical purposes—partly, no doubt, because Communists in West Germany were discredited by their association with Russian policy in East Germany. What is notable is the continued change after 1949 in the character of this party's program.[60] Its socialism ceased to be socialism in any formerly accepted meaning of the term. The capitalist economy was frankly and openly accepted when the party adopted its new basic program in 1959. At the Bad Godesberg conferences at that time, the Social Democrats voted that "the consumer's freedom of choice and the worker's freedom to choose his job are fundamentals of a socialist economic policy, while free enterprise and free competition are important features of it."[61] And in 1964 the party paid its tribute to the dynamics of the market economy.[62] Entering the grand coalition of 1966 required no new doctrinal concessions.

The British Labour party has not been so forthright in repudiating its orthodox commitment to public ownership. An effort in 1960 to revise the party constitution was abandoned, and there remains a vague commitment to socialize the means of production. But by 1964 party leaders not only ignored (as before) this commitment as long-run policy, but they also avoided any nationalization plans for specific industries except for steel, previously nationalized by the Labour government of 1945–1951 and then denationalized by the subsequent Conservative government. There was considerable doubt about Labour zeal even for this renationalization proposal, although eventually legislated, since it was muted in official party campaigning. Electorally it was assumed that any nationalization commitment was a liability.

[59] A. Joseph Berlau, *op. cit.*, pp. 12–13, 330–31.

[60] Although the change, especially in style, was most marked after the death of Kurt Schumacher, the party's first postwar leader, there were many signs of a refocussed appeal even under Schumacher. Lewis J. Edinger, *Kurt Schumacher* (Stanford: Stanford University Press, 1965), p. 90; and V. Stanley Vardys, "Germany's Postwar Socialism: Nationalism and Kurt Schumacher," *The Review of Politics*, XXVII (April, 1965), 220–44.

[61] *The Economist*, CXCIII (November 21, 1959), 737.

[62] Otto Kirchheimer, "Germany: The Vanishing Opposition," in Dahl, *op. cit.*, p. 245.

While it could not be openly abandoned because of internal party reasons, the policy was made ambiguous and indefinite.[63] The "forms of public ownership," it was said, would "vary widely." It was broadly implied that a favorite form was no more far-reaching than government ownership of shares in private firms. In this and in other ways, the Labour party was bent on convincing British voters that it would do a number of things on a larger, bolder, and more effective scale than the Conservative party but that it would not do radically different things. Gone was the time when socialism was to replace capitalism.

In order to appreciate this change, one does not have to believe that earlier Labour leaders would have socialized most of the economy as soon as they came into office. In fact, the victorious Labour leaders of 1945 had no such intention; nor did the minority Labour governments of the 1920's. But socialism, in the sense of public ownership as well as of economic egalitarianism, was the long-range goal toward which the nationalization of 1945–51 was originally seen as a first major installment. What is different about Labour in the 1960's is that any nationalization which does occur—and some is always possible—will be justified only under the particular circumstances and not as the beginning of a new order. In short, the British Labour party, like the German Social Democrats, has come to accept capitalism. The party does not seek to abolish it in the name of a propertyless class of workers. (To be fair, however, the British Labour party never did go so far in this kind of class-conscious appeal as the continental Marxist parties had.)

The same development has occurred elsewhere. Even in Austria, where the Social Democrats of the inter-war years were more militantly class conscious than either German or British socialists, the party has abandoned much of its radicalism. "No other socialist party," one observer noted, "has traveled a longer road faster from Left to Right."[64] Austrian Social Democrats have sought to become a broad and moderate national movement rather than a class-bound fighting community. "All those who work for a living" have achieved equal status in the eyes of the party since 1958.[65] And the Norwegian labor party, known for its radicalism before World War II, has also

---

[63] *Signposts for the Sixties* (London: Labour Party, 1961), p. 18.

[64] Shell, *op. cit.*, p. 4.

[65] In other words, the Austrian socialist party is becoming a more purely political organization instead of a Marxist working-class movement. About half of its membership is now estimated to be other than working-class. Uwe Kitzinger, *Britain, Europe and Beyond* (Leyden: Sythoff, 1964), p. 94. Of course, the "de-ideologization" has not eliminated all of the old organizational rigidity or sense of subculture. Frederick C. Engelmann, "Austria: The Pooling of Opposition," in Dahl, *op. cit.*, 276–77.

moderated its policies and its appeals. Generally the Scandinavian parties have found this transition easy since their commitment to nationalization was never firmly fixed. Becoming primarily the party of more social welfare, as have the Swedish social democrats, raised few problems. In fact, Swedish socialists stressed control, not abolition, of private enterprise as early as 1936.[66]

The labor parties of Australia and New Zealand are worth special attention with respect to doctrine. In their cases, there was not much socialism to begin with. The Australian Labor party, it is true, was officially socialist from 1921, when public ownership was adopted in principle by a party conference during an especially radical period, but even then there was hedging. And despite its considerable time in power, the party never did much nationalizing.[67] Finally in 1953 the new party preamble stressed social justice rather than socialism.[68] In New Zealand, similarly, socialism was gradually diluted as its electoral appeal broadened. Socialization of the means of production was hardly mentioned after 1925 and not acted on when Labour came to power in 1935,[69] although proposals for it remained in the party's constitution until 1951.[70] It can be added that the other English-speaking Commonwealth socialist party to achieve any success, namely the CCF of Saskatchewan, modified its belief in government ownership before gaining provincial power in 1944.[71]

Dilution of orthodox socialist doctrine, then, has been relatively easy.[72] Even where outright abandonment has so far been impossible, ways are found to bypass what has become a doctrinal handicap in elections. But it has not been easy, despite a nonsocialist program, to maintain or increase electoral support. The old socialist party is

[66] Carl Landauer, *op. cit.*, II, 1549–52.

[67] The objective of a socialist society was always qualified by the Australian party in such a way that the use of the term hardly appears justified. James Jupp, *Australian Party Politics* (Melbourne: Melbourne University Press, 1964), p. 117.

[68] J. D. B. Miller, *Australian Government and Politics* (London: Gerald Duckworth, 1964), pp. 84–85.

[69] It is customary to speak of "the non-socialist, non-class struggle character of the Labour party by the time it got office." W. T. G. Airey, "The Rise of the Labour Party," in Robert Chapman (ed.), *Ends and Means* (Auckland: University of Auckland, 1961), p. 38.

[70] R. M. Chapman, W. K. Jackson, and A. V. Mitchell, *New Zealand Politics in Action* (London: Oxford University Press, 1962), p. 14.

[71] Seymour Martin Lipset, *Agrarian Socialism* (Berkeley and Los Angeles: University of California Press, 1950), p. 132.

[72] Israel's Mapai party ought to be added to the list of increasingly pluralist, less doctrinal, socialist parties. Lester G. Seligman, *op. cit.*, pp. 61, 63.

likely to remain a working-class party after casting away its socialism, and this identification may become a diminishing asset in a highly developed society. At least it seems to be a diminishing asset for a party seeking majority status in national elections. This helps to explain why the labor parties of Britain, Australia, and New Zealand, where two-party competition theoretically gives the socialists the best chance for majority status, fell back after the early postwar years. In all three, socialists, of course, had won enough votes to form governments, and British Labour returned to this position in the 1960's. As in earlier years, parliamentary majorities were won without majorities of the total national vote. This is to do as well as their opponents ordinarily manage, yet it is less than what would once have been thought to be the promise of a working-class party in an industrial nation. British Labour's experience in the 1950's, when it still retained most of its old class image, is instructive. Its percentage of the popular vote declined steadily, and, as long as Labour was heavily identified with the working class, the pendulum did not swing in its favor. The newly affluent British society, notable by the late 1950's, provided the wrong workers for the old class appeal. Thus in 1959, for example, Labour received fewer votes in the new prospering manufacturing areas than in its long-established industrial strongholds. The change in party fortunes in 1964 coincided with Labour's concerted effort to appeal to a new or changed social class. It is uncertain how much the image was changed or how necessary this change was to Labour success. Any opposition party might have won after thirteen years of Conservative government, and Labour's victory involved almost no increase in its total popular vote; even the more substantial victory of 1966 fell short of Labour's vote in 1951.

Australian and New Zealand labor parties, projecting similar class images, have not been so successful electorally in recent years. The Australian Labor party has been out of power since 1949, and so has the New Zealand party, except for three years in office between 1957 and 1960. Yet in both countries the labor parties had substantial periods of dominance in the decades before 1949. One has to be careful in trying to extract any general rule about declining working-class party fortunes from this experience, since short-run forces might well account for each case separately or for all of them together. What can be said, however, is that during the fifteen years 1949–64 of rapid economic development, none of the three labor parties (British, Australian, and New Zealand) did as well as its major opposition in what had previously been established as basically two-party competition. At least this suggests that parties with working-class labels and images are handicapped in increasingly affluent societies even when their socialist doctrines are diluted or muted.

Electoral records of most working-class parties in continental Europe also support this suggestion. The German Social Democrats are an important case in point. Now the SPD has in fact increased its portion of the total West German vote in the last fifteen years, but this is not the most important thing. Some of this increase, in the earlier period, may represent votes that the Communists used to receive, although the increase from 32 per cent in 1957 to 36 per cent in 1961 and to near 40 per cent in 1965 cannot thus be accounted for. The striking phenomenon is the Social Democrats' inability to obtain a *larger* increase, when party competition seemed for the first time in German history to be falling into a two-party pattern. Its greatest increases came only after it had drastically revised its socialist commitment in 1959 and after the Christian Democrats had been in office continuously for twelve years under the aged Konrad Adenauer and then several more years under the familiar Ludwig Erhard. Polling only 40 per cent of the vote, instead of nearer 50 per cent like the British and Scandinavian parties, may of course be understood as the consequence of operating in an environment where the Catholic Church exerts a strong counter-appeal to many of the working class. But only as an even less class-conscious party do the German Social Democrats appear likely to do better electorally.

Other continental socialist parties also reached a peak beyond which they have recently been unable to go. The Belgian socialists never exceeded the 39 per cent of the popular vote they received in 1925. (Even if Communist votes are added for the years just after World War II, the percentage is just over 40 per cent.) Actually, such a large percentage is unusual for a social democratic party in multi-party competition like Belgium's. More usual is the Swiss socialist record of just above 25 per cent, at which point it levelled off after a slight increase through World War II.

The levelling off should be stressed. This has occurred at a lower point under multi-party than two-party competition, and when there has been effective Catholic counter-organization of the working class (often part of the same situation). But the levelling off has come in every advanced European society (not, or at any rate not yet, to Italy), and almost always it has left the working-class party short of majority. The Scandinavian, particularly Swedish, case comes nearest to being an exception: each Scandinavian socialist movement wins so many more votes than any other single competitor (in multi-party competition) that it tends to be dominant without receiving a majority. The socialist party's continued dominance in Sweden prevents one from claiming that there are universal signs of electoral decline in the strength of the old working-class parties. At most, it only suggests the view that rising affluence checks the growth of the working-class party, for even the Swedish social democrats, despite the most moderate of socialist doctrines, have not shown any secular trend toward increasing their percentage of the total national vote. On the contrary, their peak was in 1940 when they polled over 53 per cent; or, if we add Communist votes to those of the social democrats in order to get a total for working-class parties, the peak was in 1944 when together the two parties had almost 57 per cent.[73]

We should not expect that working-class parties in Scandinavia or elsewhere would decline so sharply as to lose their status as major parties if they had achieved that status earlier. They might decline slightly over a decade or two, but electoral loyalties established for over half a century are not going to be quickly dissipated, any more than the party's large organizational apparatus will vanish. Most of the old working class continues to support the party, and that class's decline, as a proportion of the whole community, is gradual. In fact, it is so gradual that there seems to be time for the party to change not only its doctrine but its class character so as to reverse an electoral decline. In doing so, it may become no longer recognizable as a socialist working-class party, but it would not be the first time that a political party changed its character to preserve electoral continuity. The British Conservatives during the nineteenth century, for example, changed their whole basis of support from land-owning to middle-class business.

Our general picture, then, is of the likely survival of the socialist working-class party in advanced European societies. The survival, however, involves the already largely accomplished transformation from socialist doctrine to pragmatic social welfare policies, and the slower transformation from working class to broader and more various social groups. At least where the party is already large and even fairly successful, it is reasonable to expect these changes in order to ensure survival in new circumstances. But if the expectation is correct, the old socialist working-class parties will more closely resemble other parties. No longer operating as an alien force against capitalist society, the party's mass membership will seem less of an organizational necessity. Moreover, from the workers' viewpoint there would be less point in joining an ordinary political party than a "movement."

[73] For the different pattern in Finland, partly because of Communist success, see Knoellinger, *op. cit.*, p. 219.

That membership has already become a less important feature of socialist parties is not always clear from the records. The British Labour party provides an impressive example because its dues-payers declined even when its electoral prospects improved. Noting only its direct individual memberships and not its differently responding affiliated trade-union memberships, the number enrolled reached its peak of just over a million in 1952 after a nearly steady climb from 1945. Then it began to fall, with only a small and sporadic countertrend, until it reached about 800,000 in the 1960's.[74] This pattern is paralleled in some other nations where direct individual membership can be distinguished from indirect affiliated memberships (local or national). The German Social Democrats have lost members, going from 875,000 in 1947 to a low of 585,000 in 1954 before climbing back to 624,000 in 1958 and 664,000 in 1961.[75] The lower levels of membership, it should be noted, coincided with fairly substantial electoral gains. It may fairly be suggested that the Social Democrats are thus becoming a party with a broader but less intense appeal. In accord with this suggestion is the party's tolerance of a looser membership.[76] Certainly the mass-membership base is becoming less significant. The high average age of the remaining members may even indicate a sharper decline in significance in the near future.[77] So far, however, the actual decline in numbers of members of the German Social Democratic party is much less drastic than the drop in the number of French socialist dues-payers from the postwar peak of more than 350,000 to no more than about 100,000 in the late 1950's,[78] by which time French Communist membership had also greatly diminished.

On certain socialist movements, I simply do not have the records. We can suspect declines in a few of these instances. In others for which we do have records, there is evidence of stability, as in Denmark and Finland, or even of continued increases through the 1950's, as in Austria, Israel, the Netherlands, Sweden, and Switzerland. Mostly, it is true, these increases have not been large and tended to taper off by the late 1950's. Most important, all of the parties with increasing memberships, except probably the Swiss party, either counted indirect union memberships in their totals or otherwise pro-

[74] *Report of the 65th Annual Conference of the Labour Party* (London, 1966), p. 45.
[75] *Yearbook of the International Socialist Labour Movement,* (London: Lincolns Prager, 1960), II, 130–31; Chalmers, *op. cit.,* pp. 9, 11, 194.
[76] Chalmers, *op. cit.,* p. 198.
[77] Edinger, *op. cit.,* p. 107; Vardys, *op. cit.,* p. 221.
[78] *Yearbook of the International Socialist Labour Movement,* pp. 121–22.

vided for close integration of unions in their structure. Of course, these are among the marks of a successful working-class political organization, and we must accept their continued presence as evidence that a large-scale membership base remains intact among surviving socialist parties.

6. *Summary*

This long analysis of the socialist working-class party has been undertaken to help explain the relevance of a mass membership to political party organization. First, mass membership appears to be an organizational necessity for any movement seeking to effect drastic change in the economic order by democratic means; thus every socialist working-class party with that aim developed a mass membership. Second, a large party of this type emerged in every Western nation outside of North America, but this is to say mainly in Europe, where successful socialist development began at an early stage of industrialization when conditions included pre-modern class consciousness, a delayed mass voting franchise, and widespread economic deprivation. Third, no large socialist working-class party successfully developed at an early stage of industrialization in North America in the absence of such conditions, and none appears now to be developing. Fourth, this difference between the European and American experiences is not between having or not having trade unions, but between having or not having class-conscious workers ready to support a separate political party as well as their own unions. Fifth, the European socialist working-class parties survive, in some instances as majority or near-majority parties, although the conditions responsible for their development have now altered so that economically and to some extent socially the nations in question more closely resemble the United States.[79] Party survival, in these unfavorable circumstances, has involved modifications in doctrine and in class appeal.[80]

[79] The social, as opposed to the strictly economic, change in the status of European workers may not so soon produce an "American" character. There is even some reason to doubt that economic change in status is being accompanied by a change in social relations, particularly in the perception of those relations by the middle class and by the workers themselves. John H. Goldthorpe and David Lockwood, "Affluence and the British Class Structure," *The Sociological Review*, II (July, 1963), 133–63.

[80] There appears to be a parallel in rapidly modernizing Japan, where Marxism, a formidable ideological force in the two decades after World War II, is reported to have passed its peak and to have gone into decline. Robert Scalapino, "Ideology and Modernization: The Japanese Case," in David Apter (ed.), *Ideology and Discontent* (New York: Free Press of Glencoe, 1964), p. 121.

How far these modifications will go is not clear, and in particular it is not yet clear, despite a few signs of diminishing memberships, that the organizational character of the old socialist working-class parties will change. Mass membership seems less necessary for "socialist" parties that are becoming like other democratic parties rather than remaining social movements against the existing order. But where unions and other interest groups have been organizationally integrated they may well maintain the old forms—either from simple inertia or because it provides a convenient source of funds even for a party that may now have other means as well. (The same can be said for certain European parties of the right.)

Allowing for the continuation of mass-membership organizations where they already exist is a far cry from believing that they are distinctly modern and that they are likely in the future to develop in the United States. The United States has had no large socialist working-class party and may have no mass-membership party organization now or in the future.

VII

Leadership Recruitment by Class

---

1. *Socialist and Non-Socialist*

Recruitment is an important function of political parties. It is a broad term including much more than the selection of candidates. Reserving the subject of candidate selection for the next chapter, I intend to discuss here a particular aspect of party recruitment, namely its class basis—more specifically, the special qualities of recruitment (of organizational leaders and candidates) by socialist working-class parties. The point is not merely to compare a socialist party with its principal opposition in a given nation, but also a socialist party in one nation with parties of another nation in which there is no socialist party. The question to be asked in this comparison is whether the leadership recruitment pattern in a nation with a large socialist party displays the kind of special class character that I previously attributed to such parties. Is the class background of socialist leaders distinctively different from that of other political leaders, while no such difference appears between leaders of opposing parties in nations without a large socialist movement? Or, to speak in terms of the specific comparison on which I will chiefly rely, has the class basis of British Labour party leadership differed from that of British Conservatives in a manner not paralleled by any difference between American Democrats and Republicans?

The object, it is plain, is to see whether the presumed class-conscious character of nations with large socialist parties is confirmed by data on the social backgrounds of party leaders. Viewed in this light, the class distinctiveness of a given party's leadership becomes an index of the class consciousness of the nations in which the party functions. To be more precise, it is an index of the class-consciousness that existed when socialist parties were developed on a large scale. The subject-matter consists of the political leaders recruited over the last fifty to seventy-five years. If in socialist parties this leadership turns out to be much more heavily of working-class origin than it is in other parties, the finding will reinforce the argument that socialist parties served a special class purpose in their particular societies. Then, in addition to representing the working class and its interests, socialist parties will have served as a means by which those born and raised in the working class could pursue political careers apparently unavailable through other parties. Without such distinctive leadership, socialist parties might nevertheless be class-conscious because of their programs and their appeals. But with it, they would be even more clearly class-conscious political phenomena.

This higher degree of distinctiveness might well be expected in a society sufficiently class-conscious to have a large socialist party. The very idea of workers having their own party implies that they found no place in existing parties since they too were class parties—for the middle and upper classes. And it is likely that working-class leaders, or potential leaders, would feel this earlier and more sharply than most of their fellow workers. To join a middle-class party, even if it were possible to make a career in it, would involve an uncomfortable effort to declass or reclass themselves. At least this can be hypothesized for a European class-conscious society of the early twentieth century, where conditions made for collective efforts by workers to improve their status through their own parties. As Lipset has said, "the more rigidly stratified a society, the more likely that its lower classes will develop their own strong form of political activity."[1]

Inversely, then, in a less stratified society neither the working class nor its leaders would have the same incentive for collective action. But it would not follow that workers would therefore emerge as political leaders in non-working-class parties. Lacking the basis for collective class politics, they might also lack the basis for any political career. After all, politics, notably at the level of important public office, is not a career readily available in any society to members of the working class. Educational requirements are fairly high, economic returns are small especially at the start, and expenditures of time and resources are burdensome without an outside source of income. The expectation is that high-level political leadership would come mainly from the middle and upper classes, especially from those born into such classes but occasionally from those who have moved up to them by virtue of educational or business achievements. But the latter, the "upward mobiles," are not genuine working-class leaders. They are working-class by origin, but not by present occupation or income. More nearly an exception is the trade-union leader who becomes an

[1] Seymour Martin Lipset, *Political Man* (Garden City, N.Y.: Doubleday, 1960), p. 206.

active political leader or candidate, but this is hypothesized as unusual except in the case of working-class parties.

The effect of this reasoning is to turn around the often-encountered view that the heavy middle-class and upper-class character of political leadership (say, of members of a parliament) needs to be explained because it is so "unrepresentative" of the occupational composition of the nation. When, instead, political leadership is seen as a middle-class occupation, what needs to be explained is the presence of a large number of genuine workers. Only class-conscious politics, it is suggested, can bring this about, and it depends on the special circumstances discussed in the last chapter. As Karl Mannheim wrote, there is a characteristic difference between the mode of recruitment of liberal and labor leaders: "The former rise in the political world individually, that is, the degree of influence and of political power that they achieve does not depend on the increase in power of any given social stratum. A labour politician, however, rises in the political world only if, and because, labour as an entire group rises."[2]

At least this is true for the labor politician who is himself of the working class. In the familiar phrase, he rises with his class and not from it. But workers can rise from their class even in societies regarded as relatively class-conscious or rigidly stratified. Indeed, there seems to have been almost as much general mobility in Western Europe as in the United States in the twentieth century. Studies of France, Britain, Germany, Finland, and Sweden show that roughly the same large minority as in America rise above the occupational positions of their fathers.[3] So mobility in this sense characterizes every Western industrial society. The well-publicized American opportunity pattern is not unique. Existence of a similar pattern in Britain is especially well-substantiated both with respect to the occupational rise of many sons of manual workers and with respect to the occupational fall of a lesser but still substantial number of sons of higher-status fathers.[4] Factory supervision, technical tasks, and business management in growing industrial economies have required that new and additional talents be secured. Opportunities have inevitably

[2] Karl Mannheim, *Essays on the Sociology of Culture* (London: Routledge & Kegan Paul, 1950), pp. 202–3.

[3] Seymour Martin Lipset and Natalie Rogoff, "Class and Opportunity in Europe and the U.S.," *Commentary*, XVIII (December, 1954), 562–68; and Seymour Martin Lipset and Reinhard Bendix, *Social Mobility in Industrial Society* (Berkeley and Los Angeles: University of California Press, 1959).

[4] David V. Glass (ed.), *Social Mobility in Britain* (London: Routledge & Kegan Paul, 1954), p. 20.

existed, and sons of workers (and farmers) have taken advantage of the material opportunities—in Western Europe as in the United States. In other words, American and European class structures have not differed so markedly as to support a simple explanation that class-conscious leadership appeared in Europe because of an absence of opportunity for occupational advancement in nonpolitical ways. Insofar as workers chose to rise with their class as leaders of their own party, it was not because they or other talented workers could not rise from their class. So to rise would certainly have been difficult but hardly more so than rising with their class by the political route.

Other, more complex aspects of class structure must also be taken into account in order to understand the working-class leadership of large European working-class parties. Given the similarity in American and European mobility rates, the only way of using mobility itself as even a partial explanation is to say that the really large jumps in occupational status were more unusual in Europe. The available studies do not refute or support this point, since they relate mainly to gross rises and declines in status between manual and nonmanual categories. These changes in status might be small, from skilled manualist to factory supervisor, for example. A greater change, from manualist to professional or large business management, is presumably infrequent in all nations, but perhaps less so in America. Or, moving to a different and more important possibility, the opportunities for major occupational change, for rising *from* one's class, might at least *seem* greater in the United States, which helps to explain why rising *with* one's class would be a less relevant aspiration in American society.

There is more, however, than a mythological difference between American and European patterns. Rise in occupational status takes place under different social circumstances. Successful upward-mobile Americans take pride in their modest origins and particularly in having started with menial jobs, while comparably successful men in Britain, for example, less often report their first menial jobs in biographical material.[5] What is good form to assert in one society is good form to suppress in the other. This suggests that the social class to which high-status occupations belong is more sharply defined in Europe than in America. Becoming an accepted and a secure member of that class may be more difficult in Europe, although arriving in it is just as easy. It may even be harder to identify with it politically. Thus European upward mobiles, compared with American upward mobiles, less frequently vote for middle-class parties and often remain

[5] Lipset and Bendix, *op. cit.,* p. 82.

loyal to the working-class parties of their families.[6] In other ways too, there is evidence of greater European reluctance to break former class ties: upward mobiles hesitate to break their original class links, and the established middle class is reluctant to admit them to their social relationships.[7] The latter barrier, in particular, can also be found in the United States, but it is usually more pronounced in Europe.

One reason for this is that European education is linked to the class structure. Everywhere, children of the middle and upper classes tend to have educational advantages, but these have been accentuated in most of Europe by the delayed development of widespread secondary schooling and by the preservation even now of distinctive kinds of secondary schools which, as in Britain, cater to distinct classes. It is true that typically middle-class schools always have some children of the working class—an increasing number in recent years. But most of the population, including many upward mobiles, attend very different types of school, if any at all, beyond the elementary years. The result is that those rising into the middle class, in Britain most notably, have been marked off educationally from established members of that class.[8] And the differences in education reinforced the differences in style of life and in speech.[9]

While it is possible that these class distinctions are lessening or are about to lessen, there can be no doubt that they were sharp and meaningful during the earlier years of this century. Their effect can be observed in the recruitment—that is, the self-recruitment—of working-class leadership for socialist working-class parties. There was a European but not an American basis for this kind of identification. How this difference appears in party leadership remains to be demonstrated.

2.   The British Labour Party

The British Labour party is my primary subject only partly because of the ready availability of data on it. It serves specifically to demonstrate the general point about the nature of the socialist working-

[6] Lipset, *Political Man*, pp. 254–57.

[7] David Lockwood, "The 'New' Working Class," *European Journal of Sociology*, I (1960), 248–59.

[8] T. H. Marshall, *Citizenship and Social Class* (Cambridge: Cambridge University Press, 1950), pp. 57, 63.

[9] Brian Jackson and Dennis Marsden, *Education and the Working Class* (London: Routledge and Kegan Paul, 1962), present a careful and detailed study of working-class children adjusting to the middle-class ethos of a grammar school (Britain's governmentally-supported academic school at the secondary level).

class party leadership. This is because British class differences, though unmistakably strong, have not been marked by the bitter conflict characterizing many continental European nations and tending, one would expect, to a more segregated leadership. Thus if the British party displays a distinctively working-class leadership, there is likely to be a similar pattern, in at least the same degree, in continental social democratic parties.

It is useful to be reminded that the Labour party, although officially launched in the first decade of this century, arose in an old class society. This holds both for the last few decades of the nineteenth century, when there originated the movement which became the Labour party, and for the earliest years of the twentieth century. The working class had only recently been enfranchised, and it stood far apart from the governing class—economically, socially, and educationally. To an extraordinary degree, political power was, as it had long been, the monopoly of those raised in privileged circumstances. No cabinet member had been the son of working-class parents from 1801 to 1905.[10] A majority of cabinet members had in fact been sons of the nobility, and the others, increasing in proportion during the nineteenth century, had been from substantial middle-class backgrounds.[11] Not a single exception, it must be emphasized, was available to symbolize the possibility of rising from humble origins to high office—in the manner of Abraham Lincoln. Political recruitment of the Conservative and Liberal parties was exclusively from the middle and upper classes.

With the advent of mass suffrage, extended pretty much en bloc to industrial workers, it was natural for some members of the newly enfranchised class to think that they should be represented by their own leaders rather than by those who had previously been chosen only by the middle and upper classes. Workers, in other words,

[10] Harold J. Laski, "The Personnel of the English Cabinet, 1801–1924," *American Political Science Review*, XXII (February, 1928), 12–31. The only sons of workers to achieve cabinet rank after 1905 but before the first Labour government of 1924 were John Burns, whose earlier independent working-class following commended him to the Liberal government of 1906, and Arthur Henderson, the Labour party's own representative in the coalition government of World War I.

[11] W. L. Guttsman, "The Changing Social Structure of the British Political Elite, 1886–1935," *British Journal of Sociology*, II (1951), 122–34. Much of Guttsman's thorough insightful work is relevant to the present subject. See also his "Changes in British Labour Leadership," in Dwaine Marvick (ed.), *Political Decision-Makers* (Glencoe, Ill.: Free Press, 1961), and *The British Political Elite* (London: MacGibbon and Kee, 1963). Another useful analysis is by Jean Bonnor, "The Four Labour Cabinets," *Sociological Review*, VI (July, 1958), 37–48.

should have their own elected representatives. This might or might not mean a separate working-class party. In the beginning, it seemed possible that the demand could be met by at least one of the older parties recruiting working-class leaders to its ranks—much as the Liberal party, earlier in the nineteenth century, had recruited the new businessmen to its leadership.[12] Certainly the pressure for working-class leaders themselves to be elected to public office antedated the creation of the Labour party. Movements to elect workers to the House of Commons came immediately after the enfranchisement of 1867. The Labour Representation League, founded in 1869, stated in its prospectus that there were 20 million members of the British working class, "and yet, not one actual working man has found a seat in the present Parliament." The League's principal duty was "to secure the return to Parliament of qualified working men."[13] It sponsored a dozen working-class candidates in 1874, electing two of them (both miners' union officials). Similarly the Labour Electoral Association, established under this name in 1887 after an earlier status as an electoral committee affiliated with the Trades Union Congress, said that it wanted candidates who were either workingmen or of working-class origin.[14] This was the reason for the Association's existence. Ideologically it was a Radical organization trying to elect working-class representatives to act with Liberals in Parliament.

There was no turning to a separate Labour party until after the failure of working-class leaders to gain what they regarded as sufficient representation through the Liberal party. Their failure here is instructive, since the Liberals had good political reasons for trying to adopt working-class leaders as Liberal or Liberal-supported parliamentary candidates. They wanted, as did the Conservatives on a different basis, to attract the newly enfranchised urban voters. The Liberals, in the late nineteenth century, began either to adopt, or to stand aside for, worker candidates, notably in mining constituencies. The practice would have been more widespread, perhaps widespread enough to absorb the most active working-class leaders, if more local Liberal associations had been willing to follow the advice of their national party headquarters.[15] Instead, certain Liberal associations, partly for financial reasons, rejected important proffered candidacies

[12] Guttsman, *The British Political Elite*, chaps. 7 and 8.

[13] A. W. Humphrey, *A History of Labour Representation* (London: Constable & Co., 1912), pp. 188, 189.

[14] *Ibid.*, p. 97.

[15] As Herbert Gladstone, a Liberal chief whip, said: "The long and short of it is that the constituencies, for social, financial, and trade reasons, are extremely slow to adopt Labour candidates." Quoted by Henry Pelling, *The Origins of the Labour Party 1880–1900* (London: Macmillan, 1954), p. 237.

—including those of three men, Keir Hardie, Arthur Henderson, and Ramsay MacDonald, who subsequently became the most important political figures in the early Labour party. Hardie did not form his Independent Labour Party, under whose banner he was returned to Parliament, until after a Liberal caucus had rejected his candidacy in 1888.[16] Henderson joined Hardie following his own rebuff by local Liberals in 1895.[17] And MacDonald had a similar experience in this same period.[18] The Liberals were not hospitable enough. In retrospect, this is understandable. What was asked of the Liberals was not merely to accept working-class programs, which was hard enough, but also to adopt working-class candidates in constituencies that were only partly working-class and not overwhelmingly so, as in mining areas.

After 1900, when the Independent Labour party was able to link itself to trade-union support in the new Labour Representation Committee, it was too late for the Liberals to absorb the drive for working-class representation. Thus, the 1906 bargain between Liberal and Labour headquarters, under which the two parties agreed not to oppose each other's candidates in selected districts, involved a recognition of Labour as an independent party.[19] To be sure, there were short-run advantages in this bargain for both parties, but a separate working-class movement was now institutionalized in a new way.

The Liberals' inability to prevent this accomplishment can be explained by those aspects of the British social structure that made for class consciousness on the part of both the local Liberal caucuses and the new labor leaders. Parliamentary membership was so much a gentleman's occupation that it was still unsalaried. And it was not as middle-class Liberal gentlemen that Hardie and Henderson, at least, sought parliamentary candidacies. Their terms for adoption as Liberal candidates included a continued identification as working-class leaders. They wanted to keep intact their working-class credentials, as they later could and did in their own party. They were joined by others of similar background who found satisfaction in linking the improvement of their own status with the improvement of the status of their class. Working-class leaders generally, as long as they were brought up in a society where they were as likely to exclude them-

[16] *Ibid.*, pp. 68–69.

[17] Mary Agnes Hamilton, *Arthur Henderson* (London: William Heinemann, 1938), pp. 29–30.

[18] Frank Bealey and Henry Pelling, *Labour and Politics 1900–1906* (London: Macmillan, 1958), pp. 30, 128.

[19] Philip P. Poirier, *The Advent of the British Labour Party* (New York: Columbia University Press, 1958), chap. x.

selves from middle-class status as they were to be excluded by others, had their most comfortable political home in a workers' party. In a way, it is true, many of these men did achieve a kind of middle-class status as successful Labour party leaders, but their continued identi-fication as workers remained. Significantly, for example, British trade-union officials, whose ranks supplied the working-class political lead-ers, have never received the high salaries of American union officers.

Except for a few famous socialist intellectuals, whose role was not primarily in political organization or candidature, the original Labour party leadership was almost exclusively working-class. Only when the party was already well launched, after trade-union support had been secured, did Labour attract important politicians from the middle and upper classes. Their influx dates mainly from the sharp decline of Liberalism at the end of World War I, when Labour was about to become the official opposition and soon afterward to form a minority government.[20] By then, it was decidedly attractive to men of higher-born status, particularly from the radical wing of the Liberal party. Similarly, in subsequent decades, Labour attracted aspiring middle-class politicians of a variety of non-Conservative views. But, important though some individuals have been, they were simply ac-cretions to a party that was a going concern and that had been, in its first generation, primarily a vehicle for men of the working class. In 1906, all twenty-nine of Labour's parliamentary contingent, and all but one of the party's fifty candidates, were of working-class origin.[21] As late as 1918, 90 per cent of the members of the parliamentary Labour party had had no full-time education beyond elementary school—virtually a sure sign of working-class background. This per-centage, incidentally, was still about 70 in the 1930's.[22]

More revealing of the nature of early Labour leadership, if less im-pressive statistically, is the biographical material on the first Labour cabinet of 1924. Despite Prime Minister MacDonald's deliberate ef-fort to raise his government's level of experience and prestige by the inclusion of very recent and even dubious converts to Labour, thus diluting with newcomers the top ranks of his party's old leadership, eleven of the twenty cabinet members were plainly of working-class

[20] Catherine Ann Cline, *Recruits to Labour* (Syracuse, N.Y.: Syracuse Uni-versity Press, 1963), has assembled considerable biographical data on the party's new leaders of 1914 to 1931, notably those recruited just after World War I.

[21] Henry Pelling, *A Short History of the Labour Party* (London: Macmil-lan, 1961), p. 16.

[22] J. F. S. Ross, *Elections and Electors* (London: Eyre & Spottiswoode, 1955), pp. 412–14.

origin.[23] Eight of the other nine (the exception was Sidney Webb) had had virtually no previous Labour party experience. Thus the eleven, all of course old Labour men, did represent the most success- ful of the party's early twentieth-century leadership. Their lives and backgrounds typify those of the men who built the party, and they reveal much of what it meant to have been born into the British working class between the late 1850's and the early 1870's.[24] Full- time education ended early. Except for the special cases of MacDon- ald and Snowden, who prolonged their school years by remaining as "pupil-teachers" until they were eighteen and fifteen respectively, this group of Labour leaders had turned to manual work, most often mining, at ages ranging from eight to thirteen.[25] Education after that age was part-time at best, and while evening classes became available in the developing worker's education program, much had to be pain- fully acquired by individual effort in public libraries. This working- class generation did have an advantage denied to its predecessors: elementary school, as provided by the Education Act of 1870. The crucial tools of literacy were supplied to children before they went into the pits or mills, and for men of native ability this schooling was enough to allow, even to encourage, the further self-education neces- sary to ascend from manual work to white-collar jobs—and, more particularly, to leadership positions in the growing trade-union move- ment.

Men of this background continued to loom large at the top levels of the Labour party well beyond 1924. This was true of the Labour government of 1929, when eight (possibly nine) of nineteen cabinet members could point to up-by-their-own-bootstraps careers. Even in the governments of 1945 and 1950, half of each Labour cabinet con- sisted of men with the familiar pattern in which manual labor had put a stop to full-time education at the elementary level (see Table 1). This is not surprising in light of the fact that political leaders as

[23] That *only* eleven cabinet members, and fourteen of twenty-four junior ministers, were of proletarian origin was a source of parliamentary complaint. Richard W. Lyman, *The First Labour Government 1924* (London: Chapman & Hall, 1957), p. 104.

[24] Two important early party leaders not in the Labour cabinet had similar backgrounds. They were Keir Hardie, already dead, and Robert Smillie, who refused office in 1924. Hardie, the son of a ship's carpenter, had started work at age 6, and Smillie at age 9. See Hamilton Fyfe, *Keir Hardie* (London: Gerald Duckworth, 1935), and for Smillie the 1931–40 *Dictionary of Na- tional Biography* entry by Mary Agnes Hamilton, pp. 813–15.

[25] Data on the lives of these and other Labour leaders are from the appropriate volumes of the *Dictionary of National Biography*, occasionally from other biographical or autobiographical works, and, where necessary for late figures, from the British *Who's Who* or the *Times Guide to the House of Commons*.

Table 1

WORKING-CLASS BACKGROUND OF LABOUR PARTY LEADERS

Year	Total Membership	Working-Class Background*
1924 Cabinet	20	11
1929 Cabinet	19	8
1935 Shadow Cabinet†	14	7
1945 Cabinet	20	10
1950 Cabinet	18	9
1951 Shadow Cabinet†	14	3
1955 Shadow Cabinet†	14	4
1959 Shadow Cabinet†	14	4
1964 Cabinet	23	5

* "Working-Class Background" is a classification conservatively arrived at from standard biographical sources indicated in note 25. For Labour leaders so classified there was ordinarily evidence indicating a working-class father and a career begun as a worker or without formal education beyond the elementary years. In the shadow cabinets of the 1950's, for which standard biographical information is not always available, there is one doubtful case that would raise the number with working-class background by one in each of the three years. And in the 1964 cabinet there are three trade-union officers who are not counted as working class because they were grammar-school graduates who evidently did not begin as manualists. For the cabinets of the 1920's, of 1945, and 1950, it is possible to compare the tabulation here with Guttsman's (cited in note 11). His two most thoroughly working-class categories produce a total for each cabinet that is no more than one higher or lower than the figures in the table above.

† "Shadow Cabinet" is here limited to the elected Executive Committee (including the leader and deputy leader) of the parliamentary Labour party. This excludes those M.P.'s who, especially in the 1950's, were added by leadership appointment to Labour's opposition front bench.

late as 1950 would have been born in the 1880's or 1890's and so have been raised under essentially the same conditions, certainly educationally, as men born ten or twenty years earlier. The Labour party's successes of the second quarter of the twentieth century were made by the generation whose careers had started before the reduction of class barriers in the 1900's. The lives of Ernest Bevin and Herbert Morrison, and even of the younger Aneurin Bevan, are leading examples.[26] Bevin, the oldest, had the harshest time. His father

[26] Others, for whom biographical material is readily available, are George Tomlinson and Emanuel Shinwell. See Fred Blackburn, *George Tomlinson* (London: William Heinemann, 1954), and Shinwell's own *Conflict Without Malice* (London: Odhams Press, 1955). Aneurin Bevan portrays some of his self-education in *In Place of Fear* (New York: Simon & Schuster, 1952).

unknown and his impoverished mother dead when he was only eight, Bevin left school at eleven to become a farm laborer and subsequently a van boy in Bristol. Subjectively as well, Bevin's working-class identification was clear and definite. As he told a group of employers in 1917, by which time Bevin spoke for his trade union:

> You have had one set of education for yourselves and another for us. I had to work at ten years of age while my employer's son went to the university until he was twenty. You have set out for me a different set of conditions. I was taught to bow to the squire and touch my hat to the parson; my employer's son was not. All these things have produced within me an intense hatred, a hatred which has caused me to organize for my fellows and direct my mind to a policy to give to my class a power to control their own destiny and labour.[27]

No better text than this self-portrait could be found to illustrate the theme that the Labour party was built by men who were the product of the pre-modern class structure of nineteenth-century Britain. Bevin even experienced the impact of pre-industrial rural England. This was shared, although in less difficult personal circumstances, in the youthful careers of other early Labour leaders.

Herbert Morrison's background may, by comparison, seem only marginally working-class. His father, it is true, was a London police constable, but the family's means were so much like those of working-class neighbors that Morrison's formal education was assumed to end at fourteen when he went to work as an errand boy in his brother's grocery. "Secondary education," Morrison writes, "was hardly thought of by parents of my class and time."[28] Despite a considerable subsequent self-education, Morrison's origins distinguished him from middle-class politicians, certainly at the start of his career. He could be at home in the Labour party in a way that he would have found impossible in the established parties of the turn of the century.

A working-class background has undoubtedly been a source of pride and probably an advantage for those pursuing a career within the Labour party. This remained true long after the party opened its ranks to middle-class politicians, rewarded some with cabinet positions, and even, beginning with Attlee, made a man of the middle class its top leader. To have come from the working class, handicapped though one was by lack of advanced formal education, was still a useful credential. Certainly the party leaders possessing it

---

[27] Quoted by Alan Bullock, *The Life and Times of Ernest Bevin* (London: William Heinemann, 1960), I, p. 69.

[28] Lord Morrison, *Herbert Morrison* (London: Odham's Press, 1960), p. 20.

were willing, even eager, to display it. Their biographical sketches furnished for parliamentary guides, official party histories, or *Who's Who*, ordinarily state the early ages at which they left school and their own and their fathers' manual occupations. This is significantly different from what, as I noted previously, upward-mobile British corporation directors (in contrast to American executives) report. The point is that successful British businessmen have left the working class to become middle class, and it is natural, in a class-conscious society, that they should want to make their new identification as complete as possible. On the other hand, British Labour leaders, who have risen *with* their class, even if more strikingly than their fellow-workers, have all the reasons drawn from a class-conscious society to proclaim their original status. It is the very class consciousness of Britain that made possible a successful Labour party and thereby the rise of its leadership to honored public positions. British businessmen of working-class origin have, in contrast, risen *in spite of* their society's class consciousness.

It is possible that the working-class character of Labour leadership will diminish in response to changes in those conditions that originally caused the workers to build their own political movement. While allowing for some persistence of old attitudes, a new generation of the working class, if less marked off economically, socially, and educationally from the rest of the community, would be less likely to produce able Labour leaders from its own ranks. Apart from anything else, greater educational opportunities should enable more of the highly talented sons of the working class to rise, even in public life, by non-Labour party means. This would leave the Labour party, unless it were to disintegrate, to be led more completely by middle-class politicians.[29] But it is not clear that this process is under way. The proportion of Labour M.P.s with no more than elementary schooling fell, by one reckoning, 50 per cent after World War II from the pre-war figure of 70 per cent and the 1918 figure of 90 per cent already noted.[30] More recent and not strictly comparable calculations, however, show no further diminution through the 1950's; in fact, the number as well as the percentage of Labour M.P.s with only elementary education was a little higher in 1955 and 1959 than in 1951.

[29] The difficulties created by the absence of up-from-the-ranks labor leaders, when all talented working-class children will have achieved upward mobility through university education, are tellingly and amusingly depicted by Michael Young, *The Rise of the Meritocracy 1870–2033* (London: Thames & Hudson, 1958).

[30] Ross, *loc cit.*

Those recorded as manual workers declined only slightly.[31] It was not until the 1966 election, in contrast to the 1964 election, that a large number of new M.P.s raised the educational and occupational levels substantially.[32] Labour's parliamentary representation still differed markedly from that of the Conservatives, almost all of whose M.P.s have middle- or upper-class occupational and educational backgrounds. This difference derives mainly from Labour's trade-unionist M.P.s. A study of parliamentary candidatures in the 1950's reveals that there was little difference in years of formal schooling between Conservative and non-union Labour candidates. Even between these two groups, however, there was a considerable difference in the prestige of schools attended. A much higher percentage of Conservative candidates had attended fee-paying schools.[33]

More clearly indicative of change in the inter-party social difference is the sharp drop in the working-class character of Labour's top parliamentary leadership during the 1950's and early 1960's. This contrasts with the absence of any such change from 1924 to 1950.[34] Table 1 shows clearly that the shadow cabinets of 1951, 1955, and 1959 had significantly fewer members of working-class background than either the Labour governments of 1945 and 1950 or the shadow cabinet of 1935. And the 1964 cabinet displays the same tendency in even sharper form. Still more evidence of a change from 1950 to 1964 comes in the comparison of executive appointments (cabinet, non-cabinet ministers, and lesser ministerial personnel) in the two Labour governments. In 1950, twenty-eight of eighty appointees, or 35 per cent, had the distinctive working-class mark of only elementary education. The 1964 figure was only seventeen of 119, or 14 per

---

[31] Data on Labour M.P.s in the 1950's come fom the Nuffield studies by David E. Butler, *The British General Election of 1951* (London: Macmillan, 1952), pp. 38, 39, 41, and *The British General Election of 1955* (London: Macmillan, 1955), pp. 41, 42, 43, and by David E. Butler and Richard Rose, *The British General Election of 1959* (London: Macmillan, 1960), pp. 128, 129, 130. The basis for classifying by educational levels in the Nuffield studies apparently differs from Ross's (cited above), since in 1951, for which year both have data, Ross's percentage of Labour M.P.s with only elementary education is much higher than Butler's. For this reason, no direct comparison is made here between Labour M.P.s of the 1950's and those of the earlier period.

[32] David E. Butler and Anthony King, *The British General Election of 1964* (London: Macmillan, 1965), p. 237, and *The British General Election of 1966* (London: Macmillan, 1966), p. 210.

[33] Austin Ranney, *Pathways to Parliament* (Madison: University of Wisconsin Press, 1965), chap. 7.

[34] The absence of change in the social composition of Labour cabinets from 1924 to 1950 is confirmed by Guttsman, *The British Political Elite*, p. 241.

cent. Plainly, the dominant group at the leadership levels is now of fairly high middle-class status, usually by origin but in some cases by upward mobility from lower status as a result of university scholarships following grammar school education.

Whatever has happened since 1950, there can be no doubt of the large element of working-class leadership during the first half-century of the Labour party. Men for whom some kind of upward mobility would have been likely in any case chose to associate their career success with that of their class. If fewer now choose to do so or if middle-class leaders are now more useful, it would only be a sign that British class consciousness is not as it used to be.

3. Other Socialist Parties

Data on the class basis of leadership in socialist parties other than the British Labour party have not been tabulated specifically for the purpose at hand. But several studies illustrate the same recruitment theme as that developed for British Labour: socialist party leadership heavily derived from a working class previously unrepresented in non-socialist parties.

A leading illustration is the German Social Democratic party. Here, in fact, there was never any question about the distinctive working-class character of most of its leadership.[35] Except for a few admittedly important middle-class intellectuals, the German Social Democrats were always the workers' party with respect to membership and votes as well as leadership. Michels observed this when he studied the party before World War I. It is true that he went on to say that working-class leaders became middle-class in their outlook after establishing themselves in party positions. Indeed, Michels thought that this change was inevitable because it was impossible for a party leader to remain an actual manual worker once he became a salaried employee of his union or party.[36] There is no need to dispute this view. Whether or not those who started as working-class leaders remained socially in their original class does not affect the argument that a working-class party, and only a working-class party, provided the opportunity for them to become political leaders.

Michels went even farther to accept the view that "hardly any other way," presumably non-political or political, offered "an intelli-

[35] The point is not diminished in its import by the fact that Social Democratic leaders, like most of the party's members, were drawn from among the better paid workers. Seymour Martin Lipset, *The First New Nation* (New York: Basic Books, 1963), p. 291.

[36] Robert Michels, *Political Parties* (Glencoe, Ill.: Free Press, 1949), p. 299.

gent German workman" such rapid opportunities for improving his
own condition as did his "service in the socialist army."[37] He cited
both the historian Ferrero and Prince Bismarck to the same effect.
Becoming a socialist leader was an attractive career possibility open to
talented workers. Michels compared this possibility to the traditional
ascent offered peasants and petty bourgeois by the Catholic Church.[38]
For some workers, too, the Church might have offered similar opportunities. And so might the industrial and business establishment that
was growing in Germany as elsewhere in Western Europe. Therefore, it is hard to go as far as Michels in regarding the Social Democratic party as an upward mobility channel generally more attractive
than non-political channels. What remains, however, is that the Social Democratic party was *the* political channel and that it was used
by many working-class leaders. In fact, more evidently than in Britain, there were great difficulties about any other kind of political
career for a worker at about the turn of the century. German public
life, no less than British, was for the leisured and moneyed classes.
For example, German parliamentary deputies, like British M.P.s of
the same period, were not paid governmental salaries until 1906.[39]
Therefore, it was only through the Social Democratic party, which
paid salaries to its own deputies, that a worker could become a member of the Reichstag.

More recent studies than Michels's show the persistence of working-class leadership in the Social Democratic party even after World
War II. In the first Bundestag (1949) elected in the West German
Federal Republic, almost one-third of the Social Democratic members
had been manual workers. The proportion in other parties was
much smaller although, by this time, the Christian Democrats had a
trade-union following represented by some deputies.[40] Much the same
difference appeared in the Bundestag elected in 1953. Here, using a
method of classification not strictly comparable to that of the 1949
study, 44 per cent of the Socialist members were identified by early
training or social origin as "labor," while 21 per cent of the Christian
Democratic members were so identified. Another telling characteristic
of the 1953 findings is that over half of the Socialist members and
less than one-third of the Christian Democrats had had only primary

[37] *Ibid.*, p. 273.
[38] *Ibid.*, pp. 278–9.
[39] *Ibid.*, p. 121.
[40] Otto Kirchheimer, "The Composition of the German Bundestag, 1950,"
Western Political Quarterly, III (December, 1950), 595.

school education.[41] So far, it has to be admitted, it is not only the persistence of the Socialist working-class leadership that is striking, but also the presence (probably in contrast to the past) of a smaller but significant number of working-class background, occupationally or educationally, in the major non-socialist party. This must be regarded as a mark of Christian Democratic success in mobilizing a section of the working class behind its own leadership, and thus accomplishing as a confessional party what would have been difficult for any other non-socialist party to do in a class-conscious society.

The Christian Democratic recruitment of working-class leaders thus tends to strengthen the argument concerning the relation of a class-conscious society to political recruitment. In such a society, any party seeking to win working-class support will find it profitable to have working-class leaders. The socialists remain, as they do in Germany, the prime example of this recruitment pattern, but it is emulated by a successful competitor under favorable circumstances.

A specific study of a select German leadership group brings out similar findings. As of 1956, among twenty-three Christian Democratic cabinet members and parliamentary leaders and among twenty-nine Social Democratic executive committee members, just over one-quarter of the Christian Democrats and almost 60 per cent of the Social Democrats had no more than secondary education. And just over one-fifth of the Christian Democrats and almost half of the Social Democrats had social origins labelled as "labor" rather than middle-class or aristocracy.[42] The authors of this study, it is true, do not stress this large working-class element or the substantial difference between the two parties in this respect. Their concern is mainly to show that leadership in all parties is now heavily middle-class, with very few residual aristocrats and not many workers outside the Social Democratic party and the similar trade-unionist bloc in the Christian Democratic ranks. And their data do certainly support their emphasis and lend credence to the idea that the class character of German politics is diminishing. Yet it is also fair to say that their data illustrate how much of the old character remains. Interestingly, this old leadership pattern, long exhibited by the Social Democrats, was not followed by the National Socialists of the 1930's. Their leadership, as of 1936, tended to be of considerably higher educational background than that of the Social Democrats, and in fact to resemble that of a

[41] Karl Deutsch and Lewis J. Edinger, *Germany Rejoins the Powers* (Stanford, Calif.: Stanford University Press, 1959), p. 68.

[42] *Ibid.*, pp. 136, 139–40.

middle-class party.[43] Socialists—that is, the German Social Democrats —seem to have had a class base for their leadership unlike that of any non-leftist German party—including the Nazis, whose electoral appeal crossed class lines.

Even more convincing evidence is available about French parties of the left in relation to their competitors. Here the data, presented by Dogan, are limited to parliamentary deputies, but they are especially relevant because they were originally assembled to illustrate the class basis for leadership recruitment. From 1871 to 1900, before the rise of a socialist party, very few French deputies were of working-class origin. As late as 1900, only thirty could be said to have had modest social origins—a broader term than working class. The middle classes predominated, although the nobility was still fairly well represented. In the next (and last) forty years of the Third Republic, the picture greatly changed. While the parties of the right and center (including the Radicals) had only small minorities of working-class background, the Socialists at first and then the Communists had many deputies clearly of this background. Taking all the deputies serving between 1898 and 1940, Dogan shows that 84 per cent of the Communists and 47 per cent of the Socialists were of working-class origin and that similar percentages in each case had had only primary education. In the Fourth Republic, 1945–58, the Communist deputies remained heavily working-class, two-thirds of them being so classified, but the Socialists, continuing a trend started between the two wars, were now largely a party with middle-class deputies.[44] The Communist party, by 1945 having the votes and members to displace the Socialists as the major working-class party, now displayed the leadership pattern the Socialists had also followed between the wars (and earlier) when they had been *the* working-class party. Because Communists were numerous in most of the Fourth Republic's assemblies, there was still a strong working-class contingent among deputies. But, unlike the trend during the last decades of the Third Republic, there was no over-all growth in the proportion. In France, as elsewhere in Western Europe, there were signs that a high-water mark had already been reached in the class consciousness responsible for the development of working-class leadership.

[43] Lewis J. Edinger, "Continuity and Change in the Background of German Decision-Makers," *Western Political Quarterly*, XIV (March, 1961), 23.

[44] Mattei Dogan, "Political Ascent in a Class Society: French Deputies 1870–1958," in Dwaine Marvick, *op. cit.*, pp. 67–78. For a brief reference to similar Italian data, see Samuel H. Barnes, "Italy: Oppositions on Left, Right, and Center," in Robert A. Dahl (ed.), *Political Oppositions in Western Democracies* (New Haven and London: Yale University Press, 1966), p. 317.

The available Swedish data do not relate to this likely trend, but in a limited way they support the previously established distinctiveness of socialist leadership. The data are from the Riksdag of 1955, whose members were classified according to their own occupations (not their backgrounds). In this count, there were only forty-five "workers" among the 380 members, but forty of them were Social Democrats (of whom there were a total of 188).[45] The proportion of workers in the one party was significant in a way that it was not in any other Swedish party.

Another European socialist party can be cited—the Norwegian Labor party. Although in this case the available studies are tangential to the purpose at hand, they do show evidence of the heavily, but of course not exclusively, working-class character of the party leadership. Of sixteen Labor party chairmen between 1887 and 1958, thirteen began their careers as workingmen. And in the same study, it is reported that most party leaders were men who worked with their hands and belonged to trade unions.[46] The latter point is supported by another study showing that half of the party's parliamentary candidates in 1957 were affiliated with trade unions.[47] Still another study, especially interesting despite the fact that it goes beyond leadership ranks, shows that a higher proportion of Norwegian workers (and farmers) than middle-class citizens are active political participants. The authors, Rokkan and Campbell, find that this contrasts sharply with the United States, where political participation is largely a middle-class activity. They theorize that the larger proportion of politically active Norwegian workers can be explained by a political system that has class-distinct parties, like Norway's, rather than socially and economically heterogeneous parties, like the American. In their own party, as in their trade union, workers with little formal education would not be discouraged in competing for leadership positions, as they would in a party of the middle class or of diverse classes.[48] The result is paradoxical from a democratic standpoint since it means that political participation is decreased by a higher degree of national in-

[45] Nils Andren, *Modern Swedish Government* (Stockholm: Almqvist & Wiksell, 1961), p. 58.

[46] Bruce Millen, "The Relation of the Norwegian Labor Party to the Trade-Unions," in Everett M. Kassalow (ed.), *National Labor Movements in the Postwar World* (Evanston, Ill.: Northwestern University Press, 1963), p. 129.

[47] Henry Valen and Daniel Katz, "The Norwegian Party System" (Paper delivered at the American Political Science Association meeting, Washington, 1962), p. 29.

[48] Stein Rokkan and Angus Campbell, "Factors in the Recruitment of Active Participants," *International Social Science Bulletin*, XII (1960), 69–99.

tegration of social classes. Of this paradox, the distinguished authors of the Norwegian-American comparison are well aware. In fact, they think that with apparent trends toward more national integration in Norway—that is, less consciousness of class distinctions—there will probably be less active political participation by members of the working class.[49] Whether this is to be deplored depends on one's view not just of worker participation but also of the social and political system that encourages participation. The word "encourage" is important. It is not the word Rokkan and Campbell use in this connection; they speak of workers in the United States being "discouraged" from political participation. The implication is that there might be something wrong, or insufficiently democratic, about American circumstances. On the other hand, if one says that workers in the United States are not encouraged to participate, all one implies is that class consciousness is so much less than Norway's that workers feel less reason to become active.

Australia and New Zealand have working-class parties whose leadership recruitment patterns resemble those of the European socialist parties. Everything that is known about the Australian Labor party, in particular, would lead to the expectation of such a finding. The class character of both its electoral base and its parliamentary representatives has been shown to resemble the class character of the British Labour party, rather than that of any large American or Canadian party.[50] This class pattern holds for the higher leadership group, as is revealed by a study of 243 Australian party leaders, 180 of whom were federal ministers between 1901 and 1951 and 63 of whom were state ministers from 1945 to 1958. (The combination is curious, but the data are convincing nonetheless.) Dividing the whole group by party, 42 per cent of the 101 Labor ministers, compared to only 1 per cent of the non-Labor ministers, had been manual workers. These working-class ministers were usually trade-union officials. The data, impressive though they are, may understate the extent to which the Australian Labor party served as a means of upward mobility. Not tabulated as manual workers are those who might have been sons of manual workers but who moved up the occupational ladder by legal or other professional training before entering politics. There were, in fact, several Labor ministers classified as lawyers who had achieved that status by part-time study while working at non-profes-

---

[49] *Ibid.*

[50] Robert R. Alford, *Party and Society* (Chicago: Rand McNally, 1963), pp. 97–98.

sional jobs. But it should not be thought that there was an absence of educational difference between Labor and non-Labor leaders. Only twenty of the Labor ministers, compared to sixty-four of 142 non-Labor ministers, had formal training beyond the secondary level.[51]

From this study of Australian ministers, it is not clear whether there has been any recent decline in the distinctive class character of Labor party leadership. But there are indications of such a decline among members of parliament. The percentage of manual workers among Australian Labor M.P.s, above 70 per cent early in the century, was down to 50 per cent by 1917 and has gone even lower since then.[52] The figure is still high enough to make the Labor party very different from its competitors, but the difference is being eroded.

The same kind of difference and the same apparent diminution is found in New Zealand when Labour M.P.s are compared with M.P.s of the chief opposition, the National party. But it must be noted that New Zealand Labour was never as heavily working-class in either its leadership or other respects as the Australian. The type is similar but the degree is different. According to a careful study of the parliaments of 1935 to 1960, the high-water mark for "workmen and trade union secretaries" came in the 1930's when they constituted about one-third of the Labour party M.P.s. At that time, as later, there were no working-class members (with one exception) among National party M.P.s. The proportion among Labour M.P.s declined to about one-quarter by the late 1950's, but this slight decline becomes more significant when one appreciates that only about one-fifth of the *new* Labour M.P.s between 1949 and 1960 were of the working class, compared to almost half of the new Labour M.P.s in 1935.[53] The proportion of teachers and other middle-class leaders has been rising in the New Zealand Labour party so that its class character has become less sharply different from that of the National party. That some difference remains, however, is plain from a study of candidates in the 1960 general election. Slightly more than one-quarter of Labour's candidates were blue-collar workmen or trade-union secretaries, while none of the National candidates were in those categories. A parallel difference between the two parties was reflected in the educational backgrounds of the two sets of candidates; the majority in both parties

[51] S. Encel, "The Political Elite in Australia," *Political Studies*, IX (February, 1961), 32–33.

[52] *Ibid.*, pp. 34–35.

[53] Austin Mitchell, "The New Zealand Parliaments of 1935–1960," *Political Science*, XIII (March, 1961), 34–36.

had secondary or university education, but Labour had a larger minority without such education.[54]

In all the cases examined, in Australasia and Europe, the findings support the opinion, originally substantiated in the British experience, that socialist parties have had a distinctive class basis for their leadership recruitment. The demonstration might have been more convincing if data were supplied from all Western nations with large socialist parties. But the number examined seems sufficient to be representative.[55] There is no reason to expect other major socialist parties to be markedly different. Potentially more restrictive methodologically is the use of studies that cannot provide strictly comparable findings. It would have been better to have produced a single study of similar or closely related party leaders in each of our several nations, employing the same definition of class status and the same time period. Such systematic cross-national analysis might have made it possible to relate the degree of a nation's class stratification, measured by certain socioeconomic criteria, to the degree of working-class leadership found in each socialist party. Fortunately, however, this refinement has not been of primary concern. All that needed to be shown was that socialist parties generally have had a considerable, although varying, working-class leadership.

4. The American Contrast

To rest content with the limitation of the foregoing analysis is to retain the emphasis on the difference in the class base of leadership recruitment between any nation with a large socialist party and a nation, like the United States, that does not have such a party. There are two related aspects of this American contrast.

The first is that in the United States, there was always an opportunity for a small but symptomatically significant number of men of modest social origins to rise in politics, resembling the more frequent rise in occupational status in the professions or business. For the presocialist political world of the nineteenth century, this meant that the United States differed from European nations whose privileged classes still monopolized high-level political careers. The difference, as dis-

[54] R. M. Chapman, W. K. Jackson, and A. V. Mitchell, *New Zealand Politics in Action* (London: Oxford University Press, 1962), pp. 145–46.

[55] Japan, if included in our universe, would add confirmation, since in its postwar diets about one-third of the substantial socialist party contingent have been trade-union officers. Robert Scalapino and Junnosuke Masumi, *Parties and Politics in Contemporary Japan* (Berkeley and Los Angeles: University of California Press, 1962), p. 70; and James R. Soukup, "Japan," *Journal of Politics*, XXV (August, 1963), 737.

cussed earlier, may or may not have involved a greater American mobility generally. The important point is that American mobility of the nineteenth century included a mobility through political careers. And these rising political careers were part of the typically American pattern of rising out of one's class, not with it, to become an important political figure—just as one also, often simultaneously, rose to middle-class occupational and income status. It was not through a working-class party that Abraham Lincoln was recruited for political leadership. Nor was Lincoln recruited as a workman or workers' leader. Rather he was already a lawyer, distinctly arrived in the middle class, when he became an active politician in a middle-class party (or a classless party, if one prefers).

The second aspect of the American contrast is the smaller number of men of modest social origin who became political leaders during the first decades of the twentieth century. This is not because of any discernible decline in the American proportion. It seems much the same as the nineteenth century's fairly small figure. What happened, as indicated in the previous section, was that European socialist parties provided the means on a really large scale for working-class men to rise as their parties rose.

Looking back at the earlier period, one can see much of the difference reflected in Joseph Schneider's well-known comparative study of American and British careers. Covering the 300 years before 1900 and all careers, political and nonpolitical, as distinguished in entries in the standard biographical dictionaries, Schneider found that a significantly higher percentage of famous Americans than of famous Englishmen had originated from lower social groups (chiefly yeomen and farmers)—19 per cent as opposed to 4 per cent. The difference was reversed with respect to the elite classes, from which 38 per cent of the famous Americans and 54 per cent of the Englishmen had come.[56] Because business, crafts, and labor are lumped as one class in Schneider's tabulation, with only a slight American-British difference, it is impossible to say much about urban working-class origin in relation to career success in the two nations. Generally, of course, most famous persons in both Britain and the United States came from the middle and upper classes, but the higher American proportion from the yeoman-farmer class suffices to demonstrate the difference between the two societies. Especially relevant in reporting this difference is Schneider's point that those from lower status groups more frequently achieved fame through politics in the United States than

[56] Joseph Schneider, "Social Origins and Fame: the United States and England," *American Sociological Review*, X (February, 1945), 52–60.

in Britain. He specifically attributes this to the American "institution of political democracy."[57]

Again, it is worth emphasizing that this political manifestation of traditional American upward mobility did not involve the movement into higher levels of public life by men who were occupationally identified as manual workers or as similarly low-status employees. It was their fathers who had the modest occupations. The sons had by education or other means achieved at least middle-class status. Thus, when President Andrew Jackson is said to have democratized the elite by appointment of new men to top positions in the national government, what happened was that he appointed cabinet members and high civil servants whose origins, not their own occupations, were frequently humbler than those of their predecessors appointed by John Adams and Thomas Jefferson.[58]

Neither then, nor before, nor after in American history has a large proportion of top office-holders come from humble origins. There were just enough of them to be noticeable in contrast to their total absence in nineteenth-century Britain. Data assembled by Donald Matthews bear directly on this point. Surveying the 311 politicians who served as president, vice president, or cabinet members from 1789 to 1934, he found 4 per cent who were sons of wage-earners and 38 per cent who were sons of farmers (many of whom might have been prosperous and even of high social status).[59] Similar findings come from C. Wright Mills's study of 513 men who between 1789 and 1953 were Supreme Court justices, speakers of the House of Representatives, or any of the executive officers included by Matthews. Although Mills's purpose was to show the high status of most of this elite, which is certainly the case, he does find that 18 per cent originated in "lower-class families." Within this category, 13 per cent of the total came from "small-business or small-farming families that did not do so well, but could readily hold their heads above dire poverty." Five per cent came from "the class of wage workers or destitute small business-men and farmers."[60] Even the last figure is large enough, like Matthews's 4 per cent who were the sons of wage-earners, to score the point advanced here.

Incidentally, there is reinforcement in a more recent study by Mat-

[57] *Ibid.*, p. 56.

[58] Sidney H. Aronson, *Status and Kinship in the Higher Civil Service* (Cambridge: Harvard University Press, 1964), pp. 178, 199.

[59] Donald R. Matthews, *The Social Background of Political Decision-Makers* (Garden City, N. Y.: Doubleday, 1954), p. 23.

[60] C. Wright Mills, *The Power Elite* (New York: Oxford University Press, 1957), pp. 400–2.

thews. He found that 5 per cent of the 180 U.S. Senators serving between 1947 and 1957 were sons of industrial wage-earners.[61] Here
perhaps one should say "only" 5 per cent, because the figure is for
the middle of the twentieth century, when European parliaments
show a much higher working-class percentage, whether measured by
social origins or by the members' own prior occupations. But the
"only" is not appropriate in relation to the whole of American historical experience, for which the 5 per-cent figure seems fairly typical, or
in relation to nineteenth-century British experience, which displayed
almost no working-class mobility of this kind.

Turning to the twentieth century, when the American proportion
of political leaders of working-class background seems relatively small,
it is advisable to look for signs that the established parties began to
recruit working-class leaders on the really large scale of European
socialist parties. In particular, has the electoral mobilization of trade
unionists by the Democratic party, at a later date than such mobilization was undertaken by European socialists, shown a leadership
pattern like that of the socialists? Or has the Democratic party leadership remained almost entirely middle class (as measured by prior occupation, not social origin)? At the very top level, for cabinet and
Congress, we already know that there has been no marked change.

Whether we are right to confine ourselves to this level might be
questioned. Cabinet positions in the United States are roughly comparable with cabinet positions in European nations, and therefore it
is significant that there are fewer workers in twentieth-century American cabinets than in socialist party cabinets. But comparing members
of legislative bodies is more doubtful. The American Congress is independently more powerful than legislatures in parliamentary systems, and so to be an American congressman is individually more
important than to be a European legislator. Moreover the Congress,
especially in the Senate but even in the House of Representatives, is
small for a legislative body in so large a nation. The British House of
Commons, serving a nation with less than one-third the American
population, has more members than both houses of the U.S. Congress. Other European parliaments are smaller than the British and,
in absolute numbers, usually smaller than the American, but they too
tend to be larger relative to population than the American. American
congressmen, in other words, represent large constituencies. There
can really be no doubt that the Congress is not only more powerful
but more select than European parliaments. It may, therefore, be

[61] Donald R. Matthews, *U. S. Senators and Their World* (Chapel Hill:
University of North Carolina Press, 1960), p. 20.

tilted against working-class membership in a way that European parliaments are not.

Leaning backward, away from the argument, it is worth while to
look at the membership of American national party committees,
where the work is less time-consuming than in Congress and where
working-class leaders could function without leaving their union positions. Of course, the total membership is even smaller than Congress's
since each national committee has usually had only two members
from each state, one man and one woman, although the Republicans
have added a state chairman in certain cases. In studying the backgrounds of those serving between 1948 and 1963, only one labor
leader (a Democrat) was found on a national committee. No one
occupationally classified as a worker was among either the 265 Democratic or 352 Republican committee members. Educationally also,
there was little sign of an inter-party difference. Sixty per cent of the
Democrats and 67 per cent of the Republicans had at least one college degree.[62] No distinctively working-class leadership of a party is
to be discerned at this level. Perhaps none should have been expected. But if it is not in the national committees, any more than in
cabinets or in Congress, where is it to be found nationally?

If the answer, as it appears, is not to be found nationally at all,
would it be worth while searching at the state level? Surely, one
should approach a comparison of state legislatures to European parliamentary leadership with considerable skepticism. While American
congressmen may be too high and mighty to be compared with European parliamentary deputies, American state legislators do not seem
high and mighty enough. Their districts are usually small, their turnover high, the legislative sessions often brief, and their general importance in the community ordinarily much less than that of national
figures in any country. Furthermore, there is good reason to believe
that American state legislatures have always contained many members of modest social origins and even of modest occupational status
(farmers, however, more frequently than industrial workers). Now,
however, the number of lawyers and other urban middle-class men
seems to be increasing at the expense of farmers in particular. If, as
is possible, the number of industrial workers or ex-workers has also
increased, it is not so marked as to blur the general professionalizing
trend. The available data, however, are not entirely clear. As of 1949,
when all of the states were surveyed, it was found that less than 5 per
cent of the legislators were listed as laborers or craftsmen. Farmers

[62] Cornelius P. Cotter and Bernard C. Hennessy, *Politics Without Power*
(New York: Atherton Press, 1964), pp. 47, 51–52.

were 22 per cent of the whole group, but lawyers, merchants, and other middle-class occupations predominated.[63] The laborers and craftsmen were more frequent in certain (but not all) industrial states than in the country as a whole. It is also known, from other studies, that these manual workers are usually Democrats.

A few studies of particular states are useful on this score. V. O. Key has shown that one-quarter of Michigan's Democratic legislators and one-fifth of Pennsylvania's were listed as manual workers, 1945–51, while almost none of the Republican legislators in either of these industrial states were so classified.[64] The Pennsylvania finding is confirmed in a later study by Frank Sorauf. For the legislature elected in 1958, Sorauf found fairly substantial differences between Democratic and Republican legislators in educational background and occupational status. Of the 212 Pennsylvania legislators, only fourteen held blue-collar jobs, and all fourteen were Democrats. Blue-collar occupations were also more numerous among the fathers of Democratic legislators.[65] Much the same pattern was clear for the Wisconsin legislature in 1957. As in Pennsylvania, manual (or blue-collar) workers were not generally numerous, but the few manualists (about 7 per cent of all legislators) were almost all Democrats. The larger numbers who were sons of manual workers also were more heavily Democratic than Republican but, as in Pennsylvania, not overwhelmingly so.[66] Both parties, judging by these legislative contingents, served in the customary American manner to recruit leaders who had moved via nonpolitical means from the working class to the middle class. But for the smaller number coming into politics directly from the working class, often as union officials, the Democratic party seems to play the role performed by a European socialist party.

Not too much should be made of this, however, since the role is minor compared to that of a European socialist party. The number of manual workers recruited is small, and the positions for which they are recruited are not on a level with the parliamentary and cabinet positions obtained by European manual workers. Often the manualists among state legislators come from small homogeneous urban constituencies in which there are no middle-class politicians. Further-

[63] Belle Zeller, *American State Legislatures* (New York: Crowell-Collier, 1954), p. 70.

[64] V. O. Key, Jr., *American State Politics* (New York: Alfred A. Knopf, 1956), pp. 259–60, 262.

[65] Frank J. Sorauf, *Party and Representation* (New York: Atherton Press, 1963), p. 78.

[66] Leon D. Epstein, *Politics in Wisconsin* (Madison: University of Wisconsin Press, 1958), pp. 192–93.

more, not all industrial states show the same pattern.[67] The most systematic comparative study indicates hardly any urban manualists among legislators in the four states, including three industrial states, which the authors surveyed.[68] A substantial number (16 per cent) of the fathers of these legislators had been manual workers, but this only serves to confirm the same recruitment pattern always thought to be characteristic of non-class or multi-class American parties.

The truth is that at no level can American political recruitment be found to resemble the working-class leadership of a European-style socialist party.[69] No large American party has been the means for large numbers of manual workers to move directly into important positions of political leadership. For example, the American parties of the Jacksonian era, which surely mobilized the votes of the working class, evidently did not recruit their leaders from the working class. At least it has been shown conclusively that both the Democrats and the Whigs of New York State retained essentially similar middle and upper-middle class leadership during the Jacksonian period.[70] However much the American working class may have electorally supported and benefitted from the programs of a particular party, it did not use a party to rise in status *as a class*. In this respect, the working class differed from ethnic groups in the United States. Various minorities, from the Irish through the Italians and Jews to Negroes, have sought and secured political leadership positions as a form of recognition for their groups. Of course no such group was ordinarily large enough to dominate a national or even a state party in the manner of an industrial working class. But American parties, especially the Democratic party, find it politically important to extend recognition, in the form of candidatures and party positions, on the basis of

[67] Thomas R. Dye, "State Legislative Politics," in Herbert Jacob and Kenneth Vines (eds.), *Politics in the American States* (Boston: Little, Brown, 1965), pp. 168–69, has assembled data on legislators in seven states which show the variation mentioned. Relevant information on Michigan's Democratic convention delegates and state central committeemen is provided by Robert Lee Sawyer, Jr., *The Democratic State Central Committee in Michigan, 1949–1959* (Ann Arbor: University of Michigan Institute of Public Administration, 1960), pp. 8, 46–57.

[68] John C. Wahlke *et al.*, The Legislative System (New York: John Wiley & Sons, 1962), pp. 489–90.

[69] It is possible that even the recruitment of precinct leaders in the United States represents a distinctive pattern. For a description and analysis of this recruitment in a major metropolitan area, see Samuel J. Eldersveld, *Political Parties: A Behavioral Analysis* (Chicago: Rand McNally, 1964), pp. 69–71.

[70] Lee Benson, *The Concept of Jacksonian Democracy* (Princeton: Princeton University Press, 1961), pp. 64 ff.

ethnic rather than of class membership.[71] Ethnic minority recognition might coincide with working-class recognition if the ethnic group leader should happen to be a manual worker, but more often the ethnic leader obtaining party recognition has previously achieved a middle-class position in the usual American way.

Regardless, however, of the class membership of the ethnic group leader, there can be no doubt of the primacy of ethnic over class recognition in American leadership recruitment. The reason is not hard to discover, and it throws light on the whole contrast between class in America and class in Europe. In the United States, ethnic minority groups, as later and culturally disadvantaged arrivals, carried the marks of status differentiation in a way that simple working-class membership did not. Borrowing the well-known Weberian terminology, economic class differentiation was not the same as status differentiation,[72] and because it was not so in the United States there was much less basis for working-class leadership than there was in Europe. It might even be argued that ethnic status differentiation itself made class-based status differentiation less likely by cutting across classes or by dividing the working class. Some such influence may be allowed without forsaking the view that class consciousness would have been less anyway in the United States for a variety of historical reasons.

It is necessary to resist the temptation to see in the political rise of American ethnic minority leaders an exact parallel to the rise of European working-class leaders. There is no reason to believe that American ethnic leaders were themselves of the working class. No group that they represented was large enough to have its own party. And, except for the Negroes, every substantial minority was pretty rapidly recognized with leadership positions by one or both established parties. The rapidity contrasts with the slowness and apparent inability of the old British parties to give adequate leadership recognition to working-class leaders.

Negroes, admittedly, are a special case in the United States. Neither in party leadership nor in other more important ways have they been given the recognition commensurate with their numbers (about 10 per cent of the American population). Clearly in status American Negroes are much more like the late nineteenth-century European

[71] This process of ethnic group mobility in politics can be contrasted with the widespread exclusion from social clubs portrayed by E. Digby Baltzell, *The Protestant Establishment* (New York: Random House, 1964), p. 20.

[72] H. H. Gerth and C. Wright Mills, *From Max Weber* (New York: Oxford University Press, 1946), pp. 180–95.

working class than were any other groups in the United States. Even their full-fledged citizenship, notably the right to vote, has been delayed in a large section of the United States, just as that of the European working class had been delayed a century before. Interestingly, as that citizenship is finally being extended in the 1960's, it coincides with a growing Negro political militancy in much the same manner as the European working-class militancy in response to the suffrage near the turn of the century.[73] One difference, however, remains overwhelmingly important in destroying the parallel between American Negroes and European workers. The Negroes are not numerous enough in the United States to form their own party on the European working-class scale. The best that the Negroes can do by way of national political action of their own is to form non-party pressure groups of various kinds.

5. Canada

The same kind of contrast to the working-class leadership of socialist parties should be found in Canada, which, like the United States, has been largely if not so completely dominated by two non-socialist parties. The class character of the leadership of those two parties should resemble the American rather than the British pattern, and it is with this expectation that the backgrounds, occupations, and education of Canadian ministers from 1867 to 1957 were analyzed in comparison with the similar data, previously discussed, on British and American cabinets.[74] The comparison cannot be precise, since the Canadian data cover a somewhat different period of time and are classified in slightly different ways. But there is enough similarity to permit the comparison to be relevant.

Of the 275 individuals to occupy Canadian ministerial positions from confederation in 1867 until the beginning of 1957, no more than six can definitely be categorized as of working-class background by finding, in standard biographical sources, that the minister's education went no further than elementary school, that his first major adult job was as a manual worker, or that his father was a manual worker. But to this figure of six might well be added four more with

[73] Edward C. Banfield and James Q. Wilson, *City Politics* (Cambridge: Harvard University Press and MIT Press, 1963), p. 299.

[74] The names of the Canadian ministers are taken from the *Guide to Canadian Ministries Since Confederation to 1957*, published by the Canadian Privy Council, and biographical data are from *Wallace's Dictionary of Canadian Biography* (2d ed., 1945), the *Canadian Who's Who* and *Who's Who in Canada*. These are the sources used in Tables 2 and 3.

farm backgrounds and a fairly large share of fifty-one whose class backgrounds must be considered uncertain because of inadequate biographical information. By this rough method, we arrive at a substantial minority of 8–12 per cent of the 275 individual ministers who could be said to be of modest or humble social origins if not exactly from working-class backgrounds. Almost all of the remaining ministers appear to have come from the middle or upper class, mainly the former. Thus the over-all Canadian pattern resembles the American in having a sprinkling, but no more, of top political leaders recruited from working-class backgrounds. More significantly, the resemblance extends fairly evenly to the whole period from 1867 to 1957. When the data are arranged by ministries, those with working-class, farm, and uncertain backgrounds are represented in roughly the same proportions in each period. There has been no increase in the twentieth century to parallel that brought about by the British Labour party.

Table 2

OCCUPATION OF CANADIAN MINISTERS, 1867–1957, BY PARTY

Party	Lawyer	M.D.	Other Prof.	Journalist	Business	Farmer	Manual & Clerical	Uncertain	Total
Liberal	76	4	16	8	29	7	4	1	145
Conservative*	64	12	5	6	36	4	0	3	130
Total	140	16	21	14	65	11	4	4	275

* "Conservative" includes ministers listed as "Liberal-Conservative" in the early years of the Canadian Confederation.

While the background information is especially important, so much of it is uncertain that detailed tables are omitted because they would promise an exactness that our background data do not possess. One can have more confidence, however, in the data that measure background less directly. There are fewer uncertainties especially about the occupations of ministers themselves. Thus, in Table 2 it can be seen that the great majority had middle-class white-collar jobs. Fully 64 per cent were professionals, mainly lawyers, and most of the rest were businessmen. Only 7 per cent at most (19 of the 275) could be said to have had anything but middle-class occupations, and to get this percentage we have to count farmers (some of whom might have had farm businesses of considerable size) and those listed as uncertain.

Again, as in the the background data, there was no substantial increase (or decrease) in these working-class indicators during later years. The uniformity over time is striking, but it is not presented here in tabular form. The uniformity between the two parties is evident in Table 2. On the latter point, however, it is possible that the Liberal concentration of even the small number in the manual-clerical occupations indicates a party difference in receptivity of trade unionists over the last several decades. But the instances are so few that nothing should be made of the point. Altogether, in fact, there appears to be no greater movement of workers through trade-union channels to political leadership in Canada than in the United States. Rather, the upward mobility to be observed in politics is the conventional American kind.

Table 3

EDUCATION OF CANADIAN MINISTERS, 1867–1957, BY PARTY

Party	University*	Secondary	Elementary	Uncertain	Total
Liberal	110	13	4	18	145
Conservative†	89	17	2	22	130
Total	199	30	6	40	275

* "University" includes various post-secondary schools along with universities strictly speaking, but most are in the latter category.

† "Conservative" includes ministers listed as "Liberal-Conservatives" in the early years of the Canadian Confederation.

The Canadian educational data are in accord with this pattern. From Table 3 it is apparent that only very few men became ministers without having had the educational advantages enabling them to secure middle-class status first if they had not been born to such status. Mostly this meant university-level education, even more so in recent years than earlier, when secondary education often served the same purpose. But at no time has elementary education alone been represented with any frequency. This would still be a safe statement if the "uncertains" were added to the elementary group. Neither separately nor together is there an increase in numbers in recent years. In other words, there have been no signs of a change in class recruitment like that brought about by British Labour and other European socialist working-class parties. As in the United States, leadership continues to be recruited from the same classes, mainly but not entirely middle and upper classes, from which it has always been recruited.

6. Conclusion

At its simplest, the showing is that the socialist working-class party is distinctive in recruiting a large share of its leaders from the working class and, especially, in recruiting those whose own education and occupation (not just their fathers') were working class. The pattern contrasts with that of non-socialist competitors and with the major parties in the United States and Canada. The latter have a history of recruiting as leaders small but definite numbers of persons of modest origin who had individually achieved middle-class status. In this respect, the North American parties differed from nineteenth-century European parties. Yet it is true that in the twentieth century, comparing the United States and Britain, "the more equalitarian of the two societies" has "fewer members of the lower social strata among its decision-makers than the more rigid and class-bound society."[75]

Should this lead one to say, as have Lipset and Bendix: "Opportunity to enter the political elite through the electoral path is greater in Europe than in America, a fact which stems from the difference in the political-party systems on the two continents"?[76] Since the frequency of entering the political elite from the working class is greater, it might also be said that the "opportunity" is greater, provided the word is meant only in the sense of the special opportunity provided by a working-class party. But the reason for a working-class party in the first place is related to the absence of opportunity for entering the political elite through the older established parties or through any others not distinctively working class. That so many workers did choose to rise politically in a working-class party when it came into existence is an argument for the importance of the opportunity made possible by such a party. The degree of motivation might also be important. Perhaps workers in a society class-conscious enough to produce a working-class party would be more highly motivated to become political leaders than would workers in the United States. In other words, a working-class party may be needed in some societies (but not in others) to provide an outlet for leadership. The opportunity might be largely irrelevant in less stratified societies. Not everywhere do parties have the same kind of function in leadership

[75] Matthews, *The Social Background* . . . , p. 48.
[76] Lipset and Bendix, *op. cit.*, p. 73.

recruitment that Duverger attributes to them as the creators of new elites.[77] In this as in other ways, the socialist working-class party is far from characteristic.

In closing this analysis, it is well to note that the distinctive working-class leadership of socialist parties may hold mainly for the limited period of roughly the first half of the twentieth century. The findings, while by no means indisputable on this point, show that the working-class component of socialist party leadership tended to decline in certain nations after about 1950. This may be another symptom of the diminishing force of working-class politics in Western nations.

[77] Maurice Duverger, *Political Parties*, trans. Barbara and Robert North (New York: John Wiley & Sons, 1954), p. 425.

VIII

Candidate Selection

1. *Patterns*

The selection of party candidates for elective office is a mechanism through which one kind of political recruitment takes place. In Chapter VII, I discussed the extent to which socialist parties recruited a new elite from the working class and the extent to which American parties recruited new and upwardly mobile members of the middle class, but without noting the *methods* of candidate recruitment. At most, it was implied that the methods, especially the degree to which they were open or closed to new social classes, might be related to the distinctive social bases of party recruitment. That implication can now be explored and, along with it, the effect of mass-membership organizations on the selection of candidates. My central theme is that these organizations provide one means, but decidedly not the only one, for selecting candidates in a democratic political system.

Among Western democratic nations, the American method of choosing candidates differs from all of the others. As I have noted in earlier chapters, the United States is alone in so regulating parties as customarily to give those who are not formally organized in a party the opportunity to determine party candidates, consequently providing electoral competition in one-party situations. Everywhere else the selection of party candidates is basically a private affair, even if there are legal regulations. The number of participants varies greatly among nations, localities, and particular parties. A handful of leaders or many dues-paying members may exercise the choice. But, except in the United States, the organized party in some form is conceded the legal power to name candidates. This is true not only in a system like Britain's, where there are no party labels on the ballots and so no legal recognition of the parties' electoral status, but also in a system like West Germany's, where party names are on the ballots (as always with party-list proportional representation) and where, for this and other reasons, parties are subject to legal regulation (particularly the requirement of a secret ballot when choosing candidates). But in West Germany no less than in Britain party organizations choose their own candidates. No effort, legal or otherwise, is made to give non-members a role in candidate selection. Mere party voting, no matter how regular, is rarely, outside of the United States, regarded as a sufficient basis for participation in candidate selection.

Although the American method contrasts with all the others, it is primarily the American-British contrast that I shall explore here, because of the accessibility of material on British and American practices. Some of what is known about candidate selection in other nations will be discussed near the end of the chapter in order to elucidate the difference emerging from the American-British analysis. In focussing on the contrast between American and other methods, the danger is that the difference will be so exaggerated as to conceal certain basic similarities. Primary election is the system generally used in American states, and while widely established it may not be widely effective. Indeed, it is possible that in the United States candidate selection is in all practical respects in the hands of a few party leaders. It may also be so in Europe. There is no certainty about the effects of either American primary laws or European party provisions for dues-paying member participation. An oligarchy may be crucial in both situations. It cannot be assumed that the legal contrast makes for an equally sharp political contrast.

One other qualification is in order. Although the main theme concerns the degree of significance of the contrast already mentioned, there can be other important differences as well. There is no need to be limited to those differences flowing from selection by primary voters as opposed to selection by organized membership. There is also the question of national versus regional or local control. Although the American primary method seems linked to local control, in the sense of party voters in a given constituency having the power of selection, the European method could coincide with control at any level. Allowing an organized membership to select candidates might mean national or regional control, if the particular party were thus centralized, or it might mean control by strictly local organizations. Dealing with central-local relations in candidate selection raises a subject different from the breadth of participation as legally or customarily prescribed. But the subjects are not totally unrelated. It is unlikely, at least, that central control is compatible with selection by rank-and-file party members, even by dues-paying members. The odds are against a membership itself exercising the central control. Rank-and-file members have a better chance to exercise choice if candidate selection is left to the constituency.[1] This assumes a fairly small legislative constituency. The larger the unit the more difficult the arrangements for rank-and-file participation, unless a primary election is held.

2. The United States

What is called candidate selection in Europe is called nomination in the United States. American parties are said to nominate candidates whether they do so in conventions or in primary elections. In the comparative context, however, it is better to adhere to the general and European usage even when discussing American practices. That way the process by which parties label candidates, of principal concern here, can be distinguished from the process by which an individual obtains a place on the ballot with or without a party label. The latter can be dismissed in a few words by saying that it involves individual "nomination" in the sense of meeting legal requirements for a certain number of signatures on a petition, and that in the United States this kind of nomination is necessary for filing both as a candidate in a primary and as an independent non-party candidate in a general election. A similar legal requirement exists in Britain for candidates whether or not they are selected by the organized parties. I shall limit the term "nomination," then, as do the British, to the simple process of meeting this legal requirement. Thus "party nomination" in ordinary American usage becomes "candidate selection" in the present terminology.

The safest point that can be made about American practices of candidate selection is that they vary greatly at governmental levels (national, state, and local), among states, by parties, and between urban and rural areas. This is not merely because legal regulations differ, especially from state to state, but also because the social bases for political activity differ within the United States.

The best known variation is the formal legal one between the convention and the primary method. Although primaries are required for all state and local offices in all but five states, there is also the notable exception of presidential candidate selection by national party conventions. Still, there can be little doubt that the primary has become the standard form, and it is advisable not to make a major point of the variation resulting from the persistence of the convention. In addition to the fact that it *is* the exception, the convention method is not so radically different from the primary method as are both of

[1] Maurice Duverger, *Political Parties*, trans. Barbara and Robert North (New York: John Wiley & Sons, 1954), p. 357.

these American methods from the European. Even the convention is regulated by law in a way that candidate selection in other nations is not. This is clear for the national party conventions, whose delegates are chosen either in primaries or in state and district conventions according to state-prescribed procedures. But the surviving candidate selection by state conventions is also regulated by statute. So, for that matter, were the old conventions in states that subsequently adopted the primary. The long-established American practice had been to prescribe by law the manner of electing delegates to a convention whose selection of candidates conferred the party label appearing on the subsequent election ballot. And the tendency has been to give party voters a role in the election of convention delegates.

Thus, even before the adoption of the primary early in the twentieth century, it was possible for ordinary Republican or Democratic voters to participate in their party's selection at least to the extent of choosing the delegates who did the selecting, even though they held no formal party membership. This is not to say that large numbers of voters ever participated in this way, but the provision of the opportunity to do so is similar to the much more ample provision of the primary method. The basic similarity is apparent in the term "direct," originally and often still used to modify the word "primary." Adopting the "direct primary" meant that voters, previously given only an indirect voice in candidate selections, would now be given direct legal control. The change was considerable, but compared to practices in other democratic nations, it was only a more extreme version of the American tendency to treat parties as public rather than private organizations and to define their "membership" in an open and broad sense.

Blurring the primary-versus-convention distinction in this way is not to retreat from the generalization that American methods of candidate selection vary greatly. It only means that a particular variation is not overwhelmingly important in our comparative context. Neither is the familiar distinction between open and closed primaries. Again, one method, that of the primary open to voters without regard even to registration by party, is simply a more extreme manifestation of the general American tendency to legal openness of candidate selection. How open any of these legal provisions have actually made American candidate selection can be questioned. Here, in fact, there is a substantial variation within the United States. In some places, even with long-established primaries, candidates are selected by a handful of party leaders or even by a party boss. They still have to win the primaries in order to secure the formal party label for the subsequent general election, but they are virtually assured of victory because of the strength of organizational support from the leaders who did the prior selecting. Chicago's Democratic party is the most frequently cited case of this effective organizational control of the selection process, but there are many others. It may still be usual in many large cities. Another related but newer kind of organizational control arises in those few areas where membership parties exist. They may endorse candidates running in primaries and then lend their organizational support, which, while more ideological and less patronage-oriented than the old machine's, can similarly help the endorsed candidates. If regularly effective, this practice could convert American candidate selection to the European model. In practice, membership organizations would do the selecting, provided that their candidates customarily won the primaries, and consequently nothing would be left of the distinctive American method except the *de jure* existence of the primary to confirm the *de facto* choice of an organized party.

The United States is now a long way from this. Not only are membership organizations present in relatively few jurisdictions, but they do not always effectively control their party primaries when they are present. In both California and Wisconsin, where dues-paying organizations are most fully developed, there have been striking and important primary failures by endorsed candidates.[2] It is not clear that the formal endorsement possible in these states is any more effective than informal leadership support for particular candidates. Machine-style support, often formal as well as informal, may be assumed to be more effective, but its importance is likely to diminish as the old-style machines themselves decline in importance.

The fact is that there are large areas of American politics in which candidate selection is not controlled by any regular party process. Especially below the national and state levels, even in many urban places, there is no effective organizational control. Rather, party candidatures are simply assumed by individuals and groups able to win primary elections. In winning, they are likely to seek at least the informal help of those identified as party leaders or workers, but in much the same way as they seek the help of others outside party ranks. There may be no "party" to approve or disapprove of candidatures. As V. O. Key has said of state organizations: "Often party is

---

[2] The Wisconsin failures are noted in Leon D. Epstein, *Politics in Wisconsin* (Madison: University of Wisconsin Press, 1958), pp. 94–95. In California, there was a conspicuous failure in the Democratic senatorial primary of 1964.

in a sense a fiction. No finger can be put on any group or clique that has both the power and the inclination to exercise leadership in party affairs or to speak authoritatively for it in any way."[3] Candidate selection can then become more individualistic, but it may also become more directly influenced by organized interest groups. On the assumption that some kind of organization has advantages over none, then in the absence of a meaningful party organization another organized group would be likely to assume local control.[4] It is widely believed that this has happened in the United States, but the subject has not been recently explored.

In other respects as well, the knowledge of organizational activity in American candidate selection tends to be spotty. There have been a few intensive studies of legislative candidate selection in particular states. The results show a variation from strong party organizational control in Pennsylvania, where old-style machines have been maintained in many places, to considerably less control in Wisconsin and Oregon. Even in Pennsylvania, however, party control was greater in urban than in rural counties. This suggests, as the author of the study indicates, that the political party does not, on its own, set the political style so much as its style is determined by the environment.[5] Not only is the rural environment less hospitable to organizational control of candidate selection; it may be that the entire American environment is less hospitable than other national environments. The United States does not seem to be substituting new-style boss control. The resistance to membership organizations on this score is impressive. Party voters have occasionally rejected candidates endorsed by these organizations; and elected officials themselves have often been notably unenthusiastic about having their candidatures subject to the power of ideologically-minded groups. One important California Democrat has pointedly argued that his party's membership organization, the California Democratic Council, should stick to its issue-agitation and not endorse candidates.[6] The assumption is that issue-oriented partisans would prefer candidates of their own persuasion

[3] V. O. Key, Jr., *American State Politics: An Introduction* (New York, Alfred A. Knopf, 1956), p. 271.

[4] David B. Truman, *The Governmental Process* (New York, Alfred A. Knopf, 1951), p. 291.

[5] Frank J. Sorauf, *Party and Representation* (New York: Atherton Press, 1963), pp. 53, 55, 148. Comparable data have been reported for Indiana in Thomas Watts, "Informal Party Leadership and Its Role in Candidate Selection" (Unpublished paper, 1963).

[6] Jesse Unruh, Speaker of the California Assembly, cited by James Q. Wilson, *The Amateur Democrat* (Chicago: The University of Chicago Press, 1962), p. 296.

and that these candidates would be less appealing to the party's voters.

This is as close as anyone comes to justifying the absence of European-style membership controls of candidate selection. In most American constituencies, there are no membership organizations even to raise the question. In their absence, however, many American party reformers have wished that they existed in order to fill what they regard as a vacuum in political responsibility. The possible ideological zeal of organized partisans has seemed a virtue to reformers who want parties to take clear-cut stands on issues. Especially advantageous has been the likelihood that these partisans would select their own kind as candidates. This would strike a direct blow at the opportunism of individuals who, on their own, are able to secure the party label in primary elections.

The openness of American candidate selection has not been the only target for criticism. The decentralization of the selection process has been complained about just as much. No basis exists for doubting the fact of decentralization. No national party agency controls state or congressional candidacies. And often no state party agency controls the various local candidacies. Decentralization in this respect, as Key has said, is undoubtedly a prime characteristic of American parties.[7] What is less sure is whether the characteristic is peculiarly American, or whether it is not in large measure also true of parties in other nations. That question can be postponed until the examination of British candidate selection. What needs to be stressed here is that American party reformers have been impressed with the disadvantages of decentralization. Specifically, they have thought that nationally cohesive parties were impeded by the selection of congressional candidates according to state or local considerations. This meant that the reformers have been as dissatisfied with local organizational control, by old-fashioned city machines, as by any direct control by primary voters. The machines, oriented to local patronage if not local issues, were just as much non-national interest groups as any other constituent interest group influencing candidate selection through a convention or primary. The preferred alternative was national control. As the leading critic, Schattschneider, wrote with emphasis: "It is necessary for national party leaders *to win power within the party before it is possible to get* power within the government."[8] It is true that he also wanted parties rather than other groups to

[7] V. O. Key, Jr., *Politics, Parties, and Pressure Groups* (New York: Crowell-Collier, 1964), p. 453.

[8] E. E. Schattschneider, *The Struggle for Party Government* (College Park: University of Maryland Press, 1948), p. 36.

control the road to office, but what he meant were national parties. Therefore, Schattschneider would have had to change American candidate selection in two important ways. He would have made it the function of an organized party, or at least of its recognized leaders, and he would have centralized this organized party—that is, nationalized it for congressional candidate selection.

Specifically it is congressional candidacies that have been the main focus of attention for those who would centralize the process. Their concern, beginning especially with Democrats in the late 1930's, has been Senators and Representatives who refused to cast their congressional votes along lines set by their national parties and particularly by their presidential leader. An apparent remedy is to have a national party rather than a state or local party (in convention or primary) select congressional candidates. Or for those concerned for comparable legislative party cohesion at the state level, the remedy is to have a state party rather than a local party do the selecting of candidates.

Just how this remedy would operate, particularly for congressional candidates, has never been clear. No one has seriously proposed that a national party convention or a national party headquarters select congressional candidates. Since the candidates would still have to be elected in their constituencies, it has to be assumed that there be a constituency basis for their selection. But that basis could not be a local party organized around local concerns. Nor could it be an unorganized primary electorate. Neither method would insure candidacies suited to national party purposes. Therefore, there would have to be a new type of constituency organization, probably of dues-paying members, that would be branches of a national party organization. Its members would be oriented to national issues. They would have joined the party because of those issues. And their concern would be to select candidates similarly disposed. The national party headquarters would exercise some degree of control, perhaps through a veto power, over the candidates selected by its branches.

One needs only sketch out so centralized a system to see how radically different it is from existing American methods, which are neither centralized nor strictly party in character. Congressional districts provide the strongest cases in point. They do not even coincide with what there is of organized party structure in the United States. Rather, as one scholar has remarked, congressional districts are in a "relatively autonomous" position with respect to the main lines of attention and communication in the party structure.[9] State and

[9] Avery Leiserson, "National Party Organizations and Congressional Districts," *Western Political Quarterly*, XVI (September, 1963), 639.

county units provide the more usual focus, and these units seldom coincide with the geographic boundaries of congressional constituencies. It is not surprising that a congressman's relations with his district organization are especially unimportant. There is not much organization for him to relate to. Thus, party has been found to rank low as a decision-making pressure on a congressman after his election and to have been relatively unimportant in his original selection as a candidate and in his election campaign.[10]

In analyzing American methods, it is reasonable to put greater emphasis on the general weakness of party control than on its decentralization. The latter may be what party reformers have primarily complained about, but it seems to derive from the general weakness. Decentralization could not be eliminated without a form of stronger party control of candidate selection. This is not to claim that stronger parties would automatically mean centralization. We have had strong local parties that may have worked against centralization. But other forms of strong parties, even at the local level, might make for centralization. At any rate, there is no way for parties to centralize control if they are not organized so as to exercise control at some level. In the United States, there is now relatively little control to centralize.

For this reason, it is hard to accept federalism as a cause for the main characteristics of American candidate selection practices.[11] It is true that, in the federal system, state parties are stronger in most respects than national parties, but many state parties do not appear to control the selection of candidates for congressional or state legislative offices. Nor do local units of state parties regularly exercise this control. The looseness, the individualism, and the interest-group influences characterizing American candidate selection are state as well as national phenomena. They cannot be attributed to federalism.

Much more likely to be mentioned as a cause for the absence of organizational control is the direct primary. In fact, the primary has been blamed for the weakness of American parties generally in the twentieth century. The argument has been powerfully and persuasively advanced in the significant work of V. O. Key. He believed that the adoption of the direct primary, in the decades just after 1900, opened the road to disruptive forces that gradually fractionalized parties, facilitating the growth of cliques and personal attach-

---

[10] *Ibid.,* p. 641.
[11] David B. Truman, "Federalism and the Party System," in Arthur MacMahon (ed.), *Federalism Mature and Emergent* (New York: Columbia University Press, 1955), pp. 115–36.

ments.[12] "The new channels to power," Key wrote, "placed a premium on individualistic politics rather than on the collaborative politics of party."[13] The result, he thought, was the disintegration of statewide party hierarchies under the impact of the influences given free play by the primary. The organizational leaders could not survive the successes of nonorganizational individual candidates in primary elections.[14] There is no point in being a leader, indeed one is not really a leader at all, if one cannot control the selection of candidates.

The argument is cogent, but it is weakened by certain exceptions that Key and everyone else would grant. Not all state organizations have disintegrated to this extent. Some, despite the direct primary, have managed to maintain themselves and their control of candidacies over long periods of time. Eventually they too may be decisively weakened, but the delay has been so substantial that the direct primary could not be readily blamed as the prime cause. This suggests a slightly different explanation and a slightly different role for the direct primary. Less a cause than a symptom, the primary may have been adopted as an expression of an organizational weakness and individualism that was coming to be widely accepted in American candidate selection. Party organizations must already have been losing what strength they had, if so apparently disruptive a method as the direct primary could have been adopted. They opposed its adoption, but usually without success. In the few states where organizations did succeed, at least to the extent of limiting the primary's scope, they were subsequently able to maintain themselves more effectively. But these were states where the parties were especially strong to begin with. And, it is fair to say, these were states where strong parties were more acceptable. On the other hand, in most of the United States what was wanted were weak organizations. Adopting the primary was a way of institutionalizing this desire. Having a primary that opens candidate selection to nonorganizational factors is surely associated with weak parties. And it probably helps to foster such weakness. Still, this is not the same as saying that the primary is a principal cause for the weakness.

By treating the primary as more symptomatic than causal, I do not intend to treat it as less significant. On the contrary, I take the primary to be the most significant manifestation of the nonorganizational style of American candidate selection. It gives expression to

---

[12] Key, Politics, Parties, and Pressure Groups, p. 342.
[13] Key, American State Politics, p. 169.
[14] Ibid., p. 167.

that style even if it is not basically responsible for it. "Nonorganizational" here means non-party, or perhaps even anti-party, organization. Americans have not wanted to leave the selection of their party candidates entirely in the hands of organized partisans. The direct primary became the favored means for trying to give the power of selection to large numbers of voters. It is true that in this attempt, beginning at the turn of the twentieth century, Americans were reacting against old-style political machines and not against European-style membership parties. Specifically, it was the supposed corrupt manipulation of these machines at party conventions that prompted many reformers. But it says something important about the United States that the reformers sought to substitute the direct primary for machine-controlled conventions rather than to substitute a new kind of party organization. Candidate selection was to be turned over to the voters of a party and not to any party membership, however reformed.

This is to return to the primary's particular purpose, in accord with the American popular democratic tradition, of giving voters a meaningful choice in areas where general election victory for the candidates of one party or the other was almost a foregone conclusion. Constituencies dominated by a single party are by no means uniquely American. Rather, as described earlier, they characterize large portions of most democratic nations. Especially when constituencies are as small as are those for the British parliament, the number of safe seats is likely to be very high. Larger European multi-member districts, with election by proportional representation, provide a basis for contest since a given party, even if always the leading party in a multi-member district, would not be expected to win all of the seats when as many as four or five were at stake. But in the single-member district system, one has to expect party strength to be so distributed that there will be many virtually predetermined election results. This has been true in the United States not only for congressional and most state legislative districts, but for entire states over long periods of time. Significantly, it was especially true around 1900 when the direct primary started. Southern states were constantly Democratic, and many northern states, particularly in the upper midwest, were regularly Republican. These were the very states where the direct primary got its start.

The primary, however, has not regularly substituted clear bifactional intra-party politics for the absent inter-party competition. There is even a question about how much electoral competition of any kind occurs in a primary. The evidence varies. One study, focussing on congressional primaries in one-party districts, found numerous contests but few close ones. Of 965 safe-district primaries, only 214 were decided by margins closer than two to one.[15] Although the author's point is that primaries were thus not a competitive alternative, it might also be argued that they provided more competition than there would otherwise have been, at least in the 214 instances. A more substantial case, however, can be made on the basis of a few studies of primary competition in state legislative districts. V. O. Key found many primary contests where the majority party candidate was almost sure to win the general election. Urbanism tended to increase primary competition and incumbency to decrease it. But chiefly, he concluded, the incidence of competition was a function of the given party's likely electoral success.[16] Naturally, the absence of competition in a primary of a party whose chances are hopeless does not adversely affect the argument for the efficacy of the primary. All that is required to establish its efficacy is that there be competition in the winning party's primary.

Key's findings are confirmed by other subsequent studies in Wisconsin and Pennsylvania. The Wisconsin data show that while legislative primaries were not generally contested, they tended to be contested much more in the majority party. Moreover, for the two Wisconsin election years studied most intensively, three-quarters of the contested primaries were decided by margins of less than two to one.[17] Pennsylvania findings are similar, even to the point of showing the same curious dropping off in primary competition in districts where party majority became unusually safe.[18] Thus it is in safe but not the safest districts where primary competition most often occurs.

Critics might grant that primaries provide electoral choice in districts where the general elections provide virtually none, and still remain opposed to primaries. This involves more than their standard argument that primaries fail to provide the kind of meaningful choice that party competition provides for voters who need labels in order to distinguish intelligibly between candidates. That argument is not worth much if there is no likelihood of inter-party competition in a given district. But critics of the primary also believe that its existence, particularly *because* it provides a kind of competition, serves to deter the development of inter-party competition. When an opposition to majority-

---

[15] Julius Turner, "Primary Elections as the Alternative to Party Competition in Safe Districts," *Journal of Politics*, XV (May, 1953), 197–210.

[16] Key, *American State Politics*, p. 179.

[17] Epstein, *op. cit.*, p. 134.

[18] Sorauf, *op. cit.*, p. 114.

party incumbents or to majority-party leadership can appeal to voters through a primary election, what incentive is there to build an alternative party?[19] Certainly, the strictly local incentive would seem to be absent, although not the larger national or state concerns. Of course, the relation of the locality to the larger concerns, especially national ones, would have originally produced the one-party dominance, whether we contemplate the Democratic party in the southern Black Belt, the Republican party in rural New England, the Democratic party in industrial working-class areas, or the Republican party in wealthy suburbs. As long as the relationship making for one-party dominance persists or is thought to persist, it is unlikely that there will be much local incentive for building an alternative party, even if no primary existed. The alternative party would represent what the locality opposed in state or national politics.

Further damage can be done to the argument of those who blame the primary for the absence of inter-party competition. Not only is it likely, as indicated above, that one-party dominance rests on a deeper political basis than that provided by the primary, but it is possible to show that when that basis changes, the primary does not prevent the emergence of two-party competition. Thus, the upper Great Lakes states, long Republican bastions, became two-party competitive by the 1950's. Even in Wisconsin, where the primary was especially well established in its open form, the Democratic party succeeded in replacing an intra-Republican faction as the competitive alternative (after a period of third party effort). At most, therefore, the existence of the primary slowed the process of shifting from intra-party to inter-party competition. But more impressive is the fact that states became two-party states when their socio-political basis came to resemble that of the national parties sufficiently to support both parties. In other words, the primary, while surely a distinctive method of candidate selection, is not easily identified as a cause for perpetuating one-party politics. The United States, it may be stressed again, is not distinctive in having large areas of one-party dominance.

One other aspect of the primary as a distinctive American method needs to be explored. This is its relation to the social bases for recruitment of political leaders. Plainly, the primary is an especially open

[19] The question is especially relevant to open primaries, but it was also relevant to California's former provision for cross-filing by candidates in closed primaries—that is, permitting candidates to run and sometimes win both the Republican and Democratic primaries. The effect of this is described by Winston Crouch *et. al., California Government and Politics* (Englewood Cliffs, N.J.: Prentice-Hall, 1964), pp. 63–64.

selection method in the social as in the political sense. An aspirant for candidacy can appeal directly to the voters. In principle and to some extent in practice, he is not dependent on an established leadership to make him the party candidate. He can get the voters to do that themselves. Or at least he can try. We cannot be sure that "new men," defined as new by class or ethnic origin, would be more likely to be selected in a primary than by another method, but the primary does clearly open the door. An idea of its significance in comparative terms may be understood by imagining the possibility of new men like Keir Hardie and Ramsay MacDonald, standing in a British Liberal party primary, instead of having their candidacies rejected by local Liberal caucuses. With a primary, they could not have been so easily kept from Liberal candidatures by an oligarchical leadership. They might not have won the primaries, but they would have had an open electoral chance. Curiously, Hardie actually requested a wider poll of the local party that rejected him.[20] It is at least possible that the Liberal party, if it had adopted a more open selection method, would have been able to absorb the rising working-class leadership that eventually built the Labour party. But at the time Hardie and MacDonald sought Liberal candidatures, before 1900, the primary was not yet well established even in the United States.

It would be stretching the point, however, to suggest that the adoption of the primary in the United States, just after 1900, was a factor in precluding the rise of an American socialist working-class party.[21] We have no evidence that primaries caused the rise of working-class leaders. On the contrary, as the American data in the previous chapter show, no large or increasing number of political leaders with working-class backgrounds emerged in American politics in the twentieth century. The primary may have facilitated the rise of those with political ambitions, but that says little since the numbers were not at all like those in European socialist parties.

The effect of the primary in Britain or other nations is hard to discuss not only because the primary was never adopted outside the United States, but also because the very idea of the primary implies an openness about party organization and so about candidate selection that is peculiarly American. This openness, it may be argued, is

[20] Henry Pelling, *The Origins of the Labour Party* (London: Macmillan, 1954), p. 68.
[21] The usefulness of primaries in absorbing rising strata of American society into existing parties is suggested in the well-known study of New Haven politics by Robert A. Dahl, *Who Governs?* (New Haven: Yale University Press, 1961), p. 114.

legalistic. In practice, American candidate selection may often be decisively influenced by insiders. Nevertheless, the law prescribing open selection methods reflects an antipathy to oligarchy that is impressive even if not always successfully institutionalized. Oligarchy in candidate selection, accepted as natural for parties in other nations, remains disapproved in American politics.

3. Great Britain

The British method of candidate selection presents a sharp contrast. Its frank acceptance of private party processes is based on the assumption that inter-party electoral competition suffices to meet democratic standards. The right to vote carries with it no right to help a party select its candidates. Dues-paying membership and organizational activism are the requisites for participating in candidate selection. Ordinary voters merely choose between the privately designated party candidates. Conservative voters are presented with a Conservative parliamentary candidate, and Labour voters with a Labour candidate. This is the practical situation.

Legally, the procedure is more open. With no party labels on the general election ballot, individuals who have not been selected as party candidates may stand for Parliament on a theoretically equal basis, provided that they meet the requirements of signed nomination papers and a substantial monetary deposit (£150, returnable if one-eighth or more of the vote is polled). The deposit requirement probably limits the number of non-party candidates, but it does not eliminate them. And neither it nor any other legal requirement prevents an individual candidate from claiming, during his campaign, that he has the support of an organized group calling itself a party and seeking to operate against the major parties. Minor parties persist locally and nationally, and others quickly come and go. In the sight of the law, they are equal with respect to parliamentary candidacies; none have any recognized legal status. Technically, all candidacies are individual whether they are selected by major parties, minor parties, or no parties. The party selection process remains unknown to the law even though, in the case of the major parties, it is politically crucial because voters, in practice, choose between candidates selected and advertised by the major parties.

Leaving the party label off the general election ballot makes it especially easy for British law to ignore the selection process. No governmental decision is ever required to determine which candidate is entitled to a given party label. It is entirely a private party matter. If, for example, two candidates in the same constituency were to claim to represent the Conservative party, perhaps as a result of a division within the local Conservative association, the expectation would be that the Conservative party itself, nationally if not locally, would decide which candidate it wanted to advertise as its own. Since the candidate so designated would have no Conservative label on the ballot, but only in party advertising, the government understandably remains officially aloof from the process by which the candidate obtains his party designation. But this would be possible even if it did allow party labels on the ballot. Regulation of candidate selection certainly does not follow automatically from official recognition of party labels. This is known from the experience of other nations which, while printing party labels on the general election ballots, are much closer to the British government's non-regulation of selection than they are to the American restrictions.

Although British candidate selection is strictly in the hands of the organized party, an important remaining question is what element of the organized party exercises the power. More specifically, are candidates selected by a national or local organization, and what portion of the organized membership participates in the selection process? To say that the process is private or internal is only the beginning of the description.

First, it is useful to recall the structure of British parties within which the selection process takes place. Local organizations, called constituency associations by the Conservatives and divisional parties by Labour, are branches of the national parties. Membership in a branch constitutes membership in the national organization. British trade unionists can be members of the national Labour party without being members of a divisional party, if their unions are affiliated to Labour nationally. But they can also be members locally either by joining individually or by local affiliation through their unions. The local branches of dues-paying members differ from the Conservative associations chiefly in that, like the national Labour party, they are federative in structure. Thus a divisional Labour party consists of various membership units, particularly in wards or in locally affiliated unions, and these membership units send representatives to a general management committee which acts as the constituency association.[22] On the other hand, the Conservative association is itself a membership body meeting annually. It too, however, is broken down into ward units. And, more important, there is an elected executive council, comparable to Labour's general management committee, and this

[22] Robert T. McKenzie, *British Political Parties* (London: William Heinemann, 1963), pp. 538–42.

council functions regularly for the Conservative association. Thus, the two organizations are basically similar in their delegation of authority to elected representative bodies. They are also similar in having officers and executive committees charged with considerable responsibility. These executive committees are much smaller than the broad executive council, on the Conservative side, or the general management committee, on the Labour side. All of this leadership, it must be noted, is chosen locally. The national party or the related national headquarters does not designate local party leaders.

It would still be possible for local parties and their leaders to be directed by national agencies. In the matter of candidate selection, this has sometimes been assumed to be the case, even though the branches are the selection agencies. The assumption developed in part because it had been observed that members of parliament adhere most consistently, even rigidly, to their parliamentary leadership— that is, to their national party. Given this unmistakable and uncontested adherence, it seemed reasonable to believe that the national party somehow controlled the selection of candidates in order to secure properly loyal M.P.s. It was even more plausible when one considered that in both parties there are national agencies designated to play some part in candidate selection. The Conservatives have a central advisory committee maintaining a list of approved persons from which it hopes local associations will draw their candidates, and there is a centrally appointed vice-chairman of the national party who recommends names for inclusion on the list and who consults with local leaders when they seek suggestions. Labour also has a central committee that lists approved prospective candidates, and it has somewhat greater formal powers than the Conservatives for national influence on the actual selection. Although even on the Labour side candidates need not be selected from the approved lists, they usually are. Moreover, Labour has a formal requirement of national endorsement before a locally chosen candidate becomes the party's official choice.[23] And the Conservatives have nearly the equivalent in a national endorsement which in principle could be withheld. Still other apparently centralizing features impinge on candidate selection. There are model procedures established by each national party, and area or regional agents are employed by the national party to advise local parties in using these procedures.

Yet, despite this formidable central apparatus, there is little doubt among close observers of British politics that candidates are really

[23] Austin Ranney, *Pathways to Parliament* (Madison: University of Wisconsin Press, 1965), chap. 5.

selected by the local branches. In practice, there are sharp and meaningful limits to the central party's use of its apparent power. It cannot ordinarily impose its own choice against that of the local party. It can only urge that a particular candidate be adopted, but in doing even this much, great care is exercised to avoid offending the local party. The fact is that the local party is acknowledged to have the selection power. It is really *the* power of the local party organization, and national party advice has to take this into account. As one Conservative national party chairman said to a local organization, "Please be extremely careful about your selection of candidates. As you know, we in Central Office do not interfere with your jealously guarded rights in the matter. We are, if asked, prepared to give advice."[24]

Apart from procedure, the "advice" can take several forms. One is advice against a particular person. It is this which can be backed by the ultimate power of the national party to refuse to approve an objectionable choice. As far as we know, this kind of advice is exceptional. The clearest known cases involve the national Labour party's refusal to approve the candidacies of those believed to be Communists. The second kind of advice is *for* a particular person, notably for an important leader whom the national party wants returned to the House of Commons. There can be no doubt that both national organizations foster such candidacies, but they are not simply imposed on local parties. Even an important party leader, losing or surrendering his seat in one constituency, has to satisfy the local party in another constituency before becoming its candidate. The national party organization can do no more than help. An appearance of dictation is generally thought to affect adversely a candidate's chances.[25]

A third kind of central advice concerns the type of candidate. Here, both through general statements of preference and through lists of approved candidates, there is an opportunity to influence without seeming to dictate. Given the absence of a residential requirement, the opportunity might well be used by national leaders eager to have certain kinds of M.P.s. Conservative leaders have wanted their associations to adopt more trade unionists in winnable seats, and Labour leaders have wanted more young intellectually trained candidates.

[24] The statement is by Lord Hailsham (Quintin Hogg as he had been and became again) in a speech delivered on November 15, 1958 (news release from the Conservative Central Office, London).

[25] Austin Ranney, "Central Guidance of Parliamentary Candidate Selection in Britain" (Paper delivered at Sixth World Congress of the International Political Science Association, Geneva, 1964), p. 4.

But close study of national party efforts leads to the conclusion that central guidance has not achieved these objectives.[26] This is at least *prima facie* evidence of limited national influence on the selection process. On the other hand, it has to be granted that the *prima facie* evidence runs in the other direction with respect to important individual leaders seeking to regain places in Parliament by securing adoption in winnable seats. The fact that many of these leaders do secure seats would indicate the possibility, at least, of national party help.[27]

Altogether, then, candidate selection remains surprisingly local in view of the monolithic parliamentary parties to which successful candidates belong. Clearly the loyalty of M.P.s to their national leadership cannot be attributed to their selection by it.[28] Rather, it has to be said that local selection turns out to be compatible with national party purposes. This is understandable, since the local parties share those purposes. They too want M.P.s loyal to the cause as defined nationally. The point is overwhelmingly important. It means that the absence of central control and the sharp limits on central influence are not politically crucial. The vital effect of centralization is achieved without organizational centralization. It matters relatively little that the candidates adopted locally are not always those preferred by the national party as long as they are prepared to accept the party's parliamentary program and the discipline accompanying it. Some M.P.s, it is true, oppose the parliamentary party position on exceptional occasions, but not primarily because of local considerations. The reasons are almost always national ones, and when they are also such as to put the rebelling M.P.s closer to the opposition party, the local parties as much as national party headquarters are likely to disapprove.

How is it that local parties thus voluntarily serve national party purposes? The brief answer is that the local parties consist of national partisans. More specifically, their leaders are national partisans zealous enough to give time and effort to party activity. And it is this leadership which in practice selects the candidates. Both the Conservatives and Labour, at the local level, have small selection committees that produce short lists of candidates, perhaps three to six, often after screening a considerably larger number of suggestions. The potential candidates on the short list are themselves presented to the larger committees of thirty to a hundred members (the Conservative

---

[26] *Ibid.*, p. 9.
[27] *Ibid.*, p. 7.
[28] Ranney, *Pathways to Parliament*, chaps. 2, 3, 5, and 6.

executive council or the Labour general management committee) where the selection takes place. Decisions by these committees are final, at the local level, in form and in fact on the Labour side. The Conservatives have the additional step of approving the choice at a general membership meeting of the local association, but except in rare instances the step is only a formality.[29]

The types of local leaders dominating the process vary from party to party and from locality to locality. They may, for instance, be trade-union leaders rather than just political activists. But in any case they are relatively few in number. Candidate selection is not the business of the party rank and file. Not only are ordinary party voters outside the process, but so are most of the dues-paying members. These members, as many as a few thousand in some units, do not ordinarily exercise a choice between possible candidates. The choice is made for the members by their local leaders. There is no need—in fact, it is usually regarded as undesirable—for aspirants to campaign before the membership. Candidate selection is meant to be oligarchical.

Oligarchical control is not unlimited. The leaders who choose the candidates are, in this as in other matters, the elected representatives of the local membership. They could be displaced. So much is implicit in any representative arrangement. It can be an effective limitation, despite the ordinary passivity of most dues-paying members. All that is needed is an alternative leadership group prepared to take advantage of an apparently unpopular decision by the existing leadership. There is no reason to think that an alternative leadership, actual or potential, does not exist within local parties. But there are few known instances of its success in revolting against the candidate selected by the machinery of the local party. Perhaps the instances are few because the selection does adequately represent what the local party wants.

"Local party," it must be stressed, cannot mean any wider group than dues-paying members. There is no role whatsoever for ordinary party voters. And even within the dues-paying membership, it is usually impractical to carry an appeal against the leadership beyond the few dues-payers who attend meetings. In local Conservative parties, it is in the general membership meeting, called to ratify the executive council's choice of candidate, that revolt is most feasible if there is going to be any revolt at all. The meeting, attended by several hundred members, may refuse to accept the proposed candi-

---

[29] *Ibid., passim.*

date.[30] This resembles the equally infrequent action of a stockholders' meeting reversing its board of directors. The fact is that attendance at a general association meeting corresponds closely, in general type and even in actual persons, to the composition of the executive council. Activists predominate in both groups, and typically the same thirty or seventy are in control. It is no wonder that there are only scattered instances of associations overruling their executives. No more frequent are instances in which the executive submits more than one name to the general meeting so that the Conservative choice is made directly by the larger group.[31] The executive ordinarily selects the candidate reasonably assumed to represent the association.

The rarest of all the means for appealing from oligarchical candidate selection involves going to the larger portion of dues-paying members than that which attends meetings. Here again the instances are Conservative. They involve rejected aspirants, notably incumbent M.P.s, who want polls of the entire local membership, including as many as a few thousand passive dues-payers as well as the few hundred expected to attend meetings. In one case, a poll was arranged at two convenient locations to allow local Conservative party members to choose between their sitting M.P. and a new candidate preferred by the executive council.[32] In another case, exceptionally well advertised, the poll was conducted by mail so as to obtain the response of an even larger percentage of the membership to the executive's decision to reject the candidacy of the sitting M.P.[33] Both M.P.s lost their appeals to the membership, by only a narrow margin in the second instance. The main point, however, is that such appeals are irregular

[30] Two instances are described by Allen M. Potter, "The English Conservative Constituency Association," *Western Political Quarterly*, IX (June, 1956), 365–66. Another case arose from the complicated troubles of Montgomery Hyde, M.P., with his Belfast North constituency; he was rejected in 1959 by a general meeting of his Ulster Unionist (Conservative) association after the appropriate committee had, by a divided vote, recommended Hyde for readoption. *The Times* (London), March 26, 1959, p. 8.

[31] An example is indicated by Potter, *op. cit.*, p. 366.

[32] This curious event took place prior to the 1950 general election in Hampstead, a prosperous, middle-class, and then safely Conservative London borough. The poll was held because the rejected M.P., a perfectly orthodox Conservative, objected to the local executive's preference for a more important public figure. Details are most fully presented in the *Hampstead and Highgate Express*, July 15, August 5, 12 and 19, 1949.

[33] Here, in Nigel Nicolson's Bournemouth experience, is the most publicly available record of constituency-M.P. relations. The early stages are described by Nicolson himself in *People and Parliament* (London: Weidenfeld and Nicolson, 1958). The climactic poll is reported in *The Times* (London), February 27, 1959, p. 9.

as well as exceptional. The Conservative party no more than the Labour party provides in principle for a membership poll by mail or otherwise. The local leadership can properly refuse to conduct a poll. Only a rejected incumbent would seriously request the membership poll, and even he can be refused.[34] It is true that there are not many refusals, but this is because very few occasions arise. One reason is the infrequency with which sitting M.P.s are rejected by their associations. But this infrequency seems the consequence of satisfaction, on the part of local party leaders, with their originally selected candidate.

In that original selection, at any rate, the process is unmistakably in the hands of a small number of local activists. They are assumed to be entirely appropriate agents for choosing party candidates. The local oligarchy is not suspected of machine-style corruption. Despite recent grumbling about narrow-minded local oligarchs, there are hardly any signs of the American-style progressive or populist beliefs that might lead to a British counterpart of the direct primary. Having party leaders between the voters and their parliamentary candidates is inoffensive. No disposition exists to transfer the power of candidate selection to any larger portion of the electorate than the activists of a local party.

Maintaining this kind of oligarchical control has important national consequences even though the oligarchies are local. What counts is their national orientation, which makes them reliable custodians of the national party cause. They do not have to be controlled by national party headquarters. They serve well enough without being controlled. Significantly it is only in those unusual circumstances when the local parties do not thus serve that there is much chance of interference by central party authorities. Thus it was the public embarrassment over an association's apparent intolerance in rejecting its sitting M.P. that caused Conservative party headquarters to help arrange the mail ballot referred to earlier. And when the national party is even more directly embarrassed by an unsuitable candidate, like a Communist on the Labour side or a fascist on the Conservative side, central interference is overt.[35] But such situations are most exceptional. So, curiously, are the more readily predicted situations of dissident M.P.s selected and supported locally but opposed by their national parties.

[34] Thus Montgomery Hyde (see note 30) was denied his request for a poll despite the very recent Bournemouth precedent.

[35] As it was in the instances of the Labour M.P.s suspected of Communist affiliations in the late 1940's and who were consequently expelled from the Labour Party and so eliminated as potential official party candidates.

The latter requires extended explanation. Surely from time to time there are dissident M.P.s—that is, M.P.s who refuse on a given issue or set of issues to vote with their party in the House of Commons but who seek to remain in the party fold. Do not they become a source of conflict? Are there not local parties that continue to support dissident M.P.s when national headquarters would like to eliminate them or at least pressure them to be loyal? The answer is yes, occasionally, but hardly ever so as to represent a significant local-national conflict. Such a conflict could be significant only if it were over an M.P. whose parliamentary votes or (more likely) abstentions indicated a position closer to that of the opposition than that of his own party. But that almost never arises as the basis for conflict. Local party activists would be at least as troubled as the national party leaders by that kind of disloyalty. Indeed, over the Suez issue of 1956, when there were several defections in the direction of the opposing side, the local parties reacted more strongly against the offending M.P.s than did the national leaders. Local parties do not react so strongly, however, when their M.P.s dissent in the opposite direction—toward the extreme position and away from that of the opposition. Thus, also on the Suez issue before and just after 1956, there were Conservative M.P.s who wanted a stronger imperial policy than did either their government or the opposition Labour party. They were tolerated, sometimes enthusiastically, by local parties sharing their Suez views. But they could also be tolerated, if not enthusiastically, by the national leadership, since they did not threaten to help the opposition to power.[36] The Labour party exhibits the same related phenomena. Its parliamentary rebels sharing Conservative views are reacted against at least as promptly and vigorously by their local parties as by national leadership. But there have been very few such cases. The more numerous Labour rebellions have been by left-wing M.P.s, Bevanite in the early 1950's, claiming to be more socialist than their leaders and so often popular with party activists. The local acceptability of left-wing positions probably helped to impose a limit on the punitive action taken by national leaders, who might have preferred to be rid of at least some of these left-wing dissidents. But getting rid of them was not as imperative as it would have been in the case of M.P.s moving toward the Conservative position.[37] Then the local parties could be counted on willingly to serve the national party pur-

[36] Leon D. Epstein, *British Politics in the Suez Crisis* (Urbana: University of Illinois Press, 1964), chap. 6.

[37] More details are provided by Leon D. Epstein, "Cohesion of British Parliamentary Parties," *American Political Science Review*, L (June, 1956), 371–72.

pose. Because of the predictable reaction, it is understandable that not many M.P.s rebel in this way.

Another sign of local parties acting in accord with the national party is that they tolerate moderate M.P.s even when they might, at a time of intra-party conflict, prefer extremists—left-wing in the Labour case and right-wing in the Conservative. Many constituency Labour parties of Bevanite persuasion regularly re-adopted their anti-Bevanite M.P.s in the early 1950's.[38] Given vacancies, however, it is possible that they did adopt left-wing candidates. But they did not carry their preferences so far as to eliminate right-wing incumbents. Similarly, Conservative associations are not known to have tried to purge moderates in favor of right-wing or imperialist candidates. To do so, except when moderates happened to offend against the parliamentary leadership as well, would tend to destroy the national character of the party. And that is what British local parties do not do. Their chief effect, through candidate selection, is to reinforce the national parties. They accomplish this initially by choosing candidates who support the national leadership, and subsequently (apart from idiosyncratic non-political instances) by re-adopting previously elected candidates unless, as M.P.s, they have been disloyal to the extent of offending against the national party's cause as understood by *both* national and local leaders.

What must still be stressed is that when local parties react against their M.P.s, as they did in the Suez crisis, their action is self-generated, even though it is in the national party's cause. They are not simply told by national party headquarters to get rid of an offending M.P. Indeed, their zeal caused them to be criticized for an intolerance that national leaders did not appear to have. In responding against an M.P., even by the implicit threat to displace him as a candidate if he persisted in rebellion, a local party seems crudely and bluntly to be trying to exact conformity. It is then said to violate the Burkean maxim that an M.P. should be treated as a representative rather than a delegate.[39] But the local party's violation of the maxim is hardly more than another facet of its violation by customary parliamentary party discipline. The chief difference is that the local party can effectively take away the M.P.'s seat while, technically, the parliamentary party can do no more than remove the whip—that is, put the M.P. outside the fold. Also there is thought to be something less offensive about punishment administered by one's own peers than about pun-

[38] David E. Butler, *The British General Election of 1955* (London: Macmillan, 1955), pp. 45–46.
[39] McKenzie, *op. cit.*, pp. 253, 556–57.

ishment handed out by constituents. Altogether it is fair to say that the orthodox British view is that local parties should not exert pressure for conformity. Thus Robert McKenzie, in the 1963 edition of his standard work on British parties, grants that such pressure, previously thought unlikely, was displayed in the exceptional Suez instances, but he argues that this introduces an additional rigidity which the system does not need and ought not to have.[40] McKenzie prefers that M.P.s be allowed a little more freedom to differ with their parliamentary parties than is possible with local party pressure added to national pressure. In other words, he asks that local parties tolerate the same differences the national parties are willing to tolerate.

This does not ask a great deal of the local parties: only that their loyalty to the national cause be no more zealous than that of the national leadership. Almost everyone would agree that local parties usually observe this restraint. However, on the unusual occasions when they do not, it must be said that they are still trying to serve the national party's cause. Perhaps they try to serve it too well. But the point is that no local interest provides the motivation. Whatever national preferences caused the local party to adopt a nationally acceptable candidate in the first place remain the basis for displacing or threatening to displace the candidate when he becomes a parliamentary rebel associated with the policies of the opposing party. The local party oligarchy has a built-in partisanship serving the national party without central dictation.

4. Other Nations

Although British candidate selection is the prime illustration of the strictly internal party method used outside the United States, it does not resemble practices in other Western nations in all respects. The basic similarity, it should be stressed, is significant relative to American methods. But the differences within the large Anglo-European category are worth discussion. Oligarchical control of candidate selection is usual, but it is not always managed in the same way. Leadership groups vary in size and in degree of centralization. Generally, candidates are selected compatibly with national party purposes—notably the cohesion so needed in a parliamentary system—but the compatibility is often achieved through greater central or regional control than that characterizing British practice.

To a considerable extent, greater centralization is associated with a nation's electoral system. By definition, the larger multi-member con-

[40] *Ibid.*, p. 631.

stituency used for proportional representation cannot have as local a control as is possible, at least, for a single-member constituency. In an extreme case like Israel, where the entire nation is treated as a single constituency to elect the whole parliament according to party-list proportional representation, candidates are plainly national candidates selected by national party organizations. Each party submits a list of candidates up to the number to be elected.[41] Not only are the names determined centrally, but so is the order in which the names are listed (and the order in which candidates will be rewarded with seats won by the party). The central authority in each party is its executive committee or comparable inner circle.[42] The fact that this committee tries to provide geographical representation on the party list does not mean any less centralized control over the selection process.

Similar procedures are followed in countries where multi-member constituencies are regional rather than national. Then the centralization itself is likely to be regional. This seems to be true in West Germany insofar as there is central authority in candidate selection. The German situation is complicated by having half the members of the Bundestag elected by proportional representation and half in single-member constituencies. It is the former that produces the centralization of control, at the level of the *Land,* the unit for which lists are submitted (although these lists may subsequently be combined at the federal level). Each *Land* party organization selects its list of candidates to represent the party in competition for votes in that *Land.* For the single-member constituency, on the other hand, each party's constituency organization selects the candidate. Here, interestingly, little effective influence by central party agencies has been exercised.[43] Centralization of candidate selection corresponds only with centralization of electoral units. So in the multi-member constituency of the *Land,* the *Land* party is in control. Nowhere does the national party control selection, although it may influence it, in the British manner.

Because parties in West Germany are indicated on election ballots and because they have certain other forms of legal recognition, they are subject to some governmental regulation. Unlike the British practice, German candidate selection is not left entirely to custom. Regulation, however, is not onerous. And it certainly does not resemble

---

[41] Oscar Kraines, *Government and Politics in Israel* (Boston: Houghton Mifflin, 1961), pp. 84–93.

[42] Lester G. Seligman, *Leadership in a New Nation* (New York: Atherton Press, 1964), p. 67.

[43] Uwe Kitzinger, *German Electoral Politics* (London: Oxford University Press, 1960), p. 64.

American legal efforts to remove control from party organizations. The major German requirement is that selection be by secret ballot at both the constituency and *Land* levels. In the constituencies, the ballot can be either of all (dues-paying) party members or of a selection committee chosen earlier by the membership. At the *Land* level, where the party list for election by proportional representation is selected, the secret ballot is by any duly constituted party body.[44] Thus the law does not require that dues-paying members themselves select the candidates; the task may be delegated to smaller committees or conferences. There is only the possibility of larger numbers of German than British participants in the selection process. Oligarchical decision-making is still acceptable.

Also similar to the British situation is that the non-national character of candidate selection is compatible with the operation of essentially national parliamentary parties. West German local parties, especially those naming candidates in single-member constituencies, exercise their own preferences, but this does not lead to preferences for candidates likely to revolt against the national leadership. Sitting members may be replaced, as were twenty to twenty-four Christian Democrats in 1957, but the local parties make the replacements not for policy reasons, their own or the national party's, but in order to secure abler or more active members.[45] Again, the German experience illustrates that a dues-paying membership, itself or usually through its leadership, tends to select candidates suited to national party purposes. The fact that the membership functions in its own locality or region is simply not divisive.

Scandinavian politics appears to support the same point. In Norway, with party-list proportional representation, parliamentary candidates are selected at the provincial party level by delegates from local organizations. The delegates represent party activists and are activists themselves. National party leaders do not control the selection and their direct influence is limited. Nor do provincial leaders control the locally chosen delegates.[46] District committees in each party select the candidates after receiving suggestions from individual members and from local organizations. Although the process is thus oligarchical, in that the final decision is made in committee, the non-socialist parties of Sweden usually consult the entire dues-paying membership by mail

---

[44] *Ibid.*, pp. 30–31. Also Douglas A. Chalmers, *The Social Democratic Party of Germany* (New Haven: Yale University Press, 1964), pp. 155–56.

[45] Kitzinger, *op. cit.*, pp. 62, 64.

[46] Henry Valen and Daniel Katz, *Political Parties in Norway* (Oslo: Universitetsforlaget, 1964), pp. 21, 57–58, 90–91.

ballot. The Swedish socialists used to go further, requiring that the district slate be submitted to party members. Since 1940, however, this is required only if one-fourth of the delegates so request.[47] The balloting by party members in Sweden is often called a primary, but it should not be confused with the American primary. It is a private party affair, only for dues-paying members. If, however, the mail ballot in a large membership party, like the Swedish Social Democrats, were used at all frequently to overturn selection by delegates, then at least the oligarchical aspect would be substantially qualified. But this does not appear to be the case. Regardless of whether formal membership approval is required, it has been confidently declared that "the constituency party leadership remains on the whole in full control of the final draft of the list of candidates."[48] The important matter here, however, is not so much leadership control as the uncontested fact that the control is local. The approval of the national party has not been required even by Swedish Communists.[49]

Information on candidate selection in other European nations is more fragmentary. But it tends to confirm that local parties do control candidate selection, whether it is said to be oligarchical, as in Sweden, or more popular as in Norway. The Italian Christian Democratic party, despite the formal control of its national directorate, has been found reluctant to purge candidates from local lists even when some candidates failed to pledge primary allegiance to the national party program. The explanation is that party factions with local bases cannot practically be overridden.[50] The Belgian experience is of a different kind but yet consistent with the local control found elsewhere. Belgian parties conduct their own primaries, unregulated by the government, and in this manner allow their dues-paying members (but only such members) to select candidates from lists submitted by party leaders.[51]

On Australia, New Zealand, and Canada, there are findings more

[47] Dankwart A. Rustow, *The Politics of Compromise* (Princeton: Princeton University Press, 1955), pp. 149–50.

[48] Nils Andren, *Modern Swedish Government* (Stockholm: Almqvist & Wiksell, 1961), p. 33.

[49] *Ibid.*

[50] Raphael Zariski, "Intra-Party Conflict in a Dominant Party: The Experience of Italian Christian Democracy," *The Journal of Politics,* XXVII (February, 1965), 22.

[51] Maurice-Pierre Herremans, "Les Candidats," in Camille Deguelle (ed.), *Les Elections Legislatives Belges du 1 Juin 1958* (Brussels: Les Editions de la Librairie Encyclopédique, 1959), pp. 58–66. There is a mention of Irish selection procedure by Basil Chubb, "Ireland 1957," in David E. Butler (ed.), *Elections Abroad* (London: Macmillan, 1959), pp. 195–96.

specifically devoted to candidate selection. These nations, unlike those of continental Europe, use the single-member district. Nevertheless, Australia and New Zealand display somewhat greater central participation in selecting candidates than do Britain or the continental nations. The Australian pattern gives the state but not the national parties a major role. In the Labor party, endorsement by a state party executive is crucial in selecting candidates for both state and national parliaments.[52] There is, in other respects, considerable variation in the Australian Labor party's selection procedure. In some states, it is supposed to be by ballot among dues-paying members, choosing from a list proposed by the executive.[53] At times, this has been a fairly wide-open affair, with facsimile ballots printed in union newspapers and cast in large numbers by union members.[54] At other times, the ballot has hardly been used, even when formally provided.[55] But whether it is used at all or whether delegate conferences have the selection authority, as in some state Labor parties, there remains a considerable element of central—that is, state party executive—authority. In the Liberal party, delegate conferences or conventions are the regular means for candidate selection.[56] The Liberal conferences, like Labor's, are arranged so as to give state party executives a direct authority.[57] The Liberals accomplish this, at least in metropolitan areas, by having constituency conferences include not only delegates from local branches but also a two-fifths minority from the state party executive.[58]

New Zealand's Labour party resembles the Australian parties in its candidate selection. Here, given the non-federal structure of the country, the central element is national rather than state. Selection is made by a committee of six in each constituency—three appointed by the national party executive and three local delegates. While the selection takes place before a meeting of local party members, it is

[52] J. D. B. Miller, *Australian Government and Politics* (London: Gerald Duckworth, 1964), pp. 83–84.

[53] A. A. Calwell, "The Australian Labor Party," in the *Australian Political Party System* (Sydney: Angus and Robertson, for the Australian Institute of Political Science, 1954), pp. 76–77.

[54] James Jupp, *Australian Party Politics* (Melbourne: Melbourne University Press, 1964), pp. 62–64.

[55] D. W. Rawson and S. M. Holtzinger, *Politics in Eden-Monaro* (London: William Heinemann, 1958), p. 57.

[56] Louise Overacker, *The Australian Party System* (New Haven: Yale University Press, 1952), pp. 252–54.

[57] William MacMahon, "The Liberal Party," in the *Australian Political Party System*, p. 45.

[58] Rawson and Holtzinger, *op. cit.*, pp. 57–59.

the committee that makes the choice.[59] Deadlocks on the committee may be resolved by the national executive, but this happened only twice from 1951 to 1960. The same degree of central authority is not present in the National party of New Zealand. Practical authority is in the hands of a local selection committee consisting of delegates somewhat loosely chosen by party branches.[60] It is true that the names considered by the local committees have already been approved by the central authority of the National party, but control remains local.[61] In this respect, the National party of New Zealand more nearly resembles the pattern in Britain and in much of Europe than it does the pattern of centralization established in different ways by the New Zealand Labour party and the Australian parties. As concerns keeping selection within party circles, however, all Australian and New Zealand parties are in the Anglo-European pattern.

Canada comes closer to being an exception on this count, perhaps close enough to be categorized with the United States. Parliamentary candidates are chosen by special party meetings called in each constituency. There seems little doubt that practically final authority is exercised by these local meetings. Approval by the party executive at the provincial level is taken almost for granted.[62] No national party approval is required although national as well as provincial leaders may try to place particular candidates or candidates of a particular type. So far this description sounds like the British practice of local party autonomy. However, a difference arises out of the fact that the major Canadian parties do not usually have regular dues-paying members. Consequently, a constituency party meeting has an ill-defined eligible attendance. Often there may be little interest and only a handful of activists to ratify a choice made by the party leaders. But on occasion the meeting is an open convention in fact as well as name. One of these, held by Liberals in 1962 in an urban constituency, has been carefully described. The local party allowed any local "Liberal supporter" to attend to help choose the party candidate, and 1,200 appeared.[63] It was not quite an American primary

[59] Louise Overacker, "The New Zealand Labor Party," *American Political Science Review*, XLIX (September, 1955), 719–20.

[60] R. M. Chapman, W. K. Jackson, and A. V. Mitchell, *New Zealand Politics in Action* (London: Oxford University Press, 1962), pp. 153–54.

[61] Robert N. Kelson, "The New Zealand National Party," *Political Science*, VI (September, 1954), 26–30.

[62] John Meisel, *The Canadian General Election of 1957* (Toronto: University of Toronto Press, 1962), pp. 120–21.

[63] Howard A. Scarrow, "Nomination and Local Party Organization in Canada: A Case Study," *Western Political Quarterly*, XVII (March, 1964), 55–62.

election, but neither was it merely an organized group of party activists. So large and open a selection meeting was probably unusual, but it is important to note this possibility of involving relatively unattached partisans in candidate selection when there are democratic norms but no regular dues-paying members to exert or delegate authority. The skeletal or strictly electoral party organization, which exists in Canada as in the United States, does not provide a popular or an acceptable oligarchical basis for selecting candidates. Canadian candidate selection, while mainly oligarchical, is sprinkled with the relatively democratic open convention. The convention, incidentally, is in another respect an importation from the United States. Canadians have also adapted something like the American presidential convention in selecting their party leader instead of leaving this task to parliamentary parties in the British manner.

5. *Summary*

The purpose in concluding this analysis with the special Canadian experience is to emphasize the relation of organized membership, or its absence, to candidate selection. Where such membership is standard, it is also standard to leave the candidate selection to the members or their delegates. The selection appears close enough to democratic norms, especially when memberships are large, even if mainly inactive. But where there are virtually no organized members, as in the United States and Canada, there is a tendency to open the selection process. The tendency is much more marked in the United States, because of the direct primary, than in Canada. It might be argued that the absence of the direct primary in Canada means that political parties there need hardly any democratic alternative to candidate-selection by membership organizations. Canadian parties manage without primaries and without membership organizations. Consequently, it is fair to suggest that European parties without mass memberships could select candidates without using, as is most improbable, direct primaries. Indeed, many European conservative parties have thus managed their affairs for years. Socialist parties might have more difficulty in meeting internal conceptions of democratic legitimacy if their leaders chose candidates without being able to claim a mass-based representative role, but it seems reasonable to think that the difficulty could be overcome. In practice, the selection is oligarchical anyway.

On the other hand, it is true that American direct primaries tend to deprive party organizations of one of their characteristic functions, candidate selection, and so to provide one less reason for these organizations to exist. In fact, primaries were intended, by many of their proponents among progressive reformers, to serve exactly that purpose—namely, to weaken the old big-city patronage machines. Whether they actually did so, and whether primaries subsequently checked the growth of non-patronage organizations as well, are debatable propositions. Large and well-organized parties based on patronage or ideology might have ceased being suited to American circumstances in any event. Direct primaries would then be seen mainly as a convenient (and perhaps uniquely American) way of adapting to democratic expectations with respect to candidate selection. Similarly, the European method, as employed by socialists and others eager to meet democratic norms, could be viewed as an adaptation to mass-membership organizations, existing as they did for other purposes.

IX

Counter-Organizational Tendencies

Having argued that the provision of a particular method of candidate selection is insufficient reason for mass-membership organizations to exist, it is possible to examine the relevance of these organizations in other, broader respects. Previously, I have discussed them as responses to European circumstances of the late nineteenth and early twentieth centuries, especially to those circumstances associated with class-conscious socialist movements. I do not consider these parties as normal for Western societies generally, and particularly not for the United States. Neither, however, have American parties so far been presented as normal for European nations. It is still not desirable to assert so radical a view. But I will suggest that certain new political techniques tend to substitute for large-scale membership organizations, and that these techniques appear further advanced in American society than in the European. The fact that they are also present in Europe is nevertheless significant. It means that the theme is not a simple one of Americanization.

In brief, the new techniques involve increasing use, and increasingly skilled use, of the mass media for political and other kinds of communication. Their use is advanced by material developments, especially in television, and by behavioral research in popular responses. Moreover, increased formal education and a pervasive home-centered middle-class life style make for a large audience that is responsive to direct appeals about politics as about everything else. An organizational apparatus intervening between candidates and voters may be less necessary, or at any rate less efficient, as a vote-getting device.

1. Techniques of the Mass Media

Political communication via the mass media, like the media themselves, is not brand-new, but it is not so old as to be coincident with the beginning of democratic government. Television was not widely used until the late 1940's in the United States and the middle and late 1950's in other Western nations. Radio is no more than about two decades older. Only the press can be viewed as a long-established means of mass communication about politics as about other matters. But even the press's history of reaching a large public is less than one hundred years old. Mass literacy in urban societies had first to be achieved, and this did not occur until the late nineteenth century even in the United States. In the post-Civil War decade, the largest circulation a New York newspaper even claimed was the *Herald's* 100,000, and this claim was disputed. As late as 1892, only ten papers in four American cities had circulations over 100,000.[1] Not until 1900 did newspapers in the United States become really big-business enterprises. Circulation made its first massive increases in the 1880's and 1890's, when it began to grow more rapidly than the American urban population itself.[2] At about the same time, newspapers changed from heavy political partisanship to a more independent editorial stance. Editorial opinion itself was less tied to a particular party's cause, and news coverage was more frequently separated from editorial opinion (whether partisan or personal). Accompanying these developments, and perhaps prompting them, was the popularization of news content so as often to de-emphasize serious political news.[3] Inevitably, it now seems, this characterized the growth of mass-circulation newspapers. But this did not mean that newspapers ceased to be a means for communicating political cues to voters. Now they did so to less politically differentiated publics than those which had subscribed to the smaller-circulation partisan papers. In other words, the press became a mass medium in the full sense of the term. A largely although not entirely parallel development occurred in Western Europe slightly later. Italy remains in many ways exceptional in that it continues to have a limited independent press.[4]

Politically, then, parties and candidates during almost all of the twentieth century have had to adjust to at least one powerful means of mass communication. They did not monopolize the means for reaching the mass electorate. Not only have politicians often had to compete against hostile editorial policies, but they have had to try to use newspapers, hostile or otherwise, to reach voters through press

[1] Frank Luther Mott, *American Journalism* (New York: Macmillan, 1962), pp. 403, 546–47.

[2] Alfred McClung Lee, *The Daily Newspaper in America* (New York: Macmillan, 1937), pp. 69–70.

[3] Edwin Emery, *The Press and America* (Englewood Cliffs, N.J.: Prentice-Hall, 1962), p. 317.

[4] Joseph La Palombara, *Interest Groups in Italian Politics* (Princeton: Princeton University Press, 1964), p. 102.

releases and advertisements. American presidents as early as Theodore Roosevelt and Woodrow Wilson sought deliberately to exert the force of their personalities through the Washington press corps. The development of the presidential press conference became a powerful means for political communication, especially for Franklin Roosevelt.[5] Even when political organizations were highly developed, in the manner of the American big-city patronage machine or the European social democratic party, the use of the mass media coexisted with the membership apparatus. But this admission is not at odds with the argument for the increasing relative importance of the mass media. To accept that argument does not require one to make the absurd assumption that mass media have only recently been used for political purposes. Nor does it require the almost equally absurd belief that an increasing use of mass media would eliminate party organization. All that is meant is that contemporary communication techniques, along with the social conditions in which they operate, are now such that the mass media bulk considerably larger among the agencies available for influencing the electorate. It would follow that membership organizations become *relatively* less important, but not that they disappear.

The extent to which techniques of the mass media now perform political functions is likely to be greatest in the United States,[6] both because the American techniques themselves are so highly developed and because of the pre-existing weakness of American party organizations. This latter factor may encourage reliance on the mass media, but it can also be said that the availability of the media renders organizations less necessary. Neither explanation has to be exclusively adopted. Basic social changes can be responsible at once for the decline of organizational methods and for the rise of media communication. The point was made about American politics at least as long ago as an important study of the 1948 election.[7] Voters are supposed to have become less susceptible to appeals for party regularity—traditionally made in door-to-door solicitation—and more susceptible to candidate-centered campaigns conducted through the mass media.[8] There is even a little hard evidence that television is more effective

[5] Elmer E. Cornwell, Jr., *Presidential Leadership of Public Opinion* (Bloomington: Indiana University Press, 1965), pp. 31, 96–97, and 192.

[6] Stanley Kelley, Jr., *Professional Public Relations and Political Power* (Baltimore: Johns Hopkins Press, 1956), pp. 2–4.

[7] Bernard R. Berelson, Paul F. Lazarsfeld, and William N. McPhee, *Voting* (Chicago: The University of Chicago Press, 1954), pp. 178–79.

[8] Frank J. Sorauf, *Political Parties in the American System* (Boston: Little, Brown, 1964), p. 55.

than party organizational work. A careful study of political activity in Detroit has disclosed that citizens heavily exposed to television but without any party contacts show a higher percentage of awareness of voting decisions than any group not similarly exposed even though it had party contacts. As the author concludes, this demonstrates that in one respect television is more functional with respect to the party's electoral task than is the party organization itself.[9] Perhaps newspapers have also been more functional in this way, notably for the better educated citizens known to be oriented more strongly to print than to the broadcast media,[10] but the finding with respect to television seems potentially more significant because of the broader mass impact of the newer medium.

The nature of the impact of television, like that of radio, is affected by the absence of partisan identification. Whether privately owned, as in the United States, or government-owned, as is usual in Europe, radio and television outlets have politically undifferentiated audiences even more completely than do modern mass-circulation newspapers. This does not prevent broadcasting facilities from being used more effectively and more frequently by one party, notably the office-holding party, than by another, but it does mean that, with few exceptions, radio and television stations (or networks) avoid partisan commitments.[11] In this respect, they are at the opposite extreme from the older highly committed newspapers whose readers tended to be self-selected partisans. By broadcasting, politicians can reach uncommitted voters and even opposition voters subject to conversion. It is true, however, that there is nothing radically different, with respect to the nature of the audience, between this opportunity and that provided by advertisements in mass-circulation newspapers, whose partisan identification may be of little significance in its readership appeal.

More sharply different is the directness of appeal that radio and television make possible. The politician can reach voters much more personally than he can through the press. Television, in particular, is the mass equivalent for the now often impractical person-to-person communication. It would be surprising if a television appeal by the candidate in the voter's living-room did not reach more voters than

[9] Samuel J. Eldersveld, *Political Parties: A Behavioral Analysis* (Chicago: Rand McNally, 1964), pp. 517–18.

[10] Leo Bogart, "Newspapers in the Age of Television," *Daedulus*, Winter, 1963, p. 123.

[11] Some of the reasons for this are discussed by D. W. Rawson, *Australia Votes* (Melbourne: Melbourne University Press, 1961), pp. 115–16.

the aggregate of canvassing visits by local party activists. Television seems the more efficient way to reach voters in their homes. Whether this is true or not would be hard to prove from American experience alone.[12] Television appeals in the United States have been developed in the absence of much systematic organizational canvassing. It is in a nation like Britain, where large-scale canvassing existed at the advent of television, that any subsequent diminution of organized membership efforts would establish a stronger *prima facie* case for the superiority of television appeals. So far, however, there is no more than informed observation to support this view from British experience.[13] Even in Fifth Republic France, where television has been assumed to be especially important in establishing President de Gaulle's direct relations with voters, the one available study, limited to an attempted measure of the relation between Gaullist votes and the density of television-set ownership, did not show a positive correlation.[14]

Probably nothing like so definite a connection should ordinarily be expected. What we know in general about the mass communication media indicates that they are much more important in confirming or reinforcing existing opinions than they are in changing opinions.[15] The leading American student of media influence makes this point especially in accepting the findings from voting studies. These studies show little change in voting preferences produced by mass communications *during* political campaigns. But he insists that we do not know whether the use of the media over longer periods between campaigns would not produce significant changes. Over such periods, there might be less of the campaign-time tendency to expose oneself only to communications in accord with one's existing opinions and to avoid what one dislikes.[16] Still, there is little doubt that we should be wary of the easy exaggerations of the influence of mass communi-

---

[12] There is no doubt about the extensive use of the broadcasting media in the United States. Fourteen million dollars were spent for radio and television in the 1960 presidential campaign. Edward C. Dreyer, "Political Party Use of Radio and Television in the 1960 Campaign," *Journal of Broadcasting*, VIII (Summer, 1964), 211–17.

[13] Robert T. McKenzie, *British Political Parties* (London: William Heinemann, 1963), p. 648.

[14] René Remond and Claude Neuschwander, "Télévision et comportement politique," *Révue française de science politique*, XIII (June, 1963), 325–48.

[15] Martin Harrison, "Television and Radio," in D. E. Butler and Anthony King (ed.), *The British General Election of 1964* (London: Macmillan, 1965), chap. x, p. 150.

[16] Joseph T. Klapper, *The Effects of Mass Communication* (New York: Free Press of Glencoe, 1960), pp. 17, 19–20.

cations, television in particular. In any event, one need not claim an overwhelming persuasiveness for any mass medium in order to make the case for its import for political campaigning. All that is required is evidence, abundantly available, of their increasing use relative to other means of attracting votes. After all, there has never been any hard evidence to demonstrate that large numbers of votes were won by the efforts of canvassers to convert the reluctant.

It is not just the mechanism of television or other mass media that may displace functions of mass-membership organizations. The need for professional staffs to manage mass-media campaigns is also in some way at odds with the talents available from party members recruited on the basis of ideology or patronage. Neither amateur activists nor ward-heelers can supply the technical skills needed in much contemporary campaigning. They may, of course, carry on as before in their conventional organizational roles, but these suffer by comparison with the work of the new professionals. The professionals are not just television technicians. Many are specialists in public relations, advertising, opinion surveys, speech-writing, dramatics, substantive governmental policy fields, and even organizational management. Characteristic of all these specialists is that they are generally developed for a variety of nonpolitical business and academic purposes and are simply employed by politicians, especially during election campaigns. As Sorauf has said, parties—meaning apparently the organizational cadres—"find themselves technologically replaced as campaign instruments by new kinds of knowledge and by its open availability."[17]

Party employment of professional staffs between election campaigns is rather small-scale in the United States. Michigan's Republican party appears to be exceptional in having had fifteen professional employees.[18] One or two in each party is more typical. And even national party staffs have been small except at election time. This limited regular staffing, however, drastically understates the professionalization of American politics. Party organizations, especially between elections, are not the place to look for political activity. When one comes to campaign organizations established by individual candidates or parties, professional talent is more evident. True, it is talent only temporarily taken from non-political occupations, but that is all the more reason to view it as a substitute for organizational activism. It

[17] Sorauf, op. cit., p. 109.
[18] Charles E. Schutz, "Bureaucratic Party Organization Through Professional Political Staffing," Midwest Journal of Political Science, VIII (May, 1964), 127–42.

may simply be less expensive to employ outside specialists for a few months than to create party staffs.[19]

In Europe, professional staffs, while also increased at election time, are more likely to be regularly employed by a party headquarters when they are used at all. The British Conservative party is a good case in point. Not only has it had a large number of full-time professional agents at regional and constituency levels, but it has had a sizable central research staff and it has used outside advertising specialists for its pre-campaign as well as campaign publicity. Mass-media advertising was deliberately chosen in preference to party-distributed pamphlets in order to reach beyond the committed.[20] Interestingly, British Labour was slower to adjust to this professional pattern, especially in its public relations activity, but by the 1960's it was following the Conservative lead.[21] In this as in other respects, the party of the right, at least in Europe, appears to adapt most readily to the techniques of the mass media.[22] The UNR, de Gaulle's party, is another illustrative case. In both the 1958 and 1962 elections, it made many innovations—with the largest headquarters staff in France, including public-relations experts, and technicians rather than enthusiasts directing its campaign.[23] As was said of its notably successful 1962 effort: "Systematically utilizing modern organizational techniques, polls, and lots of money, it had the most effective posters, the best electoral propaganda. Essentially a group of political technicians, unencumbered by the traditional ideological burden, it can be all things to all men."[24] Of course, the UNR also had the advantage of its identification with de Gaulle. But the successful personalization of the party's appeal, which such identification made possible, is itself an element in the use of mass-communication techniques.

It is likely that this personalization is a necessary element in the

[19] Winston Crouch *et al.*, *California Government and Politics* (Englewood Cliffs, N.J.: Prentice-Hall, 1964), p. 87.

[20] David E. Butler and Richard Rose, *The British General Election of 1959* (London: Macmillan, 1960), p. 21, and Richard Rose, "Pre-Election Public Relations and Advertising," in Butler and King, *op. cit.*, pp. 372–80.

[21] Richard Rose, "The Professionals of Politics," *New Society*, August 8, 1963, pp. 10–12, and Anthony Howard and Richard West, *The Making of the Prime Minister* (London: Jonathan Cape, 1965), pp. 138–39.

[22] In the Australian election of 1958, however, it was Labour that made the most use of television. Rawson, *op. cit.*, p. 123.

[23] Philip Williams and Martin Harrison, "France 1958," in David E. Butler (ed.), *Elections Abroad* (London: Macmillan, 1959), p. 57.

[24] David B. Goldey, "The French Referendum and Election of 1962: The National Campaigns," *Political Studies*, XI (October, 1963), 307.

full exploitation of the newer techniques. If a Charles de Gaulle is unavailable, a counterpart may have to be developed. This appears to have happened in postwar West Germany, where Chancellor Konrad Adenauer served the purpose for the Christian Democrats. He served so well that the Social Democrats, after failing to compete with a less personal and more traditional reliance on an ideological organization, finally turned in the 1960's to a personality of their own, Willy Brandt, who was thought capable of challenging Adenauer (and his successor) as a popular leader. Brandt's appeal was meant to transcend strictly party concerns. He was to seek voters, not converts.[25] He was to win their confidence, not to mobilize them for a cause. A later and more successful example of personalizing a party's appeal was British Labour's Harold Wilson.

Admittedly, the personalization of political appeal was not used for the first time in the democratic politics of the 1950's and 1960's. Long before the era of Eisenhower, de Gaulle, Adenauer, Macmillan, Kennedy, and Wilson, there were parties that found it expedient to seek votes by emphasizing the personal popularity of their leading candidate (Gladstone or Jackson, for example). Even some large, highly organized parties did so. But what is new is the facility with which this can be done. It is easier, technically if not financially, to make a personality familiar to millions of voters. Television, in particular, is well suited to the purpose. And it is doubtful whether this medium is nearly as well suited to any other political purpose. Certainly, it is not a likely means to convey the ideological politics of mass-membership organizations. Thus, it is not surprising that television campaigning, like all the public-relations politics of which it is part, should be regarded suspiciously by the practitioners of an older style. It is not only the American machine politicians who feel displaced by the new professionalism. Social democratic ideologists are similarly threatened. This helps to explain the resistance by European parties of the left. For example, the British Labour party's campaign of 1959 still used less professional talent than did the Conservative partly because there was strong internal party opposition to the newer techniques.[26] The preference was for policy debates and organizational support—at least until Harold Wilson's day.

Much of the criticism of the newer techniques is centered about the enterprise of public relations as such. The idea of selling candidates like soap is offensive to all those who, in the liberal as well as

[25] Douglas A. Chalmers, *The Social Democratic Party of Germany* (New Haven and London: Yale University Press, 1964), pp. 147–48.

[26] Butler and Rose, *op. cit.*, pp. 25, 27.

socialist political tradition, believe in the capacity of voters to absorb information and to make reasoned decisions on the basis of that information. Using the professional skills of public relations in political communication seems to involve an unusually frank rejection of rationalist assumptions about political behavior. Yet a defender of this use of public relations has claimed that "public relations is issue politics"[27] and so an improvement over American machine politics, at any rate. The point is dubious, in light of the emphasis on "selling" personality and the accompanying simple brevity of issue presentation. The great popularity of frequent spot announcements, as opposed to full-length speeches, adds to one's doubts. On the other hand, it is by no means clear that the methods of public relations, even as adapted to television, really lower the standards of political discourse. It may simply extend that discourse to a portion of the public not otherwise reached at all, at least not by political presentation at a higher level. Citizens previously interested enough to learn about issues may continue to do so. All that would be displaced would be some organizational work, and in the United States this has almost never been regarded as desirable work by champions of rational and informed discourse. In Europe, it is true, social-democratic parties could make a case for the issue-orientation of their organizational politics. But this is to speak of internal party communications among members. It is irrelevant to argue for its superiority over public relations techniques since the latter are intended for an audience beyond the ranks of active party members.

Entirely apart from any inherent merits or demerits of public relations in political communication, there can be little question that they add to the advantages of incumbent office-holders. Governmental publicity is itself a major enterprise, notably in the United States, and its entirely legitimate purpose of informing citizens about programs and policies is bound to provide numerous opportunities for elected officials to appear before the electorate or prospective electorate.[28] In this way, incumbents have access to the mass media at public expense. Any head of government, be he president, prime minister, or chancellor, has the whole period between election campaigns to make use of the new techniques of direct personal appeal. How successful he is in this use depends on his potential for popularity as well as on the techniques themselves.

There does seem to be an uncontested belief that the political ex-

---

[27] Kelley, *op. cit.*, p. 47.
[28] Scott Cutlip, *Effective Public Relations* (Englewood Cliffs, N.J.: Prentice-Hall, 1964), chap. 22.

ploitation of public relations is further advanced in the United States than elsewhere. Certainly the European intellectuals who regard such "advance" as a sign of American depravity would not deny this. They, as well as almost everyone else, accept as a fact that professional public relations, generally as well as politically, is more fully developed in the United States. It may even be that this greater general development itself suffices to account for the greater political use. Accordingly, American political communication via the mass media becomes just one more example of the pervasiveness of commercialism in American life. Since this commercialism is conceded by friend and foe to be growing in Western Europe, whether or not it is called Americanization, then it might be expected that its impact on European politics would grow at the same rate. That this may be happening is suggested by the reported West German, British, and French experiences of recent years. Still, the scale of European political exploitation of the new techniques may not be as rapid as the American or as closely correlated with the use of these techniques for general commercial purposes in Europe. The fact that the nations of Western Europe have mass-membership parties, performing more functions than most twentieth-century American party organizations, may retard, while not entirely preventing, the reliance on the mass media. In other words, the very absence of effective party organizations in the United States, by the 1950's, could have helped to expedite the use of new techniques.

2. *Financing*

The extent to which new mass-media techniques and the mass-membership organization provide alternative campaign means can be observed in party financing. Broadly speaking, there have been two usual ways of raising money. The first is to obtain large sums from a few wealthy contributors, and the second is to collect small sums, conveniently in the form of regular dues, from many people. Some parties have used both methods, but characteristically the first method has been used by business-oriented parties of the right and the second by socialist working-class parties. Indeed, for the latter it has been necessary to have many dues-paying members in order to compete at all. The dues themselves, however, have constituted just one part of the working-class party's counterpart to business financing. The other has been the volunteer activities of a substantial minority of the members. The dues alone may never have been a match for the large contributions available to conservative parties. But, before the expenses of the mass media, a socialist dues-paying party probably did well enough. Duverger believed this to be the case just after World War II, when, he thought, the mass-subscribed parties of the left often spent more than parties of the right.[29] This was at the time when European membership organizations appeared to be at their peak in size and in campaign importance. Conservative parties were, in effect, imitating socialists in an effort to compete.

In retrospect, as already noted, this looks like a temporary phase. Parties of the right did not continue to develop primarily in this way. Instead, as they began to exploit the new techniques of the mass media, they sought the necessarily large sums from heavy contributors. Although the data on party finances are by no means easily available, there is some evidence to support this generalization. Even the British Conservative party, particularly frustrating to scholars (and to its opponents) because it does not publish its accounts, is known to spend a great deal more than what it gets from dues.[30] This holds for constituency units as well as the national party. There is even a question whether it is economical for the Conservatives to collect dues at all.[31] Information on the German Christian Democratic party is more exact. Like the British Conservatives, it sought to build a mass-membership party in the postwar years, but it does not support even its regular apparatus from dues alone. In fact, dues provide no more than one-fifth of the necessary amount, the remainder coming from various kinds of individual and business contributions.[32] Campaign funds are presumably similarly derived. The business contributions came especially through "sponsors associations," really trade associations helping non-socialist parties and the Christian Democrats in particular. In 1957, these associations provided more than half the campaign funds for the four non-socialist parties.[33] Less definite information is available on the Italian Christian Democratic party, but from what little is known there can be no doubt that here too most of the financing of plainly expensive campaigns came from outside a dues-paying membership. In fact, the Italian Christian

[29] Maurice Duverger, *Political Parties*, trans. Barbara and Robert North (New York: John Wiley & Sons, 1954), p. 366.

[30] J. D. Hoffman, *The Conservative Party in Opposition* (London: Mac-Gibbon and Kee, 1964), p. 89.

[31] Martin Harrison, "Britain," in Richard Rose and Arnold J. Heidenheimer (eds.), *Comparative Political Finance*, issue of the *Journal of Politics*, XXV (August, 1963), 668.

[32] Arnold J. Heidenheimer, "German Party Finance: The CDU," *American Political Science Review*, LI (June, 1957), 369–85.

[33] Uwe Kitzinger, *German Electoral Politics* (London: Oxford University Press, 1960), p. 215.

Democrats did not begin to have a substantial membership organization until after their first electoral successes of the late 1940's, and they only later built an organization comparable in numbers to that of their left-wing opponents. Yet they have been able to draw on greater material assets by means of contributions from external private groups—Catholic and business.[34]

The use of the non-party group or association as the source of Christian Democratic contributions in both West Germany and Italy differs from the typical dependence on large individual contributions by American parties (and perhaps by the British Conservatives). But the difference is more procedural than substantive. The sponsors' associations are only intermediaries between the parties and the wealthy but few individual contributors. These contributors are thus not like contributing trade-unionists, a portion of whose union dues go to a political party as though they were party members (as affiliated British trade unionists actually are). Raising money through sponsors' associations, in other words, does not convert a party to anything like a mass-membership base. Rather, its financial sources are distinctively wealthy and generous contributors outside the formal party organization. These contributors may be business corporations as such, rather than the individual owners and managers who do the contributing in the United States, where corporation contributions are illegal. The process is facilitated when businesses are allowed to deduct their contributions as expenses for tax purposes.[35]

The assumption behind this presentation of recent financing practices of European parties of the right is that these practices, admittedly extensions in scale of long-established practices of non-socialist parties, are well adapted to the expensiveness of new campaign techniques. If this is correct, it might follow that established financing methods of mass-membership parties are inadequate to the same purpose. To support this point, there is limited circumstantial evidence from recent European experience. Insofar as socialist parties have relied almost entirely on dues, they have sometimes failed to compete successfully with their better-financed opponents. Admittedly other factors could also account for this failure. But it is persuasive that socialist parties, in seeking electoral successes, have begun to secure funds beyond those coming from dues.

The British Labour party is an interesting case in point because it

[34] Stefano Passigli, "Italy," in Rose and Heidenheimer, *op. cit.*, pp. 727, 732.

[35] Business may also advertise directly, as has British steel in its massive campaigns against nationalization, and count the expenditure as a cost for tax purposes, as it would other advertising.

has traditionally been supported by an unusually large number of dues-payers and was, therefore, well supported by most earlier standards. The large numbers have been accounted for by the indirect affiliation of 5–6 million trade unionists through their national organizations, in addition to as many as a million direct constituency party members. Despite low per-capita dues, the total has been large enough to maintain a modest headquarters and certain related organizational activities between election campaigns. The campaigns themselves almost always needed additional funds, and recently the need rose, without any commensurate increase in the number of dues-payers. Nor was there any likelihood of meeting this need by increasing per-capita charges. Consequently the Labour party turned to other sources. The main one, given the party's continued alienation from most of the business community, has been lump-sum campaign donations from trade unions, over and above their annual payments in the form of dues. Gifts of this kind have come both to the national organization and to some of the constituency branches. Some local Labour parties have also raised money by conducting gambling enterprises, usually football pools, and have thus been able to maintain their own headquarters and a local party agent.[36] But the major change is at national headquarters. Not only has it needed more money for the campaigns, but also for the long pre-campaign periods in which the Conservative opposition invests much of its image-making effort. In a sense, the increased funds have come from the same old source: the trade unions. But the manner of contribution now includes more large lump-sum donations.

A somewhat parallel shift from nearly exclusive reliance on dues-paying contributions may be observed in recent West German Social Democratic experience. With a large dues-paying membership (650,000, more than two and a half times as large as that of the Christian Democrats) but without indirect union members, the post-war German Social Democrats continued to finance two-thirds of their normal non-election-year expenses from dues. But between 1953 and 1961, the party had to depend more and more on additional contributions to finance its campaigns. It is not clear how much more successful the Social Democrats are than British Labour in getting these contributions from business groups (as opposed to unions), but the party's level of expenditures has come nearer to the Christian Democratic level without any substantial increase in income from dues. German Social Democrats are now helped by direct govern-

[36] Martin Harrison, in Rose and Heidenheimer, *op. cit.*, p. 675.

mental subsidies to parties, which have been possible since the 1950's.[37] For left-wing parties, this is one kind of answer to the problem of collecting funds to compete with business-financed groups. The Italian Communists have found another: to conduct profitable commercial activities, especially in trade with Communist nations of Eastern Europe. Thus the Italian Communist party, despite its large membership, finances 80 per cent of its activities from sources other than dues.[38]

It is not impossible for a party of the left, at least of the moderate left, to obtain substantial help from business interests as well as from trade-union sources. The Australian Labor party, for example, receives contributions from retail traders, consumer-goods manufacturers, brewers, and betting establishments. Donations of one kind or another play a large part at both state and federal levels.[39] Perhaps this is a by-product not only of Australian Labor's relative moderation, particularly its non-socialist outlook, but also of the fact that the party has been in power for long periods.

Whatever sources left-wing parties use, there is no doubt that the successful ones do not depend primarily on dues. Even in Israel, where party membership figures are extremely high (as a proportion of the voting population) and where per-capita dues are often high as well, additional financing is required. Partly, this need is a consequence of unusually expensive campaigns. Mapai, the moderate socialist party and Israel's largest single party, receives no more than half of even its regular budget from dues. It has a few individual contributors, besides income from substantial economic enterprises it operates.[40] The latter source, while in some respects distinctively Israeli, is worth noting as one of several ways in which a party of the left can secure funds. Mapai's business enterprises have something in common with those of the Italian Communists and with the British Labour football pools. All of these sources are relatively new ones for parties of the left. But perhaps what is really new is the scale of these left-wing enterprises. There may always have been modest fund-raising by games of chance conducted at party gatherings, but these efforts did not go beyond party members, and they did not raise much money.

[37] Ulrich Duebber and Gerald Braunthal, "West Germany," *ibid.*, p. 784.
[38] Passigli, *ibid.*, pp. 728–29.
[39] Colin J. Hughes, "Australia," *ibid.*, pp. 651–53, and D. W. Rawson and S. M. Holtzinger, *Politics in Eden-Monaro* (London: William Heinemann, 1958), pp. 52–54.
[40] Emanuel Gutman, "Israel," in Rose and Heidenheimer, *op. cit.*, p. 710.

Another way in which parties of the left can seek parity with the more easily financed conservative parties of the business community is through governmental intervention. This takes many forms. American experience indicates that one method—legislation limiting the size of individual contributions and campaign expenditures—is clearly impractical. What these limitations have in common is their ineffectiveness. Similarly useless, at least for parties of the left, is any governmental allowance of income-tax deductions for political, as for charitable, contributions. If these are allowed up to relatively high figures, the only parties likely to benefit are business-oriented ones with the greatest access to heavy contributors. And if the deductions are limited to certain initial amounts (say, the first $10 or $20 contributed), the inducement is limited for all parties. On the other hand, the proposed American legislation of 1966, allowing taxpayers to designate a dollar amount of federal tax for a national party contribution, might benefit Democrats and Republicans. Unquestionably a party of the left would benefit from a direct government subsidy, as is now provided in West Germany. It matters little whether the subsidy is in cash or kind. Free television or radio time, either on government-owned networks or on private networks by government direction, is the most obvious advantage that can be given a party that is poorly financed for purposes of conducting mass-media campaigns. Of course, free broadcast time (as in Britain) does not entirely equalize the situation. It still costs a good deal to produce the appropriate programs as well as to mount related public-relations efforts through other media. Nevertheless the help is substantial. For a party of the left, whose mass-membership base could not conceivably expand sufficiently to support the new campaign styles, government subsidy of this kind is a promising way to compete without a compulsory transformation into a party attractive to the business community.

So far almost nothing has been said about American party financing, which must be studied in a different way. Mainly this is because there has been no major American party with a large dues-paying membership. The closest parallel to European dues-paying has been the not entirely voluntary payment from patronage appointees to their party machines, but this ceased to be characteristic or important even before the recent large increase in campaign costs. For some time, if not always, both Democrats and Republicans and their major candidates have depended heavily on large contributions from relatively few wealthy and interested individuals. It is true that at least since New Deal days there have been times and places in which the Democratic party has had less access than Republicans to such individuals in the business community. But it has always had some access to them, particularly if they belonged to ethnic minorities.

Democrats also compensated for their relative disadvantage by securing very large contributions from national trade unions—$2 million in 1956, for example.[41] These contributions, it should be noted, are not apart from the practice of collecting large amounts of money from a small number of people. While the union money derives from union membership contributions, what is turned over to the Democratic party is lump sums allotted by the union leaders. No regular party dues, direct or indirect, are thus established for union members.

Of greater potential significance, but of less material benefit to American party financing so far, is the new interest in raising money in small amounts from many individual contributors. This interest is in addition to the related sporadic development of dues-paying organizations. Curiously, this interest in small contributors seems to have come at about the same time, during the 1950's, that European parties, even those of the left, realized that they had to extend their financial base beyond the small contributions that came from party dues. But the impetus for both the European and the American developments was the same: the rising cost of campaigning in the era of mass communications. Parties on both continents simply began to look for new sources of financial support. The need in the United States was especially obvious because campaign costs, already high, rapidly rose as a result of the virtually complete commercialization of radio and television time for political as for other purposes. Both the Republican and Democratic parties, especially the latter at the national level and in some states, responded by money-raising efforts on a mass scale. In addition, it may be assumed that individual candidates, always raising a good deal of money for their own campaigns,[42] sought small as well as large contributors.

The best-known party effort was the "Dollars for Democrats" campaign conducted under the auspices of the Democratic National Committee in 1959. The idea was to reach many party voters each of whom would give a few dollars. State organizations, through their local units, collected the money, which was to be divided into equal thirds for national, state, and county organizations. The campaign was not a complete failure, and in certain states like California, where

---

[41] Nicholas Masters, "The Organized Labor Bureaucracy as a Base of Support for the Democratic Party," Law and Contemporary Problems, XXVII (Spring, 1962), 257–58.

[42] Alexander Heard, The Costs of Democracy (Chapel Hill: University of North Carolina Press, 1960), p. 271.

the new amateur kind of party organization existed, there were numerous contributions. Altogether, however, the National Committee received less that $110,000 as its share. This contrasted with the Committee's collection in the same non-election year of more than four times that amount in contributions of $1,000 each. Even at the state level, the "Dollars for Democrats" campaign did not provide a significant portion of organizational income in many places.[43] Generally, the results made it seem doubtful whether enough money was raised to justify the effort.

There is less doubt about the admittedly modest system by which both Democrats and Republicans help maintain their national, and in some instances state, organizations. Under what is known as the sustaining membership plan, individuals contribute from $10 to $100 a year to help keep headquarter staffs in operation between campaigns.[44] A mass appeal, like the "Dollars for Democrats," is not necessary for this program. The total sought is small enough, and the amount asked of each individual is large enough, so that only a modest number of potential contributors has to be reached. Nevertheless, even this number may be larger than the special and narrow group ordinarily conceived as really large contributors to American campaigns. Perhaps American parties have found a new middle or upper-middle layer of financial supporters. Something of this kind seems to have happened during campaign years, especially for the Goldwater Republicans in 1964. Before Goldwater, however, the percentage of Republican and Democratic national committee contributions in amounts of less than $500 rose from 1952 to 1960 (although it was still only 42 per cent of the total).[45] The plain fact is that many Americans can readily afford the middle-sized contributions of fifty to a few hundred dollars, and these amounts are large enough to justify the effort to collect them. Thousands, not millions, of individual contributors are involved, and naturally they are heavily concentrated in the upper income brackets.[46] The Republican opportunity here seems greater than the Democratic, but the minority of Democratic sup-

[43] Bernard C. Hennessy, "Dollars for Democrats, 1959," in Paul Tillett (ed.), Cases in Party Organization (New York: McGraw-Hill, 1963), pp. 161–81.

[44] Cornelius P. Cotter and Bernard C. Hennessy, Politics Without Power (New York: Atherton Press, 1964), p. 175.

[45] Herbert E. Alexander, "Trends in American Political Finance: A Stock-Taking" (Paper delivered at International Political Science Association, Geneva, 1964).

[46] Almost one-third of those with annual family incomes over $10,000 have been reported as contributors in the political campaign of 1956. Heard, op. cit., p. 83.

porters among upper-income families is large enough to provide substantial funds.

Certain characteristics of this type of money-raising should be commented on. It represents a way to secure funds from non-traditional sources without having to develop mass-membership organizations either to furnish dues-payers or door-to-door collectors (as in the "Dollars for Democrats" appeal). A small staff can handle the solicitation work among several thousand, or several hundred thousand, potential contributors. Therefore, despite the broadening of their financial base as a result of new campaign needs, American parties do not really seem headed in the direction of traditional European membership organizations at the very time that these organizations have passed their peak in size and importance. Nowhere do the inherently expensive new campaign techniques lead to a greater dependence on a mass-membership party. If parties pay for these techniques, they must raise larger sums than can be secured in small individual amounts. And if governmental subsidies can be arranged to pay the costs, then there is a financial solution in which a dues-paying membership plays no part one way or the other.

3. The Mass-Membership Response

From what has just been said about the evident irrelevance of mass-membership organizations to the demands, financial and otherwise, of campaigning through the mass media, it might well be expected that organizations of this kind would decline. Even allowing for the considerable inertia that we know helps to maintain social entities after their functional usefulness has diminished, it is likely that there would be signs of lessened vitality if a membership apparatus really did have less to do in winning the elections. How to measure vitality is obviously difficult. So is the problem of relating any lessened vitality to the growth of the alternative campaign techniques. If membership organizations have declined, it may be the result of other more general social causes.

This question of causal relationship may be illustrated from American experience. It is true that this experience is not with mass-membership organizations of the European type. But the closest American parallels, namely the old patronage organizations, have certainly declined. Not only has their vitality diminished, but they have almost disappeared in many places.[47] This has coincided with the development of mass media and public relations campaigning, but it has also coincided with so many other possibly related phenomena (the

[47] As described in New York City by Nathan Glazer and Daniel P. Moynihan, *Beyond the Melting Pot* (Cambridge: M.I.T. Press, 1963), p. 273.

growth of the civil service, for example) that it would be extravagant to insist on a single-factor explanation. All that can reasonably be claimed is that many of the old organizational campaign activities have been taken over by methods requiring cash outlays, in V. O. Key's phrase, instead of precinct workers.[48] The sequence has been such, however, that the new campaign methods may be seen just as readily to have filled a gap caused by the decline of patronage organizations as to have superseded the organizations and so caused their decline.

European mass-membership organizations not only lasted into the middle of the twentieth century in a way that American patronage organizations did not, but appeared to be at their peak in the early 1950's. Any subsequent decline would in fact have coincided with the development of mass-media campaigning in Europe. It would be tempting to assume a connection between the two phenomena. First, however, it is necessary to demonstrate that there has in fact been an organizational decline. Membership figures provide a convenient and plausible basis for measurement. Fewer members probably mean less organizational activity and less interest by leaders and candidates in using the party's organizational activities rather than other campaign techniques.

I have earlier presented data for socialist working-class parties in Britain, France, and West Germany that show substantial decreases in membership in the 1950's. The finding was not uniformly confirmed by the experience of similar parties in other nations, but the British, French, and West German cases seemed especially significant because of the advanced economic and social status of those nations. What I did not make clear was whether these decreases were primarily socialist phenomena rather than general party phenomena. Here and there, however, there has been occasion to note smaller memberships in non-socialist parties after apparent organizational peaks in the early postwar years. The British Conservatives have already been observed to have lost a half-million members from the early 1950's to the early 1960's (from about 2.8 million to about 2.3 million), while the Labour party dropped from about 1 million to about 800,000 direct dues-paying members. This decline was closely observed in microcosm by an intensive study of the changing character of one constituency party.[49]

Other data, not previously noted, are also available to sustain the

[48] V. O. Key, Jr., *Politics, Parties and Pressure Groups* (New York: Crowell-Collier, 1964), p. 494.

[49] Frank Bealey, J. Blondel, and W. P. McCann, *Constituency Politics* (London: Faber and Faber, 1965), pp. 95, 100, 405-7.

case for general party membership losses. The West German experience is notable. Here, in the land where the mass-membership party may be said to have originated, not only the Social Democrats lost members. Party membership generally, at a peak in the immediate postwar years, declined into the 1950's and then leveled off.[50] The Christian Democrats, although they never had as many members as the Social Democrats, fit the picture of relative de-emphasis on membership in the 1950's. By the early 1960's, a scholarly review of German party membership began with the fact that German parties generally were not attractive enough to secure large numbers of members. The authors themselves deplored this fact and attributed it to the parties' failure to fulfill basic needs or material interests. West Germans now saw little reason to join parties, and the ratio of members to voters (one in thirty) was lower than in many other European nations. An important exception was the German Refugee party, whose membership was large relative to its votes, and this was attributed to its close affiliation with various refugee groups and so to its character as an interest group.[51] In other words, a party had to have more than an electoral purpose to attract many members. The point is entirely consistent with the thesis of this book. And it can be accepted without deploring the low-membership appeal of the major German parties as some kind of deficiency peculiar to those parties or to postwar German politics. On the contrary, the recent membership record of the major German parties is similar to that of party organizations in certain other Western nations. Moreover, the exceptionality of the Refugee party's experience really strengthens the point. Not only has that party been untypical because of its interest-group quality, but it has declined as refugees cease to constitute a distinctive group, so that the party is much less important than it was in the 1950's.

Altogether, the German experience supports the broad generalization that large membership organizations are characteristic of parties which are interest groups as well as electoral agencies. The old Social Democratic party, based as it was on a distinctive working-class consciousness, is a much more significant illustration than the Refugee party. As the Social Democrats sought, in ways already observed, to appeal more broadly to the community, their organized membership declined in relative size and relevance.

[50] Wolfgang Hartenstein and Klaus Liepelt, "Party Members and Party Voters in West Germany," in Stein Rokkan (ed.), *Approaches to the Study of Political Participation* (Bergen, Norway: Chr. Michelsens Institut, 1962), p. 46.
[51] *Ibid.*, pp. 45–46.

A different but not contrary interpretation of mass-membership decline has been presented in a study of Norwegian parties. There was a gradual decline in Labor party membership from 1949 through the 1950's, and stagnation in Conservative party membership by the late 1950's after initial postwar growth.[52] In the Labor case, about which there is more information, the decline was especially marked among individual members and in the youth branch of the party. But it was not accompanied by any loss of Labor votes at election time. The author's explanation of membership decline is that loyalties to parties are no longer tenacious enough to cause as many people to join the party for which they vote. In support of this explanation, there is evidence that the bourgeois-socialist distinction between Norwegian parties is now regarded, at least by a sample of university graduates, as mainly historical. There are now, the author believes, strong cross-party loyalties at odds with this historical distinction. Like the scholarly critic of German party membership, the Norwegian author is concerned with what he regards as the ill effects of decreased citizen participation in party organizations, since he believes that such participation is essential to a vital political system. On this point, there is room for argument. Political systems, notably the American, can work without large membership parties. They work differently, to be sure, but no worse or better. In any event, there is little use in deploring the trend toward less membership participation. If the trend results from a simple lessening of ideological fervor or from the diminution of intense interest-group (or class-conscious) politics, it is hardly practical to suggest a restoration of the old style. Parties, it can be argued, successfully win votes, perhaps more votes, with fewer organizational members. The new campaign techniques may at least facilitate the electoral task.

French party membership figures show even sharper declines than those cited for other European nations, but they have to be treated with more caution since the period of diminution coincides with an unusual instability of parties and of the constitutional system in which the parties function. The risk is not entirely avoided by staying within the era of the Fourth Republic, 1946–58. Still, it is worth noting that during those years, every important French party lost members. Even the Communists, by far the largest party in 1958, had dropped to about 500,000 after being over 900,000 in 1946.[53] The

[52] Ulf Torgersen, "The Trend Towards Political Consensus: The Case of Norway," *Approaches to the Study of Political Participation*, pp. 166, 168–69.

[53] E. Drexel Godfrey, Jr., *The Government of France* (New York: Crowell-Collier, 1961), p. 71.

Socialists went from a postwar peak of 354,000 to not much over 50,000 by 1958. The Catholic-oriented MRP declined from 400,000 to under 40,000. The Radicals, not traditionally a mass-membership party, did briefly have 100,000 members under Mendès-France in the middle 1950's, but this was short-lived. The case differs only slightly from the parties whose declines were continuous from the late 1940's until the end of the Fourth Republic. The continuity of membership decline seems characteristic, at least of parties of the left and center, where membership organizations customarily existed in France. The Gaullist party also followed the pattern in some respects. When the party began, in 1947, it emulated the then standard European practice of building a large membership organization. It actually secured 1 million members in 1948, the largest total ever achieved in France, but it dropped to less than half this figure in the next two years and then still more after the 1951 election, when the Gaullist party as such began to disintegrate.[54] Significantly, when Gaullism revived at the inception of the Fifth Republic, its new embodiment, the Union for the New Republic (UNR) did not build a mass-membership organization. Neither did it do so during its electoral success of the early 1960's. Instead, as previously observed, the Gaullists emphasized new campaign techniques to win votes for their leader and for themselves.

While the French experience, with its dramatic declines in party membership, cannot be regarded as typical, its direction is in accord with the British, West German, and Norwegian findings for the same period. Together, the examples are convincing, although it must be granted that certain smaller European nations present exceptions, usually in multi-party situations where parties are also interest groups. The characteristics of another exception really strengthen the argument that advanced social circumstances lead to diminished organizational activity. This is the case of Italy, where mass-membership parties grew during the very period of their decline in the other large nations of Western Europe. The model is provided by the large Communist party organization, whose ability to attract members did not diminish during the 1950's or early 1960's.[55] Furthermore, the Christian Democrats have built a parallel organization which, in 1964, claimed 1.6 million members,[56] somewhat more than the Communists.

[54] Philip M. Williams, *Crisis and Compromise* (London: Longmans Green, 1964), p. 139.
[55] Norman Kogan, *The Government of Italy* (New York: Crowell-Collier, 1962), pp. 55–57.
[56] *The Economist*, CCXI (June 27, 1964), 1462.

Thus, we face the fact that it is in the least advanced nation of Western Europe that mass-membership parties have come to prosper in the 1960's. The explanation is clear. Italy is the one European nation whose social and economic circumstances continue to provide a base for a highly class-conscious workers' party, even a revolutionary one like the Communists, and so for an equally zealous opposition to defend the established order. The ideological or intense interest-group loyalties, which in West Germany or Norway no longer sustain party memberships in the former manner, exist in meaningful form in Italy. There, organized members are useful agents for reaching the electorate. And, more to the present point, Italian campaigning through the mass media is not technically so developed as elsewhere in the West. Nor is such campaigning as suitable to Italian political and social circumstances as it is to nations where individuals are more detached from intense group loyalties and more susceptible to generalized electoral appeals.

That the thriving Italian mass-membership parties are the exception proving the rule is substantiated by the similarity of thriving party organizations in various developing nations. Admittedly the developing nations, exemplified by the newly self-governing African countries, are not as Western or Westernized as Italy. Admittedly too, their politics tend to follow the pattern of a single large party without substantial competitors. But a similarity does exist with respect to the nature of party organization. African parties, as Hodgkin has shown, are often mass-membership organizations generating a wide range of activities besides the simple electoral ones. As such, they seem to fulfill the needs of a not yet modernized society. Significantly, the African mass parties in their initial stages regard European socialist and Communist parties as models.[57] Like them, the new African parties are movements originating in behalf of an alienated majority against a ruling class. The African mass-party organizations have provided both a new elite and a political base for this new elite. In the decolonization period, as Hodgkin indicates, these larger and more fully organized parties superseded the smaller and looser parties of older leadership groups.

There can be no question that organizationally, the mass parties, in Africa as in Europe, represent more developed phenomena. They appear better adapted to certain circumstances—namely, the rise of a new and large class or new and large nation previously deprived (like

[57] Thomas Hodgkin, *African Political Parties* (Harmondsworth: Penguin, 1961), pp. 74–75.

the nineteenth-century European working class) of political power. The fact that the new nation is defined racially rather than by economic class is not crucial with respect to the usefulness of the mass-membership party. It may be crucial, however, in establishing the monopolization of power that seems to follow. With the departure of imperial rulers and the legitimatization of popular support as the basis for government, there is no rival to the party representing the racially defined nation. That is, there is no *party* rival. The military or the tribe is another kind of rival. The mass party claims to be *the* national party much as the successful revolutionary Communist party has claimed, in Eastern Europe, to be *the* party of a working class regarded as synonymous with the nation. Such monopolistic assertions have not been made in Western Europe, where Communists have so far failed to secure power and where socialists, if in power, have been constitutional democrats, not Leninist democrats.

The fact that mass-membership parties are organizationally more developed, whether or not they become monopolistic holders of power, does not mean that they belong to the most modern or advanced societies. The very fact that these parties have become so developed in several African countries ought to be convincing on this point. And, being convincing here, it should be easier to appreciate that the Italian mass parties, larger in the 1960's than those in most other West European nations, represent political responses to what might be called early modernizing forces rather than later advanced ones. One does not have to regard Italy as more like Africa than like Western Europe, but one does have to acknowledge that Italy of the 1960's resembles other West European nations of a few decades earlier. According to this argument, it will follow that Italian mass-membership parties will decline as the nation becomes still more modern. Nothing like this, at least in the near future, can be predicted for mass parties in African or other developing nations. For one thing, monopolistic one-party control tends to perpetuate mass membership, since it is used for non-electoral purposes in the one-party state—be it Communist, fascist, or just nationalistic. Thus even the most advanced modernizing forces would not have the same effect that they have apparently had on competing parties in the West. Italian mass party organization might also escape this effect if the Communists were to achieve power and so make their party the monopolistic ruling agency. Otherwise, however, there is good reason to expect the same decline in mass memberships and in their political significance when party competition becomes less class-conscious and when election campaigns can be fought more effectively through the mass media.

4. *Contagion from the Right?*

While mass-membership organizations are usually believed to have originated and to have developed most fully on the left, there is an almost equally apparent "contagion from the right" in the case of the counterorganizational tendencies described in this chapter. Just as Duverger is correct in regarding working-class parties as the necessitous pioneers in mass political organization—except for the earlier and somewhat different efforts of American patronage machines and of British Liberals and Conservatives after 1867—so it is reasonable to view business-oriented middle-class parties as the pioneers of the new style of campaigning via the mass media. They may not have been pioneers in the sense of always being the first parties to use the mass media. But they appear to have used the media more fully, and then to have been followed in this use by their rivals.

Britain, West Germany, and, to a lesser extent, France all provide evidence of this contagion from the right. More can and will be said about the nature of this experience, but a word ought to be added about how American phenomena fit the theory. There can be little doubt that both American parties, embracing various individual candidacies, have been in the forefront in using heavily financed mass-media campaigns. In fact, they have been identified so closely with such campaigns that their use or approximate use in Europe is often regarded as Americanization. "Madison Avenue" as a synonym for the hard political sell has become an international term. Pioneering in this respect might well have been expected. Not only were the mass media and the accompanying advertising and public relations businesses especially advanced in the United States, but both parties were mainly middle-class cadre-type organizations, at least by the middle of the twentieth century, and they did not have the mass memberships to provide an alternative means of conducting campaigns. The absence of such memberships might have been taken, as it was by Duverger, as a sign of political backwardness,[58] but it was so only in the narrow organizational sense imposed by a European socialist perspective of a given period. The very fact that American parties had only a few members, once patronage organizations had declined, meant that they had special cause to use the mass media in order to convey their electoral messages. By being organizationally backward, or even retrogressive compared to an earlier day, they were well suited to be especially advanced in campaign techniques.

[58] Duverger, *op. cit.*, p. 5.

Perhaps this seems to stand Duverger's theory of "contagion from the left" wrong-side-up. But as Marx said of his conversion of Hegelian idealism to dialectical materialism, what may be done here is to stand Duverger right-side-up. European mass-membership organizations, like the old American patronage machines, were only modern and advanced relative to particular circumstances of time and place. They cease to be so when class-conscious movements lose their significance and when there is a broad public to be reached most efficiently through the mass media. Similarly in these circumstances —which after all have obtained for a longer time in the United States than in Europe—the skeletal or cadre-type American party becomes the modern prototype in certain vital respects. Its leaders are middle-class politicians, and its relatively few organized followers are also likely to be middle class. There are many chiefs, but few Indians.

The closest European parallel is the German Christian Democratic party. Despite its pre-1914 denominational origin and its subsequent anti-Marxist ideology, both of which would tend to produce characteristics of a mass-membership party, the Christian Democratic party did not have a highly developed organization when it came to power in West Germany in 1949.[59] What organization they did build resembled that of the Social Democrats only formally. Membership was smaller. It was predominantly middle class, and it did little for the party. Dues were not regularly collected; they were not needed, in view of large collections from sponsors' associations, and indeed the dues would have been virtually irrelevant.[60] There was even an advantage in having few active members. It made it easier to impose a central and efficient direction of campaigns by professionals.[61] On the other side, among the Social Democrats, the tradition of activist membership was less clearly compatible with broad public communication through the mass media. The old self-sufficient party of the working class provided an alternative campaign means through its internal communication network.[62] This method was even a rival to the broader means of appeal since emphasis on the one meant less attention to the other. And insofar as campaigning was organizational and internal, it was likely to be in traditional working-class terms and thus useless, or even harmful, to the party's need to obtain broader

[59] Arnold J. Heidenheimer, *Adenauer and the CDU* (The Hague: Martinus Nijhoff, 1960), pp. 187–88.

[60] Arnold J. Heidenheimer, *The Governments of Germany* (New York: Crowell-Collier, 1961), p. 71.

[61] Kitzinger, *op. cit.*, pp. 101–2.

[62] Chalmers, *op. cit.*, p. 30.

support.[63] It is understandable that the Social Democrats finally began to change their emphasis to extra-organizational campaigning after 1959, but it is also understandable that they should have been delayed in doing so in a way that the Christian Democrats were not.

Contagion from the right has been a little less marked in the British case, but the general trend in the late 1950's and early 1960's is clear enough. The fact that the British Conservatives, unlike the German Christian Democrats, had first built a large membership organization, whose volunteer campaign work continued to be used, did not mean that they failed to pioneer (in the 1950's) in the employment of new campaign techniques. And the Labour party, a little more slowly than the German Social Democrats but finally in 1966 with great success, followed the Conservative pattern.[64] France's experience is less convincing since, at least into the early 1960's, only the UNR emphasized the new techniques—with great success. More significantly, the UNR's emphasis on new techniques coincided with its deliberate decision not to build a membership organization (such as de Gaulle's RPF had had in the late 1940's).[65] The absence of such an organization has been called the "new-styled pragmatism" of the UNR, and as such it has been criticized as democratically defective because it does not involve a more developed mass organization whose members could participate in policy-making.[66] This criticism, however, presupposes a mass-membership model, probably of the old socialist working-class party, that never existed in the United States and that appears now to be less significant in Europe. For France as for other Western nations, the UNR's skeletal arrangement, with its heavy use of mass media by the leadership, appears much more likely to be imitated.

Having suggested so strongly that organizationally there is a contagion from the right, it is well in conclusion to clarify what is *not* contagious. Certainly I do not conceive every feature of traditional middle-class or business-oriented parties, American or European, as being of contemporary or future relevance to other parties or even to those of the right. A prime example of what is *not* relevant is the decentralization of party authority in state or local units. Much more

[63] *Ibid.*, p. 227.

[64] Mark Abrams, "Party Politics after the End of Ideology," in Erik Allardt and Yrjo Littunen (eds.), *Cleavages, Ideologies and Party Systems* (Helsinki: Academic Bookstore, 1964), pp. 56–63.

[65] Roy Macridis and Bernard E. Brown, *The De Gaulle Republic* (Homewood, Ill.: Dorsey Press, 1960), pp. 294, 297.

[66] Henry W. Ehrmann, "Direct Democracy in France," *American Political Science Review*, LVII (December, 1963), 901.

characteristic of American than European parties, this decentralization shows no sign of becoming widespread. Even in the United States it is subject to diminution as all politics become more national in orientation.[67] It is by no means certain that national party committees or other centralizing agencies will take over from state and local power centers. To do so would require a major shift in party finances. But even without any change from decentralized parties in America, no one would argue that centralized parties elsewhere are at all likely to follow the American pattern in this respect. If there is a trend in any direction, it is surely toward nationalizing and centralizing.

What remain, by way of a contagion from the right, are the strong counterorganizational tendencies represented by the increased use of new campaign techniques involving mass media, professional skills, and large financial contributions. These techniques substitute for mass-membership organization where it does not exist, and they tend to displace certain existing membership functions.

[67] This is the thesis of E. E. Schattschneider, "United States: The Functional Approach to Party Government," in Sigmund Neumann (ed.), *Modern Political Parties* (Chicago: The University of Chicago Press, 1956), pp. 194–218.

X

The Programmatic Function

A programmatic party, or what is more commonly called an ideological party, is undoubtedly associated with mass-membership organization. The relation is reciprocal. In order for a party to attract regular dues-payers and especially the fairly numerous activists at the heart of a dues-paying organization, it is useful if not essential to have a program to which loyalty can be given over a period of time, between elections as well as during campaigns. Particular candidates and policies chosen for particular elections are not enough to sustain regularized volunteer activism, although often they are enough to stimulate campaign exertion on a given occasion. As distinct from public office-seekers and professional staff employees, where material benefits can be sufficient to justify their party work, the volunteer activist associated with a dues-paying organization needs to have a *cause*. It is hard to imagine a mass-membership party without a long-range program. Patronage aside, there is no other basis on which to build a large-scale organization. Belief in a cause is the substitute for material interest.

The reciprocal quality of the relation emerges from the likelihood of a mass membership exerting pressure to maintain or even extend the program that attracted the members, especially the activists, in the first place. While a program seems necessary for a large-scale organization, the organization itself becomes concerned with the continued prominence and purity of the program. As already observed, the membership may thus limit the flexibility of campaign tactics. Being interested in programs, not merely in winning elections for the sake of holding office, volunteer activists may be at odds with the candidates attempting to lead the party. There is a potential conflict here that does not exist in the absence of mass membership. A nonmembership party, even if with a well-developed program (as is unlikely), would have little trouble changing or discarding it when expedient for electoral purposes.

Using the term "programmatic" instead of "ideological" or "doctrinal" does not avoid all of the problems associated with those other terms. "Programmatic" is also imprecise. In the broadest sense, all parties have programs, perhaps even more evidently than all have ideologies or doctrines. The most one can say is that some parties are more programmatic (or more ideological or more doctrinal) than others. American Republicans and Democrats, as well as traditional European socialists, would then all be programmatic in one degree or another. However correct this might be semantically, the usage violates common understanding of the difference between the major parties of the United States, on the one side, and the European socialist parties, at the other extreme of democratic parties. If the difference is only in degree, it is one so great as to justify calling it a difference in kind.

One must distinguish "programmatic" from the ordinary presentation of policies during campaigns. All parties and candidates present policies, and the differences in emphasis do not seem crucial in and of themselves. What is crucial is whether the policies are part of a settled long-range program to which the party is dedicated in definite enough terms to mark it off from rival parties. To be programmatic, then, requires an intellectualized perspective but not necessarily an elaborate or sophisticated one. "Public ownership of the means of production," involving belief in the superiority of socialist to capitalist society, is definite enough. And so is the commitment to private capitalism when such a commitment is in opposition to a major socialist program. Conflicting value systems, each capable of enlisting considerable support in a given society, are thus essential to the existence of major programmatic parties. Nothing so deep-going or so long-lasting is required for opposing party policies at particular times.

On the other hand, opposing party policies are more likely to be prominent when there are also programmatic differences. Parties with programs will emphasize policies more. Policies are simply more important to them. They view their policies not just on the merits, but also as elements in a long-range social purpose.

There remains the question why "programmatic" has been adopted as the descriptive term instead of "ideological" or "doctrinal." Plainly, "programmatic" is less far removed from policy than are the other two words. "Ideology" and "doctrine" convey much more commonly the meaning of value system, fixed long-range purpose, intellectualized position, and even rigidity. But this is the very reason for not using them. They usually convey too much to be readily accepted as terms fitting all of the parties here called programmatic. For example, the British Conservative party denies that it is ideological or doctrinal, and the denial is ordinarily and reasonably taken at face value. The Conservative party has not been ideological or doctrinal in the manner of even the British Labour party or another social democratic party. But the Conservative party has surely been programmatic, if in lesser degree than Labour, in a sense that neither of the major American parties is. Over a long period of time, the Conservatives have stood for a program designed to preserve capitalist society against a perceived major opposition. Activist members have been recruited and retained on this basis just as clearly as Labour has recruited and retained volunteers for its cause. The same can be said for such European parties as the Christian Democrats. To be sure, their programs (like their membership organizations) have often been less highly developed than those of their socialist opponents, but they have had qualities missing on any regularized basis from the major American parties.

"Programmatic" is a less offensive and less emotive term than "ideology" or "doctrine." At least this is true in the United States and probably in Great Britain. While some politically conscious citizens take pride in professing an ideology or a doctrine, there are others for whom the words suggest the alien or rigid. No one appears to feel this way about having a program. It is almost never regarded as a bad thing. Usually it is regarded as a very good thing. So it is for many who seek to preserve mass-membership parties. What they cherish primarily is the program on which the membership is based. The one is necessary for the other, but the program, not the membership as such, is the object of devotion. Similarly, those who want to build new party organizations, in the United States for example, advocate both programs and mass memberships—the former to recruit the latter, and the latter to help maintain the former.

It is this programmatic advocacy that is to be examined in the present chapter. The standpoint for examination is like that adopted for mass-membership organizations: programs fit parties in certain circumstances but not in others, and non-programmatic parties may function more effectively for some purposes. Neither type is treated as necessarily more advanced than the other, although each may belong to a different stage of economic and social development in a given Western society. That point need not be labored since it has already been made repeatedly with respect to organizational phenomena. What I shall emphasize is the difficulty of reconciling programmatic parties with the underlying realities of competitive democratic politics, notably when the competition is between only two parties.

1. *Parties as Policy-Makers*

At the root of the belief in programmatic parties is the assumption that parties should be primarily policy-makers. Of course, as previously acknowledged, there can be party policies, even ones that are carried out after winning an election, without these policies being part of a program in the full sense of that term. But unless the party is programmatic it is most unlikely to be *primarily* a policy-making agency. It may present policies incidental to the business of winning elections—of putting particular candidates into office. But the believer in the programmatic party thinks of policies in a much more important way. They, and the program from which they come, are the party's *raison d'être*. Elections are to be won in order to carry them out.

To fulfill this function, a party must have an apparatus capable of generating policies or at least of deciding what policies are consistent with the party's basic objectives. How much internal democratic procedure the apparatus should include is an open question. It could be entirely consistent with the purpose of a programmatic party to have its policies made by a small group of leaders, assisted by specialized staff, as long as consent was obtained from the organized membership. The resulting policies could still fairly be regarded as those of the membership. There is no need, despite some precedents, to posit an improbable degree of intra-party democracy as a necessity for a programmatic party. Operating within the programmatic commitments of an organized membership involves problems even for a fairly oligarchical policy-making apparatus. It means that policies cannot be merely *ad hoc*, designed variously for marginal voters outside the party. And it means that policies cannot be merely general, designed to please almost everyone in the electorate. They must have a special meaning in terms of the program to which members are presumably devoted and for which they joined the party and continued to work in it.

While obviously it is possible for a party to have a policy-making apparatus for this purpose, it is by no means clear that parties are readily adapted to the purpose. The policy-making function may ill suit certain kinds of parties, or ill suit other functions of parties. Certainly, some parties make virtually no policy and yet are successful by other standards. The Democratic and Republican parties have almost never been regarded as policy-makers. In fact, they have often been criticized for not having policies (except *ad hoc* ones). The criticism has been part and parcel of a broader attack on American parties as nonprogrammatic and unorganized.[1] Yet it can be countered that American parties have been highly successful, as judged not only by the criterion of winning elections (that is, of electing candidates under the given party labels) but also by the criteria of longevity and stability. Their very successes in these respects may owe something to their nonprogrammatic character and the consequent absence of coherent policy-making.

The fact that American parties have not been policy-makers, in the present sense of the term, hardly means that there has been no policy-making for and by government authorities. Even the critics of American parties do not go this far. They grant that policy is made somewhere. Often, they do not like what is made or how it is made, and would like parties to assume more of this burden in order to ensure what they regard as more favorable results. But it is always granted that policies are proposed by some groups and individuals in the political process. Congressmen, interested specialists, pressure groups, particular governmental administrators, and of course the political executives are all operative. In some instances, they may have advantages over parties as policy-makers. Most policy is complex and specialized. Why should one assume that parties, notably programmatic parties, are especially well qualified for the task? Of course, no one assumes that they are in any literal way. Parties are never expected to have large specialized staffs capable of developing policies on a wide variety of complex subjects. To a great and meaningful degree, policies have to originate among outside experts whose full-time non-party occupations provide them with the necessary knowledge and skill. Parties draw on these experts for generally desired policies, as determined by programmatic considerations. Admittedly, however, this can be a great deal more than nonprogrammatic parties find necessary. It does involve party policy-making even though non-party persons are used.

Whether party policy-making in this feasible sense is always appropriate remains in question. Why should parties assume the kind of coherent policy-making that being programmatic implies? In particular, why should parties so function when, as is thought to be the case for American parties, coherent policy-making might interfere with successful electoral campaigns by narrowing political appeals? I do not raise the question cynically. There is an entirely respectable and defensible democratic political theory that holds that the electorate cannot and should not decide policy questions but should de-

[1] James MacGregor Burns, *The Deadlock of Democracy* (Englewood Cliffs, N.J.: Prentice-Hall, 1963), p. 323.

cide only on the office-holders who will do the policy-making.[2] In this perspective, party policies are at best unnecessary and at worst misleading, since the voters to whom parties are appealing should concentrate on the individuals to be elected. Parties still present candidates, who if elected may collectively decide on policy matters as they arise, but the parties do not have to stamp their candidates with settled policy commitments. As Schumpeter so well puts it, a party need not be defined by its principles any more than a department store by its brands.[3] Following this argument, as Anthony Downs has done, leads to a model of party behavior in which policies are viewed as *ad hoc* expedients to attract votes on given occasions.[4] Candidates may also believe in the policies and even do something about enacting them into law after an election. But Downs is surely right in thinking it conceivable that policies be decidedly subordinate to the business of electing individuals to office. Parties can thus operate consistently with a theory of democratic political competition. Indeed, Downs is able to construct a most rational model of election contests in which parties find it to their advantage, for purposes of winning elections, *not* to have fixed policies derived from a program.

Such a model is not only rational in the sense that it permits parties to adopt just those policies designed to win votes, or even to adopt no clear-cut policies at all in order to maximize votes. It is also rational in the sense of serving the purpose of democratic elections insofar as those elections are assumed to be held primarily to elect individuals to office rather than to decide policy questions. The individuals may still be of one party rather than another, and so committed in some degree to work together. They may even be committed to political tendencies loosely distinguishing one party from another. There is evidence of such a policy distinction between American Republican and Democratic county leaders in a state whose politics have not been known for their ideological intensity.[5] But the absence of strong policy commitments by respective party leaders or

[2] Joseph A. Schumpeter, *Capitalism, Socialism, and Democracy* (New York: Harper & Bros., 1950), p. 269.

[3] *Ibid.*, p. 283.

[4] Anthony Downs, *An Economic Theory of Democracy* (New York: Harper, 1957), p. 28.

[5] The state is Ohio. Thomas A. Flinn and Frederick M. Wirt, "Local Party Leaders: Groups of Like Minded Men," *Midwest Journal of Political Science*, IX (February, 1965), 77–98. Similar evidence concerning party leaders, especially at the top echelons, is provided in a study of politics in the Detroit metropolitan area. Samuel J. Eldersveld, *Political Parties: A Behavioral Analysis* (Chicago: Rand McNally, 1964), pp. 184–85.

candidates would not be fatal. Parties could function with little more than their labels to distinguish one set of candidates from another. That is, they can function in this way as long as their goal is primarily to win elections. If, instead, the goal is to enact the policies of a party program, then a large measure of intra-party policy agreement among candidates is necessary.

Basically different conceptions of party functions, it is plain, are involved when policy-making is urged on parties. They are asked to subordinate vote-getting to programmatic considerations. Winning and holding office is a means to another end. Of course, it is always so in the sense that anyone elected to office wants to do something by way of policy-making. But for a party as such primarily to have policy objectives is not so universal. There are certainly instances when a party becomes a vehicle for a particular policy.[6] Yet a party may have its functions defined in such a way as to leave policy-making to the individuals whom it helps elect. The party then appears as a more sharply differentiated political agency—that is, more differentiated by its functions. Instead of combining policy-making with election campaigning, it simply concentrates on the latter.

The customary argument against this kind of differentiation is that it deprives the electorate of a chance to express a preference for a given set of policies. Certainly it is true that the electorate is not given this chance if parties do not stand for coherent programmatic policies. But it is not true that non-programmatic parties are what deprive the electorate of this opportunity. What reason is there to believe that the electorate would have this chance anyway? It is conceivable only under exceptionally simple circumstances. Two, and probably only two, rival parties would have to stand for sharply and clearly opposing policies on a given public question, and a majority of voters would have to make their choice for a given party's candidates on the basis of that question in order for the winning party to have a majority mandate to carry out its policy. While some voters in a party's majority could have other reasons for casting their ballots as they did, they would at least have had to agree with the party on the given policy question in order to be counted as part of the basis for the mandate. Any voter who chose the party's candi-

[6] Such an instance is described in an account of the adoption of imperial preference policies by the British Conservative party in the 1930's. Samuel H. Beer, *British Politics in the Collectivist Age* (New York: Alfred A. Knopf, 1965), p. 301. A less successful effort to convert a party to a fixed policy position is illustrated by the campaign of Mendès-France in the 1950's. Francis De Tarr, *The French Radical Party* (London: Oxford University Press, 1961), pp. 185, 200, 242.

dates despite disagreement with, indifference to, or ignorance of the particular policy is not part of the policy-majority. Clearly, then, an electoral majority for a given policy would be most unlikely. Certainly one could never assume it existed because a given party won a majority of votes for its candidates. Even programmatic parties win some voters who favor only certain of its policies and not others, and perhaps some voters who merely prefer individual candidates or leaders.

The difficulty of reading majority policy preferences into majority electoral victories is well stated by Robert Dahl: "Strictly speaking, all an election reveals is the first preferences of some citizens among the candidates standing for office."[7] These first preferences, Dahl adds, cannot be interpreted as first choices for a specific policy presented by the winning candidates. He is thinking of American national elections, which provide the readiest and most convincing examples of the complexity of voter choice, but much the same phenomenon has been found in a considerably simplified issue-oriented state election.[8] And there is no reason to think that it is much easier to read clear-cut policy preferences into European electoral decisions. Even apart from multi-party situations, which ordinarily do not permit clear majority decisions on policies since they do not allow majority decisions for any one party, the more programmatic European parties do not solve the problem. For example, a British party's majority (rare, incidentally, in terms of popular votes) represents a majority preference for the party generally, and not for particular policies to which it is committed and by no means for its entire program. The party may act as though it has a mandate for all its policies, but it is well understood that not all of its voters really preferred the party's stand on every policy.

The point is so obvious, when one thinks about it, that there seems no need to expound it. Curiously, however, it is lost sight of when parties are urged to be policy-makers. A party's majority, or near majority, of voters is simply assumed to favor the policies which that party has submitted to the voters. This assumption ignores the much more likely contingency of an electoral majority composed of several minorities each interested in a different issue (or personality), plus some hereditary party voters interested in no current issue.[9] But per-

[7] Robert A. Dahl, *A Preface to Democratic Theory* (Chicago: The University of Chicago Press, 1956), p. 125.
[8] Leon D. Epstein, "Electoral Decision and Policy Mandate," *Public Opinion Quarterly*, XXVIII (Winter, 1964), 564–72.
[9] Dahl, *op. cit.*, pp. 131–32.

haps this is not quite the right way to put the position of the believer in majority party government.[10] He could allow for there being
less than a clear majority for each particular policy advanced by a
party, as long as the general party program was, in a broad way, supported by a majority. In that case, one is back to the heart of the argument for a programmatic party. But there is really no way to know
whether the electorate has endorsed a broad program when it votes
for party candidates, any more than there is a way to know whether
the electorate has endorsed particular policies. The one as much as
the other asks too much of an electoral decision.

Without the possibility of demonstrating majority support for
party policy-making, there is no basis for believing in the inherent
superiority of programmatic parties. Surely they are by nature no
more democratic. They may even be less so if their programs are developed by zealous minorities of program-oriented members, and
then pressed in the name of a nonexistent electoral majority. But one
does not have to accept this danger as real in order to appreciate the
point being made here: that parties, given their electoral functions,
are not especially well qualified to assume the additional functions
of policy-making. Issues would have to be unusually simple for parties thus to qualify.[11] Or there would have to be many more than
two parties—enough, in fact, to provide specific policies for each substantial set of preferences within the electorate. This is not an impossible goal, as can be observed from certain multi-party situations,
but it is not what the advocates of majority rule by a given victorious
party have in mind.

American advocates of responsible party government, no less than
European believers in a socialist party, are thinking in terms of majority support for a program. Anything less than that defeats the purpose for which the party exists: to enact its programmatic policies
into law. It is true that there is a special difficulty about the fulfillment of this purpose in the United States. Even apart from the size
and diversity of the nation, there is the problem of bridging two
legislative chambers and the vital executive-legislative separation of
powers. The American constitutional structure provides a hostile en-

[10] E. E. Schattschneider has bluntly stated the majoritarian belief: "If
democracy means anything at all it means that the majority has the right to
organize for the purpose of taking over the government. Party government is
strong because it has behind it the great moral authority of the majority and
the force of a strong traditional belief in majority rule." *Party Government*
(New York: Rinehart, 1942), p. 208.

[11] J. Roland Pennock, "Responsiveness, Responsibility, and Majority Rule,"
American Political Science Review, XLVI (September, 1952), 801–03.

vironment for those who would have office-holders, elected under a given party label, enact a given set of policies. The office-holders enjoying majority status in one branch of government may belong to a different party from those controlling another branch. Or even if the same party controls both legislative chambers and the executive branch, the various office-holders do not have the same incentives to join in support of given policies as do parliamentary party representatives whose continuous support is needed to keep an executive in power. The very difficulty imposed by the American structure, however, helps to explain why reformers have sought to make parties responsible policy-making agencies. They are meant to bridge the gaps in the structure, imposing a unity among elected office-holders in different branches of government. There is something to this appealing idea. Everyone would admit that when elected office-holders of the same party control all branches, and as long as there is intra-party agreement on policies, there is likely to be more concerted policy-making. The problem is not just to win party control of all branches; it is also to obtain intra-party agreement on policies. Recognizing this, the reformers would obtain the agreement by making parties essentially programmatic.

It follows, then, that elected office-holders of a given party would be committed to certain policies. This seems commonplace in a parliamentary system like Britain's, where members of the House of Commons support their party's policies even when they disagree with them, but it is by no means the same in the American system. The individual American congressman may have political incentives working against loyalty to his party's policies. Even if most of his votes are simply responses to his party label, there may be crucial increments which he receives because he is distinguished favorably from his party or from its policies.[12] Purely personal considerations may also be important in his vote-gathering. Not all of the incentives against party policy commitments need be attributed to the separation of powers in order to appreciate the degree to which American legislators customarily regard themselves as independent of party policy commitments. Perhaps there is simply an especially strong element of individuality about the relations between an American representative and his electors. Whatever is responsible for the relative inde-

---

[12] This possibility has been demonstrated for legislators deviating from their parties (in this instance, for the less conservative Republicans and the less liberal Democrats in a state legislature). Duncan MacRae, Jr., "The Role of the State Legislator in Massachusetts," *American Sociological Review*, XIX (April, 1954), 191.

pendence, it is not readily broken down by the apostles of party programmatic regularity. American politicians are not easily convinced that it is uniformly in their interests to have fixed party policy commitments.

There is even a basis for doubting whether policy commitments have much to do one way or the other with the election of American congressmen. From a study of the 1958 congressional election, it is apparent that voters did not know the policy records of their congressman or his party. The overwhelming majority of voters did not reward or punish their congressman because of his acceptance of, or deviation from, the party program. Only 7 per cent of the electorate gave issue-oriented reasons for their vote. Most of the electorate simply voted for the candidate of their preferred party, and the remainder responded to various personal campaign appeals or congressional services.[13] What is most significant among these findings is that the party label evidently commands support in the absence of its identification with definite policies. Perhaps this is expected for the United States. A similar finding is therefore more striking in Great Britain, where parties have been regarded as highly programmatic by comparison. The evidence here is limited to a study of a single constituency in the 1955 general election. It shows, as anticipated, voting intention strongly associated with views as to which party had the best policy for the voter himself. But when party and policy were separated, many voters did not know which party had which policy, and many also disagreed with a particular policy that their preferred party was advocating.[14] As in the American study, it turns out that voters knew their party but not its policies.

This strikes another blow at the theory of electoral representation that underlies the belief in parties as programmatic policy-makers. Party majorities are not mobilized for policies as such. They are mobilized for candidates standing under a given label. The candidates, and party leaders generally, may have policies more or less in common, but the electorate is not voting primarily for those policies. This is not to say that the electorate, especially the voters for the winning party, is against any set of policies of a party leadership. It may be no more than understandably ignorant of this part of the office-holders' business. By virtue of voting for candidates of a given party, there does seem to be a built-in preference for many policies which that

[13] Donald E. Stokes and Warren E. Miller, "Party Government and the Saliency of Congress," *Public Opinion Quarterly*, XXVI (Winter, 1962), 536.

[14] R. S. Milne and H. G. Mackenzie, *Marginal Seat, 1955* (London: Hansard Society, 1958), pp. 117–21.

party's elected office-holders subsequently advance.[15] Party preferences, as Duverger has rightly observed, help to structure public opinion on given issues.[16] But this occurs as readily after as before an election. It has nothing to do with the notion of a party receiving an electoral mandate for specified policies. Voters tend simply to follow their respective parties on policy positions as on other matters.[17] Entirely consistent with this tendency is the finding, from American data, that party leaders have more clearly defined policy commitments than do ordinary party voters.[18]

2. Foreign Policy

So far, the difficulties in the way of programmatic parties have been presented solely in terms of domestic policy-making. The argument, in effect, has been that even in the domestic area a party is unlikely to have genuine majority support for any particular policies. At most, a winning party can claim authorization for the enactment of policies that its office-holders prefer. Whether the voters also prefer those policies is really another matter. Their preference for a given party's candidates cannot be assumed to be synonymous with preferences for specific policies of that party. Only in the most general—and largely meaningless—sense can voters be said to favor party policies. Both the variety of reasons for choosing candidates and ignorance of policy positions make an election of office-holders different from an issue referendum. The difficulties loom still greater

[15] This seems to be the way to reconcile the important findings of V. O. Key with other American survey data analyses. Key, in studying presidential voting behavior from 1936 to 1960, found large numbers whose votes were "instrumental to their policy preferences." These voters, he reported, did appraise governmental actions and did relate their ballots to the appraisal. *The Responsible Electorate* (Cambridge: Harvard University Press, 1966), pp. 58–59.

[16] Maurice Duverger, *Political Parties*, trans. Barbara and Robert North (New York: John Wiley & Sons, 1954), pp. 372, 378.

[17] The clearest evidence of this phenomenon is in Bo Sarlvick, "The Role of Party Identification in Voters' Perception of Political Issues: A Study of Opinion Formation in Swedish Politics 1956–1960" (Mimeographed paper delivered at International Political Science Association, Paris, 1961), pp. 8, 14, 20. See also the American data reported for the influence of party (and party leaders) on the foreign-policy views of party identifiers. V. O. Key, Jr., *Public Opinion and American Democracy* (New York: Alfred A. Knopf, 1961), pp. 450–51.

[18] Herbert McClosky, Paul J. Hoffmann, and Rosemary O'Hara, "Issue Conflict and Consensus Among Party Leaders and Followers," *American Political Science Review*, LIV (June, 1960), 406–27.

when foreign policy is introduced—as it surely ought to be in light of the overwhelming importance of international questions, including defense considerations, in the politics of the lesser as well as the greater powers of the twentieth century.

It must be emphasized that the manner in which foreign policy complicates the projected task of programmatic parties is not solely the result of most voters' ignorance of the subject. It is true that the nature of the subject, removed as it is from the voters' perceived interests and experience, probably makes for even less knowledge than that which exists with respect to most domestic issues. But the difference is only in degree, and this may not be at all large—as between ignorance of monetary policy, for example, and an aspect of foreign policy. The far-away nature of international questions does not put them much further beyond the reach of ordinary voters than many technical domestic questions. Perhaps the need to take the responses of foreign governments into account seems a new dimension, but it is only something else that voters cannot know in much the same way that they cannot know, for other practical reasons, about many subjects. Similarly, the fact that security considerations prevent public access to information on the military aspects of foreign policy is only an additional impediment to what is bound to be limited voter knowledge of any complex subject.

There is a different basis altogether for treating foreign policy as a special source of trouble for those who would have programmatic parties. Foreign policy appears peculiarly unsuitable for discussion in the arena of electoral competition, not just because it is difficult and complex, but mainly because it is seldom such as to allow for genuine alternatives. In this respect, foreign policy does differ in kind from domestic policy. Even if changes in a government's domestic policy are usually only incremental in actual practice, the possibility of a sharply different policy exists. That much is essential if there are to be programmatic parties. Their policies must be different in order to be meaningful even to their respective leaders and activists. But any such significantly different foreign policies threaten the coherence and continuity of the nation's pursuit of its national interests. Radically changing a nation's foreign policy or even threatening to change it in any but the slightest and most gradual way ordinarily appears out of the question. Certainly the idea of asking the electorate to change foreign policy by preferring one party over another is well outside the experience of most democratic nations. International commitments are difficult to change by unilateral action based on an electoral verdict.[19] Party promises to make a change, therefore, are almost certain to be specious if they are made at all.

Still another problem arises. Insofar as a party should develop its own distinctive international program, specious or not, there is no assurance that its electoral appeal here will coincide with its appeal on the domestic front. There is difficulty enough in assuming that separate domestic policies attract all of a party's voters. But they at least may be derived from a common programmatic commitment to certain broad interests—say, the industrial working class or the business community. When foreign policy—not to mention more than one such policy—is added, its appeal may be irrelevant to those interests and so to the party's usual programmatic following. Without any essential programmatic linkage between domestic and foreign policies, despite futile efforts to develop a socialist as opposed to a capitalist foreign policy, the addition of foreign policy to a party program is almost certain to complicate the derivation of an electoral mandate for any policy. How can voters for a given party's candidates be said to favor that party's foreign or domestic policies when both are part of the party's program? If it is unwarranted, as already argued, to assume a voter preference for any policy just because of a preference for a party's candidates, so it is surely unwarranted to assume a preference for both the foreign and domestic policies of such a party.

Historically, parties have tended to develop their programs primarily around domestic issues and so to attract members as well as some voters on the basis of those issues. If a party subsequently adopts foreign-policy positions, its followers would be asked to support positions having little to do with the party's original programmatic attraction. In that event, a party could serve to provide cues for its followers—suggesting partisan reasons for supporting a foreign policy that otherwise there would be no reason to support or oppose. Party identification, in other words, might structure opinion. On occasion, this can be done most dramatically and divisively, as it was in Britain during the Suez crisis of 1956 when Conservative voters and Labour voters were nearly polarized into pro-Suez and anti-Suez blocs by respective party stands.[20] More typically, however, parties serve to strengthen rather than weaken a national consensus on for-

[19] Leon D. Epstein, "Democracy and Foreign Policy," in William N. Chambers and Robert H. Salisbury (eds.), *Democracy Today* (New York: Collier, 1962), pp. 175–77.

[20] Leon D. Epstein, *British Politics in the Suez Crisis* (Urbana: University of Illinois Press, 1964), chap. 7.

eign policy.[21] Disagreement between major parties is often confined to the question of more effective administration of a generally accepted policy.[22] Neither in the United States nor in Britain have democratic parties been found, over any period of time, to generate divergent attitudes on international matters.[23] The Suez case in Britain was decidedly exceptional.

It must be granted that the absence of divergent party positions on foreign policy does not prove that such divergence is impossible in a democratic society. But it does suggest that the factual situation is in accord with the expectation that foreign policy would be ill suited to basic inter-party disagreement. Even an otherwise programmatic party might have good reason to avoid an essentially partisan foreign policy. Here is an area in which, more than others, the electorate is asked to choose individuals to make governmental policy according to their own judgment and only within the confines settled by a broad bipartisan or nonpartisan consensus. At least such a consensus is regarded as essential if a nation is to have an effective foreign policy. The substance of the foreign policy, as opposed to its administration, is not supposed to be open to significant change in response to electoral verdicts. Moreover, wide public support is itself an element of strength for the policy being pursued. Altogether, then, there is an incompatibility between the foreign-policy-making model, now widely accepted in Western democracies, and the programmatic party model.

3. The Interest-Group Relationship

Returning to the domestic ground on which the case for the programmatic party ordinarily rests and apparently must rest, there is a real problem to be solved if we regard parties as ill suited to the task of expressing or mobilizing majority support for a given policy. Given the desideratum of popular expression with respect to domestic affairs at least, how are elected office-holders to be informed of electoral desires? It is admittedly not enough to answer that office-holders are elected to exercise their own judgment. That answer might have to prevail, within broad limits, in foreign affairs, but there is not the same demonstrable need to be satisfied with it in do-

[21] V. O. Key, Jr., *Public Opinion* . . . , p. 446.
[22] Warren E. Miller and Donald E. Stokes, "Constituency Influence in Congress," *American Political Science Review*, LVII (March, 1963), 45–56.
[23] Morris Davis and Sidney Verba, "Party Affiliation and International Opinions in Britain and France, 1947–1956," *Public Opinion Quarterly*, XXIV (Winter, 1960), 590–604; James N. Rosenau, *National Leadership and Foreign Policy* (Princeton: Princeton University Press, 1963), pp. 216–17.

mestic matters. Presumably democratic office-holders, executive or legislative, are expected to regard themselves not only as responsible to the electorate for the policies they adopt, but also as responsive to the wishes of the electorate (or of some portion of it) when adopting policies. The problem is not solved by substituting the individual office-holder for his party as the agent commissioned by the voters to carry out policy. This commission is hardly clearer in the case of a majority election of an individual candidate than it is for several candidates of one party. An election, as has already been stressed, is not a single-issue referendum. The argument against the theory of a majority-party policy mandate is just as applicable against such a policy mandate for a single elected official. The argument rests on the same crucial fact about the function of elections: their majorities are for the individuals elected, not for any of their particular policies, and this is so whether votes are accorded by party label or by personal preference for candidates.

It should be well noted that this argument is about *majority* election, and so when applied to parties it is about those with a *majority* bent. In other words, it concerns two-party competition or something close to it, because only then is there the serious possibility of a party securing a majority verdict on any basis whatsoever. Such a verdict, of course, is essential to the claim that a programmatic party should be responsible for the enactment of policies in the name of its voters. Multi-party competition, on the other hand, virtually rules out this claim. It is true that parties that are engaged in multi-party competition are much more likely to be programmatic. And they are much more likely to be able to interpret their votes as preferences for specific policies and not just for candidates and party labels. The simple fact of minority status, characteristic of parties in a multi-party situation, allows or even encourages a narrowly focussed appeal around more particular policies than a party with a majority can afford. Thus, while even the votes for a minority party cannot be counted absolutely as endorsement for the party's particular policies, they are more likely to provide this endorsement.[24] Especially are they more likely to do so for a party whose orientation is exclusively around one set of issues and interests. The French Peasant party is an example, and not the most extreme. What characterizes such a party is that its very specificity, while allowing a policy mandate, also ensures that this mandate is in behalf of only a minority of the total electorate. The more specific the policy, the smaller the minority.

[24] Downs, *op. cit.*, p. 127; Sarlvick, *op. cit.*, p. 10.

It cannot be denied, however, that multi-party competition provides a partial answer to the question of how office-holders (legislators, at any rate) are to reflect electoral preferences on policy matters. Each of several minority parties can be genuinely programmatic. And each of several may be closely linked to highly differentiated economic, social, or religious organizations. Such is plainly the case in Belgium, where Catholic, Liberal, and Socialist movements are "spiritual families," with separate institutions, and not just political parties.[25] Given multi-party competition, no single party can enact its programmatic policies on its own. Coalition bargains have to be struck, but the function of party representation of policy preferences is served even though parties cannot be policy-makers in the full sense. As we know from the frequency of multi-party competition in Western democracies, this function cannot be dismissed as abnormal or unimportant. On the other hand, it is a function that parties do not perform in the same way when there are only two of them. The degree to which parties are programmatic depends on the system—not just on whether there is two-party or multi-party competition, but also on the social divisions which make for one kind of competition as opposed to another.

There remains the question of how policy preferences are represented when there is two-party competition. The answer is that organized interest groups may then fulfill some of the functions served by parties elsewhere. Interest groups exist to champion particular policies, and they may be highly programmatic. They need not have a majority bent either in a two-party or in a multi-party environment. They do not seek to elect candidates under their own labels, but at most to help candidates favoring policies of concern to their members. To this end, interest groups may even seek to help entire parties whose slates of candidates are sympathetic. But, by definition, interest groups are not parties. At least they are not so in a two-party competitive situation. By way of contrast, interest groups are often, as observed in Chapter III, nearly synonymous with certain of the minority parties in a multi-party situation. The way this point was made in discussing the number of parties was to say that parties in a multi-party situation often perform the functions that are divided between parties and interest groups in a two-party framework. Electing candidates and representing definite policy preferences are simultaneously feasible for minority parties in a way that they are not for

[25] Val R. Lorwin, "Conflict and Compromise in Belgian Politics," (Mimeographed paper delivered at American Political Science Association, Washington, 1965), pp. 1–4.

parties of a majority bent. Two-party competition makes for a sharper functional differentiation between parties and interest groups. Or, in one respect, it affords parties a more limited range of functions.

At the same time, two-party competition imposes a considerable burden on interest groups to perform a representative function concerning policy. Although they have a similar function in any democratic society, the importance of their performance is magnified when the function is more nearly exclusively theirs. This is so despite the fact that interest groups almost always have other functions, often of much greater importance to their members, than the political function of influencing government policy. For example, trade unions bargain collectively with industrial employers and also seek favorable labor legislation; farm organizations conduct informational and insurance programs besides pressing for larger governmental subsidies; trade and professional associations provide various mutual advantages in addition to those secured from government; veterans organizations exist for social purposes as well as for public pensions; and even the more directly political groups, like the numerous ones devoted to various civic causes, may serve their memberships in other ways than by pressing for particular governmental action. Nevertheless, only the political pressure is of concern here.

For this function of representing policy positions, interest groups have great advantages over major political parties. Without the party's need to attract as many as possible of the electorate, an interest group can limit its appeal to those who support its program. The group's dues-paying members, unlike a party's, can be synonymous with its clientele. And it is consistent with its political purpose to remain small and specialized. Intensity of membership commitment may be more useful than a large heterogeneous following. Some interest groups, however, are large and relatively diverse. So-called peak associations, representing all businesses or all unions, are examples. These associations have trouble, somewhat analogous to that of parties, in committing themselves to particular policies about which their respective memberships can be assumed to agree. Consequently, their policies often have to be fairly general, but still it is possible to be more definite than a party which must appeal to an even wider combination. In any event, these peak associations, while attracting considerable attention because of their size, are not necessarily the most important form of interest-group representation.

It is hard to deny that specialized interest groups provide the most suitable means for policy preferences to be represented in a complex modern society. How else are individual citizens—with desires, economic or otherwise, for governmental policies favorable to them or to some cause with which they are identified—going to communicate those desires? It is really no answer to say that they can do so through political parties. They would have to find a way to influence the party, and even for this task an organized group is essential. More important, a major party cannot manage a clear-cut identification with a single set of interests if it is successfully to fulfill its electoral function. Where parties do attempt such an identification, they are rightly regarded as failing to aggregate interests in the manner of a party whose electoral function is more highly differentiated. Italy is a case in point.[26]

An interest group, separated from a party, is a means for influencing governmental office-holders (legislative, executive, and even judicial) directly and indirectly. The techniques include not just the well-known practice of legislative lobbying, but also everything from large-scale public-relations campaigns to administrative consultations. From substantial recent scholarship, we know that these activities, with varying emphases, are carried out in Western democracies generally and not just in the United States. It can even be suggested that the non-encapsulation of interest groups by parties is an advanced stage of development.[27]

Naturally, interest-group activity has received more attention in the United States, perhaps because so much of the activity takes place in the relatively open circumstance afforded by non-disciplined legislative parties. Their discovery by scholars owes something to the relatively larger development of American political science, and their acceptance as useful rather than wicked may also be attributed to the particular nature of American political science—especially to the pluralism characterizing so much recent scholarship. Yet even in the United States some scholars have been reluctant to concede the legitimacy of representation through interest groups. One reason for this reluctance can be traced to the tendency of the responsible-party school to think of interest groups as rivals that parties must overcome. But there is such rivalry only if parties are conceived as policy-makers. If, instead, they are seen in more exclusively electoral terms, as mobilizers of majorities for candidates and not directly for policies,

[26] Joseph La Palombara, *Interest Groups in Italian Politics* (Princeton: Princeton University Press, 1964), pp. 84–85.
[27] Lester G. Seligman, *Leadership in a New Nation* (New York: Atherton Press, 1964), p. 100.

then the function of interest groups in promoting policies is no more than a sensible division of labor that frees parties for the task of mobilizing majorities to elect candidates.[28]

Now it is well known that even in this circumstance political parties find it expedient to adopt various policies. American parties, despite their non-programmatic character, still have platforms promising a legislative and executive output. The platforms themselves are part of the effort to mobilize majorities, as well as to provide inexpensive solace to various party supporters. The policies of the platforms are instrumental for the purpose of winning elections. The parties are not primarily trying to promote the policies. That remains the task of interest groups. It is to win the support of the interest groups, or their members' support, that parties adopt policy positions. Thus a prospective majority of voters may be partly composed of several separate minorities attracted by separable policy commitments. But this is not how a programmatic party is supposed to operate. The instrumentalist view not only leaves the development and promotion of policy to interest groups, but it also makes no claim for the kind of majoritarian mandate for a given policy that a programmatic party makes when it wins an election. The significance of this difference can be best seen in the sharp contrast between an American party and a traditional European socialist party whose policies are designed to serve the interests of a working class comprising a majority or potential majority of the community. It is in this latter perspective that a party asserts a majoritarian mandate for its policies. And for the assertion to be accepted it is necessary that there be a genuinely majority-class interest. Not only must it exist, but it must also be perceived by members of the class. These are difficult conditions to meet in a complex society where many interests divide even an industrial working class.

In a complex society of this kind, interest groups provide the persistent programmatic qualities that parties with a majority bent cannot afford. This is not only a matter of promoting special economic policies of benefit to particular groups. An altogether different kind of interest group is exemplified by an American organization, the National Committee for an Effective Congress, active in supporting candidates during the 1950's and 1960's. This organization was the means by which non-Marxist liberals concerned with civil rights, internationalism, and increased government services could support similarly concerned congressional candidates in either major party.

[28] David B. Truman, *The Governmental Process* (New York: Alfred A. Knopf, 1951), p. 272.

The Committee has been aptly called an electoral interest group in a most careful and insightful study of its activities.[29] It raised money from wealthy contributors and from larger numbers of prosperous middle-class professionals, and then allocated the money in certain marginal elections, especially for the Senate, in which a liberal had a fighting chance. Although most of these liberal candidates, like the liberal contributors, were Democrats, they were not all of the one party. Anyway, for the contributors and the small Committee staff, whose Democratic partisan leanings were mixed with distrust of parties generally, the objectives were programmatic. Election of their favored candidates was for the purpose of fostering fairly well-defined policies. Unlike a party's function, the Committee's was that of any politically engaged interest group. The goal was policy, and election was instrumental.

Most interest groups do not use the electoral process in this manner. Specialized groups may enjoy direct access to policy-making without having to play a role in elections. Then, the division of labor between interest groups and parties is even sharper. From what we know especially of American politics, it is usual for this division to exist. For example, in a scholarly study of state educational policy, it has been shown that professional interest groups are regularly the innovators and articulators. They work to keep the parties out of their policy realm, under the rubric of keeping politics out of education. The politics then can be those of the groups most concerned with the educational policy results. Insofar as the public becomes involved, it is mobilized by the interest groups rather than by the parties.[30]

A similar picture emerges from a detailed observational study of politics, along with other matters, in a small American town. The local party organization is found to be important only in getting out the vote. It has virtually nothing to do with policy formation at city, state, or national levels. This function belongs to interest-group organizations continuously concerned with substantive policies. They inform citizens of the issues, gather support for their policies, and attempt to communicate with governmental policy-makers.[31]

[29] Harry M. Scoble, "Political Money: A Study of Contributors to the National Committee for an Effective Congress," *Midwest Journal of Political Science,* VII (August, 1963), 229.

[30] Nicholas A. Masters, Robert H. Salisbury and Thomas H. Eliot, *State Politics and the Public Schools* (New York: Alfred A. Knopf, 1964), pp. 265, 268, 272.

[31] Arthur J. Vidich and Joseph Bensman, *Small Town in Mass Society* (Garden City, N.Y.: Doubleday, 1960), p. 227.

While these examples are drawn from the American experience, there is every reason to believe that the division of labor is duplicated to a large degree in Europe, despite the presence there of programmatic parties.[32] Not only is a good deal known about the political activity of interest groups in European nations, but it is also known that even in Britain a major party is not so monolithic as always to be able to perform the policy-making function in the manner envisioned for a programmatic party.[33] There is every reason to accept Samuel Beer's judgment that strong parties do not make for little influence by interest groups.[34] The most that might be said for the British party as a policy-maker, given its considerably greater cohesion in government, is that important interest groups may find it more advantageous to concentrate on winning a party, as such, over to its policy goals. How this can be managed is neatly illustrated by the study of the success of commercial-television advocates in gaining Conservative support for their policy during the early 1950's.[35] Another equally important point emerges from this case. The policy not only originated in an interest group, but was fostered by that group, who persuaded sufficient Conservative office-holders to adopt it so that its enactment was ensured. And this was done without any direct electoral mandate for commercial television. The Conservative party never submitted the policy to the electorate.

The plain fact of the matter is that a cohesive party, assuming an organizational responsibility for governing in the style of a British parliamentary party, is only somewhat more of a policy-maker than a loose American party. It may enact policies as a party in a way that an American party cannot regularly manage, but the policies may be the product of particularized interest groups rather than of any programmatic commitments backed by majority support. Britain's generous agricultural subsidies are another excellent case in point. They represent a governmental response, at least as ample as the American, to the pressure of an interest group.[36] An electoral factor plays a part in this response, but it involves a party bid for the votes of an inter-

[32] A leading case is the intense interest-group activity of French peasant organizations, beginning in the 1930's, along with the activity of a peasant party. Gordon Wright, *Rural Revolution in France* (Stanford, Calif.: Stanford University Press, 1964), p. 40.

[33] Richard Rose, "Faction and Party: The British Example" (Mimeographed paper delivered at American Political Science Association, Washington, 1962).

[34] Beer, *op. cit.*, p. 351.

[35] H. H. Wilson, *Pressure Group* (London: Secker and Warburg, 1961).

[36] J. Roland Pennock, "Agricultural Subsidies in England and the United States," *American Political Science Review*, LVI (September, 1962), 621–33.

ested minority and certainly not of a majority mandate for the given policy.

Recently, it has become usual to speak of parties, especially in circumstances of two-party competition, as performing an aggregative function with respect to interest groups. Unable to obtain the essential optimum number of votes by identifying with any one interest, a party is said to put together a combination of interests that together form a majority. The winning party is the more successful aggregator. Closely enough defined, this aggregative function is compatible with the division of labor between parties and interest groups. Aggregating means bringing together—additively, not collectively or organically—a variety of interests championing particular policies. Those that any one party brings together for any one election, or even for a series of elections, are likely to share certain tendencies and seldom to be squarely contradictory. Their followings may overlap. But the result is still a combination of specialized interests whose several policies have been adopted by the party, and not a following drawn to the party by preconceived program.

Undoubtedly the extent and diversity of a major party's aggregation vary from country to country. For a party to win elections in the United States or Canada, in comparison to Great Britain, it has seemed necessary to combine such different interests as to appear to be much less coherent even in policy tendencies. Given our view of the limited policy-making function essential for a party, this less coherent result is not troubling in the way that it has often been for many intellectual commentators more interested in policies than in elections. Still, the need for very broad aggregation must be recognized as making for distinguishable party characteristics. Parties responding to their environments by attempting to be very broadly aggregative cannot even *seem* programmatic. Instead they have to be admired, if they are at all, for their pragmatic compromising spirit. It is on this basis that American parties have occasionally been idealized. Contrary to the critical view that it is unhealthy to be without settled principles, the very diversity of each American party has been observed to be highly functional in the American political system. This is the theme of Herbert Agar's treatment of parties. Their customary flexibility in compromising opposing interests and principles is praised in sharp distinction to their one great failure preceding the American Civil War. Agar makes no attempt to universalize the usefulness of the American party's role as a compromiser. Indeed, he regards this role as especially suited to a large federal community like the American: "Instead of seeking 'principles,' or 'distinctive tenets,' which can

only divide a federal union, the party is intended to seek bargains between the regions, the classes, and the other interest groups. It is
intended to bring men and women of all beliefs, occupations, sections,
racial backgrounds, into a combination for the pursuit of power. The
combination is too various to possess firm convictions."[37] Agar specifically contrasts this situation to Britain, where he believes parties of
principle are appropriate.

If this assumes that British parties are entirely without the bargaining and compromising character of American parties, the contrast is
too sharply drawn. To perform their electoral function, or to be what
Agar calls "a combination for the pursuit of power," some bargaining
and compromising is in order. But the diversity of interests to be
brought together may be appreciably less in a smaller and more
homogeneous nation—so much less as to enable a party to seem
programmatic. On the other hand, whatever provides the basis for
social and structural federalism is likely to work against programmatic parties. The Canadian example illustrates this as clearly as does
that of the United States. Historically, the major Canadian parties
sought to bridge sectional interests by economic programs not sharply
distinguishable from each other.[38] The more successful party, the
Liberal party in the twentieth century, was the one that contained
and combined the most diverse sectional and class interests under its
broad tent. It has even been bluntly stated that the "fact that a party,
to be successful, must draw its support from two or more regions accounts for the opportunism and lack of principles in the Canadian
parties."[39] This "opportunism," which could better be called flexibility, was the mark of Canada's long-time Liberal prime minister, Mac-
Kenzie King, whose biographer describes him as regarding it as very
important for a party to secure the consent of its internal rival forces
at the expense of shelving or modifying party principles. This function led King to make "enormous concessions to preserve the unity of
the Liberal party."[40]

The purpose of calling attention to the unusually broad American
and Canadian party compromises is not to emphasize any unique as-

[37] Herbert Agar, *The Price of Union* (Boston: Houghton Mifflin, 1950),
p. 689.
[38] Frank H. Underhill, "The Development of National Political Parties in
Canada," in Frank H. Underhill (ed.), *In Search of Canadian Liberalism*
(Toronto: Macmillan of Canada, 1960), pp. 21–42.
[39] H. McD. Clokie, *Canadian Government and Politics* (Toronto: Longmans, Green, 1944), p. 80.
[40] Robert MacGregor Dawson, *William Lyon MacKenzie King 1874–1923*
(Toronto: University of Toronto Press, 1958), p. 319.

pects of politics in federal societies. Rather, it is to emphasize by the clarity and extremity of these examples what seems to be functional for a major party in any democratic nation: the bringing together of diverse interests in order to win elections. It is true that the function may be much less pressing and difficult in nations with less complex and less divergent interests, but it is hard to believe that any modern society is really so simple as to permit a party with a majority bent to avoid compromising altogether. In some degree, the function that Agar attributes to American parties must be universal in two-party competition.

The degree of similarity of American and British parties in this respect can be presented in another way. Not only are British parties likely to have some of the compromising pragmatic character that is characteristic of American parties, but it is also true that American parties, no matter how much they compromise diverse interests, probably represent some kind of societal cleavage. Indeed, during an American election campaign it is often this supposed distinctiveness, at least in policy tendencies, that each party stresses. The distinctiveness may not be programmatic, in the sense the term has been used here, and its actuality may vary from election to election. But each major American party asserts a traditional posture, complete with a great many ceremonial and symbolic trappings. After all, a party competing in a democratic system cannot be completely consensual or totally aggregative of all interests. Its supporters and even its voters must recognize distinctive qualities. By definition, a competitive party is bound to be partial to some extent. This need not blur the distinction between programmatic and non-programmatic parties unless policy tendencies are confused with programs.

4. *The General Direction*

In suggesting that parties are often usefully nonprogrammatic and in citing American experience most notably in this connection, I have tried to avoid suggesting that there is any trend in the American direction. I do not believe that the relatively sharp division of labor between policy-making interest groups and electorally purposive parties, characteristic of the United States, is a necessary consequence of any particularly advanced stage of economic, social, or political development. Nor is it, as many scholarly critics would have it, a sign of backwardness or immaturity. The closest to a normative view is in the description of the difficulties, in a complex modern society, of obtaining a genuinely majoritarian election mandate for a given party policy. But these difficulties cannot be assumed to prevent parties from attempting to obtain such a mandate or from claiming to have obtained it.

It is time, however, to refer to evidence of a trend away from the programmatic party function in Western democracies. Whether any such trend is toward a norm does not have to be decided. In any event, the evidence is by no means overwhelming. It comes from a few West European nations where, beginning in the late 1950's, the social democratic parties in particular began to have less clear-cut programmatic commitments. The phenomenon has been much remarked on, especially in Britain and Germany, as the decline of ideology or doctrine. Sweden is also a case in point.[41] The West German Social Democrats appear to have made the sharpest turn, partly because of the previous prominence of doctrine and partly because they were simultaneously in the process of changing from multi-party to two-party competition. It is the West German experience, along with others, that Otto Kirchheimer had in mind in describing "the shrinking of the ideologically oriented nineteenth-century party."[42] In its place, he saw parties reduced to rationally conceived vehicles of interest representation. Or, as Kirchheimer and a colleague have written specifically about German parties in the 1960's, they have become less interested in ideology and abstract goals, and far more interested in maintaining stability and in fulfilling the mandates of the assorted interest groups that support them.[43]

Even though the decline-in-ideology school is usually thinking about no more than the decline in socialist ideology, this change is nevertheless significant, since so much of European programmatic politics has in fact concerned socialism and the ideological response to it. And where the Marxist doctrine underlying socialist programs has withered, no comparably significant doctrine has arisen to replace it. Conversely, where another doctrinal basis is still important for a major party, as Christian Democracy is in Italy, socialist doctrine also remains more meaningful than it is in West Germany or Britain. In the latter case, the decline in programmatic difference between the two major parties evidently continued into the 1960's. The proportion of the British electorate perceiving little distinction between the Con-

[41] Herbert Tingsten, "Stability and Vitality in Swedish Democracy," *Political Quarterly*, XXVI (April, 1955), 140–51.

[42] Otto Kirchheimer, "The Waning of Opposition in Parliamentary Regimes," *Social Research*, XXIV (Summer, 1957), 153.

[43] Otto Kirchheimer and Constantine Menges, "A Free Press in a Democratic State?: The Spiegel Case," in Gwendolen M. Carter and Alan F. Westin (eds.), *Politics in Europe* (New York: Harcourt, Brace & World, 1965), p. 90.

servative and the Labour parties rose from 34 per cent in 1959 to 49 per cent in 1964.[44] Even in Israel, notable for its ideological cleavages, there is a suggestion of declining intensity. Israeli parliamentary party leaders, in particular, are reported to be drifting away from the old ideologies as a result of experience in dealing with immediate problems and of a growing differentiation of society generating new specific demands.[45] The success of the largely non-ideological UNR in France seems to illustrate the effect of the same forces.[46] Insofar as there is a trend in Western societies for politics to become less ideological (or parties less programmatic), David Apter has proposed an appealing general explanation: "Advanced development communities are no longer in the process of changing from traditional to modern forms of social life. As a consequence, they look beyond programmatic ideologies with their simplified remedial suggestions. One of the outstanding characteristics of such communities is broad agreement on fundamentals and corresponding magnification of minor issues."[47]

Not every observer welcomes a decline of programmatic parties. On the contrary, the diminution of the ideological base for such parties is often deplored on the ground that it means a less active role for individual citizens in shaping policy. With the decrease in fundamental differences among West German party platforms, for example, voters are said to feel less effective.[48] They still cast their ballots, apparently in as large numbers as ever, but they no longer can play a role, as party members, in making the policy of the party for which they vote. That this really makes for less effectiveness, or feelings of less effectiveness, can be questioned even if one assumes that large numbers of members did actually participate in making policy for programmatic parties. The opportunity to make policy as a member of an interest group, in turn capable of influencing party or governmental policy, can be a more than adequate substitute. Insofar as such matters can

[44] David E. Butler and Anthony King, *The British General Election of 1964* (London: Macmillan, 1965), p. 155.

[45] Seligman, *op. cit.*, p. 88–89.

[46] Georges Lavau, "L'UNR-UDT au lendemain de sa victoire," *Revue Française de Science Politique*, XIII (June, 1963), 433–45. In a nation where programmatic interest has customarily been low, there is testimony that it remains so. James Jupp, *Australian Party Politics* (Melbourne: Melbourne University Press, 1964), p. 208.

[47] David Apter, *Ideology and Discontent* (New York: Free Press of Glencoe, 1964), p. 30.

[48] Renate Mayntz, "Citizen Participation in Germany: Nature and Extent" (Mimeographed paper delivered at International Political Science Association, Paris, 1961), p. 10.

be measured, it seems that American citizens, without programmatic parties, nevertheless believe in their own political efficaciousness to a greater extent than do citizens in three other Western nations (Britain, Germany, and Italy) for which there are comparable data. In an imposing cross-national study, a higher percentage of American respondents said that they can do something about local and national government regulations.[49] They do not claim to be able to do so through political parties, but significantly neither do many British, German, or Italian respondents. This American finding is confirmed in a Detroit metropolitan area survey showing that 57 per cent of the respondents thought that the best way to participate in community affairs was through non-party groups, and only 25 per cent through parties.[50]

In this matter of the citizen's sense of efficaciousness, it may thus matter little whether or not the party's programmatic function is declining. Citizens have other means, probably preferred and perhaps better, for expressing their policy preferences. Nor, as American experience also indicates, need the parties suffer in the performance of their electoral function because they have no programs. Voters are regularly and habitually attracted anyway. Parties may even succeed more fully in their electoral function, including the aggregation of interests, if they are freed from an identification with programmatic concerns. "Norm-oriented movements" need not be carried out by or even through parties.[51]

[49] Gabriel A. Almond and Sidney Verba, *The Civic Culture* (Princeton: Princeton University Press, 1963), pp. 185–86, 191–92.

[50] Eldersveld, *op. cit.,* p. 441.

[51] Neil J. Smelser, *Theory of Collective Behavior* (New York: Free Press of Glencoe, 1963), pp. 274–75.

XI

Program, Policy, and Organized Membership

1. The Relationship

I propose here to examine a major problem inherent in the performance of the programmatic function of political parties. The examination is partly theoretical, but it also includes reference to the experience of parties (and of one in particular) that have been plainly programmatic. The subject is not so much how a *program* is adopted. A program, as the term has been defined, may be so broad or so traditional as to be beyond the realm of intra-party controversy. But there is a serious question about deciding on policies that apply a party's program to particular issues and so to future governmental decisions. Policy-making in this sense presents the programmatic party with the problem of how and by whom decisions are to be made.

It may be argued that any party faces this problem. Even a non-programmatic party presents policies from time to time. But these do not have to be more than *ad hoc* policies, unashamedly designed to meet the interests of voters as estimated by candidates for public office. On the other hand, the programmatic party, while also seeking to appeal to voters, has the important additional concern of developing policies that fit its broader commitments and are deducible from them. This is not to say that such a party always develops policies on this basis or that all of its policies are so developed. Among major parties, at least, we may assume that there are no pure cases of programmatic policy-making. Election campaigns may inspire opportunistic policies from any party. All that is suggested is that parties committed to programs will have some appreciable concern with politics designed to carry out the programs. Perhaps the policies will only *seem* designed for programmatic purposes. But the concern is there.

What I have just said implies that within the programmatic party there is a *special* concern with policy-making. This concern relates to the basis for the existence of a non-patronage, mass-membership organization. Although an organization of this type might also be recruited by a non-programmatic party, there can be no doubt that it regularly accompanies a major programmatic party. The two phenomena—program and mass membership—are in part responsible for each other. Program provides a cause for joining although there is no hope of direct material reward for party service, and the members thus recruited may be expected to sustain the program and the policies derived from it. It is thus understandable that the intellectual reformer advocating programs for American parties also urges that there be a dues-paying membership "united chiefly by their common faith in their party's tradition, doctrine and policy."[1] If the membership is not always accorded an actual policy-making role, it is nevertheless certain that it is a potential claimant to the role. It could hardly be otherwise with a group whose organized existence owes so much to a programmatic commitment. The problem of how policy is made in a programmatic party revolves around the part to be played by the organized membership. This is not a simple matter of leaders versus rank-and-file members. A better way to state the problem is to distinguish between the party's public office-holders (plus candidates for public office) and the organized party membership. The latter's leaders may not be the same men as the public office-holders or at least they may not be the dominant office-holders. So there are at least two possible loci of policy-making in a party with mass membership attracted by the party program: the public office-holders, actual or potential, and the organized membership. Neither locus has to be regarded as monolithic. There may be important differences among the public office-holders, and among the organized members. Nor does it have to be assumed that there is always a conflict between the two centers of decision-making power. Agreement on policy is surely possible, perhaps even usual, and it is also possible that one locus of power is regularly dominated by the other.

Yet the point remains that the public office-holders and the organized membership have inherently separate bases for claiming policy-making authority, and these separate bases can conflict. The office-holders, individually or collectively, are likely to regard themselves as representative of, and primarily responsible to, a broad electorate of which their party's organized members constitute only a small though active minority. On the other hand, there may be spokesmen for the organized membership who regard themselves as representative of, and primarily responsible to, this smaller and special segment of party supporters. The latter, it must be stressed, have cer-

[1] James MacGregor Burns, *The Deadlock of Democracy* (Englewood Cliffs, N.J.: Prentice-Hall, 1963), p. 328.

tain democratic credentials for challenging the claims of the party's public office-holders. These credentials do not exist in a cadre or skeletal party, where there is no substantial membership to provide the numerical basis for a democratic claim. Although even in the skeletal organization party managers (or party "bosses") may attempt, perhaps successfully, to establish policy for office-holders, they have no inherently separate popular basis for their policy-making claims.

It is such a basis that a dues-paying mass membership clearly provides. Organized, as it tends to be in democratic parties in democratic nations, so that there is an annual meeting of several hundred to a few thousand elected representatives, plus a smaller interim executive committee chosen by the annual meeting, its policy pronouncements carry the weight of numbers. Even the several hundred to a few thousand delegates are impressively numerous, more so than the party's public office-holders as a group. This holds even though the delegates may in fact often represent small or inactive party branches and so be virtually self-appointed representatives of rank-and-file members. Their views on policy may thus be mainly those of an activist minority of a membership counted as a few million. Still, the delegates are fairly assumed to represent some members other than themselves, and so to constitute a significant body of opinion.

Much more numerous are the non-dues-paying voters of a major political party. But they are unorganized and thus must be inarticulate on policy. Office-holders can only cite what they believe this electorate wants or will accept. The citations may now include, it is true, the fairly hard evidence of electoral opinion as determined by sample surveys, lending a numerical base to any argument for considering the views of the broader electorate. But surveys cannot settle the general question of who *ought* to make party policy in the face of two conflicting claims, each based on a kind of popular legitimacy.

These claims, it is useful to reiterate, need not always conflict. A party's public office-holders may want the same policy as members do. They may think that their electorate agrees on policy. They may be the effective regular leaders of the organized membership as well as office-holders. The membership may be docile. Or there may be a combination of these possibilities making for policy agreement. Clearly, for the public office-holders, agreement is desirable. Their electoral purpose is served by having the relatively united support of party members. But they cannot count on always achieving agreement without having to accept policies desired by the organized membership but not by the electorate and/or themselves as office-holders. The electorate with which they are concerned is not just the regular party voters, but also marginal voters who might vote for the party's candidates in favorable circumstances. Surely public office-holders will want to consider this electorate. Whether they ought to give it priority over their organized following is the contested point.

In many respects, this controversial point is at the heart of theorizing about the place of a party in a democratic political system. Two conflicting theories of representation are involved. In the older and more traditional one, elected public office-holders, individually or collectively, decide policy. This need not be put in specifically Burkean terms, in which the elected representative was not supposed to respond to the wishes of his electors any more than to his organized followers. The office-holder might or might not respond to the assumed preferences of his electorate. The point is that he would pay attention to those preferences insofar as he followed any preferences other than his own. In the second theory, however, the office-holder is considered the agent, although he may also be a leader, of an organized following that determines policy. Thus there may be an enforced policy agreement among a party's elected office-holders, but it is well to emphasize that it is just one way and by no means the only way to achieve such agreement. The elected office-holders of a party can simply achieve agreement through their own caucus. Thus the essence of the second theory of representation is not that it makes for policy agreement among a party's office-holders, but that it makes for this agreement as the result of decisions of an organized party membership.

One or the other of these two theories of representation appears to underlie the studies of the policy-making relationship between public office-holders and organized party members. Ostrogorski, most emphatically adopting the older theory in a rigidly individualistic form, found much to criticize in late nineteenth-century efforts of organized American and British parties to determine policies for their elected representatives.[2] Michels, on the contrary, is critical of the tendency of parliamentary representatives of the early twentieth-century labor and social democratic parties to free themselves from the influence of their highly organized memberships in order to respond to the unorganized mass of constituency voters.[3] Duverger, for different reasons, also appears to favor the second theory; unlike Michels, however, he regards the maintenance of external party organizational

[2] M. Y. Ostrogorski, *Democracy and the Organization of Political Parties* (London: Macmillan, 1902), Vol. I, chaps. 4–5.

[3] Robert Michels, *Political Parties,* trans. Eden and Cedar Paul (Glencoe, Ill.: Free Press, 1949), p. 181.

control as realistic and indeed as already achieved by the most modern parties.[4]

Understandably, almost all of twentieth-century work on this relationship grows out of European experience. Earlier American experience with old-style party machines, about which Ostrogorski wrote, is not germane. The machines did not advance the same kind of democratic claim to policy-making, or much interest in policy-making. Even in Europe, it should be added, not only have mass-membership organizations been less important in some nations than others, but they have been much more significant on the left than on the right.

A qualification needs to be introduced here. The difference between the two theories of representation, at least in their application, tends to diminish when a party's organized membership approaches the same size and nature as its usual and anticipated portion of the electorate. A minor party with little voter appeal beyond its zealous members is obviously an example. So, to some extent, is a highly organized major party in a multi-party state. The presence of several large parties, instead of only two, means that each is likely to attract a narrower segment of voters more nearly coinciding with the party's organized or organizable following. There is simply a better chance that organized members will have the same policy preferences as party voters when the party has a narrow rather than a broad electorate. Furthermore, multi-party competition means there is less likelihood that public office-holders will find it profitable to appeal to voters outside of their own traditional following. So there is less likelihood of conflict between office-holders and membership. Naturally, this would not hold when multi-party competition is on the verge of becoming two-party competition, with at least one and probably two parties displaying a majority bent. Otherwise, however, it is fair to expect the problem of an organized membership in relation to policy-making to be most clearly revealed in a two-party competitive environment.

The ideal case for examination, therefore, is a labor or social democratic party operating as one of two major competitors. Such a party in such a situation can be expected to display the conflicting policy-making claims of an organized membership and a group of public office-holders concerned with the larger electorate. But party policy-making even in this example ought not to be understood exclusively, or predominantly, in terms of a conflict between organized members

[4] Maurice Duverger, *Political Parties*, trans. Barbara and Robert North (New York: John Wiley & Sons, 1954), p. 185.

and public office-holders. Indeed, in any general concern with the process of party decision-making one would grossly oversimplify and mislead by focussing only on these two loci of power. There are party interests and groups which, on particular issues, seek to influence either the membership or the office-holders or both. In any event, it would be unrealistic to expect all of the membership to be aligned against all of the office-holders on any issue. Fortunately, nothing like this unreality is here implied. It may even be allowed that each of these bases, or loci, of power is simply used by various interests in and around a party. Having an organized membership, then, provides a second and alternative institutional route, to that of electoral pressure on public office-holders, through which interested groups may seek to influence party policy. Admittedly, the dual institutional framework, through which party policy-making takes place, is of interest here rather than the whole complex process of party policy-making.

The meaning and perhaps the significance of this analysis can be clarified by analogy to a more familiar institutional study. Just as an organized membership and public office-holders are two loci of power in internal party policy-making, so in American government have the presidency and congress been viewed as potentially and often actively competing claimants. Surely they have provided a useful focus for understanding American government, even though it is fully appreciated that the presidency and congress are themselves the targets and the possible instruments of various policy-oriented interests.

2.   *The British Labour Case*

From what has been said about an ideal case for the institutional examination of internal party policy-making, it is apparent that the British Labour party is eminently qualified. Not only has it operated in essentially two-party competition for about four decades, but it has had non-coalition governing experience. Although Labour has been in power for relatively few years of its existence, it has had enough experience and been close enough to power the rest of the time so as clearly to be a party of majority bent. In addition, however, Labour is a socialist working-class party that originated as a "movement" outside of governing circles. As such, it certainly has had a program, a mass membership, and a commitment to the proposition that this membership should have a role in policy-making. This last characteristic distinguishes it from the Conservative party. The Conservatives have been programmatic (if less so than Labour), and they have had a mass membership. But they have not subscribed to the view that the membership should make party policy. This does not mean that the Conservative membership never tries to make or influence policy. On occasion, it may even succeed in doing so. But it is not meant for the purpose. And it makes no regular claim, through its annual conference or other agencies, to be able to commit elected Conservative office-holders to policies of which they might disapprove.[5] In this respect, the Conservative organization conforms to the British tradition of deference to leadership—meaning here the parliamentary leadership that originally created the external membership to serve its campaign purposes. Labour, on the other hand, formed its extra-parliamentary organization in an effort to win parliamentary representation that it did not yet have. So elected office-holders could be viewed, originally at least, as servants of the movement. Reinforcing this outlook was the egalitarianism accompanying British working-class politics.

Insofar as Labour has accorded a policy-making role to its organized membership, it has been exceptional in British politics. Before Labour became a major party, both the Conservatives and the Liberals had settled on parliamentary party domination of policy-making. Only briefly in the late nineteenth century had there been any doubt about where Conservative and Liberal party power should and did rest.[6] This meant that the Labour party of the twentieth century often appeared to challenge what was virtually a British constitutional principle of parliamentary party responsibility. Critics who believed that Labour really intended its parliamentary policies to be made by an external organization attacked the procedure as unconstitutional. Other critics, while agreeing on the unconstitutionality, insisted that Labour did not seriously mean to follow any such procedure. Within the Labour party, however, there were many who believed not only that extra-parliamentary party policy-making was constitutional, but also that it was the true form of democratic representation. They asserted their view often enough so that it came to be widely regarded as the orthodox or conventional Labour doctrine even though its acceptance in principle was never complete and its acceptance in practice was hard to substantiate.

The truth is that Labour has preserved a considerable ambiguity about its commitment to policy-making by the mass membership. While the ambiguity is enough to distinguish Labour from other major British parties, it would surely be an exaggeration to say that

[5] Robert T. McKenzie, *British Political Parties* (London: William Heinemann, 1963), pp. 152, 193, 220.
[6] Duverger, *op. cit.*, pp. 188–90.

the distinction was absolute and clear-cut. The Labour party constitution, dating from 1918, is most ambiguous. Clause V, labelled "Party Programme," reads as follows:

1. The Party Conference shall decide from time to time what specific proposals of legislative, financial or administrative reform shall be included in the Party Programme.
No proposal shall be included in the Party Programme unless it has been adopted by the Party Conference by a majority of not less than two thirds of the votes recorded on a card vote.
2. The National Executive Committee and the Parliamentary Committee of the Parliamentary Labour Party shall decide which items from the Party Programme shall be included in the Manifesto which shall be issued by the National Executive Committee prior to every General Election. The joint meeting of the two Committees shall also define the attitude of the Party to the principal issues raised by the Election which are covered by the Manifesto.[7]

This language plainly enough makes the external organization, through its annual conference of representative delegates, responsible for the party *program*. But it is not so clear with respect to "policies." If these were only particular items of the program included in the election manifesto, the parliamentary Labour party (PLP) would be given what looks like an equal authority and so, practically speaking, a veto over the content of any commitment before the electorate. On the other hand, the program itself, not just the portions put into the manifesto, could be regarded as the substance of the general policies to which the party as a whole, in and out of parliament, would be committed.

It is no wonder that the party's constitutional authority is interpreted differently at different times, even by the same person. The principal example is provided by Clement Attlee, who led Labour for the longest period. At first, Attlee appeared authoritatively to assert the external organization's power. Describing what he regarded as the democratic superiority of the Labour organization to the Conservative, he said that the Labour conference, representing the membership, "lays down the policy of the Party and issues instructions which must be carried out by the Executive, the affiliated organizations and its representatives in Parliament and on the local authorities."[8] His assertion was not unusual among Labour pronouncements

[7] The party constitution appears in the *59th Annual Report of the Labour Conference* (London: Labour Party, 1960), p. 304.

[8] Clement Attlee, *The Labour Party In Perspective* (London: Gollancz, 1937), p. 93.

on the subject,[9] and it was never openly challenged by fellow party members. On the other hand, Attlee seemed to be saying something very different in 1945 when he denied a Conservative campaign charge that the parliamentary Labour party received its orders from an outside body. It is true that the outside body now in question was not the party conference as a whole but its National Executive Committee (whose chairman, Harold Laski, had claimed that the leader's authority was limited by the NEC).[10] Yet Attlee's rejection of external dictation by the NEC seems applicable to the conference as well. Moreover, his actual behavior as party leader, notably while he was prime minister, displayed considerable control of policy-making through the parliamentary party.

What should be stressed about this aspect of the Attlee era and about most of the rest of Labour history before 1960 is that the parliamentary leadership's control, while real enough, was achieved without any major direct clash with the claims of the party conference. There was fairly regular agreement between the parliamentary leaders and the conference, and this agreement was by no means accidental. The PLP was well represented on the National Executive Committee, especially on its policy subcommittees.[11] The leader himself was an *ex officio* member of the NEC. As an actual or potential prime minister, he was in a strong position to wield influence in the external apparatus as he was in the parliamentary ranks.[12] Not only could he and his fellow parliamentary leaders draw directly on the respect and the loyalty of conference delegates, but through their role on the NEC they had a great deal to do with how and which policy resolutions were presented to the conference and with how they were interpreted. This is not to say that the conference never approved a resolution against the desires of the parliamentary leadership and of the NEC. But the odd instance was handled without forcing the leadership either to adopt in parliament what it did not want or to reject flatly the conference policy.

So it was with the minor issue of tied cottages (farmhouses owned by landlords and let to agricultural workers as long as they were in the landlord's employ). Twice during the Labour government of the late 1940's, the party conference, against the advice of the leadership,

[9] McKenzie, *op. cit.*, p. 10.

[10] A good account of the Attlee-Laski affair is provided by Herbert Morrison, *Government and Parliament* (London: Oxford University Press, 1954), pp. 140–44.

[11] McKenzie, *op. cit.*, pp. 422–23.

[12] *Ibid.*, p. 384.

approved resolutions urging legislation abolishing the tied-cottage system. Speaking for the government, Aneurin Bevan, ordinarily a conference favorite, could not dissuade the conference. What Bevan did, however, was to explain that the parliamentary party could, without flouting conference policy-making authority, nevertheless fail to carry out the conference resolution on tied cottages. He managed this explanation by claiming that the PLP retained the power to decide the timetable for the introduction of legislation even though it was for "the Conference to lay down the policies of the Parliamentary Party."[13] The parliamentary leadership, while it never in its three subsequent years in power found the time appropriate to introduce legislation, still allowed the conference's policy-making authority to stand in principle. The tied-cottage issue hardly justified a direct confrontation even though the leadership's control over timing amounted to a veto over conference policy-making.

More consequential issues of wider interest might not have been manageable in the same oblique way. On these, however, the leadership, in the important two decades before 1960, was ordinarily able to secure the defeat of embarrassing resolutions and the support by the conference for policy resolutions favored by most of the parliamentary party. There were some close calls, as in 1954 when the conference voted by the narrow margin of 3.27 million to 3.02 million to approve the Attlee leadership's policy on German rearmament.[14] And there was at least one instance of the leadership's accepting, after earlier opposition, a policy supported by a party conference. This occurred after the 1944 conference approved a motion, from the floor, to add heavy industry to a list of private enterprises which the NEC was proposing for public ownership. Later, within the NEC's campaign committee, this conference policy was cited as authority for inclusion of the steel industry among the industries that Labour, in its 1945 election manifesto, was promising to nationalize. But it was a parliamentary party leader who cited the conference as authority. Thus, the subsequent addition of iron and steel to the manifesto's list cannot be regarded solely as a conference victory over the parliamentary leadership, which itself seems to have been seriously divided on the issue and so open to pressure or, at any rate, persuasion from the outside.[15] Surely this is not a case of a fairly well united parliamentary

[13] 47th Annual Report of the Labour Conference (London: Labour Party, 1948), p. 214.
[14] 53rd Annual Report of the Labour Conference (London: Labour Party, 1954), pp. 92–108.
[15] Samuel H. Beer, British Politics in the Collectivist Age (New York: Alfred A. Knopf, 1965), pp. 174–78.

leadership, backed by the bulk of the parliamentary party, having a policy imposed on it by the external organization. Nor, of course, is it an instance to illustrate the complete impotence of the conference.

Neither of these sharp alternatives emerged as long as Labour's leaders in parliament were also effectively the leaders of their organized membership. They remained in command despite an open ideological rift in the 1950's between most of the PLP, notably most of its leaders, and many of the delegates at the annual party conferences. The parliamentary leadership appeared increasingly moderate and pragmatic in its socialist professions, perhaps so as to be hardly socialist at all, while many conference delegates championed a more distinctive left-wing socialism emphasizing nationalization of industry. Furthermore, the leadership was dedicated to the foreign and defense policies of the Atlantic alliance, toward which the left was adverse in varying degrees. There were times in the early and mid-1950's when left-wing viewpoints predominated in conference delegations from the constituency parties. These delegations were observed to elect left-wingers as their representatives on the NEC, particularly during the period of the Bevanite revolt against the Attlee leadership, and they were also thought to propose and to vote for left-wing policy resolutions. Subsequent careful studies have shown that this left-wing militancy was neither so consistent or complete as was once assumed, and by the end of the 1950's or at least by 1960 there is great doubt whether these delegates were distinctively left at all in relation to the trade-union delegates whose votes were always about five-sixths of the conference total.[16] But there were occasions when many constituency party delegates wanted more fully socialist policies, domestically and internationally, than the parliamentary leadership was willing to provide. The leadership was nevertheless able to secure conference approval for its moderate policies and thus avoid the problem of conflict with the representative body of the external party organization. Its success in this respect derived from the continued support of enough of the largest trade unions which, through their leaders, provided massive bloc votes sufficient to overwhelm the votes of constituency delegations even in the unlikely event that all of the delegations opposed policies of the leadership. Never was this a simple matter of all the trade-union votes supporting the leadership, any more than all constituency votes opposing. There were always left-wing union lead-

---

[16] Richard Rose, "The Political Ideas of English Party Activists," *American Political Science Review*, LVI (June, 1962), 360–71. Considerable evidence of moderation among activists in a single constituency was found by Frank Bealey, J. Blondel, and W. P. McCann, *Constituency Politics* (London: Faber and Faber, 1965), pp. 294–95.

ers just as there were right-wing constituency delegates. The fact remained, however, that the larger share of the trade unions stood with
the parliamentary leaders, and this larger share was sufficient to provide conference victories for moderate policy resolutions even if, as
suspected, the majority of constituency delegates occasionally voted
against them.[17]

What this meant in practice was that the parliamentary leaders
needed only to maintain a working arrangement with a few key officials in four or five of the big trade unions. Their confidence and
support would always be sufficient to prevent a hostile conference
resolution on a significant issue. Thus, armed with what seemed a
built-in majority, the parliamentary leaders could accept the doctrine
of conference policy-making without having to pay any price by way
of actual surrender of power. At any rate, no such price was paid as
long as the key trade unionists were not imposing their policy on the
parliamentary leaders. They may well have done so on occasion, particularly on distinctly trade-union issues, but they were otherwise regarded as supporters of policies made in the parliamentary party. Of
course, some important trade unionists were themselves in parliament,
in which case they too were policy-makers. But this was very different
from using their dominant position in the external organization to impose policies on the parliamentary party. No doubt the trade unionists
often had to be persuaded, and this itself meant that there were limits
to the freedom of the parliamentary leaders. The limits, however,
were not those which would have been inherent in submission to
policy-making by relatively large numbers of zealous amateurs. The
trade-union leaders, like the parliamentary leaders themselves, were
professional wielders of power likely to share the views of their party
counterparts.

So it seemed through most of the 1950's, as it had in less frequently observed ways earlier, but by 1960 it was clear that there was
nothing immutable about the right-wing or moderate posture of
most trade-union leaders. In retrospect, it is possible to see that this
should have always been appreciated, since even in the 1950's there
had been a substantial minority of trade unions committed to left-
wing positions, even extreme left-wing positions in a few instances,
at party conferences and elsewhere. And in the late 1950's a change
in the top leadership of the largest single union, the Transport and
General Workers, shifted sharply to the left this old bulwark of support for moderate parliamentary policies. The shift of one or two

[17] McKenzie, op. cit., p. 505.

other large unions was capable of destroying the conference's moderate majority even if most constituency associations rallied to the parliamentary leadership. This is exactly what happened in 1960, and the events of that year exposed the problem of Labour's conflicting sources of policy-making authority in a way that had previously been avoided.

The sharpness of this exposure provides excellent illustrative material. It would be hard to imagine a clearer example of the difficulties arising from the respective claims of an external membership organization and of an office-holding leadership. The actual circumstances of the conflict must be briefly described.[18] They begin with the third successive defeat of the Labour party in the 1959 general election, and the ensuing renewal of controversy between the moderate parliamentary leadership under Hugh Gaitskell and its left-wing opponents, who were outnumbered in the PLP and who sought to gain a mandate for their policies from the party conference. As in the 1950's, the controversy concerned both domestic and foreign affairs. On the domestic front, where Gaitskell hoped to modify the party's constitution so as to eliminate the traditional full-fledged dedication to public ownership, the left scored a victory even before the 1960 conference, when Gaitskell, conceding that he lacked the votes to force the constitutional change, accepted a restatement of party objectives that did not abandon the commitment to nationalization. But this concession was in the general party program rather than in any specific policy.[19] In agreeing not to press for the removal of the broad commitment to public ownership, Gaitskell and the PLP did not thereby bind themselves to particular policies of which they disapproved, or even to any program that they had not been vaguely bound to before.

The foreign-affairs issue was another matter. Here there was no doubt whatsoever that the left sought to use the 1960 conference to impose its policy preferences on the parliamentary party. And there was no doubt that Gaitskell and the majority of the Labour M.P.'s disapproved of those left-wing preferences. Specifically, the left proposed a unilateral nuclear disarmament policy involving the cessation of Britain's participation in American and NATO nuclear defense. In short, neutralism was advanced as a substitute for the Atlantic alliance, and it was this policy that seemed to have won

[18] A fuller description is provided in Leon D. Epstein, "Who Makes Party Policy: British Labour, 1960–61," *Midwest Journal of Political Science,* VI (May, 1962), 165–82.

[19] *59th Annual Report of the Labour Conference,* pp. 12–13.

enough support from trade-union leaders during the spring and summer of 1960 to represent the majority view at the October conference.

In anticipation of its success in securing the adoption of unilateralism by the 1960 conference, the left first presented a procedural resolution seeking to resolve the ambiguity about party policy-making by asserting the final authority of the conference.[20] But before the passage of this resolution an official spokesman for the NEC blandly asserted that the NEC accepted the resolution on the understanding that it did not (and presumably could not) alter the usual PLP freedom from conference instruction.[21] Thus the resolution meant sharply different things for each side when it was approved by a two-to-one margin.[22]

The successful preservation of the old ambiguity about conference authority allowed each side to claim, in the year that lay ahead, to be in accord with the party's procedural principles. As expected, the 1960 conference rejected the NEC's defense policy statement, which reflected the PLP position, and adopted instead two unilateralist, neutralist resolutions. Although the left-wing margin in each case was narrow, there were three separate victories over the advocacy of the parliamentary leadership (and of the conference's own NEC, which presented the defense policy of the parliamentary leadership).[23] The left could now point to a neutralist unilateralism as the policy of the organized party membership, and so argue that the parliamentary party leadership was bound by the doctrine of conference supremacy to adopt the same policy. On the other hand, the parliamentary leadership could simply argue that it was not bound by a conference policy in conflict with its own. After the conference, there was only a slight possibility of avoiding this direct confrontation of the two separate claims to policy-making authority. It would have required new PLP leadership willing at least to compromise or gloss over its defense policy disagreements with the conference resolutions. But the effort within the PLP to substitute this kind of leadership failed when Gaitskell was re-elected parliamentary leader soon after the conference.[24] He left no doubt that he would continue to maintain a PLP defense policy sharply at odds with the desires of

[20] *Ibid.*, p. 159.
[21] *Ibid.*, pp. 159–60.
[22] *Ibid.*, p. 168.
[23] *Ibid.*, pp. 176, 178.
[24] *The Times* (London), October 21, 1960, p. 12; October 26, 1960, p. 12; and November 4, 1960, p. 12.

the 1960 conference.[25] In fact, Gaitskell had indicated at the conference itself that it was impossible for him and the bulk of his PLP colleagues to change their convictions in response to party resolutions: "What sort of people do you think we are? Do you think that we can simply accept a decision of this kind? Do you think that we can become overnight the pacifists, unilateralists and fellow travellers that other people are?"[26]

The poignancy of Gaitskell's queries drives home the impossibility inherent in any expectation that public office-holders can be forced by their outside supporters to adopt important policy with which they flatly disagree. Not only would such a procedure require a reversal of personal convictions, as Gaitskell stressed, but it would also mean a reversal of electoral commitments. Gaitskell and most of his fellow Labour M.P.s had been elected to the House of Commons as supporters of established Atlantic defense policies, not as unilateralists and neutralists. Did not the PLP owe a responsibility to the bulk of its voters, who showed no signs of sharing the unilateralist views of the conference majority? And without this sense of responsibility, would the Labour party be able to compete successfully in subsequent general elections?

Gaitskell's unequivocal answers to these questions became the official PLP position in the parliamentary session following the 1960 party conference. But there were between one-quarter and one-third of the Labour M.P.s who took the unilateralist position either from general conviction or from the belief that conference resolutions ought to be followed by the PLP. Whichever basis these M.P.s really acted on, they could cite the conference resolutions as authority. For this reason as well as because of their numbers, it was exceptionally difficult—impossible, really—to discipline these left-wing M.P.s when they refused to vote with their parliamentary leaders on defense policy questions.[27] The left, although a minority in the PLP, now represented the majority view in the external party organization.

Both because the rift provided a firm basis for open PLP division and because of the generally bad impression created by hostility between a parliamentary leadership and its organized following, it is

[25] The National Executive Committee also refused to follow the conference's new policy.

[26] 59th Annual Report of the Labour Conference, p. 15.

[27] The most conspicuous revolt was the deliberate abstention of 72 Labour M.P.'s from an official party motion. 632 H. C. Deb. 219–354 (December 13, 1960). The list of abstainers was published by The Daily Herald (London), December 15, 1960, and by The Daily Telegraph (London), December 14–15, 1960.

doubtful whether it would have been much more practical for Gait-skell to continue indefinitely to reject conference policy than to surrender to it. Either course looked politically disastrous. The only happy way out of the difficulty was to get the 1961 party conference to reverse its defense policy. This is what Gaitskell meant to do when he told the 1960 conference: "We will fight and fight and fight again to save the Party we love."[28] During the ensuing year, he and his followers organized support so successfully in the constituency associations and in certain crucial trade unions that by the 1961 conference they secured a handsome margin for a resolution representing the leadership's anti-unilateralist views of defense policy.[29] So ended the rift between the conference and the PLP.

Despite the fact that this result represented a triumph for PLP leadership, in accord with party experience before 1960, it is not so certain just what the whole experience establishes with respect to the freedom of the PLP from the external organization. The PLP did, it is true, function for a year in defiance of conference policy. Presumably, therefore, it could do so on another occasion. This surely indicates a considerable measure of freedom. But it does not establish that the freedom is complete. For that to have been established from the events of 1960–61, the PLP would have had to persist in defiance beyond the single year. Of course, it did not have to decide whether to do so because conference policy changed to accord again with its own. What if conference policy had not changed? Would the PLP have persisted in its contrary policy? One close and scholarly observer has suggested that it could have done just that. Even he, however, grants that the PLP could not remain permanently at odds with the conference except at the price of breaking up the party.[30] This means a kind of concession to the authority of the conference. Gaitskell seems, in effect, to have recognized this when he devoted so much effort to getting the 1961 conference to reverse the policy of the previous year. It would have been a much clearer indication of PLP supremacy if he had simply ignored conference policy—not just by continuing to pursue the established PLP policy but also by refusing to consider conference resolutions worth the trouble of trying so hard to change.

---

[28] *59th Annual Report of the Labour Conference*, p. 201.

[29] *60th Annual Report of the Labour Conference* (London: Labour Party, 1961), pp. 162–94.

[30] McKenzie, *op. cit.*, p. 624. There was a significant exchange of opinions between McKenzie and R. H. S. Crossman in *The New Statesman*, LXI (June 23 and June 30, 1961), 1007, 1010, 1044.

Political practicalities, as already suggested, ruled out this latter course as well as any surrender to conference dictates. The ethos of the Labour party did not allow the outright rejection of the policy-making authority of the representatives of the organized membership. That authority had to remain no less than ambiguously important. On the other hand, it could be no *more* than ambiguously important. Even during a single parliamentary session, the PLP could not accept conference supremacy over its own policy-making without abdicating its responsibility before the electorate. There was really nothing, therefore, for the Labour party to do except tolerate its traditional ambiguity while hoping, at least at the leadership level, that the ambiguity would wither away in favor of PLP power. Fulfillment of this hope, it is often argued, would bring Labour in accord with established British constitutional practice.[31] The parliamentary system is supposed to require that authority be in the hands of the elected members of the House of Commons and their chosen leaders. Much the same can be said, however, for any democratic system. All elected public office-holders are usually assumed to be responsible to those who elected them rather than merely to their own organized followers. Britain is not unique in presenting difficulties for the policy-making claims of an organized party membership.

3. The Limited Non-British Experience

The difficulties of reconciling the policy-making claims of an organized membership with the electoral responsibilities of public office-holders are illustrated much less fully from the experience of other nations besides Great Britain. Although many democratic parties, chiefly socialist, began as movements subscribing to membership participation in policy-making, none provides so clear an instance as does the British Labour party of a clash between this value and the other democratic value of representing an electorate. Either the issue has not arisen or the evidence of it is not available.

The United States provides virtually no illustrative material. Certainly in national politics no major American party has even pretended that its policies, legislative or executive, were established by an organized membership. More to the point, there has been no nationally organized membership to claim policy-making power. Party policies, insofar as they have developed at all, remained the business of office-holders and office-seekers. In the few instances of large organized memberships at the state level, there is little evidence that

[31] McKenzie, *op. cit.*, pp. 628, 635.

these memberships succeed in establishing a claim to policy-making. The most that can be said is that such claims have occasionally been made. They seem to have been part of the new amateur politics of principle that became prominent although hardly successful in the 1950's. The amateurs did want to convert the brokerage parties to principled or programmatic parties, and their way of doing so was to build an organized membership devoted to clear-cut principles and policies based on them.[32] It must be recognized that this was precisely the reasoning of the founders of programmatic parties in other nations. A devoted and sizable non-professional membership ordinarily accompanied the very idea of a party designed to develop policies to carry out a program. Intra-party democracy appeared as a nearly essential means for social democrats as it has for the party reformers in the United States. In neither instance has an organized membership in and of itself been the main purpose. Its existence provides a basis for the principled or programmatic policy-making that American reformers, like European socialists, have often wanted. In the United States, as in Europe, it is not unrealistic to assume that if many amateur partisans were organized, they would attempt to make more sharply defined policies than would election-minded politicians seeking to attract diverse voters.[33] Except sporadically, however, the assumption has not been tested in American experience.

In apparent contrast is Australia. Notably its Labor party, a major force in Australian politics for several decades, has often been thought to subscribe to the doctrine of policy-making by an extra-parliamentary organization.[34] The party has certainly had such an organization, dominated even more clearly by trade unions than the British Labour party, and this organization has claimed a supremacy over Labor's parliamentary representatives. There is "a presumption of right on the part of the outside authority, a right to interfere if the parliamentary party and its cabinet (or either of them) are not doing what is in the interests of Labor."[35] How this interference works,

[32] James Q. Wilson, *The Amateur Democrat* (Chicago: The University of Chicago Press, 1962), pp. 1, 342.

[33] This does not contradict the substantial findings of a sharper policy difference between Republican and Democratic leaders than between ordinary Republican and Democratic voters. Herbert McClosky, "Consensus and Ideology in American Politics," *American Political Science Review*, LVIII (June, 1964), 361–82. Neither of McClosky's groups (leaders or voters) coincides with the hypothesized amateur activists.

[34] Duverger, *op. cit.*, pp. 196–97.

[35] J. D. B. Miller, *Australian Government and Politics* (London: Gerald Duckworth, 1964), p. 114.

however, is not so clear. No one suggests that the outside authority is responsible for Labor's strict parliamentary discipline. It stems from the parliamentary party's own caucus, whose decisions the Labor candidate has pledged to follow in his parliamentary voting.[36] Nor is there substantial evidence that the caucus adopts policies handed on to it by the external organization. Party conferences are not even regarded as policy-forming bodies, in the manner of British Labour conferences.[37] Interference, then, is more likely to originate in the executive agency of the external organization, particularly among the trade unionists dominating the executive. Yet even here, the extra-parliamentary control was found, in one study, to be ineffective at the national level. The explanation given is the federal character of the Australian Labor party's national executive. Its members represent state Labor parties that do not share the same policies and therefore can impose none on the national parliamentary party.[38] This leaves open only the likelihood that at the state levels there is external organizational control of parliamentary parties.

Despite the considerable uncertainty about the degree of extra-parliamentary policy-making in the Australian Labor party, the claim has been substantial enough to raise a controversy similar to that in Britain. This has occurred despite the fact that it was the executive rather than the conference that claimed to make policy. The difference may not be so significant, since an executive's authority presumably rests on the same intra-party democratic base, only one step removed, as that of a conference of representative delegates. At any rate, it is not unusual for a close observer to find that the Australian Labor party displays the "endemic conflict" between the tradition of external control and the conventions of a parliamentary-cabinet system.[39] Insofar, then, as there may be organizational policy-making, it raises in Australia as in Britain the basic question of whether it can be properly and practically imposed on public office-holders.

A closer parallel to the British Labour experience is provided by the New Zealand Labour party. Unlike its Australian counterpart, New Zealand rests any claim for external organizational policy-making in a conference rather than in an executive agency. And in New Zealand, as in Britain, the claim has generally been subordinated

---

[36] *Ibid.*, p. 110.

[37] S. Encel, *Cabinet Government in Australia* (Melbourne: Melbourne University Press, 1962), p. 194.

[38] Aaron Wildavsky, "Party Discipline Under Federalism: Implications of Australian Experience," *Social Research*, XXVIII (Winter, 1961), 437–58.

[39] Encel, *op. cit.*, p. 191.

in practice while maintained in principle. The policy and objectives of the Labour party are supposed to be drawn up by the annual conference, a gathering of 400–500 delegates stated to be the "supreme governing body of the Party."[40] But the party's constitution is not any clearer than British Labour's on whether the parliamentary party is bound by any specific directives from the conference. What is binding is the policy contained in the party's election manifesto, but the manifesto is a product of a policy committee only theoretically responsible to the conference. This committee, while formed by the external organization's executive, is evidently dominated by the parliamentary party leader and a few of his principal colleagues. Its manifesto takes conference policy resolutions into account, but it need not automatically reproduce these. Furthermore the parliamentary party is plainly free to make its own policy whenever a subject has not been covered by the election manifesto.[41] The result is that the New Zealand practice, like the British, is a working supremacy for Labour's parliamentary leadership despite the apparent claims for conference policy-making authority. These claims, unclear though they are, are not openly rejected in New Zealand any more than in Britain, and they might therefore be raised as the basis for a revolt against a particular parliamentary party policy—as they were in Britain in 1960. The result, it is fair to assume, would be a similar disruptive conflict, since the parliamentary leadership appears as unlikely in the one instance as in the other to yield its working authority. That authority has functioned since 1935, when the New Zealand Labour party first became a governing party. Before that date, conference policy-making authority was more substantial.[42] In the last thirty years, even the claim may have withered to such an extent that it could not readily be revived. One study suggests that it does not even exist in the party's constitutional doctrine.[43] If it still does, it is certainly in disuse.

In this respect, Labour practice in New Zealand is in line with the practice of its principal opposition, the National party. The difference is solely in the degree of clarity with which the parliamentary leadership's authority is asserted. The constitution of the National

[40] Robert N. Kelson, *The Private Member of Parliament and the Formation of Public Policy* (Toronto: Toronto University Press, 1964), p. 18.

[41] *Ibid.*, pp. 19–25.

[42] *Ibid.*, p. 21.

[43] R. M. Chapman, W. K. Jackson, and A. V. Mitchell, *New Zealand Politics in Action: The 1960 General Election* (London: Oxford University Press, 1962), p. 19.

party plainly makes policy-making the responsibility of the leader himself. He is required only to consult with a policy committee technically representing the external organization but actually dominated by him and the parliamentary party. The election manifesto, announcing party policy, is produced by the leader subsequent to meetings with the policy committee.[44] Of course, there is nothing unusual about this clear-cut leadership authority in a non-labor party. Much the same is true, for example, in the British Conservative party. There seems to be no tendency for non-labor parties, even when they develop membership organizations in the same size range as labor parties, to give them any constitutional basis for policy-making authority. In other words, there is here no contagion from the left. On the contrary, the contagion, if any, runs in the other direction. The New Zealand National Party, like the British Conservative party, shows that a mass membership organization can exist without claiming to make policy for public office-holders. It is the Labour party whose practice, if not wholly its constitutional principle, resembles the non-labor party doctrine.

It is necessary to go beyond the English-speaking Commonwealth in search of other parallels to the British Labour party experience. Canada is no more likely than the United States to provide illustrative cases since its major parties, like the Democrats and Republicans, do not have large, regularized membership organizations. But in continental Europe, there are major parties, even apart from the Communists, that originated as Marxist social democratic movements outside of parliament and that long have had large parliamentary representation and occasionally governing experience. What distinguishes these parties from British Labour, however, is that they developed in multi-party situations where majority status was unlikely. Their organizations might more nearly coincide with their electorate in policy-making interests and preferences. As suggested in the earlier theoretical discussion, this would mean less chance for a clash between the wishes of the membership and the bids of candidates for electoral support. In other words, one should expect many of the social democratic or labor parties of continental Europe to persist in their commitments to policy-making by an organized membership, more so than the majority-bent parties of the English-speaking Commonwealth.

The expectation is hard to test because of an absence of available evidence. One of the few systematic studies bearing at all on the

[44] Kelson, *op. cit.*, pp. 42–46.

question is of Norway,[45] but its socialist party is by no means a typical participant in multi-party competition. Rather, the Norwegian Labor party is virtually a majority party, facing several other parties. Therefore, any organizational policy-making authority cannot readily be explained as an aspect of multi-party competition and so distinguished from the British case. The study does stress membership participation in Norwegian Labor party policy-making. This is not solely a matter of formal constitutional authority. Here, in according weight to the membership organization, the party constitution merely resembles other labor party constitutions that we have observed. But it is argued that the membership organization actually exercises its constitutional authority, not, it is true, by dictating policy to the parliamentary party, but by exerting direct influence in the discussion and presentation of proposals for the party platform. Authorities on Norwegian parties specifically state that the ascendancy attributed to Britain's parliamentary Labour party does not hold for the Norwegian in relation to its membership organization. Instead, they say, the Norwegian "party decisions are definitely the result of a mutual process of influence between the two subsystems."[46] The authors grant that membership participation varies considerably according to the nature of issues, dropping off considerably on foreign affairs. Here, as in other respects, there is not a great deal of evidence of the sort that case studies of party policy-making might provide.

It is the similar unavailability of such studies for other nations that makes it difficult to be sure how much, if at all, an organized membership effectively asserts a policy-making authority granted to it by a social-democratic party constitution. Policy resolutions are regularly debated and adopted at membership conferences. But often it is not known whether they then become parliamentary party policy or, if they do, whether they have not been the decision of a parliamentary leadership able to control the membership conference or congress. Thus, even in France, where the Socialist party (SFIO) has long been regarded as one in which the "militants" had policy outlooks distinct from those of the party's parliamentary deputies,[47] it is not at all certain how much control the former have over the latter.[48] To the right of the Socialists, no such control has ordinarily

[45] Henry Valen and Daniel Katz, *Political Parties in Norway* (Oslo: Universitetsforlaget, 1964).

[46] *Ibid.*, p. 88.

[47] Philip Williams, *Politics in Postwar France* (London: Longmans Green, 1954), pp. 367–68, and Duverger, *op. cit.*, p. 192.

[48] Joseph La Palombara, "Political Party Systems and Crisis Governments: French and Italian Contrasts," *Midwest Journal of Political Science*, II (May, 1958), 135.

been claimed. There has, however, been one striking effort to provide such control in the Radical party, and it happens that this effort has been carefully studied. The occasion was the campaign during the 1950's of Pierre Mendès-France to convert the heterogeneous Radical parliamentary delegation into a cohesive party of the moderate left. He won control of the Radical party congress, largely with the support of his own militants, and then attempted to force the deputies to follow policies the congress adopted. The latter part of the effort failed. Mendès-France was unable to convert his control over the party congress into control over the parliamentary delegation.[49] Even if he had, it ought to be noted, the result would have been less than a clear-cut victory of external organization over parliamentary leaders. Mendès-France was himself a Radical deputy, indeed the chief one at the time, and the external organization could be viewed simply as an agency being used in an intra-parliamentary party struggle. Still, the crucial point is that the organization was not effectively used.

The German Social Democrats ought to provide important illustrations of organizational policy-making. The party began as a working-class movement, it has had a large mass membership, it has seldom exercised governmental power at the national level, and it has usually competed in a multi-party environment.[50] Yet it is hard to find evidence, beyond the most inferential, of external control over policies pursued by the party's parliamentary representatives—once they became numerous. Even in the fairly early years of the party, the independence of the parliamentary leadership was noted—and criticized, for example, by Michels.[51] Much more recently, in the period after World War II, a close study emphasizes the very small part played by the party congress with respect to policy-making in the Bundestag. The congress, meeting biennially as an elected representative body, is supposed to be the highest organ of the party, but its resolutions tend to be general and its function ritualistic. The congress is not used by the membership as a policy-making authority; rather, it is used by the leadership, based in the Bundestag as well as in the external organization's executive, to secure assent for its policies.[52] Thus the Social Democratic congress, whatever its original purpose and earlier role, seems little different in contemporary prac-

---

[49] Francis De Tarr, *The French Radical Party* (London: Oxford University Press, 1961), pp. 226–32.

[50] Carl Landauer, *European Socialism* (Berkeley and Los Angeles: University of California Press, 1959), II, 1320–21.

[51] Robert Michels, *op. cit.*

[52] Douglas A. Chalmers, *The Social Democratic Party of Germany* (New Haven and London: Yale University Press, 1964), pp. 133–35.

tice from the party conference of the Christian Democrats. The latter is only more frankly subordinate to the parliamentary leadership.[53]

Comparable to the German Social Democrats in their traditional Marxist conception of the party as an extra-parliamentary movement, capable of instructing its parliamentary delegation, is the Austrian Social Democratic party. Its theory has been that policy decisions should be made democratically by party members, through the usual representative conferences or congresses, and then transmitted to their agents in the legislature or government.[54] There is no indication from the history of 1945 to 1966, when the Austrian Social Democrats were regularly a governing party, that this theory corresponds to reality. Parliamentary party leaders are believed to share power with certain outside organizations, chiefly economic interest groups related to the party, but this relationship does not pose the same problem as would arise from an attempt of an organized membership to control the parliamentary party policy.[55]

In this as in other cases, especially the German, it must be granted that the lack of evidence of organizational policy-making does not prove its non-existence. There may be conflicting claims, as in the British Labour party in 1960, or there may even be actual instances of organizational supremacy. All that can be said is that the little that is known about policy-making in continental socialist parties, excepting perhaps the Norwegian case, points in the direction of parliamentary party supremacy at least since World War II. Where the traditional authority of the organized membership remains embodied in the party constitution, it does not seem to be followed in a meaningful way.

4. Summary Observations

The inadequacy of evidence with respect to non-British party policy-making precludes anything but the most tentative and hypothetical generalizations about the actual participation of organized memberships in Western nations. As was known from the start, it is chiefly labor or socialist parties, among democratic parties, whose constitutions and traditions allow extra-parliamentary organizational representatives to claim policy-making supremacy. They do this in the name of the program that the membership, often as a movement, has

[53] Arnold J. Heidenheimer, *Adenauer and the CDU* (The Hague: Martinus Nijhoff, 1960), pp. 199, 203, 206–07.

[54] Kurt L. Shell, *The Transformation of Austrian Socialism* (New York: University Publishers, 1962), pp. 95–96.

[55] *Ibid.*, p. 125.

been recruited to support. More conservative parties, although they may also be programmatic and have large membership organizations, do not provide the same basis for the membership's claim to authority in making party policy. For this reason, I have largely ignored them. But I should add that it is not concluded that their membership organizations play no part in party policy-making. On the contrary, there is good reason to believe that their very existence, partly based on programmatic appeals, means that they constitute a pressure or influence on policies made by the parliamentary leadership. Organized followers must always be one significant element in the calculations of party leaders. Naturally this applies also to those labor parties whose membership organizations are not the supreme policy-making authorities they claim to be. Here too, probably in greater degree, important pressures must be taken into account.

Just how these pressures are taken into account in various parties lies beyond my present inquiry. Hopefully, however, the experiences cited here may be relevant to this issue. By focussing on the clash between an organized membership that does claim authority and an established public office-holding leadership, my purpose has been to show the difficulty inherent in the membership's making a policy claim. That difficulty might well exist, though in lesser degree and certainly in less dramatic form, when the organized membership had no basis for claiming supremacy and was content with simply exerting influence on policy-making. After all, its influence could be exerted in a different direction from that favored by an office-holding leadership estimating the responses of its general electorate. In this projected situation, without a membership claim to policy-making supremacy, the leadership could have its way, paying the price of strained but not impossible intra-party relations. If the price is high— that is, if relations should become very strained—the leadership might prefer conciliation and compromise. Either way, it would not entirely avoid the difficulty that flows from a programmatically based membership organization. The only way to do that is to have a thoroughly docile organization. While this appears improbable on a continuous basis for a membership attracted by programmatic interests, it may be close to realization in some conservative parties. Perhaps this means that their memberships are not so interested in programs and the policies flowing from them.

At least there is good reason for believing that these conservative party memberships are not program-oriented in the same way as the traditional recruits to labor and socialist movements are. Not only have they joined an organization inspired by an already existing party at the office-holding level—while labor and socialist recruits joined an external movement seeking to gain public offices—but they also differ in that their members joined to support the established order rather than to change it. The degree of dedication may differ significantly. In this as in other respects, the working-class party of the late nineteenth and early twentieth centuries seems a distinctive phenomenon. Its commitment to organizational policy-making was part of its broader distinctiveness. Because the working-class party, labor or social democratic, viewed itself as the representative (and the only true representative) of a presumed majority of the population, its organization of that majority seemed to provide the legitimate policy-making agency. The important thing was to maintain democracy in intra-party deliberations. A conference or congress fairly elected by party members could be the policy-maker for the working class. The party's parliamentary delegation, on the other hand, was merely to carry out the policy. Its responsibility to the organized membership did not conflict with any electoral responsibility since the membership itself was assumed to embody the will of the majority of the electorate—that is, of the working class that composed the majority.

It is only an assumption of this kind that can lend democratic credibility to an organized membership's claim to policy-making authority. Otherwise, its credentials seem much less legitimate than those of public office-holders whose policies are tailored to the electorate. The membership must itself be conceived as representing the majority of the population before it can be regarded as any more than another interest group seeking to fashion policy.

Insofar as this conception derives only from the traditions of the working-class movement, it is likely that it will lose its force as those traditions change. In particular, as labor and social democratic parties in Western nations become less class conscious, broadening their appeals beyond industrial workers, their organized members could become more like members of non-labor parties—having neither a special mission nor a special majoritarian basis for one. In thus coming to resemble others more closely, the labor and social democratic parties should also be able to avoid the difficulties, so well illustrated in the British case, of reconciling organizational policy-making claims with the responsibilities of public office-holders to their electors.

XII

The Governing Function

1. *The Impact of the Governmental System*

Reserving the discussion of the governing function of political parties until this point is not a way of reducing its significance. On the contrary, it is appreciated that this function is potentially the most significant one. But it is not clear that political parties always perform the function. There is also a serious question whether parties must perform it in every democratic political system in order for the system to be effective. As is known and will be described at length, considerable variations exist among political systems with respect to the degree to which parties assume responsibility for governing. The variation is so great that it has understandably been exaggerated in the familiar contrast between the non-responsible American parties and the highly responsible British parties. Almost no one would seriously argue that American parties, as loose collectivities, assume *no* governmental responsibility in their own and in the public's perspective. But they are thought to assume it much less fully and clearly than major parties in many other nations, notably Britain. Accepting much of this familiar contrast, as will be done here, does not mean that one has to regard it as invidious with respect to parties in the United States. It is true that both American party reformers and European critics of American politics do make the contrast invidiously. They believe that the Republican and Democratic parties fail to fulfill responsibility for governmental policy output demanded by a working political system.

This is a particular normative view of party functions to which this work does not subscribe. My starting point was that only the provision of a label to structure voting decisions is an essential party function; an entity calling itself or being called a party is such in fact if it does as much as label a set of candidates. Anything else that it does, by way of organization or governing, may be usual, even broadly (while not universally) characteristic, but it is not essential to its existence as a party. Perhaps this seems a peculiarly stubborn view. One could argue that the electoral function of labelling candidates leads by inexorable logic to a collective responsibility for governing on the part of the candidates elected under a given label. Obviously there is some connection. Even in the United States, where we have come to speak of party-in-government as distinct from party-in-electorate, we recognize that the elected office-holders not only carry the same label in government as they do in electoral campaigns but that their actions as governmental policy-makers are collectively related in some degree to their electoral concerns. But that little phrase "in some degree" is most important. The degree has not been great enough to create the collective responsibility for governing that characterizes many parties in other countries. Thus the logical progression, if such there be, from electoral to governing function is not inexorable. Parties may govern in one democratic political system in very different ways and in very different degree than they do in others.

In order that a party can fulfill a collective governing responsibility, its elected office-holders plainly have to agree regularly on common policies, either from conviction or from expediency. Rare or perhaps even occasional individual deviations are feasible, but they must be so exceptional as not to mar the impression of a party whose representatives are collectively capable of enacting and carrying out policies. Intra-party disputes among elected office-holders, as in non-governmental party organizations, presumably exist, but the important point is that they be settled by an internal decision-making process so that the party-in-government stands united. The customary term for this is cohesion, and it is used primarily with reference to legislative parties. In a parliamentary system, this is the only kind of governmental party cohesion. The achievement of cohesion by a party's legislative membership is thus sufficient for responsibility, actually or potentially. But in a system like the American one, with its separately elected executive and legislative authorities, legislative cohesion is not enough. To their own agreement, the legislators of a given party must add a unity of purpose with the executive leadership, if of their party. The complications are great, but it is not clear that they alone would be sufficient to prevent cohesion in the American system. For one thing, the difficulties of bridging the executive-legislative separation cannot explain the relatively non-cohesive character of American legislative parties in and of themselves.

Another aspect of the differential impact of parliamentary and separation-of-powers systems is worth stressing: the absence in the latter of the incentive for legislative party cohesion provided in a parliamentary system. That incentive is simply the need to support an executive leadership whose very existence, given the usual rules of the parliamentary game, requires the regular approval of a majority of legislators. The parliamentary party thus becomes the agency for executive stability. It may be so on its own if it is a majority. Or it may be one of several parties coalescing to provide the stability. Or, as a second party in two-party competition, it may be the support of a potential alternative government. In any event, there is a crucial role for a legislative party in a parliamentary system that is not available under the separation-of-powers formula. An American executive may want the continuous support of his legislative party because it is useful for the enactment of his policies, but he does not need this support in order to stay in office. He may not even need it for the enactment of his policies if he can secure enough votes from legislators outside his own party. The parliamentary system does not work that way. Shifting majorities across party lines, while technically sufficient, are not reliable enough to maintain an executive in office even if they might be mobilized to enact policies proposed by the executive. It is true that a parliamentary party does not literally have to support an executive leadership of the same party. But it has a powerful incentive to do so, certainly more powerful than any affecting a legislative party in the American system.

For this reason, the governing function of political parties is regarded as basically influenced by whether parties exist in a parliamentary or a separation-of-powers system. For the party-in-government to be cohesive in such high degree as to be clearly "responsible" is much more likely in a parliamentary system than in the United States. This argument, yet to be fully defended, is meant to reduce but not eliminate the importance of certain other factors often held accountable for differences between European and American patterns. For example, small size and great homogeneity in a nation might still facilitate cohesion. So might strongly class-conscious parties. But the evidence will indicate that these are not crucial factors. Parliamentary party cohesion can be shown to exist in their absence. Also, it ought to be stressed, such cohesion exists without programmatically-oriented mass-membership organizations. Even if this could not be demonstrated, however, it follows from the previous chapter's report on the way many parliamentary parties make their own policies that they are not dependent on external organizations for their cohesion. An organized membership can tend to disrupt parliamentary party cohesion, as it did temporarily in the British Labour case, at least as readily as it can impose its own policies. Not only is the extra-parliamentary organization unnecessary for the achievement of parliamentary party cohesion, but it may even make it more difficult in certain instances.

Analysis of the governing function of parties is roughly divided into three main sections. First, within the parliamentary frame of reference, is the established bipartisan model of Great Britain and three Commonwealth nations—Canada, Australia, and New Zealand —whose systems are close adaptations of the British. Second are the mainly continental European variations of the parliamentary system, characterized by a recent tradition of, if not current experience with, multi-partyism. This separation of the continental from the British models is not meant to indicate a basic difference. Instead, it will be argued, broadly similar incentives exist for party cohesion and governing responsibility in both, even though the achievement of responsibility, if not of individual party cohesion, is often more difficult in the multi-party situation. The third section of the analysis concerns the response of American parties to the separation of powers and how the governing function, performed so largely by parties in parliamentary systems, is discharged differently in the United States.

2. The Two-Party Parliamentary Model

British parliamentary party cohesion is the most familiar working model. It may not be any greater than in other political systems, but more is known about it.[1] And there can be no doubt about its contemporary significance in the operation of the political system. Each major British party, Conservative and Labour, maintains effective unity in its parliamentary ranks so that it is able, when a majority, to maintain a government in office, and able, when in opposition, to demonstrate its capacity to maintain a government if it became a majority. For these purposes, the unity does not have to be absolute at all times. There can be and there are instances when M.P.s do not vote with their party colleagues and leaders, but these instances are the allowable exceptions. It is important that they are regarded as exceptions to the recognized and accepted norm of parliamentary behavior. Or, stated differently, there is a norm that is not seriously questioned even by the M.P.s who deviate from it. They and their leaders view parliamentary party cohesion as the essence of the con-

---

[1] Sources for much of the British material that follows can be found in Leon D. Epstein, "Cohesion of British Parliamentary Parties," *American Political Science Review*, L (June, 1956), 360–77, and *British Politics in the Suez Crisis* (Urbana: University of Illinois Press, 1964), chaps. 5–6. In these works the subject is explored in more illustrative detail than is possible here.

temporary British system. Deviation has to be justified as exceptional, as infrequent, and, most telling of all, as undamaging to the maintenance of a government by party leaders. Thus there can be a readier toleration of deviations in an opposition party, whose reputation but not its capacity for supporting a government is at stake. Even in a majority party, however, deviations can be tolerated as long as the majority is large enough. What is intolerable is a deviation that causes the defeat of a government, either because its majority is small to begin with or because so many M.P.s fail to vote their support. One is tempted to say that this never happens in Britain, but one should be more cautious. It is convincing enough to say that no government based on a party with a majority of parliamentary seats has been forced from office by an adverse parliamentary vote during this century.

The conditional phrase, "based on a party with a majority of parliamentary seats," is worth discussion on more than one count. It had to be inserted in order to allow for the difficulty of Labour's minority government in 1924, when the government did lose a vote of confidence in the House of Commons because of the defection not of its own Labour supporters but of the third-party Liberals who had previously supported the government.[2] Clearly cohesion in the governing party is insufficient when that party lacks a majority. The absence of such a majority in 1929, as in 1924, resulted from a temporary and transitional British departure from the two-party model.[3] For a time, Britain had substantial three-party competition. That could always recur, or even a minor third party might capture, in a close election, enough seats to prevent either major party from having a majority. The fact that neither circumstance has arisen since 1929, despite a few close calls, allows us to regard two-partyism as a British norm and therefore a single party's parliamentary cohesion as crucial. This is reinforced by most, though not all, of British parliamentary history during more than half a century before World War I.

It was in the late nineteenth century, the era of Conservative-Liberal competition, that parliamentary party cohesion was established. Careful measurements of the phenomenon show that party voting in the House of Commons increased markedly after the 1860's and by the 1890's reached levels not very much below those exhibited

[2] Richard W. Lyman, *The First Labour Government 1924* (London: Chapman and Hall, 1957), chap. 13.

[3] Reginald Bassett, *Nineteen Thirty-One* (London: Macmillan, 1958), chap. 3.

in the mid-twentieth century.[4] This change reflected both an increase in "whipped divisions," that is, in the percentage of divisions labelled as party issues, and an increase in the percentage of M.P.s voting with their parties in such divisions. In other words, not only did cohesion rise, but the occasions for its existence also rose.[5] All this occurred, it must be emphasized, before the rise of the Labour party. Thus, even if the (subsequently) still greater cohesion of the mid-twentieth century be attributed to the Labour party (and Conservative solidarity in response to it), the fact would remain that most of the increase in parliamentary party unity had been accomplished without any Labour influence. So much of it was accomplished that cohesion generally can be said to have existed in its contemporary form before the Labour party made its parliamentary mark. This is to say that the phenomenon exists independently of the socialist working-class party and of any claim, on its behalf, to exert discipline derived from an extra-parliamentary movement.

Attributing cohesion primarily to the pressures of parliamentary government raises another important question. Why did this pressure not operate earlier to make British parties cohesive in the House of Commons? Already by the middle years of the nineteenth century, Britain surely had parliamentary government and two competing parliamentary parties. Yet these parties actually declined in cohesiveness from the Reform Bill of 1832 to the middle of the century, at which time they were hardly cohesive at all.[6] The fact that it was only after the 1860's that the trend was sharply upward suggests that more than parliamentary government was causal. At least two new circumstances seem relevant. One was the enlargement of the suffrage, linking parliamentary representatives to a broader electorate whose voting decisions were structured by parties, and the other was the considerable increase in the importance of the executive responsible to these parliamentary representatives. Members of parliament were, more than before, put in a position of party men elected to support a leadership that was actually or potentially the governing authority. Maintaining a government in office became their responsibility. They stood before the electorate not as independent agents but as supporters of one set of leaders or the other. Of course, extra-parliamentary party organizations grew at the same time and also in

---

[4] Samuel H. Beer, *British Politics in the Collectivist Age* (New York: Alfred A. Knopf, 1965), pp. 184–85, 257.

[5] *Ibid.*, pp. 262–63.

[6] A. Lawrence Lowell, *The Government of England* (New York: Macmillan, 1908), II, 78.

response to the new mass electorate. But there is almost no indication that these new Conservative and Liberal organizations were themselves directly responsible for the new cohesion. Indeed, their actual development lagged behind it.

But these late nineteenth-century conditions do not obliterate the importance attached to parliamentary government as an explanation for party cohesion. The pressure for cohesion remains indigenous to parliamentary government, but it becomes strongly determining only in the modern conditions of a mass electorate and strengthened executive authority. It seems more reasonable to state the case this way than to try to argue that the modern conditions are really determining. After all, they have not produced party cohesion in American government. On the other side, it is true that not every parliamentary government, in modern conditions, has produced cohesion. But the exceptions, as will be observed, are situations in which parliamentary government itself was unworkable, usually in multi-party circumstances. Where the parliamentary system endures along two-party lines, as it has in Britain, the cohesive party is characteristic.

Britain's cohesive parliamentary parties are worth extended examination. There is considerable misunderstanding about how they operate. It is easy to exaggerate the formal disciplinary apparatus. On paper, the means of discipline are formidable, especially in the Labour party, where the rules provide for the expulsion of an M.P. from the parliamentary party and ultimately even from the external organization.[7] The latter deprives an M.P. of the opportunity to stand again as an official Labour candidate. But expulsion, as either a threat or an actuality, rarely occurs. It is not necessary, in order regularly to secure party unity, nor is it really useful on the infrequent occasions when party unity is broken. Instead, parliamentary party cohesion rests on rules of the game that are accepted by the M.P.s playing the game. And the cardinal rule is to vote with one's party for the sake of the solidarity expected of any party claiming to be able to govern.

In practice, the observation of this rule means following the parliamentary party leadership. Even without the effective power to invoke the drastic sanction of expelling any offending M.P.s, the leadership exerts a strong influence over the rest of the parliamentary party. It is true that this influence in turn depends on the continued consent of most of the party's M.P.s, who collectively possess a final authority if they want to exercise it, but the leadership has the advantages of prestige, experience, and potential or actual government officeholding.

[7] 53rd Annual Report of the Labour Conference (London: Labour Party, 1954), p. 202.

The last of these advantages derives its significance from the prime minister's appointive powers. His government—ministers, under-secretaries, parliamentary secretaries, and so forth—consists of seventy to one hundred politicians of his own party, mainly from the House of Commons. Thus as much as one-fifth to one-fourth of a parliamentary party is bound to a leader, when prime minister, by executive solidarity as well as by ordinary party loyalty. And when the leader is not prime minister but only the head of the opposition hoping to become a majority, there may be an even larger share with expectations of executive appointments after a general election victory. These expectations can only be fulfilled by a prime minister. There is no other route to executive office. And, most telling in comparison to the situation of an American congressman, there is virtually no position, status, or power except such executive office that an M.P. has a chance to achieve while in the Commons. Seniority alone confers nothing like the importance attainable in the U.S. Congress, since there are in parliament no subject-matter standing committees serving as independent foci of decision-making. To be a British parliamentary committee chairman is a chore and perhaps a modest acknowledgement of judiciousness and efficiency, but it cannot rival its American counterpart in status or power. The fact is that a British M.P. must make his way into an executive position in order that his political career seem successful in the sense of exercising power. Otherwise the most he can hope for is good-humored recognition as a backbench specialist on Commons procedure and tradition, or as an individualistic performer commenting on current affairs in the House and through the press, radio, and television. These roles are available only to a few M.P.s in each generation.

The dependence of almost all politically ambitious M.P.s on appointments from their leadership does not mean that obedience is exacted as an absolute *quid pro quo*. There is one exception. When actually in a government, M.P.s are generally required to vote with their leaders as a condition for remaining in the government. Otherwise, there is usually nothing so crude as a promise of an executive position for staying in line, or the overt withdrawal of a suggested position because of deviant voting in the House. It is only that there is a general understanding that loyalty pays off. The troublesome M.P.—that is, troublesome to the party whips and so to the leadership —obviously does not receive the same favorable notice as the M.P. who both speaks and votes for his party's position. No more than occasionally is a persistent rebel so consequential that he must be given a ministerial position. Only a few M.P.s of ambition can afford the risks of that pathway to influence. Churchill, Macmillan, and Bevan are conspicuous exceptions, but they are still exceptions.

By no means all of a parliamentary party's cohesion can be explained as a result of the ambitions of its members to hold office. Many do not have this ambition. They may be too old or otherwise incapacitated, perhaps by temperament, for the responsibilities of executive office. They may prefer to be ordinary backbench M.P.s. Or they may have held executive office in the past and now regard themselves as out of the running. Their loyal voting behavior has to be accounted for on other grounds. Moreover, the number of M.P.s to be accounted for is large, probably at least as many as those whose loyalty can be partly explained by the leader's power to bestow positions. We are thrust back to the original explanation that M.P.s are simply willing participants on a parliamentary team. The party's policies are their policies. Indeed, there is a sense in which backbench M.P.s help to make those policies even if they originate with the leadership. The parliamentary party, or at any rate a majority of it, must openly or tacitly accept the policies before they are really binding on individual members, and it is unlikely that a narrow majority would override the strong feelings of a large minority. Put differently, the leadership would not often seek to impose its policies on large numbers of reluctant members. Instead, persuasion and compromise might well be employed for the sake of a willingly united party.[8]

Such informal tactics appear much more relevant than the power to dissolve the Commons. This calls into question the traditional regard for the dissolution power as a major means for the prime minister to keep his majority intact. The theory has been that the threat to dissolve in case of a vote of no confidence dissuades the prime minister's partisan supporters from such a no-confidence vote. M.P.s, it has been assumed, would prefer to keep their seats than to risk them in a general election. To protect their own political lives, they would remain loyal to the prime minister. At most, this threat could explain only the governing party's cohesion, not the opposition's. And it is doubtful whether it is really operative to discipline even the governing body. There is no recent British evidence of dissolution, or threatened dissolution, being used for this purpose. Perhaps it does not have to be so used. British parliamentary parties may achieve cohesion without it. But it is hard to see just how dissolution could be effectively used as a threat to keep one's own followers in line.

The prime minister wants, above all, to time the dissolution for the

[8] Herbert Morrison, *Government and Parliament* (London: Oxford University Press, 1954), p. 94.

maximum electoral advantage of his party—which is to say, also for his own advantage. For him to dissolve the House when his own supporters have caused him to lose a vote of confidence, or otherwise to be shaken in his majority, would hardly be politically wise. There could hardly be a time less propitious for electoral victory. He would appear before the country as the leader of a disunited party. The disadvantage is so apparent and so great that it is hard to believe that a prime minister could convince his parliamentary followers that he would dissolve if they rebelled. The prime minister's own political suicide would be much more certain than that of most of his party's M.P.s. Many of them have safe seats and would be re-elected anyway. Some, of course, would lose their seats if their party was in disarray following a more-or-less forced dissolution. But such losses would also make it likely that the party's parliamentary majority was lost and so the prime ministership. A fairly small number of marginal seats are all important to the leadership and to its hopes for maintaining itself in executive office.

One should add, as an aside, that this argument against the relevance of the dissolution power to the maintenance of majority party cohesion does not mean that it is also irrelevant to the maintenance of the occasionally useful support by a minor party's M.P.s. When the bipartisan model functions so imperfectly as to make a prime minister dependent on a party other than his own, as MacDonald and his minority Labour government were in 1924 and 1929, then it is possible that dissolution can be used as a threat against the M.P.s of the lesser party—assuming that they have more reason to fear a general election than have the prime minister and his party. Similarly, in the year and a half after the 1964 election, when Prime Minister Wilson's Labour government had so narrow a majority that it wanted the tolerance if not the support of the Liberal M.P.s, the prime minister's power to dissolve if defeated on a confidence vote might have been useful in securing the acquiescence of the Liberals as long as they were at least as reluctant as Labour to fight another general election. Thus it may be granted that there are marginal circumstances in which the power to dissolve can be used as a weapon to help maintain a government in office (and not just, as is much more usual, to time a general election for the convenience of the prime minister and his party). The marginal circumstances, however, involve the prime minister's relations with a party other than his own, and so do not affect the argument that dissolution is unemployable as a means to discipline his own party.

Should one therefore conclude that dissolution has nothing to do

with the maintenance of a majority party's cohesion? Not exactly.
Even if the prime minister does not and probably cannot, for practical political reasons, discipline his party's M.P.s by threatening a
general election, there is still the possibility that M.P.s willingly support their party leadership because they, along with the prime minister, simply do not want a dissolution that would follow from a
no-confidence vote. But this is really only another way of saying what
has already been stressed: that members of a majority parliamentary
party share in the partisan desire to maintain their leaders in office.
That is the main purpose for which they have been elected to parliament. Dissolution in politically disadvantageous circumstances, conducive to the loss of a majority in the general election, would defeat
this purpose almost as directly as the resignation of a prime minister
after a no-confidence vote. Either action would probably bring the
opposition to power. To avoid this ultimate political catastrophe, not
just to avoid dissolution, is what provides the motivation for majority
party cohesion. Losing a party majority in parliament is a blow not
only to the cause itself but also to the M.P.s, who lose their seats in
consequence of the party debacle.

This motivation may be observed to have operated regularly and
sufficiently in recent decades. On only one occasion was there anything like an exception. This was in the dramatic parliamentary division of May, 1940, when more than forty Conservative followers of
Prime Minister Chamberlain voted against him, while others ab-
stained.[9] Although even these notable defections left enough Conservatives supporting Chamberlain so as to prevent a defeat on the
motion, the revolt was so substantial and so drastic that it was at least
one of the factors leading him to resign as prime minister. But one
must remember that the partisan basis for Conservative cohesion did
not exist in the ordinary way in 1940. Not only might strict partisanship have been overridden by a patriotic concern to fight Hitler more
effectively than Chamberlain seemed to be doing, but Conservative
M.P.s also knew that defeating Chamberlain could not bring the
opposition Labour party into power. The Conservative majority was
so large that there was no chance of a Labour and/or Liberal government in the existing parliament. And dissolution, with the election of
a new parliament, was out of the question during an obviously critical stage of the war. Therefore, the most that the revolting Conservatives could bring about was the substitution of a new Conservative

[9] The special nature of the 1940 experience is compared with the parliamentary party cohesion of 1956 in Epstein, *British Politics in the Suez Crisis*,
p. 94.

prime minister capable, as Chamberlain was not, of attracting Labour into a coalition government. This was accomplished when Winston Churchill succeeded Chamberlain.

Other than the extraordinary instance of 1940, there has been no open parliamentary revolt leading to changes in the prime minister-ship or in the opposition leadership. Even if there had been, it would not necessarily provide telling evidence against the cohesion of the parliamentary party. The revolt might simply have been to secure a new party leader behind whom the party would rally more readily or effectively than behind the old leader. Changing leaders, after all, can be part of the process of maintaining cohesion.

There have, however, been revolts unproductive of change in the party leadership. They may not have been designed to produce a change but only to show a greater degree of dissatisfaction with the leadership and its policies than that demonstrated by disagreement within the parliamentary party caucus. The method, employed by individual M.P.s and by groups of M.P.s, is to abstain from voting in support of the party's official position. Also the reasons for the dis-agreement may be publicly stated (or, in other cases, the reasons may be stated even though the M.P.s decide to vote with their party). Occasional deviations of this kind, as already indicated, can be and are tolerated by British parliamentary parties as long as the deviations do not, by their numbers, threaten to destroy a majority and as long as they do not, by their frequency, threaten to destroy a party's repu-tation for sufficient cohesion to be able to govern. Thus there is no danger, even for a governing party, in allowing individual M.P.s to honor their consciences by abstaining now and then—provided that their votes are not needed to maintain the majority. Nor, in that happy situation, is there much danger in abstentions by small groups of M.P.s who want collectively to demonstrate their strong feelings. No doubt party leaders would prefer that these demonstrations not take place even though their majority is safe. Their goal is to have a party that is as cohesive as possible, but they can get along with a party that is cohesive enough to maintain a government (or, in opposition, to seem capable of maintaining a government). Except when a govern-ing party has a very narrow majority, as occurred in 1964, the strong feelings of a modest number of followers can be accommodated in the form of occasional abstentions.

It cannot be emphasized too strongly, however, that the allowable abstentions must be kept small. This means not only small enough to avoid eliminating a governing party's majority, but also small enough to avoid coming close to elimination. The limitations are well illustrated by the Conservative parliamentary majority during the Suez crisis of 1956–57. Abstentions did occur, first on the left and then on the right as the Conservative government shifted policies, but they were never sufficient to threaten the overthrow of the government. Indeed the rebels appeared to have no desire to overthrow the government; on at least one occasion they may have deliberately limited the number of abstentions in order to avoid anything that would look like a threat to overthrow. At the same time, the Conservative whips had their own good reasons for working effectively to dissuade Conservative waverers from abstaining.[10] In any event, the result was a persistent and convincing party majority voting in favor of the government, both when it went into Suez and when it came out. The principle of cohesion proved sufficient to sustain a government in especially difficult circumstances. The governing party, in other words, remained capable of governing.

The case for treating this capacity for governing as a response to the parliamentary system is strengthened by evidence from Australia, New Zealand, and Canada. In each of these nations, where parliamentary forms are close adaptations from the British model and where also the prevailing pattern has been that of near two-party competition, the cohesive parliamentary party has developed much as in the British House of Commons. It can even be argued that the Australian Labor party is more determinedly cohesive than any British party. Its discipline is formalized by an erstwhile candidate's pledge that, if elected to parliament, he will "vote on all matters connected with the Labor platform or concerned with the fate of a government in accordance with the decision of the majority of the parliamentary party."[11] Although this rule leaves a little room for individuality, there is no doubt that the intention is to secure conformity on everything important to party purposes. Nor is there any doubt about the Australian Labor party's success in fulfilling this intention. Indeed, the success has been so great and so nearly uniform as to subject the party to criticism for its rigidity. It is also charged with responsibility for imposing its disciplined pattern, derived from the party's predominant trade-union basis, on Australian parliamentary behavior in general—meaning the practices of competing parties. This charge might seem to have a historical justification in that Labor was the first Australian party to be a disciplined parliamentary force. But, in light of the rise of Britain's cohesive parliamentary parties before British La-

[10] *Ibid.,* chap. 5.
[11] J. D. B. Miller, *Australian Government and Politics* (London: Gerald Duckworth, 1964), p. 110.

bour could have been a major influence, it is hard to see why the non-Labor parties in Australia could not have developed their own cohesion quite independent of the Labor example.

The fact that both the Liberal and Country parties in Australia function cohesively in parliament is not questioned. The Country party, operating often as a minor but a necessary coalition partner of the Liberals, is reported to "preserve a party solidarity almost as complete as that of Labor."[12] The Liberals are admittedly less formally and less stringently bound to their party than are Labor M.P.s to theirs. But, while the Liberals are not pledged in the Labor manner, they "vote together from convenience and habit, and in accordance with parliamentary strategy."[13] In short, they do not choose to exercise their freedom. They are thought to do so even less than is customary among British M.P.s. Generally, however, their solidarity appears remarkably like that of the British Conservatives both in degree and in its voluntary, self-disciplined character. No more than British Conservatives do Australian Liberals need the formal disciplinary rules of the opposing Labor party in order to be united. Evidently the demands of the parliamentary system suffice.

It may seem harder to account for the cohesion of the Australian Labor party in this same way. One might infer that Labor's extra-parliamentary apparatus for controlling M.P.s is the necessary element in securing parliamentary voting regularity. Not only does Labor exact a candidate's pledge to conform, but it plainly threatens a nonconforming M.P. with reprisals—specifically, subsequent rejection of candidature. The curious feature of this arrangement is that the power to select (and reject) candidates is subject to control by the several *state* Labor parties.[14] Pressure on M.P.s from these state parties is real enough, but it cannot be said to account for the national parliamentary party's cohesion. To do so, the state Labor parties would have to exert their pressure consistently in the same direction. No such assumption is warranted, since the state parties are well known for their independent power in the federal system. Thus, if anything, extra-parliamentary control might in and of itself threaten party cohesion in the national parliament. If it does not (and apparently it does not), the explanation must lie in a willingness to acknowledge the parliamentary party's caucus decisions as binding. These decisions may themselves have been influenced by external

[12] *Ibid.*, p. 111.
[13] *Ibid.*, p. 110.
[14] L. F. Crisp, *The Australian Federal Labour Party 1901–1951* (London: Longmans, Green, 1955), p. 132.

agencies, particularly the state party executives, but once made they are regularly observed by individual Labor M.P.s. Insofar as state parties threaten to discipline deviating M.P.s, they are backing the parliamentary party and particularly its leadership. Moreover, they are backing the normal rules of the parliamentary game. All M.P.s —whether formally threatened, as are Labor M.P.s, or formally (but not always actually) free, as are Liberal M.P.s—regularly vote in support of the decisions made by the majority of their respective parliamentary party caucuses. As in Britain, there are allowable exceptions and a rare unallowable revolt.[15] But cohesion is clearly the overwhelmingly dominant characteristic.

New Zealand's two parliamentary parties are similar to Australia's. Or, more accurately, they are especially similar to Britain's since there is not even any reason for suspecting that the cohesion of New Zealand's Labour party (or of the rival National party) derives from an extra-parliamentary organization. Constituency organizations, as in Britain and Australia, can threaten rebellious or potentially rebellious M.P.s with subsequent rejection of their candidacies, but this external pressure is essentially in support of the parliamentary party.[16] The policy decisions that a party expects its M.P.s to follow are those of the parliamentary caucus. Certainly, New Zealand M.P.s follow these decisions.[17] From 1936, when the National party became the single important anti-Labour organization, until 1946, there were only two revolts in the form of parliamentary votes by M.P.s against their caucus decisions. And from 1946 to 1955, not only did all divisions result in the expected government majority (except once when absenteeism had to be rectified in a subsequent division), but out of 366 parliamentary divisions only seven involved any voting across party lines. Five of these were instances of free votes, some of which had occurred earlier as well. The other two, in whipped divisions, were small aberrations within the opposition party.[18] It is safe to regard parliamentary party cohesion in New Zealand as a fact of political life.[19]

---

[15] Dagmar Carboch, "The Fall of the Bruce-Page Government," *Studies in Australian Politics* (Melbourne: F. W. Cheshire, 1958), pp. 121, 146.

[16] Peter Campbell, "Politicians, Public Servants and the People in New Zealand," *Political Studies*, III (October, 1955), 208.

[17] *Ibid.*, p. 207.

[18] Robert N. Kelson, *The Private Member of Parliament and the Formation of Public Policy* (Toronto: University of Toronto Press, 1964), pp. 108–16.

[19] Leslie Lipson, "Party Systems in the United Kingdom and the Older Commonwealth: Causes, Resemblances, and Variations," *Political Studies*, VII (February, 1959), 19.

To what extent does this fact about New Zealand strengthen the view that cohesion is simply an accompaniment of the two-party parliamentary model? At the very least, the evidence from New Zealand is consonant with that view. It has to be granted, however, that it is also consonant with the view that the presence of a major labor party favors cohesion within a parliamentary system. In New Zealand, as in Australia, the Labour party was the first large and highly disciplined party (even though the source of the discipline is in the parliamentary Labour party rather than in the external apparatus). The opposition's discipline was not so regularly established until 1936.[20] Thus, there is at least the speculative possibility that cohesion would not have been achieved unless a labor party, for its own reasons, had already become highly cohesive. The basis for rejecting this possibility is that Britain's Conservative and Liberal parties managed to achieve considerable cohesion before the Labour party presented itself as a still more cohesive force. If parties thus developed in Britain independently of Labour influence or example, why could they not have done so in Australia and New Zealand? The parliamentary system, in a basically two-party pattern, is what all three nations have in common.

The argument is most directly strengthened by observing the Canadian experience. In Canada, parliamentary party cohesion has existed without a major labor party at any stage. The Liberal and Conservative parties became cohesive parliamentary forces during a long competitive period, and they have remained that way during recent decades of competition with third and fourth parties. Of course, one cannot conclude simply from the absence of a labor-party influence that therefore cohesion was a response only to the parliamentary system.[21] But there is another reason for coming to that conclusion: nothing except the parliamentary system distinguishes Canada from the United States in such a way as to account for the much greater cohesion of parties in the Canadian House of Commons than in the American Congress. Both Canada and the United States have federal systems. Both have important regional variations supporting a social as well as a structural federalism. Both have, at the national level, two major political parties each of which is a loose federation of state (or

[20] Kelson, *op. cit.*, pp. 108–9.

[21] The question, along with other general aspects of the Canadian party experience, is discussed at greater length in Leon D. Epstein, "A Comparative Study of Canadian Parties," *American Political Science Review*, LVIII (March, 1964), 46–59. More illustrative material is cited in the article than can be noted here.

provincial) parties. Both have had relatively large rural populations coexisting with urbanized, industrial areas. Neither nation has had large mass-membership organizations linked to major parties. And neither has been greatly influenced by the class-conscious politics of a labor or social-democratic party.

Naturally these matters, on which Canada and the United States resemble each other, do not exhaust the conceivable social, economic, and institutional circumstances that might be compared. But the matters noted are those which, if they significantly differed as between the two nations, might be said to help explain the difference between the two national legislative parties. Yet, except for the presence of the parliamentary system in Canada and its absence in the United States, no other factor can be readily related to the cohesion result. Candidate selection, it is true, is by party meetings in Canada and not by direct primary. But this difference is hardly relevant. The Canadian method is not that of a highly organized national and programmatic party. Rather, it is like the fairly open convention method, dominated by state and local considerations, used in the United States before the primary was adopted. And that older American method, prevailing until just before World War I, did not produce cohesive parties in the United States Congress. There is little reason to believe that anything like this method should be held responsible for parliamentary party cohesion in Canada. At most, the degree of party control of Canadian candidate selection could be said to be more nearly compatible with the maintenance of legislative party cohesion than the American primaries would be.

This leaves parliamentary government itself as the only likely explanation of the Canadian phenomenon.[22] While we come to this conclusion by a process of elimination insofar as the strictly Canadian-American comparison is concerned, the result is consonant with the experience reported for Britain, Australia, and New Zealand. In the four Commonwealth nations, the parliamentary system, operated in a largely two-party framework, produces cohesive legislative parties. It is true that in each of these nations it is the *British* parliamentary system, or a variant of it. Therefore, we cannot say, at least not yet, that any parliamentary system produces cohesive parties.

The Canadian case is still so crucial, at this point of the analysis, that it should be observed in more detail. Party cohesion in the Cana-

[22] The explanation, however, was regarded as unconvincing by David B. Truman, "Federalism and the Party System," in Arthur MacMahon (ed.), *Federalism: Mature and Emergent* (New York: Columbia University Press, 1955), pp. 115–36.

dian House of Commons had already been well established before World War I; it was possible for a leading constitutional scholar, Macgregor Dawson, to say in an early work, published in 1922, that "few Canadian members of parliament have shown their independence of their party."[23] He cited an important example of full Conservative party support for a prime minister despite known intra-party differences. This had become the normal practice despite three famous party splits over the preceding half-century.[24] Mainly the cohesion has been described as a matter of M.P.s following their leaders, even to the point of "subservience."[25] More broadly, cohesion is expected by the public as the "very condition of party government of the Cabinet variety."[26] The parliamentary party caucus is the place where agreement is reached, although it is unclear whether the caucus procedure is primarily consensual or strictly a leader-follower affair. Some kind of bargaining takes place in this intra-party arena.[27] But the important point is that the parliamentary party ends up voting as a unit in the House.

The regularity of this voting behavior is not in question. It has been sufficient to sustain every majority party government in Canadian history. The only instances (three before 1963) of governmental defeats leading to dissolution occurred when the prime minister, lacking a majority in his own party, was deserted by M.P.s of the third or fourth parties who had previously supported the government. Similarly, the main opposition party can count almost as regularly on unity in its ranks. In both cases, though of course more in the former, M.P.s have the strong incentive for cohesion that the parliamentary system provides. They want to make the party viable and capable of attaining its goals. M.P.s have said as much when systematically interviewed.[28] Their collective desire for the effectiveness of unity overrides all of the other divisive forces operating in so federal and so heterogeneous a society as the Canadian.

[23] Robert MacGregor Dawson, *The Principle of Official Independence* (London: P. S. King, 1922), p. 229.

[24] *Ibid.*, pp. 228–29.

[25] Hugh McD. Clokie, *Canadian Government and Politics* (Toronto: Longmans, Green, 1944), p. 135.

[26] Hugh McD. Clokie, "The Machinery of Government," in George W. Brown (ed.), *Canada* (Berkeley and Los Angeles: University of California Press, 1950), p. 307.

[27] Escott M. Reid, "The Rise of National Parties in Canada," in Hugh Thorburn (ed.), *Party Politics in Canada* (Toronto: Prentice-Hall of Canada, 1963), p. 20; and Robert MacGregor Dawson, *The Government of Canada* (Toronto: University of Toronto, 1957), pp. 243–47.

[28] Allan Kornberg, "Caucus and Cohesion in Canadian Parliamentary Parties," *American Political Science Review*, LX (March, 1966), 83–92.

3. Multi-Party Parliamentary Variants

If the argument from British and English-speaking Commonwealth experience is correct, any successful parliamentary system, even in a nation with multi-party competition, ought to produce cohesive parliamentary parties to sustain executive authority. There is no immediately apparent reason why the need for two or more parties to coalesce or otherwise work together in order to constitute a parliamentary majority should reduce the usefulness of cohesion for the working of the system. The need for cohesion in each of two or more parties forming a coalition government is no less great than the need for cohesion in one majority party. It may be granted, however, that this same logic would not hold for each of two or more separate opposition parties; the members of one of several opposition parties would not have the same pressures for unity, as a means of demonstrating capacity for sustaining an alternative government, that exist for members of a single large opposition party in the British-type situation. In multi-party competition, no single opposition party is regularly regarded as an alternative government anyway. This does not mean that opposition parties in multi-party competition are never cohesive. As will be observed, many are clearly so. But the pressures for their cohesion are not as readily attributable to the demands of the parliamentary system as is the cohesion of governing parties in either two-party or multi-party competition, or the cohesion of a single opposition party. Other pressures, besides those emanating from a parliamentary system, must play a part. A Communist parliamentary party, to take an extreme case, is obviously unified even though it may be so far short of majority status as never to seem an alternative government.

Instances of parliamentary party cohesion not readily attributable to the parliamentary system need not be discussed at length. It has never been part of the argument that other factors were regularly insignificant. All that is argued is that the parliamentary system is a sufficient force even when other factors (like a class-conscious workers' party) are absent. A direct attack on this view comes from any demonstration of uncohesive parties in a parliamentary system. Foreknowledge that there can be such a demonstration, from France of the Third and Fourth Republics if from nowhere else, provided the basis for limiting the reach of the argument to results in two-party parliamentary systems. In multi-party situations, all that can be shown is that the cohesive parliamentary party has become usual (but not universal) in most nations and that it is especially prevalent when multi-partyism verges on two-partyism.

France of the Third and Fourth Republics is the leading apparent exception. There is abundant evidence from French history of 1875–1940 and 1946–58 that uncohesive parties were customary. Only the Socialists and later the Communists were unified parliamentary forces over any considerable period of time. The Fourth Republic provides especially convincing evidence of a customary non-cohesion. On seventy-two major issues in the National Assembly between 1946 and 1956, it has been found that there were few on which the members of any party, except the Communists and Socialists, voted in anything like unified style. It is further reported that on scores of these major issues, anywhere from 10 to 40 per cent of the deputies of a party (MRP, Radical, Conservative, or RPF) voted differently from the majority of their party. In the same period, the fall of ten ministries was directly contributed to by split voting within two or three parties originally supporting the government.[29] It was not unknown in the Fourth Republic for some members of a prime minister's own party to desert his governing combination and so contribute to his fall.[30] Plainly, then, the supposed demands of parliamentary government did not operate to produce cohesion. Not only did parties as such break in their support of the government, but deputies in those parties broke from their leadership's continued support of the government. However great the parliamentary incentives for cohesion in other nations, they were certainly insufficient in the Fourth Republic. The parties of the right and center were at least as disunited as American congressional parties.

The Fifth French Republic presents a different picture. The Union for the New Republic has undoubtedly been a cohesive parliamentary force in supporting governments chosen by President de Gaulle. It was able to provide support virtually on its own after winning a majority of seats in 1962, and in the four preceding years, when it was by far the largest single parliamentary party, it had also been the main support of the government. In other words, the UNR was in the position of a majority party in two-party competition except that its opponents were divided among several parties. In addition, of course, the UNR was subject to a very special influence as the instrument of de Gaulle, whose personal and constitutional power was tremendous. Therefore, the UNR's cohesion cannot confidently be

[29] David S. McLellan, "Ministerial Instability and the Lack of Internal Cohesion in French Parties," *World Affairs Quarterly*, XXVIII (April, 1957), 3–24.

[30] Francis De Tarr, *The French Radical Party* (London: Oxford University Press, 1961), p. 222.

regarded as the simple response of a majority or near-majority party to the demands of a parliamentary system.

It might even be said that the Fifth Republic is not exactly a parliamentary system. Certainly, the independent power of the president appears incompatible with the classic parliamentary principle of executive responsibility to legislative authority. Yet that principle has been followed to the extent of a premier and his cabinet still depending on an Assembly majority in order to remain in office (and so having a general election when that majority disappeared in 1962). Thus there is the usual parliamentary incentive for cohesion by the governing party. The question remains whether this incentive is as consequential in securing UNR cohesion as is the dominance of President de Gaulle. In light of this unanswered question, the most that can be generalized from the new phenomenon of a highly unified non-leftist party is that such a response to parliamentary circumstances is at least possible in France when a party reaches majority status. French experience in the Fifth Republic is, in this respect, consonant with expectations derived from the previous observations of two-party parliamentary systems.

The more telling French evidence is still the absence of cohesion (except among Socialists and Communists) in the Third and Fourth Republics. This experience means that the parliamentary system is not always sufficient to produce cohesive parties. It is tempting to attribute this insufficiency to a French multi-partyism that precluded majority or near-majority status for any single party. Surely party competition was especially fragmented because of the cross-cleavages of religion, class, region, and regime-commitments. This suggests that it is not just multi-partyism but a particular kind of multi-partyism that makes cohesive parties unlikely even in a parliamentary system. The suggestion may be examined in reviewing the experience of other continental nations.

No other Western parliamentary system, it can be noted at the outset, displays the same non-cohesive parties as the French Third and Fourth Republics. German experience, for example, is largely to the contrary. Even in the Weimar Republic, parliamentary voting tended to be party voting.[31] This had always been true of the Social Democrats, and of course the Communists and Nazis operated as unified forces. But so for the most part did the parties of the Center

---

[31] George L. Rueckert, "Parliamentary Party Cohesion in the West German Bundestag" (Unpublished Ph.D. dissertation, University of Wisconsin, 1962), p. 6.

and the traditional Right.[32] In the Federal Republic, cohesion has been characteristic. The Social Democrats have been almost completely united on roll-call votes, and the Christian Democrats usually but not always united to a high degree.[33] The absence of complete or near-complete solidarity in the latter case is significant, since the Christian Democrats, as the leading governing party, might have been expected to respond to the demands of the parliamentary system with an especially rigorous discipline. On certain crucial issues, they appear to have done so. But at least in the Second Bundestag, which has been systematically studied, a minority of Christian Democrats deviated (often by abstention) a surprising number of times. Plainly they did not do so in sufficient numbers, or at such times, as to have seriously embarrassed their leadership. On some occasions, a few deviations made no practical difference since the coalition government had more than enough votes for majority support. But even if it had not, the government could have survived, since the German constitutional system does not require a government to resign because of loss of a majority on a policy question. Only the agreement of a majority on a new chancellor can force the resignation of the old one. This West German modification of parliamentary government may lessen the pressure for regular or continuous parliamentary party cohesion. But it by no means eliminates it. A government is still expected to have a working majority in order to be effectively in office. And so far in West Germany, in one kind of coalition or another, that requirement has been met. The Christian Democratic deputies, despite the deviations noted, play the principal role in meeting that requirement, even though some of them are actually members of the affiliated Christian Social Union (of Bavaria) rather than of the Christian Democratic Union proper.

The conditions in West Germany might, however, appear to be more nearly those of two-party competition, even under the grand coalition of 1966–67, than of multi-partyism. Only the Christian Democrats (including the Christian Social affiliates) and the Social Democrats have been serious contenders for power in the sense of presenting the electorate with alternative governments. The Free Democrats, the only third party continuing to win parliamentary seats after 1961, were, before the grand coalition, junior partners in Christian Democratic governments. Their partnership was necessary since the Christian Democrats lacked a majority of seats except from

[32] Lewis J. Edinger, *Kurt Schumacher* (Stanford, Calif.: Stanford University Press, 1965), p. 112.
[33] Rueckert, *op. cit.*, pp. 217, 285, 295, 354–57.

1957 to 1961 (when they had a very bare majority), but this made the system multi-party only in a limited sense. The Christian Democrats remained primarily responsible for governing, and the Socialists for providing the alternative in the form of a coherent opposition party (at least until they joined the coalition government in 1966). The situation differs sharply from Third and Fourth Republic France where no party seemed regularly responsible, actually or prospectively, as *the* governing party. Even if we do regard the recent German competition as approaching two-partyism, however, we may not be able to associate the generally high parliamentary party cohesion with this particular competitive pattern. The fact that cohesion existed generally in the multi-party Weimar Republic means that there must be an additional, if not alternative, explanation. In other words, German parties generally, not just the Social Democrats, appear to be cohesive in any parliamentary system. Since this has not been true for French parties, we have a French-German difference that cannot be explained simply by the number of parties in relation to parliamentary government. Whatever in parliamentary government encourages party cohesion did work in Germany, regardless of the number of parties, although it did not work in French multi-party circumstances.

In line with the German rather than the French experience of cohesion with multi-party competition is virtually all of the rest of continental European experience under parliamentary government. Multi-partyism, in one degree or another, characterizes this experience, but so does cohesion of parliamentary parties. Unfortunately, there are no detailed studies of the phenomenon, partly because it seems to have been taken for granted that two or more parties would maintain their unity, separately and together, in support of a governing coalition resting on these parties. Sometimes, it is true, the multi-partyism has been nearer the West German variety, and so nearer to two-partyism, than to the fragmentation of the Third and Fourth French Republics. For example, in the Italian Republic, there has regularly been a single large party, the Christian Democrats, with a majority or near-majority of parliamentary seats. While the Christian Democrats have governed in coalition with one or more of the lesser parties, their own cohesion has undoubtedly been of principal importance in maintaining a government—always headed by a Christian Democrat and dominated by his party. The notable fact about this Christian Democratic cohesion is its steady achievement despite the well-known factions within a distinctly heterogeneous political party. The factions have had their own organizations and social bases, at times behaving like parties within a party in propagandizing their separate programs, but in parliamentary roll calls they have displayed an essential solidarity.[34] That is, the solidarity is displayed once a prime minister and his governmental combination have been accepted, even if reluctantly and after much disagreement by certain factions. Forming an Italian government has involved intra-party as well as inter-party bargaining over its composition and character. Yet the crucial point remains: there is Christian Democratic, plus minor party, cohesion in support of the government once established.

Both Belgium and the Netherlands are clear illustrations of strong parliamentary party cohesion in multi-party circumstances where no party is near majority status. The contrast to the Third and Fourth French Republics is sharp. The five or six major Dutch parties, representing almost as much fragmentation as that which characterized earlier French parliaments, are each nevertheless strikingly cohesive. The Dutch problem in stabilizing executive authority has been only to secure agreement among enough parties to compose a majority. At times, this has taken weeks to accomplish. But when accomplished, the result has been a stable government over a considerable period of time—ordinarily for several years between general elections.[35] The parliamentary members of each governing party remain loyal to the government as long as their party remains loyal. Party cohesion is the rule. The Belgian situation is similar except that there are fewer major parties. Consequently, the existing parliamentary party cohesion may seem less remarkable, but its existence is not in doubt. The occasions for non-regularity in party voting are rare. Only four such occasions occurred between 1953 and 1959 in the two Belgian legislative chambers.[36]

Scandinavian parties are not basically different in this regard. They may seem less significant as evidence of cohesion in multi-party parliamentary government, since much of the time in recent decades a single party—labor or social democratic—has been at or near majority status and so has had what might be called the two-party incentive (as well as its working-class solidarity) to maintain cohesion. But there is every indication that the opposition parties, although

[34] Raphael Zariski, "Intra-Party Conflict in a Dominant Party: The Experience of Italian Christian Democracy," *Journal of Politics*, XXVII (February, 1965), 5.

[35] Robert C. Bone, "The Dynamics of Dutch Politics," *Journal of Politics*, XXIV (February, 1962), 23–40; and Hans Daalder, "Parties and Politics in the Netherlands," *Political Studies*, III (February, 1955), 1–16.

[36] François Perin, *La Démocratie Enrayée* (Brussels: Institut belge de science politique, 1960), pp. 73–76.

neither of majority bent nor working-class, have also maintained their cohesion. The most definite information on this point comes from a Norwegian study. A roll-call analysis of voting in the national legislative body, the Storting, shows about the same degree of cohesion for each party.[37] And that cohesion, it is specifically stated, is much greater than that displayed by Democrats or Republicans in the U. S. Congress.[38] Parliamentary party caucuses in Norway make decisions genuinely binding on members.

Beyond the usual boundaries of West European nations, there is scattered evidence supporting the association of cohesive parties with parliamentary government. Interwar Czechoslovakia appears to have had disciplined parties.[39] More is known about the recent Israeli case. Like the Netherlands, Israel has as many as five or six important parties although, unlike the Netherlands, one party—the Mapai—has been large enough to be the leading element in each government over a considerable period of time. This party, however, has been so far short of a parliamentary majority that it has had to concede a great deal to other parties in order to persuade them to join a coalition cabinet. Bargaining after each election, or after any other break in the continuity of the coalition, can be as long a process as that in the Netherlands.[40] The resulting governmental coalition, however, can depend on the solidarity of each governing party. It is the withdrawal of support by an entire party, not a division in voting within a party, that is the chief threat to stability. In other words, the advantages of stability must be seen as party advantages in a manner similar to that perceived by members of a single governing party.

In summary, it is plain that there are numerous instances to disprove any notion that multi-partyism precludes the party cohesion found in two-party parliamentary systems. More than ever, the French experience appears to be a deviant case to be explained by something special in the national circumstances. In the absence of a ready explanation of that kind, it is tempting to dispose of the French exception by stating the generalization as follows: any parliamentary government, in order successfully to stabilize executive authority and so endure in the modern world, must produce cohesive parties re-

[37] Henry Valen and Daniel Katz, *Political Parties in Norway* (Oslo: Universitetsforlaget, 1964), p. 225.

[38] *Ibid.*, p. 98.

[39] Edward Taborsky, *Czechoslovak Democracy At Work* (London: Allen and Unwin, 1945).

[40] Benjamin Akzin, "The Role of Parties in Israeli Democracy," *Journal of Politics*, XVII (November, 1955), 528.

gardless of the number of competing parties. Thus the Third and especially the Fourth Republics would not be exceptional. They would really illustrate the rule since they did not successfully stabilize executive authority and they did not endure. On the other hand, one would still have to explain their failure, or, in present terms, account for the parliamentary system's inability to produce cohesive parties in France when such parties are thought to be the expected and the usual result of the system.

4. Separation of Powers

Turning to the impact of the separation of powers on party cohesion in the legislative branch is to turn only to the United States, because, as already noted, there is among Western democracies no other clear instance of a long-established working democratic government based on the separation of powers. Having to limit observation to one nation is a decided analytical disadvantage. Large and important though the United States is in the democratic universe, it is still difficult to generalize from any one national experience. In particular, the attempt to associate the absence of cohesive legislative parties with the separation of powers would be more convincing if there were at least one other nation where the same association appeared but where other conditions more nearly resembled those of a European nation than of the United States. In the absence of any such nation, the argument must rest heavily on the fact that there is nothing about the United States, except the separation of powers, to distinguish its circumstances significantly from those of all of the nations with cohesive parties. Notably, as already stressed, American circumstances cannot be thus distinguished from the Canadian.

It can be granted that this necessary emphasis means that the separation of powers is not treated as a positive force creating uncohesive parties. The preferred statement is that the absence of parliamentary government is decisive. With it cohesive parties have regularly developed except in France. Without it, cohesive parties might still be possible, but they are not necessary. In other words, the separation of powers does not require that legislative parties assume the same collective governing role that they have under parliamentary government. The executive authority, embodied in the single elected president, enjoys tenure of office without regularized majority legislative party support. Of course he will, in the literal sense, enjoy his tenure more if he has something like that support, but he does not need it in order to exercise many of his policy-making powers.

Just how uncohesive are American congressional parties? Although there is agreement among all observers that they are much less cohesive than those in working parliamentary systems, notably the British, the contrast should not be overdrawn so as to depict American parties as unimportant rallying points for individual congressmen.[41] Indeed, as careful scholars have noted, party identification of the individual congressman is more closely associated with his roll-call voting than is any other discernible factor (section, urban-rural, ethnic, etc.).[42] On questions of order and procedure, party is almost absolutely determining. It is understood that a congressional party is entirely cohesive in organizing the legislative body, particularly in electing its officers. In this limited respect, the American party behavior resembles that which is exhibited more generally by the British parliamentary party. The explanation is simple. Only in organizing the legislature is there in the American system the same strong incentive for party unity that exists continuously in Britain for purposes of sustaining a government in office. Policy questions in the American Congress do not impose the same necessity for cohesion as they do in a system where all such questions involve votes of confidence in the executive leadership. Nevertheless on these non-organizational or non-procedural matters there is considerable pressure for party regularity in congressional voting. It is felt, as David Truman has observed, "even though frequently it may be effectively resisted."[43] The pressure is especially great and so harder to resist when it combines the force of congressional party leadership with that of presidential leadership of the same party persuasion. Often a congressman may not want to resist it. But the point remains that when he does, perhaps because of conflicting sectional or other pressures, he can do so. Furthermore, enough congressmen, of majority as well as minority party membership, break often enough from their leaders and their colleagues so as to make American congressional parties much less cohesive and so much less reliable as policy-making agencies of government.

Describing congressional parties as "mediate" groups, as Truman has done, is fitting. Each congressional party consists of individuals who share many political attitudes with each other and so with the party under whose label they were elected, but who separately and factionally are also affiliated with and depend on other groups, in-

[41] Julius Turner, *Party and Constituency Pressures on Congress* (Baltimore: Johns Hopkins Press, 1951), p. 25.

[42] *Ibid.*, p. 34; and David B. Truman, *The Congressional Party* (New York: John Wiley & Sons, 1959), p. 247.

[43] Truman, *op. cit.*, p. 285.

cluding interest groups and constituency party organizations. The risks to which congressional party members are most poignantly subject are re-election, and these risks "are not fully integrated into the shared attitudes and goals of the group, as they would be in an immediate group such as a militant labor union, a military combat group, or even a well-managed business firm."[44] Or, one might add, an immediate group like a British parliamentary party, whose risks are so fully integrated as a result of the governmental system in which such a party functions. The British M.P.'s fortunes are identical with those of his parliamentary party in almost the same sense as the fortunes of American congressmen are rightly said *not* to be identified with their legislative parties. The American congressman does not find party voting as regularly profitable as does the British M.P.

This is not to say that the American congressman's political situation would in all ways be transformed into that of a British M.P.'s by the substitution of parliamentary government for the separation of powers. Undoubtedly the American legislator would still have stronger counter-pressures, especially of a local and sectional kind, than those which are overridden in Britain. The American's situation would be more like the Canadian's, and there might be more difficulty about regularizing cohesion than exists in Britain. But the incentives for cohesion would be much greater than is now the case in the United States. In light of the Canadian experience, they would seem sufficient despite local and sectional differences among American constituencies. In any event, it may be a mistake to accept the conventional view that constituency differences produce most of the congressional party irregularity.[45] One may have been misled by the obvious instances of Southern Democratic opposition to Northern Democratic programs for civil rights, and by various intra-party splits along urban and rural lines with respect to farm price supports.[46] There is at least one important case study of congressional behavior that points in another direction. This concerns the passage of tariff legislation during the 1950's and 1960's. From numerous interviews with congressmen, eliciting their ideas as legislators on the tariff issue, what emerges is a picture of congressmen as surprisingly in-

[44] *Ibid.*, p. 293.

[45] V. O. Key, Jr., *Politics, Parties and Pressure Groups* (New York: Crowell-Collier, 1964), p. 685.

[46] It has been argued that a decline in the relative strength of Southerners among congressional Democrats will increase the cohesive potential of the Democratic party. Raymond E. Wolfinger and Joan Heifetz, "Safe Seats, Seniority, and Power in Congress," *American Political Science Review*, LIX (June, 1965), 348.

dependent decision-makers.[47] Not only was party little mentioned as a consideration in molding their voting decisions, but neither did interest groups appear to be determining in the usual sense. It is arguable, to be sure, whether this picture is correct both for the case at hand and for any fairly large number of other cases. The congressmen's perceptions, reported in interviews, might not be accurate with respect to their actual voting behavior. But insofar as there is something to the finding, it would indicate that their individual decision-making, not just their responses to local or sectional pressures, must be overcome if parties are to be cohesive. It cannot be assumed that it would be easy to overcome, but again it is generally overcome in parliamentary systems. Interestingly, however, most of the known scattered instances of deviation from parliamentary party regularity in Britain are of M.P.s acting on their own policy preferences, which may or may not be supported by their constituencies.[48]

The impact of the separation of powers on non-regularity in party voting, be it for individual or constituency reasons, can be observed in American state legislatures as well as in the Congress. Since this adds fifty cases to the single national one, it diminishes the disadvantages admittedly inherent in the availability of only one Western nation governed by the separation of powers. The fifty states share basically the same social and economic circumstances with the United States as a whole, but because each separate state tends to be less heterogeneous than the entire nation, there would seem to be a greater possibility of legislative party cohesion despite the separation of powers. At least, the constituencies represented by members of a single party are bound to be less diverse in a state legislature than in the Congress. Nevertheless, greater party cohesion is found only in certain states and in limited degree. Nothing like the regularity of parliamentary party voting is characteristic of state legislative parties. It is most plainly absent in states dominated by a single party.[49] These might well be excluded from consideration because without the spur of inter-party competition there would hardly be any more basis for cohesion in a parliamentary system than in a separation-of-powers system. Many fairly competitive states, however, have not even had the agencies for the achievement of cohesive parties. Belle Zeller reported in the mid-1950's: "In only thirteen states do majority caucuses

[47] Raymond A. Bauer, Ithiel de Sola Pool, and Lewis A. Dexter, *American Business and Public Policy* (New York: Atherton Press, 1963), p. 487.

[48] Epstein, "Cohesion of British Parliamentary Parties."

[49] Belle Zeller, *American State Legislatures* (New York: Crowell-Collier, 1954), pp. 192–93.

meet frequently and exert or attempt to exert any significant control over their members or the program of the legislature."[50] Most of these states are not just two-party competitive but also highly urban (as two-party states tend to be). Even in these states, however, legislative party cohesion is only high in comparison with less urban states. It is not high by parliamentary standards.[51]

The variation in degree of party voting, even among certain urban states, is the most marked characteristic emerging from all the comparative studies of American legislatures.[52] Thus, a recent inquiry shows more party voting in five northeastern American state legislatures than in the U. S. Congress, but considerably less in California and a few other states.[53] There is little doubt that the separation of powers allows the government to function without cohesive parties at the state as at the national level. This is in no way refuted by the finding that considerable cohesion is achieved at certain times and places. Even if this state-level cohesion were almost as complete as that in parliamentary systems, there would be no need to retreat from the view that the separation of powers *allows* uncohesive parties in a functioning government. What could not be argued is that the separation of powers necessarily produces uncohesive parties. But that has not been the argument. Cohesive parties, it may be granted, can exist under any governmental system. Social and economic circumstances in certain American states, and perhaps eventually in an increasingly homogeneous United States, might produce united parties without any change in the American constitutional order. The point remains that the absence of a parliamentary system allows either cohesive or uncohesive parties to be functional. The *necessity* for cohesive parties is not there.

A closer look at the American national government will help to explain how the system works without legislative parties assuming the governing function of European parliamentary parties. The key lies in the very nature of the independently elected executive. The president of the United States has much more policy-making power than the admittedly considerable amount that derives from his leader-

[50] *Ibid.*, p. 194.

[51] Malcolm E. Jewell, "Party Voting in American State Legislatures," *American Political Science Review*, XLIX (September, 1955), 773–91; and William J. Keefe, "Comparative Study of the Role of Political Parties in State Legislatures, *Western Political Quarterly*, IX (September, 1956), 726–42.

[52] John C. Wahlke *et al.*, *The Legislative System* (New York: John Wiley & Sons, 1962), p. 376.

[53] Thomas R. Dye, "State Legislative Politics," in Herbert Jacob and Kenneth Vines (eds.), *Politics in the American States* (Boston: Little, Brown, 1965), pp. 185–88.

ship of his party. He is more than the party leader occupying the highest office by virtue of a party majority. Not only is the majority electing him to office his own majority, in substantial degree, but it is really this election that makes him the effective party leader. In other words, his power even within his party comes largely from holding presidential office. This is not just a matter of having his leadership influence enhanced because he has appointments to make. A prime minister in a parliamentary system also gains influence in this way since he has many cherished ministerial positions to fill. But the American president is his party's leader because of his executive office, and not, like a prime minister, the holder of the executive office because he is party leader.

It is even possible to imagine an American president who would not be a party leader in any important sense. An observer of the presidential system can at least suggest such an arrangement without its seeming absurd.[54] Generally, however, the president is viewed as more, really considerably more, than a party leader. And, in practice, this has meant that he mobilizes support for his policies across party lines as well as within his own party. His office, institutionally and otherwise, provides the basis for a leadership transcending party on many domestic as well as foreign issues. His role as party leader is, in this perspective, only one of several influential roles derived from the office.[55] As a nonpartisan leader, he can and does influence congressmen regardless of their party affiliation. Congressmen have been found universally to recognize the President's functions of policy initiation and recommendation.[56] This does not mean that congressmen of the opposition party regularly follow the president's recommendations. But neither do all of the congressmen of the president's own party. It may be granted that the latter are more likely to do so. Yet the point remains that all congressmen are open to presidential influence. Party is not an absolute barrier any more than it is an absolute basis of presidential support. The president mobilizes his majorities in the manner described by an intimate observer of the process:

> Even while paying lip service to his party, a President finds himself obliged to bypass it. With the help of modern communications, he has a more direct means of contact with his public than the party's

---

[54] See Austin Ranney, *The Doctrine of Responsible Party Government* (Urbana: University of Illinois Press, 1954), pp. 139–42.

[55] Richard E. Neustadt, *Presidential Power* (New York: John Wiley & Sons, 1960).

[56] Avery Leiserson, "National Party Organization and Congressional Districts," *Western Political Quarterly,* XVI (September, 1963), 633–49.

many-layered relay system. On the compelling issues of foreign policy and defense, he inevitably seeks to clothe his policies in the respectable robes of bipartisanship. Toward such matters as fiscal and monetary policy and even civil-rights legislation, he makes constant efforts to maintain an unpartisan posture. His appointees to high office often bear little relation to the party which elected him.[57]

The modern communications, mentioned above, have not created the national nonparty role assumed by recent presidents. That role has always been available and it has long been used in varying degrees. But the "unmediated" access provided by radio and television surely makes the non-party role easier and more effective.[58] They may even make the party role less useful. It has been argued that "the more the public comes to see the President as the personification of the *nation,* irrespective of party, the less willing it is to accept the partisan side of his office."[59]

Whether or not the increased presidential use of modern communications lessens the effective exploitation of party leadership, there can be no doubt that the American president now has the means to use his status to gain non-partisan public support and so often cross-party congressional support. Nor can there be any doubt that such cross-party support has been necessary for presidential policy-making. Obviously it has been necessary when the president's own party lacks majorities in both houses of Congress—a situation prevailing in thirty-two of the years from 1861 to 1965.[60] But it has been necessary in other years as well. The table on page 347 provides the relevant data for selected recent congressional sessions in which first there was Republican control of the presidency and of Congress (1953 and 1954) and then Democratic control of both branches (1961–63).

It may be observed that the proportion of presidential victories requiring minority party votes was higher in the first two years, when the Republican majority in both houses was very small and notably remote from its leader in the White House, than in the early 1960's, when the Democratic congressional majority was fairly substantial and more closely linked to presidential leadership (although not so much so under Kennedy as under Johnson, beginning in late 1963).

[57] Douglass Cater, *Power In Washington* (New York: Random House, 1964), p. 12.

[58] Elmer E. Cornwell, Jr., *Presidential Leadership of Public Opinion* (Bloomington: Indiana University Press, 1965), p. 284.

[59] *Ibid.,* p. 300.

[60] Charles O. Jones, *Party and Policy-Making: The House Republican Policy Committee* (New Brunswick, N.J.: Rutgers University Press, 1964), p. 80.

PARTY SUPPORT ON CONGRESSIONAL ROLL CALLS
INVOLVING PRESIDENTIAL ISSUES,
1953–54 AND 1961–63*

	Presidential Issues	Presidential Victories	Victories Requiring Minority Party Votes
SENATE			
1953	49	43	38
1954	77	60	49
1961	124	100	30
1962	125	107	30
1963	115	103	33
HOUSE OF REPRESENTATIVES			
1953	34	31	20
1954	38	30	14
1961	65	54	18
1962	60	51	17
1963	71	59	17

* "Presidential issues" are those so classified by the *Congressional Quarterly* to include only those issues on which the president took a stand at the time of the congressional vote. The tabulations are all taken from the yearly volumes of the *Congressional Quarterly Almanac* (Washington: 1953–54 and 1961–63), IX, 77–78; X, 50; XVII, 619–21; XVIII, 705–7; and XIX, 712–14.

Nevertheless, two things are striking about all the sessions. One is that victories for the president constituted a large proportion of the presidential issues on which Congress voted. And the second is that this proportion would have been significantly lower in all sessions (even those of the 1960's) if minority party votes were unobtainable. The two findings together suggest that the president does effectively add cross-party support to party support in order to enact his policies. Perhaps he would do so less often when his own party had overwhelming majorities in both houses, but even in such a situation, which prevailed in 1965, there might be issues on which the president would find some of the necessary votes in the other party.

The fact is that the president can have either kind of majority: strictly party or cross-party. He can have a party majority on certain issues, and a cross-party majority on other issues. Moreover the cross-party majority need not be the same combination on each occasion. All this is another way of saying that the president, freed from exclusive reliance on a single party, is able to present some policy recommendations with considerable chance of success even though his own party would not always be sufficiently united to enact them into law.

The absence of a single regularized majority, like that provided by a cohesive parliamentary party, does not necessarily mean less frequent majority support. It may be more frequent, if also more various, and it may be obtainable on a cross-party basis when it would not be on strictly party basis even in a parliamentary situation. A prime minister can only obtain his policy goals if his own party, in caucus, agrees to accept those goals. In contrast, executive leadership based on a shifting majority may even have advantages—at least as long as an occasional defeat does not end the leadership's hold on office. The separation of powers precludes that contingency.

Nevertheless, upholding presidential cross-party leadership as superior to the cohesive parliamentary party in performing the governing function would go further than is necessary to make the point relevant to our analysis of parties. All that has to be shown is how the governing function can be performed without the cohesive party.[61] The national or non-party role of the presidency is the response under the separation-of-powers system to the need for powerful executive authority in the modern state. This response is comparable, in its functional significance, to that of the cohesive party in the parliamentary system.

5. The Nongoverning Party

Perhaps it is an exaggeration to speak of the American party as a nongoverning party. It assumes *some* of the functions of government. But it is not *the* agency of governmental policy-making. As an entity, it is unable to commit itself to a program, or even a set of policies, on which it can effectively deliver after winning the appropriate legislative and executive offices. Therefore, as has been seen, the function of governmental policy-making is performed in part by agencies—the presidency and cross-party majorities—of a somewhat different character.

The fact that the function is thus performed in the American system has not prevented reformers from advocating that the cohesive party be developed in order to assume more of the governing function. Usually the greater party cohesion, in and out of Congress, has been perceived as entirely compatible with presidential leadership. Indeed, a more cohesive party has been seen as the means for enhancing the president's policy-making capability by strengthening his

[61] Duverger, writing several years after his major work on parties, has also accepted a popular presidential regime as an alternative to a cohesive parliamentary party in mobilizing a majority in a modern democratic society. *La Ve République et le régime presidentiel* (Paris: Artheme Fayard, 1961).

strictly partisan leadership. To this end, James MacGregor Burns has urged that a president should remodel his party to make it a more effective governing instrument—presumably more effective in the support and enactment of policies he champions in his role as party leader.[62] The remodelling, while mainly of the national organization, is meant to produce a united congressional party as its principal goal.[63] As long as it is the president who helps to produce such a united party, the result is not likely to be seen as in conflict with his leadership. Yet that possibility must be allowed for. Schattschneider, at one point in his crusade for party reform, even suggested the possibility as desirable. "As long as the condition of parties in Congress remains what it is," he wrote, "Congress cannot compete with the President in the discovery and exploitation of public issues; only when the national parties are strong enough to dominate Congress will that body discover and exploit public issues so effectively that the presidency will cease to be the sole rallying point of the great public interests of the country."[64]

While this statement is exceptional and, one suspects, tangential, in the advocacy of American party cohesion, it unintentionally reveals the difficulty, or even the impracticality, of the reformers' arguments. There is really no way in which one can be sure that the cohesive majority party in both houses of the American Congress would be an instrument of presidential leadership or a means of support for it. The separation of powers not only enables a congressional majority to be of a different party from the President's, but also allows his own party majority to disagree with his leadership. In either situation, presidential leadership might be weaker if, with party reform, he faced a *cohesive* majority against his policy. The party reformers would have denied him the cross-party majority now so often available. And the desired policy outputs might be harder to realize than under the present looser parties.

This is another way of saying that the largely nongoverning party may be functional in the American constitutional system. And it may be so in any system founded on the separation of powers.[65] Although one cannot be sure that a cohesive legislative party, capable of gov-

[62] *The Deadlock of Democracy* (Englewood Cliffs, N.J.: Prentice-Hall, 1963), pp. 145, 168, 175. The references are to criticisms of Wilson and both Roosevelts for failing to change party organizational arrangements.

[63] E. E. Schattschneider, *Party Government* (New York: Rinehart, 1942), p. 137.

[64] *Ibid.*, p. 210.

[65] Jean Grossholtz, *Politics in the Philippines* (Boston: Little, Brown, 1964), p. 137.

erning in the British manner, would not work in the American Congress, there ought at least to be doubts. Even if one brushed aside those doubts, there would still be the fact that the fully governing party has not been necessary in the United States. Executive leadership, often transcending party, has provided a workable alternative.

XIII

Conclusion

By now it is clear that I have intended to place the frequently deplored American parties in a comparative frame of reference where they can be perceived as responses to circumstances at least as modern as those that molded European parties of the first half of the twentieth century.[1] What may be less clear is the relation of the loosely organized, unprogrammatic, and less cohesive American parties to democratic theory. The point is that these very characteristics allow parties to function in accord with a pluralist conception of democracy. The characteristics are deplorable only from the standpoint of a majoritarian theory, which is at the heart of the preference, so often expressed by political scientists, for a large and strong party organization able to mobilize electoral support for programmatic policies to be enacted by a party serving as a governing agency. So definite has this preference been that some of its advocates present it as a norm for political parties generally.

Before concentrating on the alternative pluralist model, it is useful to summarize the way in which I have criticized this majoritarian norm in the present work. My criticism is of two kinds. First, I have emphasized the absence of the supposedly normal party pattern over long periods of time in several nations, and the development of trends away from the pattern. Second, where the supposed norm has prevailed, I have tried to reveal its relations to given national circumstances and to point out its functional problems within a democratic political system. This approach involves, from the start, a skeptical view of normative party theory in general and especially of that version which would reform government by adopting the "right" kind of parties or the "right" kind of party system.

[1] The idea is not new. Samuel J. Eldersveld has written: "Social and political environmental conditions vary fom one culture to the next. . . . Parties are merely a particular structural response, therefore, to the needs of a social and political system in a particular milieu." *Political Parties: A Behavioral Analysis* (Chicago: Rand McNally, 1964), p. 2.

It is appropriate to have begun with a scrutiny of the well-known preference for two-party competition. Supposing it to be normal is consequential for a strong-party advocate because, wanting a majority party, he is bound also to want a competitive situation in which one party can regularly win a majority. Two-party competition, as opposed to multi-party competition, automatically produces this outcome for any given office or set of offices, and so it is obviously related to the advocacy of a majoritarian strong party. Two-party competition does not ensure a strong party, but it does ensure a majority party in a way that multi-party competition cannot. Since majority status is necessary for meaningful strength, it is no wonder that the strong-party advocate ordinarily prefers two-party competition and assumes either its existence or its likely existence. Yet the hard fact is that two-party competition is not demonstrably normal in Western democracies. Not only has multi-party competition been usual in many nations, but there are few signs of a general movement toward two-party competition. Moreover, in many places where two-party competition is ordinarily thought to exist, it is riddled with exceptions in the form of one-party areas and persistent third and fourth parties. There simply does not seem to be anything more "normal" about two-party competition than about the various other competitive patterns involving many parties, one party, or even no party.

What can be said about the non-normality of two-party competition generally can be said (even more confidently) about the kind of two-party pattern characterizing British politics. Each of the two major British parties is not only a potential majority party but also a cohesive party. To a very large degree, Conservatives and Labour suffice as representative agencies, and yet, unlike the American parties, each maintains its effective unity as a governing force. The incentive for this unity is attributed to the parliamentary system, but nevertheless the British success in this respect has not been followed consistently in larger or more heterogeneous nations. Such nations, even with working parliamentary systems, have often had more than two important (though cohesive) parties. In other words, Britain's pattern of two strongly cohesive parties may be much more nearly unique in its Britishness than its admirers have assumed.[2] Like so many other British products, it has a limited export market. New Zealand is the best customer. The least likely may be the United

[2] The point that the British system might not elsewhere produce British-type results is made by Robert A. Dahl, *Political Oppositions in Western Democracies* (New Haven and London: Yale University Press, 1966), pp. 393–95.

States. Not only are the parliamentary system's incentives lacking, but even if legislative cohesion could be achieved, it seems doubtful whether only two cohesive parties could contain all of the American political forces any more effectively than Canada's traditional two parties have been able to contain all of the Canadian forces.

There is still another aspect, although a less nearly unique one, that limits the modern relevance of Britain's two-party pattern. That aspect is the characteristically European role of a large socialist working-class party. It is true that the Labour party cannot be held primarily responsible for either Britain's two-party pattern or parliamentary party cohesion, both of which were largely developed before it existed. Yet it is probable that the solidarity characterizing a class-conscious socialist movement has tended to increase the strong-party spirit of British government. As Samuel Beer has wisely said, "The major theme of the Collectivist attitude toward representation has been party government." He rightly observes that the main socialist view is that this representation is not of individuals or even sub-groups, but "primarily the two major classes of industrial society."[3] Accordingly, the Labour party not only found Britain's already developed parliamentary party cohesion to be congenial and useful, but the party added its own theoretical justification, namely the claims of a majoritarian working class, for the maintenance of disciplined political representation. In this respect, the British Labour party resembled socialist working-class parties elsewhere, in the Commonwealth and in continental Europe. These parties, along with the Communists, have usually been more cohesive than most others in their respective nations, and when, as in France, other parties have not been cohesive at all, the socialists (and Communists) have been exceptional in their parliamentary solidarity. In other words, it could be argued that the growth of a socialist working-class party is favorable to the establishment of strong parties, British-style, on the assumption that the working-class base makes not only for socialist party cohesion but also for cohesion in an opposing capitalist party. Then, if there were a general tendency for socialist working-class parties to grow, it would appear that there was something normal about the British pattern.

The trouble with this line of argument, however, is that socialist working-class parties in Western democracies have generally ceased to grow at least in anything like their traditional doctrinal and class-conscious form. An American party of this type now appears more remote than ever. West European socialist parties have been observed

[3] Samuel H. Beer, *British Politics in the Collectivist Age* (New York: Alfred A. Knopf, 1965), pp. 79, 83.

to have greatly altered their traditional character in order to try, not always successfully, to avoid declines. A peak of European socialist party development, and of socialist-type party development, came at about 1950 in what were then, by American standards, considerably less advanced economic and social circumstances. It can be conjectured that immediately after World War II, Europe, because of the harsh impact of the war, resembled the industrial society of the early years of the twentieth century a great deal more than it did the affluent years of the late 1950's and 1960's. Even if that is not the case, there can be no doubt that Western European politics of 1950 was still heavily influenced by the conditions of an earlier industrialization and of a class-stratified society of pre-industrial times. The basis for a party representing an entire alienated class had not yet so plainly withered as it would almost everywhere in Western Europe during the next fifteen years.

It was the mistaken belief in the future success of the socialist working-class party that led certain political scientists in the early 1950's to assume that the characteristics of this type of party would become dominant in competing parties as well. This meant the triumph not only of the governing cohesion of elected public office-holders, but also of the mass-membership organization supporting the cohesion on programmatic grounds. The socialist working-class party was the model for organizational as well as for governing purposes. A highly developed party structure, based on class solidarity, represented the apparently successful "contagion from the left." The point was taken for granted by the editor of the most widely used comparative parties anthology of the mid-1950's when he wrote: "In place of *a party of individual representation,* our contemporary society increasingly shows *a party of social integration.*"[4] So it was that Duverger, the systematic exponent of the belief in the organizational contagion of left-wing parties also wrote: "The vast centralized and disciplined parties of today . . . alone suit the structure of contemporary society."[5] What then appeared so axiomatic to Duverger is now convincingly challenged both by the arrested growth of membership organizations, socialist and nonsocialist, and by their diminished relevance in nations with highly developed communications technology. The trend appears to be away from, not toward, the large socially integrated party. Duverger was right to think of the mass-membership

[4] Sigmund Neumann, *Modern Political Parties* (Chicago: The University of Chicago Press, 1956), p. 404. (Italics are Neumann's.)

[5] Maurice Duverger, *Political Parties,* trans. Barbara and Robert North (New York: John Wiley & Sons, 1954), p. 427.

party as a response to a stage of political democratization, at least in West European circumstances, but it was a response to relatively early democratization (as was the American patronage organization) rather than to the last half of the twentieth century. The same can be said for the socialist working-class party itself. It has been shown, in the background of its leadership as in its membership, to be a distinctive product of a limited time and place.

Duverger stands in relation to theories of party development much as Marx does in relation to broader social theories. There is the same kind of insightful interpretation of political development following from economic class development, and also the same kind of mistaken projection of such development. Political scientists are as indebted to Duverger as historians are to Marx. There is much to be said for any bold and systematic attempt to account for political phenomena within a general frame of reference. But there is as much responsibility in reference to Duverger as to Marx to change the theory, or develop a new one, in order to explain more recently revealed phenomena. This attitude remains genuinely respectful of Duverger's contribution. His significance is evident from the fact that he cannot be ignored.

A similar point can be made about the American scholars, particularly Schattschneider, who advanced the still popular belief in the virtues of the responsible party—meaning a highly organized, programmatic, and cohesive party.[6] The responsible-party advocacy is not quite the American version of the Duverger model. The socialist working-class organization was not available in the United States. Nor has there ordinarily been a likely substitute in the form of any other mass-membership organization. For the most part, the American strong-party advocate has had to base his hopes either on the development of such an organization where almost none existed,[7] or on the achievement of a cohesive programmatic leadership of a purely electoral following. Even in the latter, more usual case, however, the responsible-party advocate still holds, in common with the believer in the socialist working-class party, a majoritarian theory of party behavior. There is the same underlying idea that the majority should

[6] E. E. Schattschneider was frankly an advocate who thought that strong and responsible parties could be achieved in the United States. He stated this explicitly as late as his "United States: The Functional Approach to Party Government," in Neumann, *op. cit.*, pp. 194, 201.

[7] The need for national parties in the United States to establish grass-roots memberships on a card-carrying, dues-paying basis is stressed by James MacGregor Burns, *The Deadlock of Democracy* (Englewood Cliffs, N.J.: Prentice-Hall, 1963), p. 328.

control government through the agency of a political party represent-ing it.[8] The American responsible-party advocacy is linked to Euro-pean party majoritarianism by another and less theoretical connec-tion. From the days of Woodrow Wilson, American political scien-tists urging responsible parties have looked to Britain as a model. The advent of the Labour party enhanced the attractiveness of the model for the American liberal left. Parties as they function in the United States were what the responsible-party school has always wanted to change, in the British if not in a generally European direction. It is this advocacy, and the theory underlying it, with which I have almost continuously taken issue in this book.

American parties are here accepted as the responses to their cir-cumstances, constitutional as well as social, just as European par-ties are accepted as responses to theirs. I have specifically rejected the notion that American parties are in any general sense less modern than European. Older as a democracy and as an affluent industrial society than any European nation, the United States could more reasonably be assumed to have the more modern parties now, just as it had the first large parties in the nineteenth century. Indeed, this does appear to be the case with respect to certain aspects of party development—namely the lesser class-consciousness, the absence of strong opposition to the existing social structure,[9] and the more purely electoral (as opposed to membership) organization of Ameri-can parties. These aspects, fostered partly by technological change in mass communication, now increasingly characterize European parties too. But the problem is too complex for a simple Americanization theme. There are other aspects, particularly the nationalization of parties, in which American parties are coming to resemble the Euro-pean as the politics of a large and diverse nation become increasingly national in a way that British politics have been for some decades. And there are other aspects in which there is no clear or even likely trend in either direction. The leading case in point is the degree of cohesion among elected public officeholders of a given party. A con-tinued low degree of cohesion seems probable in the United States because it is functional in the particular political system, and a con-tinued high degree of cohesion seems probable in Britain because it is functional in that nation's two-party parliamentary system. Loose as well as integrated parties can serve the democratic purpose.

It is possible to go one important step further. Granting that the

[8] Austin Ranney, *The Doctrine of Responsible Party Government* (Urbana: University of Illinois Press, 1954), p. 10.

[9] Dahl, *op. cit.*, pp. 342–44.

British-style parties better serve the majoritarian democratic purpose, it can also be said that the looser American-style parties better serve the democratic purpose as it is conceived in pluralist terms. The pluralist democrat rejects the validity or legitimacy, and even the regularized existence, of a majority electorate united over the wide range of complex issues in a modern nation. Separate majorities on separate issues, or perhaps on sets of issues, there may be, but that is very different from believing in a single majority for almost all issues. Consequently, the pluralist cannot recognize the claims of a programmatic party, with or without a membership organization, to represent a coherent majority for all of its policies. Behind this denial of majoritarian-party claims lies the pluralist's disbelief in a majority-class interest, the simplest theoretical support for the strong-party school.

The pluralist's party norm involves more than the avoidance of class consciousness in the older European socialist sense. It also involves a generally non-programmatic character, a leadership capable of responding to diverse electoral considerations, and a transactional or brokerage view of political activity. A party may still be associated with particular policies and interests, presumably in accord with habitual voting patterns of large portions of the electorate, but it preserves, in theory as in practice, a loose and accommodating character. Such a party, while having had patronage-seeking memberships in the past, does not usually have large numbers of program-committed members. The brokerage party, by its nature, is unattractive to members of this kind. And it does not have the need of a majoritarian party to legitimize, through mass-membership participation, any program or policies. For electoral purposes, which are of prime importance, a cadre organization suffices.

The absence of large-scale membership participation is often deplored on the ground of its evidently non-popular character. So it is that the actual American version of the pluralist's party model is thought to represent an unfortunate passivity on the part of ordinary American citizens. They are said not to share in political action and responsibility.[10] Certainly this is correct if political action and responsibility are defined largely in terms of participation in party affairs. But parties are only one kind of possible political participation, and by no means the most significant, especially in the United States. Americans rank relatively high as participants as soon as the definition is broadened to include various other voluntary associations and

---

[10] An important example of this line of criticism is found in Gunnar Myrdal, *An American Dilemma* (New York: Harper, 1944), II, 713–17.

nonpartisan community activity.[11] It is hard to say that these other forms of political participation are less functional in a democratic political system than purely party membership and party activism. A pluralist might well argue that large-scale party activism is a symptom of dysfunction because it occurs especially when parties are organized around intense and highly divisive programs and policies, notably those associated with deep class cleavages. There is considerable evidence from Western Europe to indicate that when the intensity based on such cleavages diminishes, so does party membership and activism. This diminution is a subject of concern for some Europeans who consider it part of an unfortunate process of depoliticization. But it is possible, in line with the pluralist's conception of politics, to view the process as only de-ideologization.[12] The consequence can be to free parties from members as well as programs, but to leave them no less effective in performing the electoral function for which they have always existed. American experience shows that parties, however weak organizationally, can still structure the vote for candidates covered by their labels.

The pluralist's acceptance of the workability of parties with limited functional roles, really the acceptance of weak parties, is some distance from the individualist theory that parties should be abolished. It may not be unthinkable or even entirely undesirable for a pluralist's political system to be without parties, but it is not necessary to be without them. As long as they do not have the majoritarian pretensions so often assigned them, political parties can be clearly compatible with the pluralist democratic theory. In any case, parties in at least their limited electoral role appear to have been regular responses to mass democracy. Despite some weakening here and there, they remain very much alive in Western democracies. Surely it is difficult now to think of burying them, even though their most highly organized forms may appear neither welcome nor inevitable.

[11] Gabriel A. Almond and Sidney Verba, *The Civic Culture* (Princeton: Princeton University Press, 1963), pp. 89, 169, 177, 302, 306.

[12] Seymour Martin Lipset, "The Changing Class Structure and Contemporary European Politics," *Daedalus,* Vol. XCIII of *Proceedings of American Academy of Arts and Sciences* (Winter, 1964), pp. 280–81.

Index

Abrams, Mark, 91 n, 92 n, 259 n
Absentee ballots, 114
Activists, 117 ff., 122 ff., 222, 223, 227, 230, 231, 261; *see also* Party workers
Adams, John, 190
Adenauer, Konrad, 162, 240
Adrian, Charles R., 94 n
Africa, 3, 4; mass-membership parties in, 255–56; single parties in, 47, 256
Agar, Herbert, 283–84, 285
Aggregation, 13, 16, 55, 73–74, 75, 279, 283
Agrarian parties: Australia, 66–67; Austria, 119; Canada, 64–66; United States, 75; *see also* Farmers
Agrarian party: Norway, 118; Sweden, 120, 121
Airey, W. T. G., 160 n
Akzin, Benjamin, 119 n, 339 n
Alexander, Herbert E., 249 n
Alford, Robert R., 86 n, 87 n, 89 n, 90 n, 186 n
Alienation of working class, 136–37, 152, 156
Allardt, Erik, 47 n, 69 n, 112 n, 156 n, 259 n
Almond, Gabriel A., 13 n, 14 n, 73, 83 n, 288 n, 358 n
American Federation of Labor (A.F. of L.), 141
Andren, Nils, 185 n, 228 n
Apter, David, 165 n, 287
Aronson, Sidney H., 190 n
Asia, 3, 4
Attlee, Clement, 178, 296–97, 298
Australia, 3; candidate selection, 228, 229, 230; class voting, 86, 87; constituency associations, 329; Country party, 59, 65–66, 67, 328; financing of parties, 246; Labor party, 59, 74–75, 86 n, 89, 122, 161, 186–87, 229, 239 n, 246, 306 ff., 328–29; Liberal party, 66, 122, 229, 328–29; multi-party competition, 59; parliamentary party cohesion, 327–29; parliamentary system, 36, 61, 327–29, 331; party discipline, 327–29; party identification, 83; policy-making, 306; single-party constituencies, 229; state parties, 5, 32, 229, 307, 328–29; third parties, 65; two-party system, 327; upward social mobility, 186; working class, 86; working-class parties, 137, 138, 160, 186, 306
Austria, 3; coalition government, 69, 72–73, 119; Communist party, 69, 149; multi-party system, 59, 68, 69; People's party, 68, 74, 119, 149; policy-making, 312; proportional representation, 72; Social Democratic party, 149, 159, 312; socialist parties, 135, 149, 164; Socialist party, 68, 74, 119; third parties, 63; Trade Union Federation, 149; trade unions, 149; two-party system, 68–69, 72

Ballot, 9, 37, 77; absentee, 114; double-ballot system, 57; in Great Britain, 215, 216, 221, 222; mail, 221, 222, 227–28; nonpartisan, 43, 93 ff., party labels, 42–43, 114–15, 215, 216; public, 25–26, 229; secret, 26, 201–2, 227; in United States, 41, 93–97; in West Germany, 201–2, 227
Baltzell, E. Digby, 195 n

359